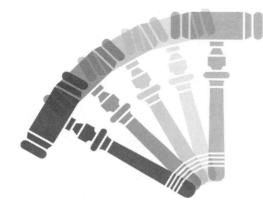

Casenote™ Legal Briefs

PROPERTY

Keyed to
Casner, Leach, French, Korngold, and VanderVelde's
Cases and Text on Property,
Fifth Edition

ASPEN
PUBLISHERS

1185 Avenue of the Americas, New York, NY 10036
www.aspenpublishers.com

This publication is designed to provide accurate and authoritative information in regard to the subject matter covered. It is sold with the understanding that the publisher is not engaged in rendering legal, accounting, or other professional services. If legal advice or other expert assistance is required, the services of a competent professional person should be sought.

— From a *Declaration of Principles* adopted jointly by a Committee of the American Bar Association and a Committee of Publishers and Associates

© 2004 Aspen Publishers, Inc.
A WoltersKluwer Company
www.aspenpublishers.com

Permissions
Aspen Publishers
1185 Avenue of the Americas
New York, NY 10036

Printed in the United States of America.

ISBN 0-7355-4535-9

1 2 3 4 5 6 7 8 9 0

FORMAT FOR THE CASENOTE LEGAL BRIEF

PARTY ID: Quick identification of the relationship between the parties.

NATURE OF CASE: This section identifies the form of action (e.g., breach of contract, negligence, battery), the type of proceeding (e.g., demurrer, appeal from trial court's jury instructions) or the relief sought (e.g., damages, injunction, criminal sanctions).

FACT SUMMARY: This is included to refresh the student's memory and can be used as a quick reminder of the facts.

CONCISE RULE OF LAW: Summarizes the general principle of law that the case illustrates. It may be used for instant recall of the court's holding and for classroom discussion or home review.

FACTS: This section contains all relevant facts of the case, including the contentions of the parties and the lower court holdings. It is written in a logical order to give the student a clear understanding of the case. The plaintiff and defendant are identified by their proper names throughout and are always labeled with a (P) or (D).

ISSUE: The issue is a concise question that brings out the essence of the opinion as it relates to the section of the casebook in which the case appears. Both substantive and procedural issues are included if relevant to the decision.

HOLDING AND DECISION: This section offers a clear and in-depth discussion of the rule of the case and the court's rationale. It is written in easy-to-understand language and answers the issue(s) presented by applying the law to the facts of the case. When relevant, it includes a thorough discussion of the exceptions to the case as listed by the court, any major cites to other cases on point, and the names of the judges who wrote the decisions.

CONCURRENCE / DISSENT: All concurrences and dissents are briefed whenever they are included by the casebook editor.

EDITOR'S ANALYSIS: This last paragraph gives the student a broad understanding of where the case "fits in" with other cases in the section of the book and with the entire course. It is a hornbook-style discussion indicating whether the case is a majority or minority opinion and comparing the principal case with other cases in the casebook. It may also provide analysis from restatements, uniform codes, and law review articles. The editor's analysis will prove to be invaluable to classroom discussion.

QUICKNOTES: Conveniently defines legal terms found in the case and summarizes the nature of any statutes, codes, or rules referred to in the text.

PALSGRAF v. LONG ISLAND R.R. CO.
Injured bystander (P) v. Railroad company (D)
N.Y. Ct. App., 248 N.Y. 339, 162 N.E. 99 (1928).

NATURE OF CASE: Appeal from judgment affirming verdict for plaintiff seeking damages for personal injury.

FACT SUMMARY: Helen Palsgraf (P) was injured on R.R.'s (D) train platform when R.R.'s (D) guard helped a passenger aboard a moving train, causing his package to fall on the tracks. The package contained fireworks which exploded, creating a shock that tipped a scale onto Palsgraf (P).

CONCISE RULE OF LAW: The risk reasonably to be perceived defines the duty to be obeyed.

FACTS: Helen Palsgraf (P) purchased a ticket to Rockaway Beach from R.R. (D) and was waiting on the train platform. As she waited, two men ran to catch a train that was pulling out from the platform. The first man jumped aboard, but the second man, who appeared as if he might fall, was helped aboard by the guard on the train who had kept the door open so they could jump aboard. A guard on the platform also helped by pushing him onto the train. The man was carrying a package wrapped in newspaper. In the process, the man dropped his package, which fell on the tracks. The package contained fireworks and exploded. The shock of the explosion was apparently of great enough strength to tip over some scales at the other end of the platform, which fell on Palsgraf (P) and injured her. A jury awarded her damages, and R.R. (D) appealed.

ISSUE: Does the risk reasonably to be perceived define the duty to be obeyed?

HOLDING AND DECISION: (Cardozo, C.J.) Yes. The risk reasonably to be perceived defines the duty to be obeyed. If there is no foreseeable hazard to the injured party as the result of a seemingly innocent act, the act does not become a tort because it happened to be a wrong as to another. If the wrong was not willful, the plaintiff must show that the act as to her had such great and apparent possibilities of danger as to entitle her to protection. Negligence in the abstract is not enough upon which to base liability. Negligence is a relative concept, evolving out of the common law doctrine of trespass on the case. To establish liability, the defendant must owe a legal duty of reasonable care to the injured party. A cause of action in tort will lie where harm, though unintended, could have been averted or avoided by observance of such a duty. The scope of the duty is limited by the range of danger that a reasonable person could foresee. In this case, there was nothing to suggest from the appearance of the parcel or otherwise that the parcel contained fireworks. The guard could not reasonably have had any warning of a threat to Palsgraf (P), and R.R. (D) therefore cannot be held liable. Judgment is reversed in favor of R.R. (D).

DISSENT: (Andrews, J.) The concept that there is no negligence unless R.R. (D) owes a legal duty to take care as to Palsgraf (P) herself is too narrow. Everyone owes to the world at large the duty of refraining from those acts that may unreasonably threaten the safety of others. If the guard's action was negligent as to those nearby, it was also negligent as to those outside what might be termed the "danger zone." For Palsgraf (P) to recover, R.R.'s (D) negligence must have been the proximate cause of her injury, a question of fact for the jury.

EDITOR'S ANALYSIS: The majority defined the limit of the defendant's liability in terms of the danger that a reasonable person in defendant's situation would have perceived. The dissent argued that the limitation should not be placed on liability, but rather on damages. Judge Andrews suggested that only injuries that would not have happened but for R.R.'s (D) negligence should be compensable. Both the majority and dissent recognized the policy-driven need to limit liability for negligent acts, seeking, in the words of Judge Andrews, to define a framework "that will be practical and in keeping with the general understanding of mankind." The Restatement (Second) of Torts has accepted Judge Cardozo's view.

QUICKNOTES
FORESEEABILITY – The reasonable anticipation that damage is a likely result from certain acts or omissions.
NEGLIGENCE - Failure to exercise that degree of care which a person of ordinary prudence would exercise under similar circumstances.
PROXIMATE CAUSE – Something which in natural and continuous sequence, unbroken by any new intervening cause, produces an event, and without which the injury would not have occurred.

NOTE TO STUDENTS

Aspen Publishers is proud to offer *Casenote Legal Briefs*—continuing thirty years of publishing America's best-selling legal briefs.

Casenote Legal Briefs are designed to help you save time when briefing assigned cases. Organized under convenient headings, they show you how to abstract the basic facts and holdings from the text of the actual opinions handed down by the courts. Used as part of a rigorous study regime, they can help you spend more time analyzing and critiquing points of law than on copying out bits and pieces of judicial opinions into your notebook or outline.

Casenote Legal Briefs should never be used as a substitute for assigned casebook readings. They work best when read as a follow-up to reviewing the underlying opinions themselves. Students who try to avoid reading and digesting the judicial opinions in their casebooks or on-line sources will end up shortchanging themselves in the long run. The ability to absorb, critique, and restate the dynamic and complex elements of case law decisions is crucial to your success in law school and beyond. It cannot be developed vicariously.

Casenote Legal Briefs represent but one of the many offerings in Aspen's Study Aid Timeline, which includes:

- Casenotes *Legal Briefs*
- Emanuel *Outlines*
- *Examples & Explanations* Series
- *Introduction to Law* Series
- Emanuel *Law in a Flash* Flashcards
- Emanuel *CrunchTime* Series

Each of these series is designed to provide you with easy-to-understand explanations of complex points of law. Each volume offers guidance on the principles of legal analysis and, consulted regularly, will hone your ability to spot relevant issues. We have titles that will help you prepare for class, prepare for your exams, and enhance your general comprehension of the law along the way.

To find out more about Aspen Study Aid publications, visit us on-line at www.aspenpublishers.com or e-mail us at legaledu@aspenpubl.com. We'll be happy to assist you.

Free access to Briefs on-line!

Download the cases you want in your notes or outlines using the full cut-and-paste feature accompanying our on-line briefs. Please fill out this form for full access to this useful feature. No photocopies of this form will be accepted.

① **Name:** _____ **Phone:** (____) _____

     Address: _____ **Apt.:** _____

     City: _____ **State:** _____ **ZIP Code:** _____

     Law School: _____ **Year (circle one):** 1st   2nd   3rd

② **Cut out the UPC found on the lower left-hand corner of the back cover of this book. Staple the UPC inside this box. Only the original UPC from the book cover will be accepted. (No photocopies or store stickers are allowed.)**

> **Attach UPC inside this box.**

③ **E-mail:** _____ **(Print LEGIBLY or you may not get access!)**

④ **Title (course subject) of this book** _____

⑤ **Used with which casebook (provide author's name):** _____

⑥ **Mail the completed form to:**   Aspen Publishers, Inc.
                                       Legal Education Division
                                       Casenote On-line Access
                                       675 Massachusetts Ave., 11th floor
                                       Cambridge, MA 02139

I understand that on-line access is granted solely to the purchaser of this book for the academic year in which it was purchased. Any other usage is not authorized and will result in immediate termination of access. Sharing of codes is strictly prohibited.

_____

Signature

Upon receipt of this completed form, you will be e-mailed codes so that you may access the Briefs for this Casenote Legal Brief. On-line Briefs may not be available for all titles. For a full list of available titles please check www.aspenpublishers.com/casenotes.

HOW TO BRIEF A CASE

A. DECIDE ON A FORMAT AND STICK TO IT

Structure is essential to a good brief. It enables you to arrange systematically the related parts that are scattered throughout most cases, thus making manageable and understandable what might otherwise seem to be an endless and unfathomable sea of information. There are, of course, an unlimited number of formats that can be utilized. However, it is best to find one that suits your needs and stick to it. Consistency breeds both efficiency and the security that when called upon you will know where to look in your brief for the information you are asked to give.

Any format, as long as it presents the essential elements of a case in an organized fashion, can be used. Experience, however, has led *Casenotes* to develop and utilize the following format because of its logical flow and universal applicability.

NATURE OF CASE: This is a brief statement of the legal character and procedural status of the case (e.g., "Appeal of a burglary conviction").

There are many different alternatives open to a litigant dissatisfied with a court ruling. The key to determining which one has been used is to discover *who is asking this court for what.*

This first entry in the brief should be kept as *short as possible.* The student should use the court's terminology if the student understands it. But since jurisdictions vary as to the titles of pleadings, the best entry is the one that apprises the student of who wants what in this proceeding, not the one that sounds most like the court's language.

CONCISE RULE OF LAW: A statement of the general principle of law that the case illustrates (e.g., "An acceptance that varies any term of the offer is considered a rejection and counteroffer").

Determining the rule of law of a case is a procedure similar to determining the issue of the case. Avoid being fooled by red herrings; there may be a few rules of law mentioned in the case excerpt, but usually only one is *the* rule with which the casebook editor is concerned. The techniques used to locate the issue, described below, may also be utilized to find the rule of law. Generally, your best guide is simply the chapter heading. It is a clue to the point the casebook editor seeks to make and should be kept in mind when reading every case in the respective section.

FACTS: A synopsis of only the essential facts of the case, i.e., those bearing upon or leading up to the issue.

The facts entry should be a short statement of the events and transactions that led one party to initiate legal proceedings against another in the first place. While some cases conveniently state the salient facts at the beginning of the decision, in other instances they will have to be culled from hiding places throughout the text, even from concurring and dissenting opinions. Some of the "facts" will often be in dispute and should be so noted. Conflicting evidence may be briefly pointed up. "Hard" facts must be included. Both must be *relevant* in order to be listed in the facts entry. It is impossible to tell what is relevant until the entire case is read, as the ultimate determination of the rights and liabilities of the parties may turn on something buried deep in the opinion.

The facts entry should never be longer than one to three *short* sentences.

It is often helpful to identify the role played by a party in a given context. For example, in a construction contract case the identification of a party as the "contractor" or "builder" alleviates the need to tell that that party was the one who was supposed to have built the house.

It is always helpful, and a good general practice, to identify the "plaintiff" and the "defendant." This may seem elementary and uncomplicated, but, especially in view of the creative editing practiced by some casebook editors, it is sometimes a difficult or even impossible task. Bear in mind that the *party presently* seeking something from this court may not be the plaintiff, and that sometimes only the cross-claim of a defendant is treated in the excerpt. Confusing or misaligning the parties can ruin your analysis and understanding of the case.

ISSUE: A statement of the general legal question answered by or illustrated in the case. For clarity, the issue is best put in the form of a question capable of a "yes" or "no" answer. In reality, the issue is simply the Concise Rule of Law put in the form of a question (e.g., "May an offer be accepted by performance?").

The major problem presented in discerning what is *the* issue in the case is that an opinion usually purports to raise and answer several questions. However, except for rare cases, only one such question is really the issue in the case. Collateral issues not necessary to the resolution of the matter in controversy are handled by the court by language known as *"obiter dictum"* or merely *"dictum."* While dicta may be included later in the brief, it has no place under the issue heading.

To find the issue, the student again asks *who wants what* and then goes on to ask *why did that party succeed or fail in getting it.* Once this is determined, the "why" should be turned into a question.

The complexity of the issues in the cases will vary, but in all cases a single-sentence question should sum up the issue. *In a few cases,* there will be two, or even more rarely, three issues of equal importance to the resolution of the case. Each should be expressed in a single-sentence question.

Since many issues are resolved by a court in coming to a final disposition of a case, the casebook editor will reproduce the portion of the opinion containing the issue or issues most relevant to the area of law under scrutiny. A noted law professor gave this advice: "Close the book; look at the title on the cover." Chances are, if it is Property, the student need not concern himself with whether, for example, the federal government's treatment of the plaintiff's land really raises a federal question sufficient to support jurisdiction on this ground in federal court.

The same rule applies to chapter headings designating sub-areas within the subjects. They tip the student off as to what the text is designed to teach. The cases are arranged in a casebook to show a progression or development of the law, so that the preceding cases may also help.

It is also most important to remember to *read the notes and questions* at the end of a case to determine what the editors wanted the student to have gleaned from it.

HOLDING AND DECISION: This section should succinctly explain the rationale of the court in arriving at its decision. In capsulizing the "reasoning" of the court, it should always include an application of the general rule or rules of law to the specific facts of the case. Hidden justifications come to light in this entry; the reasons for the state of the law, the public policies, the biases and prejudices, those considerations that influence the justices' thinking and, ultimately, the outcome of the case. At the end, there should be a short indication of the disposition or procedural resolution of the case (e.g., "Decision of the trial court for Mr. Smith (P) reversed").

The foregoing format is designed to help you "digest" the reams of case material with which you will be faced in your law school career. Once mastered by practice, it will place at your fingertips the information the authors of your casebooks have sought to impart to you in case-by-case illustration and analysis.

B. BE AS ECONOMICAL AS POSSIBLE IN BRIEFING CASES

Once armed with a format that encourages succinctness, it is as important to be economical with regard to the time spent on the actual reading of the case as it is to be economical in the writing of the brief itself. This does not mean "skimming" a case. Rather, it means reading the case with an "eye" trained to recognize into which "section" of your brief a particular passage or line fits and having a system for quickly and precisely marking the case so that the passages fitting any one particular part of the brief can be easily identified and brought together in a concise and accurate manner when the brief is actually written.

It is of no use to simply repeat everything in the opinion of the court; the student should only record enough information to trigger his or her recollection of what the court said. Nevertheless, an accurate statement of the "law of the case," i.e., the legal principle applied to the facts, is absolutely essential to class preparation and to learning the law under the case method.

To that end, it is important to develop a "shorthand" that you can use to make margin notations. These notations will tell you at a glance in which section of the brief you will be placing that particular passage or portion of the opinion.

Some students prefer to underline all the salient portions of the opinion (with a pencil or colored underliner marker), making marginal notations as they go along. Others prefer the color-coded method of underlining, utilizing different colors of markers to underline the salient portions of the case, each separate color being used to represent a different section of the brief. For example, blue underlining could be used for passages relating to the concise rule of law, yellow for those relating to the issue, and green for those relating to the holding and decision, etc. While it has its advocates, the color-coded method can be confusing and time-consuming (all that time spent on changing colored markers). Furthermore, it can interfere with the continuity and concentration many students deem essential to the reading of a case for maximum comprehension. In the end, however, it is a matter of personal preference and style. Just remember, whatever method you use, underlining must be used sparingly or its value is lost.

For those who take the marginal notation route, an efficient and easy method is to go along underlining the key portions of the case and placing in the margin alongside them the following "markers" to indicate where a particular passage or line "belongs" in the brief you will write:

N   (NATURE OF CASE)
CR   (CONCISE RULE OF LAW)
I   (ISSUE)
HC   (HOLDING AND DECISION, relates to the CONCISE RULE OF LAW behind the decision)
HR   (HOLDING AND DECISION, gives the RATIONALE or reasoning behind the decision)
HA   (HOLDING AND DECISION, APPLIES the general principle(s) of law to the facts of the case to arrive at the decision)

Remember that a particular passage may well contain information necessary to more than one part of your brief, in which case you simply note that in the margin. If you are using the color-coded underlining method instead of margin notation, simply make asterisks or checks in the margin next to the passage in question in the colors that indicate the additional sections of the brief where it might be utilized.

The economy of utilizing "shorthand" in marking cases for briefing can be maintained in the actual brief writing process itself by utilizing "law student shorthand" within the brief. There are many commonly used words and phrases for which abbreviations can be substituted in your briefs (and in your class notes also). You can develop abbreviations that are personal to you and which will save you a lot of time. A reference list of briefing abbreviations will be found elsewhere in this book.

C. USE BOTH THE BRIEFING PROCESS AND THE BRIEF AS A LEARNING TOOL

Now that you have a format and the tools for briefing cases efficiently, the most important thing is to make the time spent in briefing profitable to you and to make the most advantageous use of the briefs you create. Of course, the briefs are invaluable for classroom reference when you are called upon to explain or analyze a particular case. However, they are also useful in reviewing for exams. A quick glance at the fact summary should bring the case to mind, and a rereading of the concise rule of law should enable you to go over the underlying legal concept in your mind, how it was applied in that particular case, and how it might apply in other factual settings.

As to the value to be derived from engaging in the briefing process itself, there is an immediate benefit that arises from being forced to sift through the essential facts and reasoning from the court's opinion and to succinctly express them in your own words in your brief. The process ensures that you understand the case and the point that it illustrates, and that means you will be ready to absorb further analysis and information brought forth in class. It also ensures you will have something to say when called upon in class. The briefing process helps develop a mental agility for getting to the *gist* of a case and for identifying, expounding on, and applying the legal concepts and issues found there. Of most immediate concern, that is the mental process on which you must rely in taking law school examinations. Of more lasting concern, it is also the mental process upon which a lawyer relies in serving his clients and in making his living.

ABBREVIATIONS FOR BRIEFING

acceptance	acp
affirmed	aff
answer	ans
assumption of risk	a/r
attorney	atty
beyond a reasonable doubt	b/r/d
bona fide purchaser	BFP
breach of contract	br/k
cause of action	c/a
common law	c/l
Constitution	Con
constitutional	con
contract	K
contributory negligence	c/n
cross	x
cross-complaint	x/c
cross-examination	x/ex
cruel and unusual punishment	c/u/p
defendant	D
dismissed	dis
double jeopardy	d/j
due process	d/p
equal protection	e/p
equity	eq
evidence	ev
exclude	exc
exclusionary rule	exc/r
felony	f/n
freedom of speech	f/s
good faith	g/f
habeas corpus	h/c
hearsay	hr
husband	H
in loco parentis	ILP
injunction	inj
inter vivos	I/v
joint tenancy	j/t
judgment	judgt
jurisdiction	jur
last clear chance	LCC
long-arm statute	LAS
majority view	maj
meeting of minds	MOM
minority view	min
Miranda warnings	Mir/w
Miranda rule	Mir/r
negligence	neg
notice	ntc
nuisance	nus
obligation	ob
obscene	obs

offer	O
offeree	OE
offeror	OR
ordinance	ord
pain and suffering	p/s
parol evidence	p/e
plaintiff	P
prima facie	p/f
probable cause	p/c
proximate cause	px/c
real property	r/p
reasonable doubt	r/d
reasonable man	r/m
rebuttable presumption	rb/p
remanded	rem
res ipsa loquitur	RIL
respondeat superior	r/s
Restatement	RS
reversed	rev
Rule Against Perpetuities	RAP
search and seizure	s/s
search warrant	s/w
self-defense	s/d
specific performance	s/p
statute of limitations	S/L
statute of frauds	S/F
statute	S
summary judgment	s/j
tenancy in common	t/c
tenancy at will	t/w
tenant	t
third party	TP
third party beneficiary	TPB
transferred intent	TI
unconscionable	uncon
unconstitutional	unconst
undue influence	u/e
Uniform Commercial Code	UCC
unilateral	uni
vendee	VE
vendor	VR
versus	v
void for vagueness	VFV
weight of the evidence	w/e
weight of authority	w/a
wife	W
with	w/
within	w/i
without prejudice	w/o/p
without	w/o
wrongful death	wr/d

TABLE OF CASES

CHAPTER 1
THE NATURE AND IMPORTANCE OF PROPERTY

QUICK REFERENCE RULES OF LAW

1. **The Right to Exclude.** When nominal damages are awarded for an intentional trespass to land, punitive damages may also be awarded at the jury's discretion. (Jacque v. Steenberg Homes, Inc.)

2. **Limitations on the Right to Exclude.** Real property rights are not absolute; and, "necessity, private or public, may justify entry upon the lands of another." (State v. Shack)

3. **Blackstone and the Right to Exclude.** Trespass to chattels does not encompass an electronic communication that neither damages a recipient computer system nor impairs its functioning. (Intel Corporation v. Hamidi)

4. **Wild Animal, Natural Gas, and Water.** Property in wild animals is only acquired by occupancy, and pursuit alone does not constitute occupancy or vest any right in the pursuer. (Pierson v. Post)

5. **Wild Animal, Natural Gas, and Water.** A violent or malicious act to a person's occupation, profession, or livelihood, gives rise to a cause of action. (Keeble v. Hickeringill)

6. **Government Regulation of Wild Animals and Fisheries and the Public Trust.** Where an actor undertakes significant but incomplete steps to achieve possession of a piece of abandoned personal property and the effort is interrupted by the unlawful acts of others, the actor has a legally cognizable prepossessory interest in the property sufficient to support a claim of conversion. (Popov v. Hayashi)

7. **Government Regulation of Wild Animals and Fisheries and the Public Trust.** The owners of land and of an oil and gas lease have the right to produce as their own non-native gas from their land, which gas has previously been purchased, injected, and stored in a common reservoir by another landowner having no license, permit, or lease covering the land from which the non-native gas is produced. (Anderson v. Beech Aircraft Corporation)

8. **The Capture Doctrine, Wild Animals, and Natural Gas Water Law.** The reasonable use doctrine, rather than the absolute ownership doctrine, applies to groundwater disputes. (Cline v. American Aggregates Corporation)

9. **Property Rules and Liability Rules.** Under the reasonable use doctrine, where one lawful use of water is unreasonably interfered with by another equally lawful use, the latter must yield or be enjoined. (Harris v. Brooks)

10. **Finders and Bailees.** A finder of chattel has title superior to all but the rightful owner upon which he may maintain an action at law or in equity. (Armory v. Delamirie)

11. **Bailments**. As the possessor of property has absolute title to that property against all except the rightful owner, the possessor may maintain an action against anyone who violates that title (except for the rightful owner). (The Winkfield)

12. **Finder versus Owner of the Locus in Quo.** The finder of a chattel, clearly lost, has rights to possession superior to everybody except the true owner; the place of finding is of no consequence. (Hannah v. Peel)

13. **Finder versus Owner of the Locus in Quo.** Misplaced goods (items intentionally placed by the owner where they were found and then forgotten or left there) are deemed to be in the bailment of the owner of the property on which they are found for the true owner. (McAvoy v. Medina)

14. **Finder versus Owner of the Locus in Quo.** The finder of mislaid property acquires no rights to the property since possession belongs to the owner of the premises upon which the property is found. (Benjamin v. Lindner Aviation, Inc.)

15. **Sunken Treasure.** When a previous owner claims long lost property that was involuntarily taken from his control, abandonment must be proved by clear and convincing evidence. (Columbus-America Discovery Group v. Atlantic Mutual Insurance Co.)

JACQUE v. STEENBERG HOMES, INC.

Property owner (P) v. Company (D)

Wisc. Sup. Ct., 563 N.W.2d 154 (1997).

NATURE OF CASE: Suit for intentional trespass to land.

FACT SUMMARY: The Jacques (P) brought suit against Steenberg Homes (D) claiming intentional trespass to their land when Steenberg (D) plowed a path across their field, over their protests, in order to deliver a mobile home.

CONCISE RULE OF LAW: When nominal damages are awarded for an intentional trespass to land, punitive damages may also be awarded at the jury's discretion.

FACTS: Steenberg Homes (D) was delivering a mobile home. It found the easiest route of delivery was through the Jacques' (P) land. Despite the Jacques' (P) protests, Steenberg (D) plowed a path through the Jacques' (P) field. The Jacques (P) sued Steenberg (D) for intentional trespass. At trial, Steenberg (D) conceded intentional trespass but argued that punitive damages could not be awarded since no compensatory damages had been awarded. Though the jury awarded $1 in nominal damages and $100,000 in punitive damages, the circuit court set aside the punitive damages award. The court of appeals affirmed and the Jacques (P) appealed.

ISSUE: When nominal damages are awarded for an intentional trespass to land, may punitive damages also be awarded at the jury's discretion?

HOLDING AND DECISION: (Bablitch, J.) Yes. When nominal damages are awarded for an intentional trespass to land, punitive damages may also be awarded at the jury's discretion. Steenberg (D) argued that punitive damages could not be awarded by the jury without an award of compensatory damages as a matter of law. The Jacques (P) argued that the rationale supporting the compensatory damage award requirement is not applicable when the wrongful act is an intentional trespass to land. This court agrees. The rationale for the requirement is that if the individual cannot show actual harm, society has little interest in having the unlawful, but harmless, conduct deterred and punitive damages are inappropriate. The issue of whether nominal damages can support a punitive damage award in intentional trespass to land cases is one of first impression. This court has recognized that in certain circumstances of trespass, the actual harm is not the damage to the land, but the loss of the individual's right to exclude others from his property, and has implied that the loss of this right may be punished by a large damage award despite the lack of measurable harm. Thus, the compensatory damages requirement should not apply when the tort supporting the award is intentional trespass to land. Next, we consider whether the $100,000 damage award was excessive. The punitive award does not shock our conscience. Rather, it is the brazen conduct of

Steenberg homes we find shocking. Here the $100,000 award was not excessive. Steenberg's (D) intentional trespass demonstrated an indifference and reckless disregard for the law and for the rights of others. Moreover, such an award is necessary to deter similar conduct in the future. Reversed and remanded.

EDITOR'S ANALYSIS: The Supreme Court has recognized the interest of a landowner in the right to exclude others from his land as one of the essential property rights. The law recognizes that harm occurs in every trespass to land by the nominal damage award, whether or not actual damages are sustained. The potential harm resulting from intentional trespass to land, which if repeated might ripen into prescription or adverse possession, may result in the owner's loss of property rights. Moreover, society's interest in deterring wrongdoing supports the conclusion in this case as well.

QUICKNOTES

COMPENSATORY DAMAGES - Measure of damages necessary to compensate victim for actual injuries suffered.

NOMINAL DAMAGES - A small sum awarded to a plaintiff in order to recognize that he sustained an injury that is either slight or incapable of being established.

PUNITIVE DAMAGES - Damages exceeding the actual injury suffered for the purposes of punishment, deterrence and comfort to plaintiff.

TRESPASS TO LAND - Physical invasion of the plaintiff's property that is intended and caused by the defendant's conduct.

NOTES:

STATE v. SHACK

State (P) v. Agencies seeking to aid migrant farm workers (D)

N.J. Sup. Ct., 277 A.2d 369 (1971).

NATURE OF CASE: Appeal from a conviction of trespassing.

FACT SUMMARY: Tejeras (D) and Shack (D) entered upon private property against the orders of the owner of that property, to aid migrant farm workers employed and housed there.

CONCISE RULE OF LAW: Real property rights are not absolute; and, "necessity, private or public, may justify entry upon the lands of another."

FACTS: Tejeras (D) and Shack (D) worked with migrant farm workers. Tejeras (D) was a field worker for the Farm Workers Division of the Southwest Citizens Organization for Poverty Elimination (known as SCOPE), a nonprofit corporation funded by the Office of Economic Opportunity which provided for the "health services of the migrant farm worker." Shack (D) was a staff attorney with the Farm Workers Division of Camden Regional Legal Services, Inc. (known as CRLS), also a nonprofit corporation funded by the Office of Economic Opportunity which provided (along with other services) legal advice for, and representation of, migrant farm workers. Tejeras (D) and Shack (D), pursuant to their roles in SCOPE and CRLS, entered upon private property to aid migrant workers employed and housed there. When both Tejeras (D) and Shack (D) refused to leave the property at the owner's request, they were charged with trespassing under a New Jersey statute which provides that "any person who trespasses on any lands . . . after being forbidden so to trespass by the owner . . . is a disorderly person and shall be punished by a fine of not more than $50." After conviction for trespassing, Tejeras (D) and Shack (D) brought this appeal.

ISSUE: Does an owner of real property have the absolute right to exclude all others from that property?

HOLDING AND DECISION: (Weintraub, C.J.) No. Real property rights are not absolute; and, "necessity, private or public, may justify entry upon the lands of another." This rule is based upon the basic rationale that "property rights serve human values. They are recognized to that end and are limited by it." Here, a central concern is the welfare of the migrant farm workers—a highly disadvantaged segment of society. Migrant farm workers, in general, are "outside of the mainstream of the communities in which they are housed and are unaware of their rights and opportunities, and of the services available to them." As such, here, the "necessity" of effective communication of legal rights and of providing medical services for the migrant farm workers justifies entry upon the private property. Of course, the owner of such property has the right to pursue his farming activities without interference, but, here, there is no legitimate need for the owner to exclude those attempting to assist the migrant farm workers. Furthermore, the migrant farm worker must be allowed to receive visitors of his choice, so long as there is no behavior harmful to others, and members of the press may not be denied access to any farm worker who wishes to see them. In any of these situations, since no possessory right of the farmer-employer-landowner has been invaded (*i.e.*, since he has no right to exclude such persons), there can be no trespassing. Reversed.

EDITOR'S ANALYSIS: Generally, the right to exclusive possession is considered "the oldest, most widely recognized right of private property in land." This case, though, illustrates the central limitation on the right to possession or use of private property—*i.e.*, it may not be used to harm others. Here, the exclusion of Tejeras (D) and Shack (D) was, therefore, invalid because it would harm a very disadvantaged segment of society (the farm workers). Note, that under this principle, an owner of property, also, has no right to maintain a nuisance, to violate a building code, or to violate any "police power" laws (*i.e.*, laws for the general public welfare).

QUICKNOTES

POSSESSORY RIGHT - The right to possess particular real property to the exclusion of others.

TRESPASS - Unlawful interference with, or damage to, the real or personal property of another.

NOTES:

INTEL CORPORATION v. HAMIDI
Employer (P) v. Former employee (D)
Cal. Sup. Ct., 71 P.3d 296 (2003).

NATURE OF CASE: Appeal from injunction in action for trespass to chattels.

FACT SUMMARY: Hamidi (D) and his organization, Former and Current Employees of Intel (FACE-Intel) (D), mass-mailed e-mails that were critical of Intel Corp. (Intel) (P) to thousands of Intel employees. Intel (P) claimed that this conduct constituted trespass to chattel because it intermeddled with its personal property (computers).

CONCISE RULE OF LAW: Trespass to chattels does not encompass an electronic communication that neither damages a recipient computer system nor impairs its functioning.

FACTS: Hamidi (D), a former employee of Intel Corp. (P), formed an organization named Former and Current Employees of Intel (FACE-Intel) (D) to disseminate information and views critical of Intel's (P) employment and personnel policies and practices. Over a 21-month period, Hamidi (D), on behalf of FACE-Intel (D), sent six mass e-mails that criticized Intel (P) and invited recipients to go to FACE-Intel's (D) Web site, to as many as 35,000 employee addresses on Intel's (P) electronic mail system. Recipients could request to be removed from FACE-Intel's (D) mailing list. In sending the mass mailing, Hamidi did not breach Intel's (P) computer security. Despite Intel's (P) request that the e-mails cease, Hamidi (D) continued his mailings. Intel (P) sued Hamidi (D) and FACE-Intel (D) for trespass to chattels. The trial court entered default judgment against FACE-Intel (D) for failure to answer, and granted summary judgment against Hamidi (D), permanently enjoining him from sending unsolicited e-mail to addresses on Intel's (P) computer systems. The appellate court affirmed, and the supreme court granted review.

ISSUE: Does trespass to chattels encompass an electronic communication that neither damages a recipient computer system nor impairs its functioning?

HOLDING AND DECISION: (Werdegar, J.) No. Trespass to chattels does not encompass an electronic communication that neither damages a recipient computer system nor impairs its functioning. Such an electronic communication does not constitute actionable trespass to personal property because it does not interfere with the possessor's use or possession of, or any other protected interest in, the personal property itself. Any consequential damages, such as loss of productivity, are not an injury to the company's interest in its computers. To prevail on this particular claim, Intel (P) would have to prove injury to its computer systems—as where the quantity of e-mail (spam) overloads a system.

EDITOR'S ANALYSIS: The court emphasized that its decision did not rest on any special immunity for e-mail communications, and noted that such communications could cause legally cognizable injury under other legal theories, such as interference with prospective economic relations, interference with contract, defamation, or intentional infliction of emotional distress. As the opinion makes clear, for conduct to amount to trespass to chattels, however, there must be injury to the chattel itself, or to some right in that property.

QUICKNOTES
TRESPASS TO CHATTELS - Action for damages sustained as a result of defendant's unlawful interference with plaintiff's personal property.

NOTES:

PIERSON v. POST

Hunter (P) v. Hunter (D)

N.Y. Sup. Ct., 3 Caines 175 (1805).

NATURE OF CASE: Action of trespass on the case.

FACT SUMMARY: Post (P) was hunting a fox. Pierson (D), knowing this, killed the fox and carried it off.

CONCISE RULE OF LAW: Property in wild animals is only acquired by occupancy, and pursuit alone does not constitute occupancy or vest any right in the pursuer.

FACTS: Post (P) found a fox upon certain wild, uninhabited, unpossessed waste land. He and his dogs began hunting and pursuing the fox. Knowing that the fox was being hunted by Post (P) and within Post's (P) view, Pierson (D) killed the fox and carried it off.

ISSUE: Has a person in pursuit of a wild animal acquired such a right to or property in the wild animal as to sustain an action against a person who kills and carries away the animal, knowing of the former's pursuit?

HOLDING AND DECISION: (Tompkins, J.) No. Property in wild animals is acquired by occupancy only. Mere pursuit vests no right in the pursuer. One authority holds that actual bodily seizure is not always necessary to constitute possession of wild animals. The mortal wounding of an animal or the trapping or intercepting of animals so as to deprive them of their natural liberty will constitute occupancy. However, here, Post (P) only shows pursuit. Hence there was no occupancy or legal right vested in Post (P) and the fox became Pierson's (D) property when he killed and carried it off. The purpose of this rule is that if the pursuit of animals without wounding them or restricting their liberty were held to constitute a basis for an action against others for intercepting and killing the animals, "it would prove a fertile source of quarrels and litigation." Reversed.

DISSENT: (Livingston, J.) The dissent feels that a new rule should be adopted: that property in wild animals may be acquired without bodily touch, provided the pursuer be in reach or have a reasonable prospect of taking the animals.

EDITOR'S ANALYSIS: The ownership of wild animals is in the state for the benefit of all its people. A private person cannot acquire exclusive rights to a wild animal except by taking and reducing it to actual possession in a lawful manner or by a grant from the government. After the animal has been lawfully subjected to control, the ownership becomes absolute as long as the restraint lasts. Mere ownership of the land that an animal happens to be on does not constitute such a reduction of possession as to give the landowner a property right in the animal, except as against a mere trespasser who goes on such land for the purpose of taking the animal.

QUICKNOTES

OCCUPANCY - Period of time during which a party possesses and uses real property.

POSSESSION - The holding of property with the right of disposition.

NOTES:

KEEBLE v. HICKERINGILL
Landowner (P) v. Neighbor (D)
11 East 576, Cas. T. Holt 19, 11 Mod. 130 (1707).

NATURE OF CASE: Action to recover damages caused by trespass.

FACT SUMMARY: Keeble (P) had prepared a decoy pond on his land which attracted wild fowl. With the intention of depriving Keeble (P) of the fowl, Hickeringill (D) drove the fowl away by shooting his gun.

CONCISE RULE OF LAW: A violent or malicious act to a person's occupation, profession, or livelihood, gives rise to a cause of action.

FACTS: Keeble (P) alleged that he had a decoy pond on his land which he had equipped with decoy ducks and nets for the purpose of capturing the wild fowl attracted to the pond. He further alleged that Hickeringill (D), with the intent of depriving Keeble (P) of the yearly profit he made from the pond, drove the fowl away by discharging his gun.

ISSUE: Will a violent or malicious act to a person's occupation, profession, or livelihood give rise to a cause of action?

HOLDING AND DECISION: (Holt, C.J.) Yes. Where a violent or malicious act is done to a person's occupation, profession, or livelihood, an action will lie. In this case, the decoy was a benefit to Keeble (P). Hickeringill's (D) action interfered with Keeble's (P) exercising of his trade. There would not be an action if Hickeringill (D) had damaged Keeble (P) by setting up a decoy on his land near Keeble's (P), since he has as much right to make and use a decoy as Keeble (P). If a person sets up the same trade as another in the same town, there is damage, but it is sine injuria, for it is lawful for him to set up the same trade. Judgment for Keeble (P).

EDITOR'S ANALYSIS: The court decided that this action was not brought for property but for Hickeringill's (D) interference with Keeble's (P) occupation, and so based its decision on those grounds. In *Andrews v. Andrews*, 242 N.C. 382, 88 S.E. 2d 88 (1955), the plaintiff complained that the decoy pond, set up by the defendant on a lot adjoining plaintiff's farm, attracted wild geese, who used the pond as a base for attacking plaintiff's crops. The court held that an action would lie in nuisance. The dissent argued that the case should be dismissed, since the defendant did not have ownership in the geese, or even possession of them, to make him responsible for their actions.

NOTES:

POPOV v. HAYASHI
Baseball fan (P) v. Baseball fan (D)
Cal. Super. Ct., No. 400545, WL 31833731 (2002).

NATURE OF CASE: Action for conversion, trespass to chattels, injunctive relief and constructive trust.

FACT SUMMARY: Both Popov (P) and Hayashi (D) intended to establish and maintain control over a baseball that gave Barry Bonds his 73rd home run in 2001, but just as Popov (P) was getting it in his glove, a crowd engulfed him, and brought him to the ground. Hayashi (D), who was near Popov (P) and who also was brought to the ground by the crowd, found the ball and pocketed it. Popov (P) claimed he had established sufficient possession of the ball to gain title to it and brought suit to compel Hayashi (D) to return the ball to him.

CONCISE RULE OF LAW: Where an actor undertakes significant but incomplete steps to achieve possession of a piece of abandoned personal property and the effort is interrupted by the unlawful acts of others, the actor has a legally cognizable pre-possessory interest in the property sufficient to support a claim of conversion.

FACTS: Barry Bonds, a professional baseball player, hit a record-setting 73rd home run on October 7, 2001. On that day, Popov (P) and Hayashi (D) and many others had positioned themselves in an area of the stadium where Bonds hit the greatest number of home runs in the hopes of catching a record-setting ball (so they brought their baseball gloves with them). The ball hit by Bonds initially landed in Popov's (P) glove, but it was not clear whether the ball was secure there, as Popov (P) may have lost his balance while reaching for the ball. However, even as the ball was going into his glove, a crowd engulfed him and he was tackled and brought to the ground, with people hitting and grabbing him. Hayashi (D), who had been near Popov (P), was also forced by the crowd to the ground, where he saw the ball. He pocketed it and revealed it only when a camera was trained on him, presumably because he wanted proof that he was the owner of the ball. Popov (P), seeing the ball, grabbed for it, believing it to be his, but Hayashi (D) refused to give it to him. Popov (P) then brought suit for conversion, trespass to chattels, injunctive relief, and constructive trust.

ISSUES: Where an actor undertakes significant but incomplete steps to achieve possession of a piece of abandoned personal property and the effort is interrupted by the unlawful acts of others, does the actor have a legally cognizable pre-possessory interest in the property sufficient to support a claim of conversion?

HOLDING AND DECISION: (McCarthy, J.) Yes. Where an actor undertakes significant but incomplete steps to achieve possession of a piece of abandoned personal property and the

effort is interrupted by the unlawful acts of others, the actor has a legally cognizable pre-possessory interest in the property sufficient to support a claim of conversion. As an initial matter, there was no trespass to chattels—which requires injury to the chattel—because the ball itself was not damaged and because Popov (P) did not claim that Hayashi (D) interfered with his use and enjoyment of the ball. If there was a wrong at all, it was conversion, which is the wrongful exercise of dominion over the personal property of another. One who has neither title nor possession, nor any right to possession, may not assert a conversion claim. The key issue, therefore, is whether Popov (P) achieved possession or the right to it. "Possession," however, does not have one meaning; the meaning varies depending on the context in which it is used. Some guidelines, however, do exist, *e.g.*, that possession requires both physical control over an item and an intent to control it and exclude others from it. Here, Popov (P) clearly had the requisite intent, so the issue is whether he had exclusive dominion and control over the ball. Possession in this context is based on custom and what is physically possible. Here, "not only is it physically possible for a person to acquire unequivocal dominion and control of an abandoned baseball, but fans generally expect a claimant to have accomplished as much." Because Popov (P) did not establish by a preponderance of the evidence that he would have retained control of the ball after all momentum ceased and after any incidental contact with other people or objects, he did not achieve full possession. This conclusion does not resolve the case, however, because Popov (P) was attacked illegally by the crowd, and because, therefore, it is unknown whether he would have retained control over the ball absent the crowd's actions. Because Popov (P) has a legally protected pre-possessory interest in the ball, he may advance a legitimate claim to the ball. Hayashi (D), too, was a victim of the crowd's illegal activity, but was able to extricate himself from the crowd. Although Hayashi (D) exercised complete dominion and control over the ball, the ball was encumbered by the qualified pre-possessory interest of Popov (P). Thus, awarding the ball to either of the two parties is unfair to the other. Both have a superior claim to the ball as against all the world, but not against each other; they are equally entitled to the ball. Because the court sits in equity, it may devise an equitable solution to this problem. Here, that solution is equitable division, whereby both Popov (P) and Hayashi (D) have an equal and undivided interest in the ball. Accordingly, Popov's (P) conversion claim is sustained only as to his equal and undivided interest.

Continued on next page.

EDITOR'S ANALYSIS: The parties agreed that before Bonds hit the ball, it belonged to Major League Baseball, but that at the time it was hit, it became intentionally abandoned property. Also, to effectuate its decision, the court ordered the sale of the ball, with the proceeds being equally split between the two men. The ball ultimately sold for $450,000—Hayashi (D) estimated that his share would only cover his legal fees.

QUICKNOTES

CONVERSION - The act of depriving an owner of his property without permission or justification.

NOTES:

ANDERSON v. BEECH AIRCRAFT CORPORATION
Landowner (P) v. Adjoining landowner (D)
Kan. Sup. Ct., 699 P.2d 1023 (1985).

NATURE OF CASE: Interlocutory appeal from partial summary judgment for plaintiff in quiet title action.

FACT SUMMARY: Beech Aircraft Corp. (Beech) (D) injected gas into a reservoir, a part of which underlay the Andersons' (P) property. Beech (D) did not have any right to use that part of the reservoir. The Andersons (P) and Avanti Petroleum, Inc. (Avanti) (P)—Anderson's (P) oil and gas lessee—sought to produce the gas in the reservoir that was under the Anderson (P) property.

CONCISE RULE OF LAW: The owners of land and of an oil and gas lease have the right to produce as their own non-native gas from their land, which gas has previously been purchased, injected, and stored in a common reservoir by another landowner having no license, permit, or lease covering the land from which the non-native gas is produced.

FACTS: The Stalnaker reservoir had produced native gas, but then was depleted. The reservoir underlay the property of both Beech Aircraft Corp. (Beech) (D) and the Andersons (P). After the reservoir was empty, Beech (D) bought gas from interstate pipelines and injected it into the reservoir through wells on its property, storing the gas in the reservoir for later use. Avanti Petroleum, Inc. (Avanti) (P), an oil and gas lessee of the Andersons (P), sought to produce the non-native gas. The Andersons (P) and Avanti (P) brought suit to quiet title, to recover damages for slander of title and trespass, and for an accounting. The trial court granted summary judgment for the plaintiffs on the quiet title claim. The state's supreme court granted interlocutory review.

ISSUE: Do the owners of land and of an oil and gas lease have the right to produce as their own non-native gas from their land, which gas has previously been purchased, injected, and stored in a common reservoir by another landowner having no license, permit, or lease covering the land from which the non-native gas is produced?

HOLDING AND DECISION: (Prager, J.) Yes. The owners of land and of an oil and gas lease have the right to produce as their own non-native gas from their land, which gas has previously been purchased, injected, and stored in a common reservoir by another landowner having no license, permit, or lease covering the land from which the non-native gas is produced. This is an issue of first impression in this state. First, the law of capture applies to natural gas. This means that natural gas in the ground is part of the real estate until it is actually produced and severed, at which point it becomes personalty. Until that point, no one owns it, although a landowner (or his lessee) has the exclusive right of acquiring the gas that is underneath his property. Because oil and gas are fugitive and migratory, like wild animals, when these are restored to their natural wild and free state, they again belong to no one and resume their status as common property. In *Hammonds v. Central Kentucky Natural Gas Co.*, 225 Ky 685, 75 S.W.2d 204 (1934), the court concluded that if non-native injected gas wanders into the land of an adjoining landowner, the landowner that placed the gas in the earth is not liable for trespass as that landowner no longer owns the gas. This nonownership theory has been adopted by other courts, but has also been criticized on the grounds that once natural gas has been reduced to possession, and has been transported and injected, that gas no longer resembles native gas. Underground storage of gas is also regulated by statute. In this state, the legislature has provided that any natural gas public utility may appropriate for its use (through eminent domain) for the underground storage of natural gas any subsurface stratum or formation that is suitable for such storage and that is in the public interest. Also, the utility must obtain a certificate from the state before it can appropriate any stratum or formation for such use. Because Beech (D) is not a natural gas public utility, it does not have this condemnation power. To carry out the legislative intent, and to adopt a fair rule that is in the best interest of the people of the state, the law of capture should be applied in this case. Under the law of capture, Beech (D) lost its ownership of the stored gas after injecting it into the reservoir. Affirmed.

EDITOR'S ANALYSIS: In 1987, the Kentucky Supreme Court cast doubt on the continuing vitality of the *Hammonds* decision. In *Texas American Energy Corp. v. Citizens Fidelity Bank & Trust Co.*, 736 S.W.2d 25 (Ky. 1987), the court held that when previously extracted gas stored in underground reservoirs is capable of being defined with certainty and the integrity of the reservoirs is capable of being maintained, title to such gas (or oil) is not lost and these minerals do not become the property of the owners of the land above the reservoirs. In that case, the court rejected the wild animal analogy previously relied on to vitiate ownership by the party injecting the gas or oil underneath the land.

CLINE v. AMERICAN AGGREGATES CORPORATION
Landowner (P) v. Adjoining landowner (D)
Ohio Sup. Ct., 474 N.E.2d 324 (1984).

NATURE OF CASE: Appeal from affirmance of summary judgment for defendants in action over groundwater use.

FACT SUMMARY: Owners of land neighboring American Aggregates Corporation's (American Aggregates) (D) quarry claimed that American Aggregates' (D) pumping of its quarry pits caused dewatering and pollution of their water wells.

CONCISE RULE OF LAW: The reasonable use doctrine, rather than the absolute ownership doctrine, applies to groundwater disputes.

FACTS: American Aggregates Corporation (American Aggregates) (D) owned and operated a quarry. As part of the quarrying process, water had to be pumped from the quarry pits created by the quarrying operation. Twenty-six neighboring landowners (P), all of whom used water wells to supply their entire domestic water needs, brought suit alleging that their properties and that of American Aggregates (D) overlay a water aquifer and that American Aggregates' (D) pumping of its quarry pits unreasonably caused dewatering and pollution of their wells. The trial court granted summary judgment to American Aggregates (D) because the state's common law did not recognize a cause of action for a landowner's damages resulting from a neighbor's use of underground percolating water. The appellate court affirmed, and the state's supreme court granted review.

ISSUE: Does the reasonable use doctrine, rather than the absolute ownership doctrine, apply to groundwater disputes?

HOLDING AND DECISION: (Celebrezze, J.) Yes. The reasonable use doctrine, rather than the absolute ownership doctrine, applies to groundwater disputes. The court is asked to reexamine the state's common law as applied to groundwater. The current law, as announced in *Frazier v. Brown*, 12 Ohio St. 294 (1861), is based on the absolute ownership doctrine, which provides no correlative rights between owners of adjoining lands with regard to groundwater and which regards such water as part of the land itself, to be enjoyed absolutely by the owner of that land. This rule, also known as the English rule, fails to acknowledge advances in the understanding of subsurface waters that have occurred since the early 1800s. Also, adherence to the absolute ownership doctrine may result in uncertainty, harshness, and injustice because it may protect a more powerful neighbor who has the ability to divert water. On the other hand, advances in scientific knowledge can insure the protection of a landowner's property rights in groundwater. Therefore, the better standard to apply is the reasonable use doctrine found in the Restatement of the Law of Torts, Section 858. This doctrine provides that a landowner does not have liability for the use of groundwater on her or his property unless the withdrawal of the water: (1) unreasonably causes harm to a neighboring landowner by lowering the water table or reducing artesian pressure; (2) exceeds the landowner's reasonable share of the annual supply or total store of groundwater; (3) or has a direct and substantial effect on a watercourse or lake and unreasonably causes harm to a person entitled to use the water. This doctrine is much more equitable than the absolute ownership doctrine, which is hereby overruled. Reversed.

CONCURRENCE: (Holmes, J.) The adoption of the reasonable use doctrine will provide for greater conservation of one of our greatest natural resources in the context of our growing industrialized state. This standard preserves the general rule of nonliability—the privilege to use the water beneath one's land—while recognizing an exception when there is usually enough water for all users but one landowner removes an excess to the detriment of the others. This is a flexible standard that will meet the changing needs of users and can accommodate changes in circumstances to provide for the utilization of water where it is most needed. The rule prevents a neighbor from usurping one's source of groundwater, and promotes economic efficiency. Finally, this doctrine conforms to hydrologic fact and can conform to any future discoveries in this area.

EDITOR'S ANALYSIS: Most American jurisdictions have abandoned the English rule of absolute dominion. States that have declined to abandon this rule have done so on the grounds that such a change should be made by the legislature, or because they have been presented with insufficient evidence that the doctrine is counterproductive or has caused bad water policy.

QUICKNOTES
ABSOLUTE OWNERSHIP - Ownership of property that exists exclusively to one party.

HARRIS v. BROOKS
Riparian landowner (P) v. Adjoining riparian landowner (D)
Ark. Sup. Ct., 283 S.W.2d 129 (1955).

NATURE OF CASE: Appeal from denial of injunctive relief in riparian rights action.

FACT SUMMARY: Mashburn (P), a riparian lessee, conducted a commercial fishing and boating enterprise on a lake. The Brooks (D), lessees of an adjoining riparian owner, pumped water from the lake to irrigate rice. Mashburn (P) and Harris (P), his lessor, filed suit to enjoin the Brooks (D) from continuing to use lake water for this purpose, claiming that they reduced the lake's water level to such an extent as to make the lake unsuitable for fishing or recreation.

CONCISE RULE OF LAW: Under the reasonable use doctrine, where one lawful use of water is unreasonably interfered with by another equally lawful use, the latter must yield or be enjoined.

FACTS: Mashburn (P) leased riparian land from Harris (P) and others who owned land adjacent to Horseshoe Lake. Beginning in April 1954, he ran a commercial fishing and boating business on the lake where he sold fishing bait and rented boats to the general public. The Brooks (D) leased land on the lake from a different landowner and periodically grew rice on the land, irrigating it with water pumped from the lake. They pumped no more water in 1954 than they did in 1951 and 1952, no rice being raised in 1953. However, by July 1954, Mashburn's (P) business began to suffer and he brought suit alleging that the Brooks' (D) water use had reduced the lake's water level to such an extent as to make the lake unsuitable for "fishing, recreation, or other lawful purposes." Although the lake was below normal in August, as the result of unusually dry weather, it was not clear that this was the case in July, when the water level in the lake was below its normal level of 189.67 feet above sea level. Mashburn (P) sought to enjoin the Brooks (D) from using the lake for irrigation. The trial court denied injunctive relief, and the state's supreme court granted review.

ISSUE: Under the reasonable use doctrine, where one lawful use of water is unreasonably interfered with by another equally lawful use, must the latter yield or be enjoined?

HOLDING AND DECISION: (Ward, J.) Yes. Under the reasonable use doctrine, where one lawful use of water is unreasonably interfered with by another equally lawful use, the latter must yield or be enjoined. The court is not bound by the uniform flow theory of water use, under which Mashburn (P) would be entitled to an injunction if it was shown that the water level in the lake was at or below the normal level when the suit was filed. Other water use doctrines are the appropriation doctrine and the riparian doctrine. Under the appropriation doctrine, a government entity apportions water to contesting claimants. This theory is not consistent with this state's law. Under the riparian doctrine, as it has developed, there are two theories. The first is a natural flow theory, under which a riparian owner can take water for domestic purposes (*e.g.*, for one's family, livestock, gardening, *etc.*) only. The second theory is a reasonable use theory, under which the use of water by each riparian owner is limited to what is reasonable, having due regard for the rights of others above, or below, or on the opposite shore. Thus, an owner's right to use water is qualified only by the correlative rights of other riparian owners, or the public. This court has previously recognized the reasonable use theory to some degree, and now embraces that theory in the following form. First, the right to use water for strictly domestic purposes is superior to most other uses. Second, other than domestic use, all other lawful uses, *e.g.*, fishing, irrigation, swimming, recreation, are equal. Third, when one lawful use destroys another, the former must yield or be enjoined. Fourth, when one lawful use interferes with or detracts from another lawful use, if the interfering use is unreasonable, it may be enjoined to the extent that it is unreasonable. Applying these principles here, the Brooks' (D) use unreasonably interfered with Mashburn's use at the point at which the water level of the lake was at or below 189.67 feet above sea level. Therefore, their use is enjoined when the water level of the lake falls to or below that level, for as long as they use the lake. Reversed and remanded.

EDITOR'S ANALYSIS: The court in this case relied on the Restatement (First) of the Law, Torts, § 852. Under the most current version of the Restatement (Second), the basic rule is that a riparian owner is liable for making an unreasonable use of the water that causes harm to another riparian owner's reasonable use. Although the Restatement (Second) provides many considerations of reasonableness, some legal commentators have posited that courts will decide whether a use is reasonable by comparing the cost to the plaintiff caused by the defendant's conduct to the cost to the defendant of modifying the defendant's conduct to accommodate the plaintiff's use.

QUICKNOTES

INJUNCTIVE RELIEF - A court order issued as a remedy, requiring a person to do, or prohibiting that person from doing, a specific act.

RIPARIAN RIGHT - The right of an owner of real property to the use of water naturally flowing through his land.

ARMORY v. DELAMIRIE
Jewel finder (P) v. Goldsmith (D)
King's Bench, 1 Strange 505 (1722).

NATURE OF CASE: Action in trover to recover the value of personal property.

FACT SUMMARY: Armory (P) found a jewel which he took to Delamirie (D), a goldsmith, for appraisal, but Delamirie's (D) apprentice removed the stones which Delamirie (D) refused to return.

CONCISE RULE OF LAW: A finder of chattel has title superior to all but the rightful owner upon which he may maintain an action at law or in equity.

FACTS: Armory (P), a chimney sweeper's boy, found a jewel which he took to Delamirie's (D) goldsmith shop to learn what it was. Delamirie's (D) apprentice, under the pretense of weighing the jewel, removed the stones from the setting and told his master the value. Delamirie (D) offered Armory (P) three halfpence for the stones, but he refused. Delamirie (D) returned the setting without the stones.

ISSUE: Could Armory (P), who lacked legal title to the chattel, maintain an action to recover its value?

HOLDING AND DECISION: (Pratt, C.J.) Yes. The finder of lost property, although he does not acquire absolute ownership, does acquire title superior to everyone else except the rightful owner. Such title is a sufficient property interest in the finder upon which he may maintain an action against anyone (except the rightful owner) who violates that interest. Additionally, Delamirie (D) was liable as he was responsible for the actions of his apprentice. As for the measure of damages, if Delamirie (D) did not show the stones were not of the finest value, their value would be so determined.

EDITOR'S ANALYSIS: As to ownership, the finder is in a position similar to that of a bailee. The finder does not obtain absolute ownership, but does have the right of ownership against everybody except the true owner. Here, the chattel, the jewel, was subsequently converted against the finder. Yet the finder, if he should subsequently lose the chattel, may reclaim it from a subsequent finder. The finder has a choice of remedies. He may recover the chattel in specie if it is still in the converter's possession, or he may recover full value from the wrongdoer. Notice that an action in trover, which is an action at law, is to recover the value of the chattel. If it is desired to have the item returned, an action in replevin must be brought in equity.

QUICKNOTES

CHATTEL - An item of personal property.

TROVER - An action for damages resulting from the unlawful conversion of, or to recover possession of, personal property.

NOTES:

replevin - recover chattel

THE WINKFIELD

[1902] Ct. of App., P. 42, 1900-1903 All E.R. 346 (1901).

NATURE OF CASE: Action by bailee for damages for destruction of bailed property.

FACT SUMMARY: After the Winkfield collided with and sank the Mexican and its owners admitted liability for half the loss of the Mexican, the Postmaster-General, amongst others, filed claims for damages. The Postmaster sued for the loss of mail bags and parcels, for parcels whose owners had authorized the Postmaster to represent them, and for the value of letters and parcels whose owners did not make claim, but were lost in the accident.

CONCISE RULE OF LAW: As the possessor of property has absolute title to that property against all except the rightful owner, the possessor may maintain an action against anyone who violates that title (except for the rightful owner).

FACTS: The owners of the Winkfield, which collided with and sank the Mexican off the coast of South Africa, admitted liability for half the loss to the Mexican and paid into court 32,514 pounds. The Postmaster-General filed claim for the loss of a substantial amount of mail aboard the Mexican as follows: (1) 105 pounds for mail bags and parcels which were property of the crown; (2) 5,041 pounds for parcels whose owners authorized the Postmaster to represent them; and (3) 1,726 pounds estimated value of letters and parcels whose owners had not filed claim nor instructed the Postmaster, but who undertook to distribute this claim amongst them. While recovery was had on the first two claims, recovery was disallowed on a third ground as the Postmaster-General concededly was not liable to the senders or addressees for their loss.

ISSUE: Where a bailee brings an action against a wrongdoer who violated the title to bailed property held by the bailee, can the bailee recover the loss against the wrongdoer although he has no liability to the bailor?

HOLDING AND DECISION: (Collins, M.R.) Yes. A person possessed of goods as his property has absolute title against all but the rightful owner. One who violates that title, having no title in himself, is a wrongdoer and cannot defend himself by showing that title was in a third person, "For against a wrongdoer, possession is title." The right of the possessor to recover full damages cannot be made to depend upon the extent of his liability to the true owner as that question of liability is not relevant as between the possessor and wrongdoer. Between a bailee and a stranger, possession gives title, an absolute and completed ownership, and a right to receive the complete equivalent for his loss. Once full damages have been paid to the bailee, the wrongdoer has answered any claim by the bailor.

EDITOR'S ANALYSIS: In *Armory v. Delamirie*, 1 Strange 505 (1722), it was established that the possessor property has absolute title against all except the rightful owner, and that the possessor can maintain an action against anyone who violates his rights of possession. Early cases had established the right of a bailee to sue a wrongdoer on the basis of the bailee's liability to the bailor for the loss of the bailment. In this case, the bailee had no liability to his bailors. In fact, the bailors could not necessarily be established. Even so, as the bailee had the right to possession, he had all the rights inherent in possession against all except the rightful owner(s). Thus, it became irrelevant to the wrongdoer's argument that the bailee was not liable to his bailor. The issue was defendant's wrongful action alone. No argument could be interposed which was irrelevant to that issue. In those cases where the bailee is liable to his bailor, the bailee's recovery against the wrongdoer terminates the wrongdoer's liability. The bailor must seek his recovery against the bailee.

NOTES:

HANNAH v. PEEL

Finder of broach (P) v. Property owner (D)
1 K.B. 509 (1945).

NATURE OF CASE: Action to recover chattel (article of personal property).

FACT SUMMARY: Hannah (P), a soldier who found a diamond broach in a house temporarily requisitioned by the British Army, sought to recover the broach from the owner of the land, Peel (D), who claimed it even though he had not previously been aware of its existence nor knew the true owner.

CONCISE RULE OF LAW: The finder of a chattel, clearly lost, has rights to possession superior to everybody except the true owner; the place of finding is of no consequence.

FACTS: Peel (D) owned a house he had never occupied. Hannah (P), a soldier stationed in the house after the Army had requisitioned it, found a diamond broach covered with cobwebs and dirt loose in a crevice on the top of a windowpane. Hannah (P) turned the broach over to the police who, in turn, gave it to Peel (D). Peel (D) neither knew previously of the broach's existence nor its true owner. The true owner not having been found, Peel (D) sold the broach. Even though Peel (D) offered Hannah (P) a reward for finding the broach, Hannah (P) refused it, and sued Peel (D) for the return of the broach or its value and damages for its retention.

ISSUE: Does the finder of a chattel have a superior right to possession over everybody except the true owner, even when the chattel is found on the land of a third person?

HOLDING AND DECISION: (Birkett, J.) Yes. The court initially notes that, in surrendering up the broach, Hannah (P) did not intend to waive his claim to the article, and suggests that if the discovery had never been communicated to the defendant, the real owner of the broach could never have had a cause of action against the defendant simply because it was found in his home. Since Peel (D) never had custody over the broach, he had come under no responsibility, as he would have been had the broach been intentionally deposited in his home. The circumstances under which the broach was found indicate it was lost in the ordinary sense of the word. Furthermore, Peel (D) could claim no prior possession. The court distinguishes earlier cases which hold that a man possesses everything which is attached to or under his land by noting that the same principle does not embrace things lying unattached on the surface of a man's land even though no one else has possession. Judgment for Plaintiff.

EDITOR'S ANALYSIS: Following a traditional approach, Hannah (P) would probably not have prevailed had the broach been classified as misplaced, treasure trove or abandoned. A chattel is misplaced if voluntarily placed by the owner and then neglected or forgotten. Under this category, the land owner is in a better position to return the article to its true owner than a finder who takes the article off the premises. However, in this case, it is unlikely that the true owner would have placed the broach intentionally into the remote crevice from which it was recovered. Similarly, it is not likely the broach was a remnant of some treasure trove which in English common-law meant it was intentionally hidden or secreted and therefore reverts to the Crown. The broach is a single item of jewelry found uncovered and unenclosed. In this country, the finder has a superior right to treasure trove even over the state. Once again, the spot in which the broach was found suggests that it was not abandoned. A land owner who must suffer abandoned property should have possession of it if he chooses.

QUICKNOTES

CHATTEL - An article of personal property, as distinguished from real property; a thing personal and moveable.

POSSESSORY RIGHT - The right to possess particular real property to the exclusion of others.

TREASURE TROVE - Money, coin, gold, or silver hidden in the earth or elsewhere whose owner is unknown.

NOTES:

McAVOY v. MEDINA
Wallet finder (P) v. Barber shop owner (D)
Mass. Sup. Ct., 93 Mass. 548 (1866).

NATURE OF CASE: Action to recover money.

FACT SUMMARY: A wallet was inadvertently left at a barber shop, a customer (P) found it, and the barber (D) asserted ownership.

CONCISE RULE OF LAW: Misplaced goods (items intentionally placed by the owner where they were found and then forgotten or left there) are deemed to be in the bailment of the owner of the property on which they are found for the true owner.

FACTS: McAvoy (P) was a customer in Medina's (D) barber shop. McAvoy (P) found a wallet which was lying on a table. McAvoy (P) showed Medina (D) where he found the wallet and told Medina (D) to keep the wallet and the money in it and to give it to the real owner. Medina (D) promised to attempt to find the owner. McAvoy (P) later made three demands for return of the money, but Medina (D) refused. The wallet had been placed on the table by a transient customer of the barber shop, and had been accidentally left there. The true owner was never found.

ISSUE: Does the finder of misplaced goods on another's property obtain title to the goods?

HOLDING AND DECISION: (Dewey, J.) No. The owner of the premises on which misplaced goods are found is deemed to be the bailee of the goods for the true owner. This wallet was not lost. It had been voluntarily placed upon a table and then accidentally left there. This is different from lost property which had not been voluntarily placed by the owner where it was later found. When goods are misplaced, the finder acquires no original right to the property. Holding the owner of the premises as bailee of the goods is better adapted to secure the rights of the true owner.

EDITOR'S ANALYSIS: The focus of lost or misplaced property cases is to determine whether it is likely that the true owner can ever be found. Therefore, because the finder was the first in possession, he will have paramount rights. On the other hand, where goods have been voluntarily placed and then forgotten, the true owner is much more likely to be found. As the true owner would be more likely to return to where he remembered placing the article, the owner of the premises will be deemed a bailee for the true owner.

QUICKNOTES

BAILMENT - The delivery of property to be held in trust and which is designated for a particular purpose, following the satisfaction of which the property is either to be returned or disposed of as specified.

NOTES:

BENJAMIN v. LINDNER AVIATION, INC.
Employee (P) v. Employer (D)
Sup. Ct. of Iowa 534 N.W.2d 400 (1995).

NATURE OF CASE: Appeal and cross-appeal from declaratory judgment establishing right to mislaid property.

FACT SUMMARY: Heath Benjamin (P), who found over $18,000 in the wing of an airplane he was working on while employed by Lindner Aviation (D), appealed from holding that the money belonged to the owner of the airplane, State Central Bank (D).

CONCISE RULE OF LAW: The finder of mislaid property acquires no rights to the property since possession belongs to the owner of the premises upon which the property is found.

FACTS: In April of 1992, Benjamin (P) was employed as an airplane inspector by Lindner Aviation (D). While servicing a plane belonging to State Central Bank (D), Benjamin (P) discovered two packets wrapped in foil inside the left wing. Inside the packets was over $18,000 in twenty-dollar bills with mint dates mostly from the 1950s. The money was turned over to the authorities, and two days later Benjamin (P) filed an affidavit with the county auditor claiming that he was the finder of the currency. Pursuant to Iowa Code chapter 644, notices regarding the found money were posted and published, and Lindner (D) and the Bank (D) filed similar claims. When no one claimed the money within twelve months, Benjamin (P) filed a declaratory judgment against Lindner (D) and the Bank (D) to establish his right to the money, but the district court held that chapter 644 applied only to "lost" money and that this money was "mislaid." The court awarded the money to the Bank (D) and awarded Benjamin (P) a 10% finder's fee pursuant to chapter 644. Benjamin (P) and Linder (D) appealed, claiming that chapter 644 eliminated distinctions made at common law between various types of found property.

ISSUE: Does the finder of mislaid property acquire rights to it?

HOLDING AND DECISION: (Ternus, J.) No. The finder of mislaid property acquires no rights to the property since possession belongs to the owner of the premises upon which the property is found. Chapter 644 does not abrogate the common law classifications of found property. Mislaid property is voluntarily put in a certain place by the owner, who then forgets where it is, and it is therefore different in nature from lost property. The premises where the money was found was the airplane, belonging to the Bank (D), and not Lindner's (D) hangar. Therefore, the trial court correctly looked to the common law classifications of found property in holding that the Bank (D) was the proper owner of the money. Affirmed.

DISSENT: (Snell, J.) The money should be awarded to Benjamin (P) as the finder of abandoned property. The evidence indicates that the money had been in the wing for over thirty years, thus satisfying the legal requirements for abandonment.

EDITOR'S ANALYSIS: The dissent has a valid point; it does seem as if the money was beyond the point of having been merely mislaid. It is also important to consider, however, that the money was not discovered under a rock in an abandoned field. If all other facts were the same except that the airplane was located on the Bank's (D) property when it was being serviced by Benjamin (D) and he discovered the money, the majority's decision seems like the only fair one.

NOTES:

COLUMBUS-AMERICA DISCOVERY GROUP v. ATLANTIC MUTUAL INSURANCE CO.

Salvagers (P) v. Insurers(D)

974 F.2d 450 (4th Cir. 1992)

NATURE OF CASE: Appeal from judgment for plaintiff.

FACT SUMMARY: The district court found that Atlantic Mutual (D) and other insurance companies had abandoned their interest in sunken treasure and applied the law of finds, rather than the law of salvage.

CONCISE RULE OF LAW: When a previous owner claims long lost property that was involuntarily taken from his control, abandonment must be proved by clear and convincing evidence.

FACTS: When Columbus-America Discovery Group (P) salvaged a shipwreck that had sunk off the coast of South Carolina in 1857, over a million dollars worth of California gold and other treasures were found. Atlantic Mutual (D) and other insurance companies that had paid the owners' claims at the time of the disaster claimed ownership of the treasure. The district court found that the insurers (D) had deliberately destroyed all their records, thereby abandoning any claim of ownership, and declared that Columbus (P) was the finder and sole owner. Atlantic (D) appealed, alleging that the court should have applied the law of salvage, not the law of finds.

ISSUE: When a previous owner claims long lost property that was involuntarily taken from his control, must abandonment be proved by clear and convincing evidence?

HOLDING AND DECISION: (Russell, C.J.) Yes. When a previous owner claims long lost property that was involuntarily taken from his control, abandonment must be proved by clear and convincing evidence. The lower court erred when it found an abandonment and applied the law of finds. On remand, the court is to apply the law of salvage. The salvor is to receive compensation for its service but it did not receive any right to title to the sunken treasure. Reversed and remanded.

DISSENT: (Widener, J.) The district court's finding of abandonment and its specific finding that the underwriters intentionally destroyed all the documents proving their claim to the treasure were both supported by the evidence. Under case precedents, abandonment may be inferred from circumstantial evidence.

EDITOR'S ANALYSIS: The majority concluded that the missing documents may have been lost or stolen. The dissent assumed that the missing documents were intentionally destroyed. The law of finds has been applied only in cases where the owners expressly and publicly abandoned their property.

QUICKNOTES

SALVAGE - The value of an item of property, determined when it is acquired, that is calculated as an offset to a taxpayer's gross income when that item is no longer useful to the taxpayer's generation of income.

TREASURE TROVE - Money, coin, gold, or silver hidden in the earth or elsewhere whose owner is unknown.

NOTES:

CHAPTER 2
ACQUISITION OF PROPERTY BY CONQUEST, ADVERSE POSSESSION, AND PRESCRIPTION

QUICK REFERENCE RULES OF LAW

1. **Conquest.** Discovery gave exclusive title to those who made it. (Johnson and Graham's Lessee v. M'Intosh)

2. **Adverse Possession and Prescriptions of Interests in Land.** Title to land based on adverse possession may be obtained where the possessor performs acts of ownership for over 21 years without interruption, with the knowledge of an adverse claimant. (Ewing v. Burnet)

3. **Problems in Applying the Statute of Limitations: Tacking.** Whether a claimant's physical acts upon the land of another are sufficiently continuous, notorious and exclusive does not necessarily depend on the existence of significant improvements, substantial activity, or absolute exclusivity. (Nome 2000 v. Fagerstrom)

4. **Problems in Applying the Statute of Limitations: Tacking.** The doctrine of adverse possession does not protect parties who are ignorant of their interest in property. (Lawrence v. Town of Concord)

5. **Color of Title.** No use of land while it is owned by the state can support a claim of an easement by prescription. (Kiowa Creek Land & Cattle Co. v. Nazarian)

6. **Color of Title.** A future estate cannot be harmed during the pendency of an intervening estate. (Dieterich Int'l Truck Sales, Inc. v. J.S. & J. Services, Inc.)

7. **Adverse Possession of Chattels and Preservation of Cultural Heritage.** In the context of a replevin action for particular, unique and concealed works of art, a plaintiff has not discovered his cause of action until he learns that the works are being held by another and who, or at least where, that other is. (Autocephalous Greek-Orthodox Church of Cyprus v. Goldberg & Feldman Fine Arts, Inc.)

8. **Adverse Possession of Chattels and Preservation of Cultural Heritage.** There is no duty of reasonable diligence imposed upon the true owners of stolen art work for purposes of the statute of limitations in a replevin action. (Solomon R. Guggenheim Foundation v. Lubell)

9. **Adverse Possession of Chattels and Preservation of Cultural Heritage.** (1) The statute of limitations for bringing a claim against the government is tolled where the government has deliberately kept a plaintiff in ignorance of vital information necessary to pursue the plaintiff's claim within the statutory time period. (2) A claim of breach of implied-in-fact contract of bailment survives a motion to dismiss for failure to state a claim where it is alleged that defendant: has taken possession of the property with knowledge that it belongs to plaintiff and without claiming the property to be his own; has taken the property with the express intent of returning it to its rightful owner, and has stored and protected the property for that purpose; and has falsely declared the property to be unidentifiable, thereby breaching the contract. (Rosner v. United States)

10. **Acquisition of Rights by Public Use and the Public Trust Doctrine.** When the government unilaterally authorizes a permanent, public easement across private lands, this constitutes a taking requiring just compensation. (Opinion of the Justices—Public Use of Coastal Beaches)

JOHNSON AND GRAHAM'S LESSEE v. M'INTOSH
Investors (P) v. Grantees (D)
21 U.S. 543 (1823)

NATURE OF CASE: Appeal from judgment for defendant in action in ejectment.

FACT SUMMARY: Johnson and Graham's Lessee (P) had purportredly acquired title to land from Native-American tribes, but the United States claimed that it held title to the territory and, consequently, only it could convey good title to others.

CONCISE RULE OF LAW: Discovery gave exclusive title to those who made it.

FACTS: The Illinois Indians in 1775 purported to convey 11,560 acres to Johnson and Graham's Lessee (P) for private investment. M'Intosh (D) claimed the same land under a grant from the United States. When Johnson and Graham's Lessee (P) sued, M'Intosh (D) alleged that discovery by the European nations gave them complete sovereignty over the land they discovered and the United States acquired clear title to all such lands when it won its independence from Great Britain. The court found that, although the land was occupied by the Indians, they did not hold title and could not convey good title to the land. Johnson (P) appealed.

ISSUE: Did discovery give exclusive title to those who made it?

HOLDING AND DECISION: (Marshall, C.J.) Yes. Discovery gave exclusive title to those who made it. The British government asserted title to all the lands occupied by Indians and their rights have passed to the United States. The Indian inhabitants are to be considered merely as occupants, incapable of transferring good title to others. Affirmed.

EDITOR'S ANALYSIS: This decision contributed to the absence of bidding for Indian land. This resulted in a single buyer with no competition who obtained land at bargain prices. The Native-Americans were driven west by the European settlers.

QUICKNOTES

TITLE - The right of possession over property.

TRANSFER OF TITLE - Any transfer or conveyance having an effect on title to an interest in real property.

NOTES:

EWING v. BURNET
Landowner (P) v. Adverse possessor (D)
36 U.S. 41 (1837).

NATURE OF CASE: Appeal from denial of order of ejectment.

FACT SUMMARY: Ewing (P) contended that because his title to a lot was issued prior to the title issued to Burnet (D) from a common grantor, he had good title even though Burnet (D) had used and exercised open and notorious dominion and control over the properly for over 21 years.

CONCISE RULE OF LAW: Title to land based on adverse possession may be obtained where the possessor performs acts of ownership for over 21 years without interruption, with the knowledge of an adverse claimant.

FACTS: Symmes conveyed title to a parcel of land to Forman in 1798. In 1803, he executed a deed to the same lot to Burnet (D). Forman conveyed his title to Williams, who knew of Burnet's (D) adverse claim, but did not act on it and did not exercise control of the land. For over 21 years, the statutory period for adverse possession in Ohio, Burnet (D) controlled the land, granting leases for the use of its gravel, using the gravel himself, and prosecuting trespassers. He did so openly and notoriously. Williams died in 1824, and Ewing (P) succeeded to the land. He brought suit in ejectment, and the jury found Burnet (D) had obtained title by adverse possession. Ewing (P) appealed.

ISSUE: Does the open and notorious exercise of ownership and control over land continuously for over 21 years permit a party to assert title by adverse possession?

HOLDING AND DECISION: (Baldwin, J.) Yes. A party may obtain title to land by adverse possession if he exercises open and notorious control over land for over 21 years, to such an extent as to evidence an assertion of ownership over that of a knowing adverse claimant. The determination whether the acts of open ownership were sufficient to establish adverse possession was a determination of fact. In this case, the use of the gravel, the granting of leases, and the prosecution of trespassers clearly support the jury's finding of sufficient ownership and control, and therefore such findings must be upheld on appeal. Affirmed.

EDITOR'S ANALYSIS: The time period included in adverse possession statutes, usually 20 years, is a special type of a statute of limitations. It requires a landowner to bring suit to remove an encroaching party within the time period or forfeit the cause of action, and with it, the title to the land. The reason for allowing a party to obtain title by adverse possession is to induce the full use of land. An owner who allows his land to lie dormant for extended periods is not aiding society by exploiting his land. To induce full use of lands, society threatens the owner with loss of title to a party who will use the land productively.

QUICKNOTES

ADVERSE POSSESSION - A means of acquiring title to real property by remaining in actual, open, continuous, exclusive possession of property for the statutory period.

NOTES:

NOME 2000 v. FAGERSTROM
Landowner (P) v. Adverse possessor (D)
Alaska Sup. Ct., 799 P.2d 304 (1990).

NATURE OF CASE: Suit for ejectment and counterclaim to acquire title by adverse possession.

FACT SUMMARY: Charles and Peggy Fagerstrom (D) used a parcel of land owned by Nome 2000 (P) for various purposes from 1944 to 1987 but did not build a house on it until 1978, thereby defeating their adverse possession claim, according to Nome (P).

CONCISE RULE OF LAW: Whether a claimant's physical acts upon the land of another are sufficiently continuous, notorious and exclusive does not necessarily depend on the existence of significant improvements, substantial activity, or absolute exclusivity.

FACTS: Fagerstrom (D) used a rural parcel of land owned by Nome 2000 (P) for recreational purposes beginning in 1944. In the 1970s, Fagerstrom's (D) family began to make more substantial use of the land, adding improvements and spending more time there each year. In 1977, they built a reindeer shelter that occasionally housed reindeer. They also excluded trailers from the land and spent weekends there. In 1987, the Fagerstroms (D) built a cabin on the land and continued to use the land on weekends and vacations for recreational purposes. In 1987, Nome 2000 (P) brought suit to quiet title. The Fagerstroms (D) counterclaimed for title by adverse possession. The jury found for the Fagerstroms (D) and the court entered judgment for the entire parcel. Nome 2000 (P) appealed.

ISSUE: Does a claim of adverse possession depend on the existence of significant improvements, substantial activity, or absolute exclusivity?

HOLDING AND DECISION: (Matthews, C.J.) No. Whether a claimant's physical acts upon the land of another are sufficiently continuous, notorious and exclusive does not necessarily depend on the existence of significant improvements, substantial activity, or absolute exclusivity. Use consistent with the use by any similarly situated owner is sufficient to establish claim by adverse possession. The statute requires continuous, notorious, hostile and exclusive use of a property for ten years in order to succeed in a claim for adverse possession. Nome (P) claimed that the Fagerstroms' (D) possession only became adverse when they built the cabin in 1978, and thus they did not meet the statutory ten-year period. But the statute does not require actual improvements to the land, only sufficient use based on the type of property occupied. The land in question is rural and thus has a lower requirement of use. The Fagerstroms (D) occupied the land sufficiently that their occupation was visible in 1977. The various structures erected and the feeling of the community that the

Fagerstroms were the owners of the property meets the statutory requirement of continuous, notorious exclusive and hostile possession. Affirmed in part, reversed in part, and remanded.

EDITOR'S ANALYSIS: The court found that what the Fagerstroms (D), as Native Alaskans, believed or intended vis-a-vis the property had nothing to do with whether their possession was hostile. The hostility requirement merely means that the adverse possessor acted toward the land as if he were the owner. But the Fagerstroms (D) claim title to a large portion of the land was only partially granted by the court. The Fagerstroms' (D) use of certain trails for hiking did not constitute dominion and control over the south portion of the land sufficient to demonstrate adverse possession.

QUICKNOTES

ADVERSE POSSESSION - A means of acquiring title to real property by remaining in actual, open, continuous, exclusive possession of property for the statutory period.

EASEMENT BY PRESCRIPTION - A manner of acquiring an easement in another's property by continuous and uninterrupted use in satisfaction of the statutory requirements of adverse possession.

EJECTMENT - An action to oust someone in possession of real property unlawfully and to restore possession to the party lawfully entitled to it.

NOTES:

LAWRENCE v. TOWN OF CONCORD

Devisee of alleged adverse possessor (P) v. Owner (D)

Mass. Sup. Ct., 788 N.E.2d 546 (2003).

NATURE OF CASE: Appeal from affirmance of summary judgment for defendant in adverse possession action.

FACT SUMMARY: Frazier occupied land from 1965 to 1996 and devised the land to Lawrence (P). It was not until 1997 that the town of Concord (Concord) (D) learned that it had received a devise of the land under a will probated in 1942, and was therefore its owner. Lawrence (P) claimed title to the land through Frazier by virtue of Frazier's adverse possession.

CONCISE RULE OF LAW: The doctrine of adverse possession does not protect parties who are ignorant of their interest in property.

FACTS: Burke left land (the "locus") in the town of Concord (D) to her daughter, Burke Boyer, who conveyed her life interest to Burke's adopted daughter, Burke Frazier. Burke Frazier was married to Joseph Frazier. Burke's will had provided that if Burke Frazier were not survived by children, the property would go to the town of Concord (D). Burke Frazier died in 1965, survived only by Frazier. Frazier lived continuously at the locus for at least twenty years (the number of years required for adverse possession). Frazier devised the locus to Lawrence, who claimed to be its owner when Frazier died in 1997. The town (D), believing itself to be the owner of the property, took the property by eminent domain without compensating Lawrence (P), who filed suit claiming title to the land by virtue of Frazier's purported adverse possession. Lawrence (P) contended that Frazier had satisfied all the elements of adverse possession, in that his possession was exclusive, continuous, open, notorious, and adverse to the town's ownership for the requisite period. The trial court granted summary judgment for Concord (D), and the appellate court affirmed. The state's supreme court granted review.

ISSUE: Does the doctrine of adverse possession protect parties who are ignorant of their interest in property?

HOLDING AND DECISION: (Spina, J.) No. The doctrine of adverse possession does not protect parties who are ignorant of their interest in property. The town (D) argues that because it did not know that it owned the locus, it would be inequitable to allow Frazier to acquire title to it by adverse possession. The town also argues that because of its lack of knowledge of its ownership of the locus, Frazier's possession of the property was not sufficiently "open" and "notorious" to place the town on notice of its ownership interest. However, the adverse possession statute pertains to the owner's knowledge of an adverse possessor's use, not the owner's knowledge of ownership. The purpose of the "open and notorious" requirement is to place the true owner on notice of the hostile activity of the possession so that the true owner may take responsive legal action. Such notice, however, does not need to be explicit, and it is constructive, so that it is immaterial whether the true owner actually learns of the adverse use or not. Also, an owner's knowledge of its interest is not an element of proof of a claim of adverse possession, and an owner's lack of knowledge of ownership is not a defense to such a claim. Such a conclusion supports the purpose of adverse possession, which is to quiet controversy and sanction long continued usages of property. Moreover, Frazier had no obligation to reveal to the town (D) its true ownership. Even if he intended to conceal the truth, as many adverse possessors do, Frazier's use was open to the world to see, and he appeared to be acting as the true owner. Thus, his intent is irrelevant. An adverse possessor has no burden to reveal his intentions to the true owner absent a special relationship between the parties, *e.g.*, lessor/lessee. Here, there was no such special relationship. The town claims that Frazier's claim of adverse possession fails because he himself did not live there continuously, but rented the property for certain periods of time. However, a person claiming title by adverse possession need not personally occupy the land for the statutory period (here, 20 years); he may rely on the possession of his tenants, whose possession is his own. Even where the tenants overstay their tenancy, all that they interrupt is use of the property, not the underlying claim to ownership in fee simple; all they can claim is a leasehold estate, not a fee simple estate. For all these reasons, Frazier satisfied all the requirements for a claim of adverse possession of the locus. Therefore, Lawrence (P) is entitled to damages. Reversed and remanded.

EDITOR'S ANALYSIS: Although most courts agree with the court in this case that an adverse possessor's subjective state of mind is irrelevant to determining title by adverse possession, some courts have held that possession pursuant to a mistaken belief is not adverse, and that to be adverse, a possessor must intend to claim title to the property at issue (also known as the Maine doctrine). Most courts have rejected this stance in favor of a doctrine that holds that a mistake as to ownership is immaterial so long as the claimant conducted himself as the owner. Critics of the Maine doctrine have pointed out that it rewards the intentional wrongdoer and punishes the honest, mistaken possessor. Still, other courts take the position that only good-faith claimants may obtain title by adverse possession.

QUICKNOTES

ADVERSE POSSESSION - A means of acquiring title to real property by remaining in actual, open, continuous, exclusive possession of property for the statutory period.

DEVISE - The conferring of a gift of real or personal property by means of a testamentary instrument.

EMINENT DOMAIN - The governmental power to take private property for public use so long as just compensation is paid therefore.

KIOWA CREEK LAND & CATTLE CO. v. NAZARIAN

Neighbors (P) v. Landowners (D)

Neb. Ct. App., 554 N.W.2d 175 (1996).

NATURE OF CASE: Appeal from judgment for defendants in declaratory judgment action.

FACT SUMMARY: The Nazarians (D) purchased land from the Nebraska Board of Educational Lands and Funds four years before Kiowa (P) sought a declaratory judgment that it held an easement by prescription over a section of the land.

CONCISE RULE OF LAW: No use of land while it is owned by the state can support a claim of an easement by prescription.

FACTS: Kiowa (P) sought a declaratory judgment that it held an easement by prescription over a section of neighboring land the Nazarians (D) had purchased from the state. The district court granted the Nazarians' (D) motion for summary judgment because the statute of limitations did not run against the state, and the land had been in private ownership for less than the ten years required by law for a prescriptive easement. Kiowa (P) appealed.

ISSUE: May use of land while it is owned by the state support a claim of an easement by prescription?

HOLDING AND DECISION: (Hannon, J.) No. No use of land while it is owned by the state can support a claim of an easement by prescription, either against the state or against anyone who acquires title from the state. Just as land may not be the subject of adverse possession while the title is in the state, similarly land may not be the subject of an easement by prescription while the title is in the state. The state usually leases school lands for a period of twelve years. If the public could acquire easements by prescription over such land, the state's rights would be indirectly hampered by injuring those who buy land from it. Affirmed.

EDITOR'S ANALYSIS: The court here distinguished cases where neither party traced his rights in the property to the government. Here, the Nazarians (D) had acquired their right to the land from the state. The common law rule that government land cannot be subject to adverse possession or prescription is not followed in all jurisdictions.

DIETERICH INT'L TRUCK SALES, INC. v. J.S. & J SERVICES, INC.

Business owner (P) v. Neighbor (D)

Cal. Ct. App., 2d 388, (1992).

NATURE OF CASE: Appeal from action to quiet title in an easement.

FACT SUMMARY: The district court found that Dieterich (P) had acquired an easement by prescription for access over J.S. & J.'s (D) neighboring truck stop, but the landlord appealed.

CONCISE RULE OF LAW: A future estate cannot be harmed during the pendency of an intervening estate.

FACTS: J.S. & J. Services (D) was required to replace underground storage tanks at part of its gas station and truck stop. However, the area in question was being used by Dieterich (P) to allow his customers' trucks access to his truck repair business. Dieterich (P) filed a complaint for injunctive and declaratory relief and to quiet title to the easement. The trial court held that Dieterich (P) had acquired an easement by prescription against both J.S. & J. (D) and his landlord. The landlord appealed, claiming that since he held only a future interest, he did not have a present possessory interest in the land which could be subject to a prescriptive easement.

ISSUE: May a future estate be harmed during the pendency of an intervening estate?

HOLDING AND DECISION: (McDaniel, A.J.) No. A future estate cannot be harmed during the pendency of an intervening estate. The prescriptive period cannot commence until the future estate is vested and the lease has ended. The landlord lacked a present possessory interest in the property and was not able to legally bring an action to prevent Dieterich (P) from gaining the easement by prescription. The judgment was affirmed as to J. S. & J. (D), but reversed as to the landlord. Affirmed in part, reversed in part.

EDITOR'S ANALYSIS: The interest the landlord sought to protect was his right to possession. It was that stick in the bundle of rights which gives the landlord the power to prevent others from entering his property. To protect that interest, a possessor must bring an action in trespass or ejectment.

AUTOCEPHALOUS GREEK-ORTHODOX CHURCH OF CYPRUS v. GOLDBERG & FELDMAN FINE ARTS, INC.

Original Owner (P) v. Purchaser (D)

917 F.2d 278 (7th Cir. 1990), *cert. denied*, 502 U.S. 941 (1991)

NATURE OF CASE: Appeal from award in replevin for plaintiff.

FACT SUMMARY: The district court awarded possession of mosaics plundered from a church on Cyprus back to the Greek-Orthodox Church of Cyprus (P) when the Church sued for replevin.

CONCISE RULE OF LAW: In the context of a replevin action for particular, unique and concealed works of art, a plaintiff has not discovered his cause of action until he learns that the works are being held by another and who, or at least where, that other is.

FACTS: When the Autocephalous Greek-Orthodox Church of Cyprus (P) learned that precious artworks were vandalized and looted in churches which had come under the control of Turkish Cypriots following the Turkish invasion of the island in 1974, it sought the assistance of many international organizations and individuals in recovering the stolen art treasures and religious relics. When the Republic of Cyprus and the Greek-Orthodox Church of Cyprus (P) were notified in 1988 by a museum curator in California that mosaics from a Cypriot church dating to the fourth century were being offered for sale by Goldberg (D), an Indiana art dealer, they immediately asked for their return. Goldberg (D) refused to return them and Cyprus (P) sued for recovery of the mosaics. The district court, as a federal district court sitting in diversity, applied the law of Indiana and ordered the return of the mosaics to the Church of Cyprus (P). Goldberg (D) appealed, alleging that the six-year statute of limitations had expired before the Church of Cyprus (P) filed its complaint, and that the Church (P) had not exercised due diligence in searching for the mosaics.

ISSUE: In the context of a replevin action for particular, unique and concealed works of art, has a plaintiff discovered his cause of action before he learns that the works are being held by another and who, or at least where, that other is?

HOLDING AND DECISION: (Bauer, C.J.) No. In the context of a replevin action for particular, unique and concealed works of art, a plaintiff has not discovered his cause of action until he learns that the works are being held by another and who, or at least where, that other is. In this case, the Republic of Cyprus took substantial and meaningful steps, from the time it first learned of the disappearance of the mosaics, to locate and recover them. The mosaics were owned by the Church (P), they were removed from the Church (P) without any authorization, and Goldberg (D), as an ultimate purchaser from a thief, had no valid claim of title or right to possession of the mosaics. The elements for replevin were thus properly established. Affirmed.

CONCURRENCE: (Cudahy, Cir.J.) When the possessor of stolen or lost personal property commits fraud in the concealment, the statute of limitations does not run against the original owner until that owner has actual knowledge of the location of the property and the identity of the possessor.

EDITOR'S ANALYSIS: The concurrence here also discussed international agreements regarding the importation of cultural property. Under both international and federal law, the Cypriot mosaics would be considered cultural property warranting international protection. The cultural heritage of foreign nations is subject to special treatment regardless of whether the property was originally stolen or merely illegally exported from the country of origin.

QUICKNOTES

FRAUDULENT CONCEALMENT - The concealing of a material fact which a party is under an obligation to disclose.

REPLEVIN - An action to recover personal property wrongfully taken.

STATUTE OF LIMITATIONS - A law prescribing the period in which a legal action may be commenced.

NOTES:

SOLOMON R. GUGGENHEIM FOUNDATION v. LUBELL
N.Y. Ct. of App., 567 N.Y.S.2d 623 (1991).

NATURE OF CASE: Appeal from decision dismissing Statute of Limitations defense in replevin action.

FACT SUMMARY: The Lubells (D) appealed from an appellate court decision dismissing their Statute of Limitations defense and denying their cross-motion for summary judgment in Solomon R. Guggenheim Foundation's (Museum) (P) replevin action, contending that the Museum's (P) failure to take certain steps to recover a stolen Chagall gouache was relevant to their defense.

CONCISE RULE OF LAW: There is no duty of reasonable diligence imposed upon the true owners of stolen art work for purposes of the statute of limitations in a replevin action.

FACTS: The Museum (P) was the true owner of a Chagall gouache, valued at an estimated $200,000. The gouache was apparently stolen in the mid- to late 1960s by a Museum (P) employee. The Lubells (D) purchased the gouache from a well-known Madison Avenue gallery in 1967, displaying it in their home for over 20 years, and exhibiting it twice, in 1967 and 1981, at the gallery. The Museum (P) learned the gouache was not where it should have been in the late 1960s but claimed it did not discover it was stolen until 1969 or 1970. The Museum (P) did not notify any other museums, galleries, artistic organizations, or any law enforcement authorities of the theft. In 1986, the Museum (P) demanded the gouache's return. The Lubells (D) refused. In 1987, the Museum (P) brought a replevin action. The Lubells (D) successfully cross-moved for summary judgment based upon their Statute of Limitations defense, but on appeal, the defense was dismissed and the cross-motion for summary judgment denied on the grounds that delay alone could not make the replevin action untimely. From this decision, the Lubells (D) appealed.

ISSUE: Is the diligence of the true owner in attempting to recover stolen art work a factor in determining the statute of limitations in a replevin action?

HOLDING AND DECISION: [Judge not stated in casebook excerpt.] No. There is no duty of reasonable diligence imposed upon the true owners of stolen artwork for purposes of the statue of limitations in a replevin action. The only relevant factors in assessing the merits of the Statute of Limitations defense would be the Museum's (P) demand for the gouache's return, and the Lubells' (D) refusal to do so. State law has long protected the rights of a true owner of stolen property, even as to a good faith purchaser. The "discovery rule," which imposes a duty of due diligence, has been considered and rejected in this jurisdiction. This is prudent especially in a replevin action, where demand and refusal are substantive elements of the cause of action. There is

no consensus in the art world as to the best way to recover stolen art work, and placing the burden of locating stolen an work on the true owner would promote the illicit trafficking of stolen art. [The court still felt that the Museum's (P) conduct would still be an issue as the trial court considered the equities in the present case.] Affirmed.

EDITOR'S ANALYSIS: The court, in relieving the Museum (P) of any duty of reasonable diligence, placed the burden upon the Lubells (D) to prove that the gouache was not stolen. Ignored in the discussion, however, appears to be the role of the Robert Elkon Gallery, where the Lubells (D) purchased the gouache. Since they, as a broker of artworks, may be in the best position to control illicit trafficking, it would seem appropriate to impose some duty of diligence to inform galleries, since it appears that a simple notice could have prevented this litigation. It could also be argued that the Lubells' (D) remedy would have been to bring an action against the Elkon Gallery.

QUICKNOTES
REPLEVIN - An action to recover personal property wrongfully taken.

NOTES:

ROSNER v. UNITED STATES

Jewish victims of pro-Nazi Hungarians (P) v.
Federal government (D)
231 F. Supp. 2d 1202 (S.D. Fla. 2002).

NATURE OF CASE: Motion to dismiss in action for theft of property in Hungary during World War II.

FACT SUMMARY: Hungarian Jews (P) claimed that their property, which had been stolen by pro-Nazi Hungarians during World War II and later seized by the United States Army, was identifiable and known to belong to them, and asserted counts of (1) unconstitutional taking; (2) breach of an implied-in-fact contract of bailment; and (3) violation of conventional and customary international law.

CONCISE RULE OF LAW:
(1) The statute of limitations for bringing a claim against the government is tolled where the government has deliberately kept a plaintiff in ignorance of vital information necessary to pursue the plaintiff's claim within the statutory time period.

(2) A claim of breach of implied-in-fact contract of bailment survives a motion to dismiss for failure to state a claim where it is alleged that defendant: has taken possession of the property with knowledge that it belongs to plaintiff and without claiming the property to be his own; has taken the property with the express intent of returning it to its rightful owner, and has stored and protected the property for that purpose; and has falsely declared the property to be unidentifiable, thereby breaching the contract.

FACTS: After Nazi Germany invaded Hungary in 1944, the Hungarian government forced all Jews to turn over their gold, silver, gems, and other personal valuables to the government, which declared itself the owner of the property. Toward the end of World War II, the property was placed on a train bound for Germany, known as the "Gold Train." Before the train reached its destination, the U.S. Army seized the train outside Salzburg, Austria. American troops guarded the train for close to three months, after which the property was moved to storage facilities. Hungarian Jews (P) and their descendants claimed that the majority of the assets, with the exception of 1200 paintings, were stored in a Military Government Warehouse and that the assets were clearly identifiable because they had been placed in locked containers with the names and addresses of the owners on the outside. The Hungarian Jews (P) also claimed that the U.S. government (D) had overwhelming circumstantial evidence that the assets belonged to them. The Hungarian Jews (P) also contended that in 1946, the U.S. government (D) declared that it was impossible to identify either the individual owner or country of origin of the assets. Thereafter, unbeknownst to the Hungarian Jews (P), the U.S. government (D) sold, distributed and/or requisitioned the property from the Gold Train, and a substantial amount of property was looted from the warehouse. The Hungarian Jews (P) did not know the ultimate disposition of the property, and it was only in 1999, when the Presidential Advisory Commission on Holocaust Assets released its Report on the Gold Train, that many of the facts presented in the Hungarian Jews' (P) complaint came to light. The Hungarian Jews asserted three counts against the United States government: (1) unconstitutional taking under the Fifth Amendment; (2) breach of an implied-in-fact contract of bailment; and (3) violation of conventional and customary international law. The U.S. government (D) moved to dismiss on the grounds that the complaint was untimely and barred by sovereign immunity, that the claim relating to the violation of international law was barred because Congress had not waived sovereign immunity for such a claim, and that the takings and bailment claims failed to state claims upon which relief can be granted.

ISSUE:
(1) Is the statute of limitations for bringing a claim against the government tolled where the government has deliberately kept a plaintiff in ignorance of vital information necessary to pursue the plaintiff's claim within the statutory time period?

(2) Does a claim of breach of implied-in-fact contract of bailment survive a motion to dismiss for failure to state a claim where it is alleged that defendant: has taken possession of the property with knowledge that it belongs to plaintiff and without claiming the property to be his own; has taken the property with the express intent of returning it to its rightful owner, and has stored and protected the property for that purpose; and has falsely declared the property to be unidentifiable, thereby breaching the contract?

HOLDING AND DECISION: (Seitz, D.J.)
(1) Yes. The statute of limitations for bringing a claim against the government is tolled where the government has deliberately kept a plaintiff in ignorance of vital information necessary to pursue the plaintiff's claim within the statutory time period. As to the government's (D) argument that the suit is barred by sovereign immunity, the applicable statute of limitations for the Hungarian Jews' (P) claims is six years. The government (D) argues that because the Hungarian Jews (P) knew by at least 1947 that the U.S. Army controlled the Gold Train, the limitations period expired no later than 1953. The Hungarian Jews (P) argue that under the continuing violation doctrine, the limitations period has yet to run, and that the limitations period should be tolled based on the

Continued on next page.

27

principle of equitable tolling. Here, the continuing violation doctrine is inapplicable, because that doctrine is usually applied to claims with very short limitations periods, and is narrowly construed. Sometimes it is used where an employee fears reprisal from an employer. Here, however, none of these concerns are present. Nonetheless, the equitable tolling doctrine offers plaintiffs who have been prevented by inequitable circumstances from bringing a timely claim an opportunity to sue even after the expiration of the limitations period. Here, taking the Hungarian Jews' (P) factual assertions as true, the Hungarian Jews (P) were tricked by the government's (D) misconduct into allowing the filing deadline to pass because the government (D) deliberately kept them in ignorance of vital information essential to pursue their claims, without any fault or lack of due diligence on their part. Also, given the difficulty faced by most of the Hungarian Jews (P) after World War II, the circumstances warrant equitable tolling of the limitations period at this stage (summary judgment proceeding).

(2) Yes. A claim of breach of implied-in-fact contract of bailment survives a motion to dismiss for failure to state a claim where it is alleged that defendant: has taken possession of the property with knowledge that it belongs to plaintiff and without claiming the property to be its own; has taken the property with the express intent of returning it to its rightful owner, and has stored and protected the property for that purpose; and has falsely declared the property to be unidentifiable, thereby breaching the contract. The Hungarian Jews (P) claim that the government (D) is liable for breach of an implied-in-fact contract of bailment. To state such a claim, a plaintiff must show mutuality of intent to contract, offer and acceptance, and that the officer whose conduct is relied upon had actual authority to bind the government (D) in contract. The government (D) argues that it never communicated an intention to return the Gold Train assets. The Hungarian Jews (P) counter that all the elements of an implied-in-fact contract can be inferred from the parties' conduct insofar as the government (D): (1) took possession of the property knowing it belonged to the Hungarian Jews (P); (2) never claimed to be the owner; (3) took possession of the property with the express intent of returning it to its rightful owners; (4) stored and protected the property so it could be returned; (5) indicated that any identifiable property would be returned in accordance with U.S. policy and custom; and (6) falsely declared the property was unidentifiable, thus breaching the agreement. Based on these allegations, at this stage, and without regard to whether the Hungarian Jews (P) can ultimately prove them, the Hungarian Jews (P) have alleged sufficient facts to survive a motion to dismiss. The government's (D) motion to dismiss is denied as to this claim.

EDITOR'S ANALYSIS: Although the court has allowed the plaintiffs to pursue their claim for breach of implied-in-fact contract of bailment, if a given named plaintiff cannot prove during discovery that property on the Gold Train was identifiable and belonged to him or her, that plaintiff will not be able to further pursue the claim.

QUICKNOTES

IMPLIED-IN-FACT CONTRACT - Refers to conditions which arise by physical or moral inference: (a) prerequisites or cirucmstances which a reasonable person would assume necessary to render or receive performance; and (b) the good-faith cooperation of the promisee in receiving the performance of the promisor.

NOTES:

OPINION OF THE JUSTICES
(PUBLIC USE OF COASTAL BEACHES)
N.H. Sup. Ct., 649 A.2d 604 (1994).

NATURE OF CASE: Opinion of the state Supreme Court justices on proposed legislation.

FACT SUMMARY: The state Supreme Court justices answered three questions submitted to them by the state House of Representatives on proposed legislation recognizing a public easement in the dry sand area of historically accessible coastal beaches.

CONCISE RULE OF LAW: When the government unilaterally authorizes a permanent, public easement across private lands, this constitutes a taking requiring just compensation.

FACTS: Five justices of the state Supreme Court wrote this opinion in reply to questions submitted by the House of Representatives of New Hampshire. A bill proposed to amend a state law by inserting a new section entitled "Public Use of Coastal Beaches," recognizing a public easement in the dry sand area of historically accessible beaches. The third question posed by the House of Representatives to the court was whether this provision of the bill constituted a taking of private property for a public purpose without just compensation.

ISSUE: When the government unilaterally authorizes a permanent, public easement across private lands, does this constitute a taking requiring just compensation?

HOLDING AND DECISION: (Brock, C.J.) Yes. When the government unilaterally authorizes a permanent, public easement across private land, this constitutes a taking requiring just compensation. Except for those areas where there is an established and acknowledged public easement, prescriptive easements can only be utilized on a tract-by-tract basis, and cannot be applied to all beaches within a state. The interference with private property here involved a wholesale denial of an owner's right to exclude the public. This bill violates the prohibition contained in both the State and the federal Constitutions against the taking of private property for public use without just compensation. The state has the power to permit comprehensive beach access by using its eminent domain power and compensating private property owners, but it may not take property rights without compensation through legislative decree.

EDITOR'S ANALYSIS: The court here offered its opinion on proposed legislation. This opinion did not amount to a judicial decision. It would not be binding upon the court in the event a case arose requiring construction of the proposed statute.

QUICKNOTES

EASEMENT - The right to utilize a portion of another's real property for a specific use.

PRESCRIPTIVE EASEMENT - A manner of acquiring an easement in another's property by continuous and uninterrupted use in satisfaction of the statutory requirements of adverse possession.

TAKING - A governmental action that substantially deprives an owner of the use and enjoyment of his or her property, requiring compensation.

NOTES:

CHAPTER 3
PROPERTY RIGHTS IN CREATIVE WORKS

QUICK REFERENCE RULES OF LAW

1. **Property Rights in Personas and the Right of Publicity.** In an action for a violation of the right of publicity, likeness is a question of fact for the jury. (Wendt v. Host International, Inc.)

2. **Property Rights in Personas and the Right of Publicity.** Licensed figures or other representations based on copyrighted characters cannot infringe on the rights of actors who have portrayed those characters. (Wendt v. Host International, Inc.)

3. **Property Rights in Personas and the Right of Publicity.** The First and Fourteenth Amendments do not immunize the media when they broadcast a performer's entire act without his consent. (Zacchini v. Scripps-Howard Broadcasting Co.)

4. **Property Rights in Writings, Recordings, and Product Designs**. A preliminary injunction of a publication claimed to infringe the copyright of another publication is not proper where there is a likelihood that a fair-use defense will prevail in protecting the allegedly infringing publication and where it has not been shown that the infringing publication will cause irreparable injury to the copyrighted work. (Suntrust Bank v. Houghton Mifflin Company)

5. **Property Rights in Writings, Recordings, and Product Designs.** In order for an item to be registered as a sculptural work it must embody some creative authorship in its delineation or form. (OddzOn Products, Inc. v. Oman)

6. **Property Rights in Writings, Recordings, and Product Designs.** To be copyrightable, a work must be original and possess at least some minimal degree of creativity. (Feist Publications, Inc. v. Rural Telephone Svc. Co.)

7. **Property Rights in Writings, Recordings, and Product Designs.** The tort of conversion applies to domain names. (Kremen v. Cohen)

8. **Trademark and Tradedress.** Color alone can be a registered trademark if it has acquired "secondary meaning" such that it identifies the source, or brand, of the product. (Qualitex Co. v. Jacobson Products Co.)

9. **Trademark and Tradedress.** An expired utility patent forecloses the possibility of the patentee's claiming trade dress protection in the product's functional design. (Traffix Devices, Inc. v. Marketing Displays, Inc.)

10. **Patent Law Protection.** A micro-organism that is not naturally occurring and is the product of manufacture is patentable subject matter. (Diamond v. Chakrabarty)

11. **Property rights in Human Tissue.** Unauthorized use of human tissue in medical research does not constitute a conversion. (Moore v. Regents of the University of California)

12. **Property Rights in Human Tissue.** The exclusive right of next of kin to possess the bodies of their deceased family members creates a property interest, the deprivation of which must be accorded due process of law under the Fourteenth Amendment. (Newman v. Sathyavaglswaran)

WENDT v. HOST INTERNATIONAL, INC.
Actors (P) v. Corporation (D)
125 F.3d 806 (9th Cir. 1997).

NATURE OF CASE: Appeal from summary judgment on remand for defendant in right of publicity action.

FACT SUMMARY: Wendt (P) and Ratzenberger (P), actors on the hit television show *Cheers*, claimed that animatronic robotic figures (robots) used by Host International, Inc. (Host) (D) violated their right of publicity.

CONCISE RULE OF LAW: In an action for a violation of the right of publicity, likeness is a question of fact for the jury.

FACTS: Host International, Inc. (Host) (D) placed animatronic robotic figures (robots) in airport bars modeled upon the set from the television show *Cheers*. Wendt (P) and Ratzenberger (P), actors on the hit television show, claimed that the robots violated their state statutory and common law right of publicity. The Court of Appeals held that the state law causes of action were not preempted by federal copyright law and that disputed issues of material fact precluded summary judgment, because the district court's comparisons of photographs of the robots with photographs of Wendt (P) and Ratzenberger (P) was not sufficient to resolve the claims. On remand, the district court again granted summary judgment for Host (D), after an in-court comparison, and again the Court of Appeals granted review.

ISSUE: In an action for a violation of the right of publicity, is likeness a question of fact for the jury?

HOLDING AND DECISION: (Fletcher, Cir.J.) Yes. In an action for a violation of the right of publicity, likeness is a question of fact for the jury. Under California's Civil Code § 3344, any person who uses another's likeness for purposes of advertising or selling, without such person's prior consent is liable for any damage sustained by the person injured as a result thereof. Despite the district court's assertion that no reasonable jury could find that the robots are in any way similar to Wendt (P) and Ratzenberger (P), from this court's inspection of the robots, there are material facts that might cause a reasonable jury to find them sufficiently "like" Wendt (P) and Ratzenberger (P). Likeness need not be identical or photographic. Also, as long as plaintiffs bring claims in addition to copyright claims, such as a claim of right of publicity, the plaintiffs' claims are not preempted by federal copyright law. Here, Wendt (P) and Ratzenberger (P) are not seeking to prevent the owner of the copyright in the *Cheers* series (Paramount Pictures Corp.) (Paramount) (D) from exhibiting its copyrighted work. Therefore, summary judgment is reversed on the statutory right of publicity claim. There is also a state common law right of privacy, also referred to as the right of publicity, that includes protection against appropriation for the defendant's advantage of the plaintiff's name or likeness. At the heart of this right is the protection of a person's name and likeness from unwarranted intrusion or exploitation. This right protects more than the knowing use of a plaintiff's name or likeness for commercial purposes. It also protects against appropriation of identity by other means. Host (D) argues that the robots appropriate only the identities of the copyrighted characters on the show, not the identities of Wendt (P) and Ratzenberger (P). However, Wendt (P) and Ratzenberger (P) do not argue that they have any rights to the characters on the show, but rather, that the robots are not related to Paramount's (D) copyright of the creative elements of the characters. They argue that it is the physical likeness to Wendt (P) and Ratzenberger (P), not the characters, that has commercial value to Host (D). Actors or actresses do not lose the right of publicity merely by portraying a fictional character. Here, Wendt (P) and Ratzenberger (P) have raised genuine issues of material fact concerning the degree to which the figures look like them. The ultimate issue—for the jury to decide—is whether the defendants are commercially exploiting the likeness of the robots to Wendt (P) and Ratzenberger (P). Reversed as to the grant of summary judgment on the common law claim. Reversed and remanded.

EDITOR'S ANALYSIS: Although the court here concluded that the right of publicity claim was not preempted by federal copyright law, *Fleet v. CBS*, 50 Cal.App.4th 1911 (1996), held that an actor may not bring an action for misappropriation under California's statutory right of publicity when the only claimed exploitation occurred through the distribution of the actor's performance in a copyrighted movie. That is because the plaintiff is essentially seeking to prevent a party from exhibiting a copyrighted work, which is a claim equivalent to an exclusive right within the general scope of federal copyright. The present case was distinguished from *Fleet* on the basis of the additional elements of the complaint involving the invasion of personal rights.

QUICKNOTES

RIGHT OF PUBLICITY - The right of a person to control the commercial exploitation of his name or likeness.

WENDT v. HOST INTERNATIONAL, INC.
Actors (P) v. Corporation (D)
197 F.3d 1284 (9th Cir. 1999).

NATURE OF CASE: Dissent from order rejecting a rehearing en banc.

FACT SUMMARY: Wendt (P) and Ratzenberger (P), actors on the hit television show *Cheers*, claimed that licensed animatronic figures used by Host International, Inc. (Host) (D), violated their right of publicity and created unfair competition.

CONCISE RULE OF LAW: Licensed figures or other representations based on copyrighted characters cannot infringe on the rights of actors who have portrayed those characters.

FACTS: Host International, Inc. (Host) (D) obtained a license from Paramount Pictures Corp. (Paramount) (D)—the copyright holder of the hit television show *Cheers*—to place animatronic figures in airport bars modeled upon the set of *Cheers*. Wendt (P) and Ratzenberger (P), actors on *Cheers* who played the characters Norm and Cliff, sued Host (D) for unfair competition and violation of their right of publicity. Paramount (D) intervened, claiming that its copyright preempted the state law claims brought by Wendt (P) and Ratzenberger (P). The district court, finding no similarities between Wendt (P) and Ratzenberger (P) and the figures, granted summary judgment for the defendants. A panel of the Court of Appeals reversed, asserting that material facts existed that might cause a reasonable jury to find the figures sufficiently like Wendt (P) and Ratzenberger (P) to violate their right of publicity.

ISSUE: Can licensed figures or other representations based on copyrighted characters infringe on the rights of actors who have portrayed those characters?

HOLDING AND DECISION: (Kozinski, Cir.J.) [Dissenting] No. Licensed figures or other representations based on copyrighted characters cannot infringe on the rights of actors who have portrayed those characters. The problem is that this court's precedent pits the actors against the copyright holder insofar as the right of publicity is held to include anything that brings the actor/celebrity to mind. The parties are fighting over the same bundle of intellectual property rights—the right to make representations of the copyrighted characters. The copyright holder asserts its rights under the federal Copyright Act; the actor asserts his right under state law to control the exploitation of his likeness. So, who wins? Under the court's precedent, the actor wins and federal copyright law does not preempt state right of publicity law. The court's standard regarding the right of publicity is too sweeping, however, because it trenches on the right of the copyright holder. This is because when portraying a character who was portrayed by an actor, and who is strongly identified with the actor, it is impossible to recreate the character without evoking the image of the actor in the minds of viewers. Under the court's decision, anytime a copyright holder or its licensee uses its copyrighted character in a way that is reminiscent of the actor—even by using a new actor for the same character—the actor will have a right of publicity action against the copyright holder, that at least will survive summary judgment. Now, actors will be able to demand that copyright holders obtain (and pay for) their consent before they can use their copyrighted characters; this cannot be squared with the copyright holder's right to recreate the characters as it sees fit.

EDITOR'S ANALYSIS: The case that Judge Kozinski faults with exploding the right of publicity is *White v. Samsung Elecs. Am., Inc.,* 971 F.2d 1395 (9th Cir. 1992), in which the plaintiff was Vanna White, a letter turner on the television show *Wheel of Fortune*. White won a $400,000 jury verdict for the use of a robot that stood next to a letter board, dressed up in a blonde wig, a "Vanna-style" gown and garish jewelry. In that case, the defendant (Samsung) did not have a license from the *Wheel of Fortune* copyright holder. In this case, Kozinski takes the position that the majority has extended the right of publicity too far and has placed it on a collision course with the rights of copyright holders, especially since Host (D) did have a license to use the characters.

QUICKNOTES

COPYRIGHT ACT - Copyright Act of 1976 extends copyright protection to "original works of authorship fixed in any tangible medium of expression, now known or later developed, from which they can be perceived, reproduced, or otherwise communicated, either directly or with the aid of a machine or device." 17 U.S.C. § 102.

NOTES:

ZACCHINI v. SCRIPPS-HOWARD BROADCASTING CO.
Entertainer (P) v. Television station (D)
433 U.S. 562 (1977).

NATURE OF CASE: Appeal from judgment for defendant in suit alleging infringement of right of publicity.

FACT SUMMARY: The Ohio Supreme Court held that the television station had a privilege in reporting matters of public interest and therefore was not liable under state law for damages for infringement of Zacchini's (P) right of publicity.

CONCISE RULE OF LAW: The First and Fourteenth Amendments do not immunize the media when they broadcast a performer's entire act without his consent.

FACTS: When a Scripps-Howard (D) television station broadcast all of Zacchini's (P) "human cannonball" performance without his consent, Zacchini (P) sued for damages for infringement of his right of publicity. The Ohio Supreme Court held that as long as the television station's actual intent was not to hurt the performer, it was privileged to report on matters of public interest. Zacchini (P) appealed.

ISSUE: Do the First and Fourteenth Amendments immunize the media when they broadcast a performer's entire act without his consent?

HOLDING AND DECISION: (White, J.) No. The First and Fourteenth Amendments do not immunize the media when they broadcast a performer's entire act without his consent. The televised performance was an appropriation of Zacchini's professional property and he may be entitled to damages. Although the state of Ohio may, as a matter of its own law, privilege the press in such circumstances, the First and Fourteenth Amendments do not require it. Reversed.

EDITOR'S ANALYSIS: The court here emphasized that Zacchini (P) was not seeking to enjoin the performance, but merely to be paid for it. The right of publicity was recognized by the Ohio courts as well. The Ohio court had ruled on the basis of the constitutional privileges accorded to the press, and the Supreme Court had jurisdiction as a result.

QUICKNOTES

FIRST AMENDMENT - Prohibits Congress from enacting any law respecting an establishment of religion, prohibiting the free exercise of religion, abridging freedom of speech or the press, the right of peaceful assembly and the right to petition for a redress of grievances.

FOURTEENTH AMENDMENT - Declares that no state shall make or enforce any law which shall abridge the privileges and immunities of citizens of the United States.

RIGHT OF PUBLICITY - The right of a person to control the commercial exploitation of his name or likeness.

NOTES:

SUNTRUST BANK v. HOUGHTON MIFFLIN COMPANY

Copyright trustee (P) v. Publisher (D)

268 F.3d 1257 (11th Cir. 2001).

NATURE OF CASE: Appeal from grant of preliminary injunction in copyright infringement action.

FACT SUMMARY: Houghton Mifflin Company (Houghton Mifflin) (D) published *The Wind Done Gone* (*TWDG*), a fictional work admittedly based on *Gone With the Wind* (*GWTW*). Suntrust Bank (Suntrust) (P), the trustee of the trust that holds the copyright in *GWTW*, alleged copyright violations and sought to enjoin publication of *TWDG*.

CONCISE RULE OF LAW: A preliminary injunction of a publication claimed to infringe the copyright of another publication is not proper where there is a likelihood that a fair-use defense will prevail in protecting the allegedly infringing publication and where it has not been shown that the infringing publication will cause irreparable injury to the copyrighted work.

FACTS: The book, *Gone With the Wind* (*GWTW*), written by Margaret Mitchell, has been one of the best-selling books in the world. Suntrust Bank (Suntrust) (P) is the trustee of the Mitchell Trust, which holds the copyright in *GWTW*. Alice Randall authored *The Wind Done Gone* (*TWDG*), a fictional work admittedly based on *GWTW*, which she claimed was supposed to be a critique of *GWTW*'s depiction of slavery and the Civil-War era American South. Houghton Mifflin Company (Houghton Mifflin) published *TWDG*, and continued to do so despite Suntrust's (P) request that it stop publication. Suntrust (P) brought suit to enjoin publication of *TWDG*, alleging that *TWDG* explicitly referred to *GWTW* in its foreword; copied core characters, character traits, and relationships from *GWTW*; copied and summarized famous scenes and other plot elements from *GWTW*; and copied verbatim dialogues and descriptions from *GWTW*. Houghton Mifflin (D) did not contest the first three claims, but nonetheless argued that there was no substantial similarity between the two works or, in the alternative, that the doctrine of fair use protected *TWDG* because it is primarily a parody of *GWTW*. The district court granted a preliminary injunction, and the court of appeals granted review.

ISSUE: Is a preliminary injunction of a publication claimed to infringe the copyright of another publication proper where there is a likelihood that a fair-use defense will prevail in protecting the allegedly infringing publication and where there has not been a showing that the infringing publication will cause irreparable injury to the copyrighted work?

HOLDING AND DECISION: (Birch, Cir.J.) No. A preliminary injunction of a publication claimed to infringe the copyright of another publication is not proper where there is a likelihood that a fair-use defense will prevail in protecting the allegedly infringing publication and where there has not been a showing that the infringing publication will cause irreparable injury to the copyrighted work. The Copyright Clause of the Constitution, based on the English Statute of Anne, was intended by the Framers of the U.S. Constitution to promote learning, to protect the public domain, and to grant an exclusive right to the author of a work. In the U.S., learning is promoted by guarding against censorship and ensuring the public has access to knowledge. The Copyright Act ensures such access by providing an economic incentive for authors to publish books and disseminate ideas to the public. The Copyright Act protects an author's right in derivative works—to prevent imitation—and also only requires that a work be "fixed in any tangible medium of expression" to obtain copyright protection. A copyright is limited in time, so that eventually the work enters the public domain. Finally, an author obtains a limited exclusive right, or monopoly, in order to encourage the creation of original works. The author's ownership is in the copyright, never in the work itself. To balance the goals of the First Amendment (freedom of speech) and the Copyright Clause (limited monopoly by authors), the idea/expression dichotomy and the doctrine of fair use developed. Under the idea/expression dichotomy, copyright cannot protect an idea, but only the expression of that idea. Thus, copyright protects an author's original expression, but encourages others to build freely on the ideas and information conveyed by the work. This supports the First Amendment's goal of open debate and the free exchange of ideas. The Copyright Act also codifies the doctrine of fair use, which contains exceptions to the proscription on copying for such purposes as criticism, comment, news reporting, teaching, scholarship, or research. These exceptions allow later authors to use a previous author's copyright to introduce new ideas or concepts to the public. The issue here is largely whether a preliminary injunction was properly granted against an alleged infringer who, relying on the fair use doctrine, made use of another's copyright for comment and criticism. The answer to this question becomes an analysis of the fair use factors.

The framework for this analysis is the standard test governing the issuance of preliminary injunctions. To prevail, Suntrust (P) must prove four elements: (1) substantial likelihood of success on the merits; (2) substantial threat of irreparable injury if the injunction is not granted; (3) that the threatened injury to the plaintiff outweighs the harm an injunction may cause to the defendant; and (4) a grant of the injunction will not be adverse to the public interest. As to the first of these elements, the initial step in evaluating the likelihood that Suntrust (P) will succeed on the

Continued on next page.

merits is to determine whether it has established a *prima facie* case of copyright infringement. This, in turn, has two elements: (1) Suntrust owns a valid copyright in *GWTW* (this element is not disputed); and (2) that Randall copied original elements of *GWTW* in *TWDG*. This requires a determination of the extent that Randall copied original expression—not ideas. However, there is no bright line that separates original expression from nonprotectable ideas. Stock scenes and hackneyed characters, also known as *scenes a faire*, are considered ideas. As plots and characters become more detailed and idiosyncratic, they become original expression. A review of the two works here reveals that *TWDG* made substantial use of *GWTW*, appropriating numerous characters, settings, plot twists, and relationships from *GWTW*. Particularly in its first half, *TWDG* is largely an encapsulation of *GWTW* that exploits its copyrighted elements. Thus, a *prima facie* case has been established.

(1) Fair Use

Nonetheless, Randall's appropriation of elements of *GWTW* in *TWDG* may not constitute infringement of Suntrust's (P) copyright if the taking is protected as a "fair use." The factors for determining fair use are (1) the purpose and character of the use, including whether such use is commercial or is for nonprofit educational purposes; (2) the nature of the copyrighted work; (3) the amount and substantiality of the portion used in relation to the copyrighted work as a whole; and (4) the effect of the use upon the potential market for or value of the copyrighted work. Houghton Mifflin (D) argues that *TWDG* is entitled to fair-use protection as a parody of *GWTW*. Parody is a form of comment and criticism that may constitute fair use of the work being parodied, and is directed at a particular literary or artistic work. Thus, parody needs to mimic an original to make its point—it must borrow elements from the work being parodied. However, not every parody is a fair use, and every claimed parody must be evaluated in terms of all the elements set forth in the Copyright Act and the constitutional purposes of copyright law. *TWDG* is clearly a parody because it is a specific criticism and rejoinder to the depiction of slavery and the relationships between blacks and whites in *GWTW* that is effected through the appropriation of elements of the original work in creating a new artistic work. Given that *TWDG* meets the definition of a parody of *GWTW*, it must be assessed under the four fair-use factors.

i. Purpose and Character of the Work

First, *TWDG* is undoubtedly a commercial product, as it was published for profit. However, *TWDG*'s for-profit status is strongly outweighed by its highly transformative use of *GWTW*'s copyrighted elements. A work's transformative value is of special importance where a parody is involved, since a parody's aim is, by definition, to transform an earlier work. Here, the degree of transformation is a double-edged sword: on the one hand, *TWDG* adds new expression, meaning, and message to *GWTW*, but on the other, to succeed as a work of fiction, it must draw heavily on copyrighted elements taken from *GWTW*. Thematically, the new work provides a significantly different viewpoint of the antebellum

world, and the new work inverts the original by the way it is told and through the words that it uses to tell the new story. Additionally, the last half of *TWDG* tells a completely new story that, although involving characters based on *GWTW* characters, features plot elements found nowhere in *GWTW*. For example, in *TWDG*, nearly every black character is given some redeeming quality that their *GWTW* analogues lacked. In light of this, it is difficult to conclude that Randall simply was lazy and wanted to avoid the hard work of creating something new. Randall has, instead, used the conscripted elements of the original to make war against it. Therefore, *TWDG* reflects transformative value because it can "provide social benefit, by shedding light on an earlier work, and, in the process, creating a new one." Consideration of this factor militates in favor of finding fair use.

ii. Nature of the Copyrighted Work

Although *GWTW* is entitled to the greatest degree of copyright protection as an original work of fiction, this factor is given little weight in a parody case because parodies almost invariably copy publicly known, expressive works.

iii. Amount and Substantiality of the Portion Used

This factor presents particular difficulty in the context of a parody. Parody must take enough of an original to conjure up the original to make the object of its critical wit recognizable. Once enough has been taken to "conjure up" the original, however, any further taking must specifically serve the new work's parodic aims. Suntrust (P) argues that because *GWTW* is so popular and well known, very little reference is required to conjure up *GWTW*. Houghton Mifflin (D) counters that *TWDG* takes nothing from *GWTW* that does not serve a parodic purpose. There are numerous minor details that Randall takes from *GWTW* that arguably do not serve a parodic purpose, and numerous elements that clearly are transformative. However, in determining fair use, it must be kept in mind that literary relevance is a highly subjective analysis ill-suited for judicial inquiry. The law is clear that parodists need not take only a bare minimum amount of copyrighted material necessary to conjure up the original, as parody needs to be more than a fleeting evocation of an original to make its humorous point. Even more extensive use than necessary to conjure up the original may still be fair use, provided the parody builds on the original. How much more is reasonable depends on the extent to which the work's overriding purpose is to parody the original (here, that is *TWDG*'s *raison d'etre*), or, in contrast, the likelihood that the parody may serve as a market substitute for the original (here, based on the record at this juncture, it is not possible to conclude with certainty whether the quantity and value of the materials used are reasonable in relation to the purpose of the copying).

iv. Effect on the Market Value of the Original

This factor requires a consideration of the effect that the publication of *TWDG* will have on the market for or value of

Continued on next page.

Suntrust's (P) copyright in *GWTW*, including the potential harm it may cause to the market for derivative works based on *GWTW*— in particular the harm of market substitution. Although Suntrust (P) offered evidence that its copyright in *GWTW* and several authorized derivative works has a very high value, it fails to present evidence or argument that *TWDG* would supplant demand for Suntrust's (P) licensed derivatives. Particularly in cases of parody, evidence of harm to the potential market for or value of the original copyright is crucial to a fair use determination. In contrast, the evidence offered by Houghton Mifflin (D) focuses on market substitution and demonstrates why TWDG is unlikely to displace sales of *GWTW*. Accordingly, this factor weighs in favor of *TWDG*. In light of the weight given to these factors, *TWDG* is entitled to a fair-use defense.

(2) Irreparable Injury

There is no presumption of irreparable injury when the alleged infringer has a bona fide fair-use defense. Thus, the potential harm the copyright holders of *GWTW* will suffer from the publication of *TWDG* must be considered. Here, Suntrust (P) has failed to show, at least at this stage of the case, how the publication of *TWDG*—a work that may have little to no appeal to the fans of *GWTW* who comprise the logical market for its authorized derivative works—will cause it irreparable harm. To the extent Suntrust (P) will suffer monetary harm, such harm is not considered irreparable, as monetary damages may remedy such harm. This lack of irreparable harm, combined with the likelihood that a fair use defense will prevail, make injunctive relief improper, and the remaining factors need not be addressed, except to stress that the public interest is always served by the promotion of First Amendment values. Vacated.

CONCURRENCE: (Marcus, J.) Suntrust (P) has fallen well short of establishing a likelihood of success on its claim. First, *TWDG* is without a doubt parody. Second, in service of the book's parodic design, Randall radically reshapes what she borrows from Mitchell, and is even more transformative than the majority makes it out to be; the purpose and nature prong of the fair use analysis is thus not a close call. Third, even the preliminary record suggests that *TWDG* will not act as a substitute for *GWTW*. What little evidence there is indicates that these two books are aimed at different readerships, and that, if anything, they will complement each other.

EDITOR'S ANALYSIS: Under the current Copyright Act, most copyrights for works created after 1978 last for the lifetime of the author plus 70 years. The U.S. Supreme Court rejected claims that this extension of the copyright term (which had been shorter) violated the Constitution's mandate that copyrights granted to authors be for "limited times." With a work as old as *GWTW*, on which the original copyright may soon expire, creation of a derivative work only serves to protect that which is original to the latter work and does not extend the copyright in the copyrightable elements of the original work (§ 103(b)).

ODDZON PRODUCTS, INC. v. OMAN
Owner (P) v. Copyright Office (D)
924 F.2d 346 (D.C. Cir. 1991).

NATURE OF CASE: Defendant's motion for summary judgment challenging copyright denial.

FACT SUMMARY: When OddzOn's (P) application for a copyright was denied by the Copyright Office (D), OddzOn (P) brought this action under the Administrative Procedure Act, claiming that the refusal was arbitrary and capricious and an abuse of discretion.

CONCISE RULE OF LAW: In order for an item to be registered as a sculptural work it must embody some creative authorship in its delineation or form.

FACTS: When OddzOn's (P) applied to copyright its "KOOSH" ball as a sculptural work, the Copyright Office (D) found that it was not copyrightable because the ball was a familiar shape and its tactility—the way it feels—was a functional part of the work and therefore not copyrightable. After exhausting all administrative remedies, OddzOn (P) filed suit under the Administrative Procedure Act, claiming that the Copyright Office's (D) rejection was arbitrary and capricious, and an abuse of discretion.

ISSUE: In order for an item to be registered as a sculptural work, must it embody some creative authorship in its delineation or form?

HOLDING AND DECISION: (Ginsburg, Cir.J.) Yes. In order for an item to be registered as a sculptural work it must embody some creative authorship in its delineation or form. The Copyright Office (D) found that the "KOOSH" ball did not embody a sufficient degree of creative authorship beyond the object's basic shape to warrant a copyright. The Copyright Office (D) did not abuse its discretion in finding that the balls's tactile properties were inseparable from its utilitarian function. No authority was cited that would support the conclusion that tactility was a copyrightable aspect of a sculptural work. Affirmed.

EDITOR'S ANALYSIS: The court here explained the basic test applied for copyright of a familiar symbol or design. Although familiar symbols or designs are not subject to copyright, additional creative work beyond the object's basic shape may warrant a copyright. In this case, the mere "feel" or tactility of the ball is inextricably intertwined with its utilitarian function.

QUICKNOTES

ABUSE OF DISCRETION - A determination by an appellate court that a lower court's decision was based on an error of law.

ADMINISTRATIVE PROCEDURE ACT - Provides the standard for judicial review of agency rules.

FEIST PUBLICATIONS, INC. v. RURAL TELEPHONE SERVICE CO.

Publishing company (D) v. Phone book publisher (P)
499 U.S. 340 (1991).

NATURE OF CASE: Appeal from grant of summary judgment to plaintiff in suit for copyright infringement.

FACT SUMMARY: After Feist (D) took 1,309 listings from Rural's (P) white pages when compiling Feist's (D) own white pages, Rural (P) filed suit for copyright infringement.

CONCISE RULE OF LAW: To be copyrightable, a work must be original and possess at least some minimal degree of creativity.

FACTS: As a certified telephone service provided in northwest Kansas, Rural Telephone Service (P) published a typical telephone directory as a condition of its monopoly franchise. The white pages alphabetically listed the names, towns, and telephone numbers of Rural's (P) subscribers. Feist Publications (D) was a publishing company specializing in area-wide telephone directories. The Feist (D) directory that was the subject of this litigation contained 46,878 white pages listings, compared to Rural's (P) approximately 7,700 listings. Feist (D) approached the 11 northwest Kansas telephone companies and offered to pay for the right to use their respective white pages listings. When only Rural (P) refused to license its listings, Feist (D) used them without Rural's (P) consent. A typical Feist (D) listing included each individual's street address, while most of Rural's (P) did not. Of the 46,878 listings in Feist's (D) 1983 directory, 1,309 of those listings were identical to listings in Rural's (P) white pages. Rural (P) sued for copyright infringement. The district court granted summary judgment to Rural (P), and the court of appeals affirmed. Feist (D) appealed.

ISSUE: To be copyrightable, must a work be original and possess at least some minimal degree of creativity?

HOLDING AND DECISION: (O'Connor, J.) Yes. To be copyrightable, a work must be original and possess at least some minimal degree of creativity. This case concerns the interaction of two well-established propositions. The first is that facts are not copyrightable; the other, that compilations of facts generally are. There is an undeniable tension between these two propositions. The key to resolving the tension lies in understanding why facts are not copyrightable. No one may claim originality as to facts because facts do not owe their origin to an act of authorship. Factual compilations, on the other hand, may possess the requisite originality. Compilations were expressly mentioned in the Copyright Acts of 1909 and 1976. Even a directory that contains absolutely no protectable written expression, only facts, meets the constitutional minimum for copyright protection if it features an original selection or arrangement. If the selection and arrangement are original, these elements of the work are eligible for copyright protection. No matter how original the format, though, the facts themselves do not become original through association. There is no doubt that Feist (D) took from the white pages of Rural's (P) directory a substantial amount of factual information. The question that remains is whether Rural (P) selected, coordinated, or arranged these uncopyrightable facts in an original way. It did not. Rural (P) simply took the data provided by its subscribers and listed it alphabetically by surname. There is nothing remotely creative about arranging names alphabetically in a white pages directory. Rural (P) expended sufficient effort to make the white pages directory useful, but insufficient creativity to make it original. Thus, because Rural's (P) white pages lack the requisite originality, Feist's (D) use of the listings cannot constitute infringement. Copyright rewards originality, not effort. Reversed.

EDITOR'S ANALYSIS: In the words of the Court, copyright assures authors the right to their original expression, but encourages others to build freely upon the ideas and information conveyed by a work. This principle, known as the idea/expression or fact/expression dichotomy, applies to all works of authorship. As applied to a factual compilation, assuming the absence of original written expression, only the compiler's selection and arrangement may be protected; the raw facts may be copied at will. This is the means by which copyright advances the progress of science and art by encouraging creativity with the reward of exclusive rights for the original creation.

QUICKNOTES

COPYRIGHT INFRINGEMENT - A violation of one of the exclusive rights granted to an artist pursuant to Article I, section 8, clause 8 of the United States Constitution over the reproduction, display, performance, distribution, and adaptation of his work for a period prescribed by statute.

KREMEN v. COHEN

Domain name owner (P) v. Domain name thief (D)

337 F.3d 1024 (9th Cir. 2003).

NATURE OF CASE: Appeal from summary judgment for defendant in action for, inter alia, conversion and conversion by bailee.

FACT SUMMARY: Cohen (D) forged a letter that caused Network Solutions, the domain name registrar, to transfer the domain name "sex.com" from its rightful owner, Kremen (P), to Cohen (D). Kremen (P) sued Network Solutions for, *inter alia*, conversion and conversion by bailee.

CONCISE RULE OF LAW: The tort of conversion applies to domain names.

FACTS: Kremen (P) registered the domain name sex.com with Network Solutions (D), the domain name registrar. Con man Cohen (D), seeing great potential in that domain name, forged a letter that he sent to Network Solutions (D) indicating that Kremen (P) and his company, Online Classifieds, had decided to abandon the domain name and transfer it to Cohen (D). Although the letter's claim was less than believable, *e.g.*, it claimed that a company called "Online Classifieds" had no Internet connection, Network Solutions (D) accepted the letter at face value and transferred the domain name to Cohen (D), who went on to turn sex.com into a lucrative online porn empire. Kremen (P) sued Cohen (D), but could not collect the $40 million in compensatory damages and $25 million in punitive damages that the court had awarded, as Cohen (D) flagrantly ignored court order after court order and became a fugitive from justice. Although the domain name was returned to Kremen (P), he sought to recover his losses from Network Solutions (D) and sued it for, *inter alia*, conversion and conversion by bailee. The district court granted summary judgment in favor of Network Solutions (D), finding that the tort of conversion does not apply to intangible property, such as a domain name. The Court of Appeals granted review.

ISSUE: Does the tort of conversion apply to domain names?

HOLDING AND DECISION: (Kozinski, Cir.J.) Yes. The tort of conversion applies to domain names. To establish the tort of conversion, a plaintiff must establish ownership or right to possession of property, wrongful disposition of the property right, and damages. The threshold issue, therefore, is whether registrants have a property right in their domain names. They do, because a domain name is a well-defined interest, like stock; because ownership is exclusive insofar as a registrant alone decides where those invoking the domain name will be sent on the Internet; because domain names are valued (being bought and sold for millions of dollars sometimes); and because registrants have a legitimate claim to exclusivity—like laying claim to a plot of land. Therefore, Kremen (P) had an intangible property right in his domain name and a jury could have found that Network Solutions (D) wrongfully disposed of that right to Kremen's (P) detriment when it transferred the domain name to Cohen (D). The district court held that intangibles are not subject to conversion. However, almost every jurisdiction has discarded this rigid limitation. Some courts, and the Restatement (Second) of Torts § 242, hold that an intangible is merged in a document when the right to possession of a chattel and the power to acquire such possession is represented by the document, or when an intangible obligation is represented by the document, which is regarded as equivalent to the obligation. Applying this test, the court found no evidence that Kremen's (P) domain name was merged in a document. However, there is no indication whether the "merged with" requirement is a part of California law. A review of California law reveals that it does not follow the Restatement's strict merger requirement, and that, in fact, it rejects a tangibility requirement altogether. Federal cases applying California law take an equally broad view. Even assuming that California retains some minimal vestigial merger requirement, Kremen's (P) domain name falls easily within a class of property that requires only some connection to a document or tangible object—not representation of the owner's intangible interest in a strict sense. The relevant document is the Domain Name System (DNS), a database that happens to be stored in electronic form. Therefore, Kremen's (P) domain name is protected by California conversion law. There is nothing unfair about holding a company, such as Network Solutions (D), liable for giving away someone else's property even if it was not at fault—"the common law does not stand idle while people give away the property of others." Finally, Kremen's (P) conversion by bailee claim does not state a cause of action independent of his conversion claim. This is not a distinct tort, but is merely the tort of conversion committed by one who is a bailee, so Kremens (P) gains nothing by showing that Network Solutions (D) is a bailee. Reversed and remanded (on the conversion claim).

EDITOR'S ANALYSIS: The Court of Appeals soundly rejected the district court's concern that allowing a conversion claim for domain names would increase the threat of litigation and stifle the registration system by requiring further regulations by Network Solutions (D) and potential increases in fees. The Court of Appeals reasoned that given that Network Solutions' (D) regulations allowed it to hand over a registrant's domain name on the basis of a facially suspect letter, further regulations would be a good idea. It also opined that an increase in fees to increase security would not be regarded as a negative by registrants.

QUICKNOTES

CONVERSION - The act of depriving an owner of his property without permission or justification.

INTER ALIA - Among other things.

QUALITEX CO. v. JACOBSON PRODUCTS CO., INC.
Producer of dry cleaning press pads (P) v. Rival company (D)
514 U.S. 159 (1995).

NATURE OF CASE: Certiorari review of trademark case.

FACT SUMMARY: Qualitex (P) sued Jacobson Products Co., Inc. (D) (hereinafter, Jacobson) for trademark infringement. Qualitex (P) claimed that the green-gold color it used for its product was its trademark and, therefore, Jacobson (D) could not use the same color on its product. The District Court ruled in favor of Qualitex (P), but the Appeals Court set aside the verdict, noting that color alone could not be a trademark. The Supreme Court of the United States granted certiorari review of the issue.

CONCISE RULE OF LAW: Color alone can be a registered trademark if it has acquired "secondary meaning" such that it identifies the source, or brand, of the product.

FACTS: Qualitex (P) uses a green-gold color on the press pads it produces, which it sells to dry cleaning companies for use in the dry cleaning process. Jacobson (D) began production of press pads of the same green-gold color. Subsequently, Qualitex (P) registered the green-gold color of its pads with the Patent and Trademark Office and filed a trademark infringement suit against Jacobson (D). The District Court ruled in favor of Qualitex (P), but the Court of Appeals set aside the judgment, noting that color alone could not be a registered trademark. The Supreme Court of the United States granted certiorari review of the issue.

ISSUE: Can color alone be a registered trademark?

HOLDING AND DECISION: (Breyer, J.) Yes. Jacobson (D) advanced four arguments why trademark law should not allow color alone to be used as a trademark. First, Jacobson (D) contended that the use of color as a trademark would result in "shade confusion" as companies attempted to decide what variations on a color of a similar product did or did not infringe upon a trademark. The Court rejected this argument because determining the difference between two colors is no different from determining the subtle differences between words and phrases, such as has always been done in trademark infringement suits. Jacobson's (D) second argument is that there are a limited number of colors and that, as companies appropriate them as trademarks, the color supply would be depleted. The Court found this argument to have no merit because it believed there were plenty of colors for competitors to choose from. In addition, the Court stated that the doctrine of functionality would prevent the problem Jacobson (D) projected. Next, Jacobson (D) argued that several Supreme Court cases supported its position. However, the cases Jacobson (D) cited were found to be interpretations of trademark law made prior to the Lanham Act of 1946. Finally, Jacobson (D) argued that it was not necessary to have color as a

trademark, as the color would be protected as trade dress. This argument was found unpersuasive, because trademark protection provides additional benefits that trade dress protection does not. Because the Court found that a color can come to identify a particular brand and was not persuaded by Jacobson's (D) arguments, it found that color alone can be a registered trademark. Reversed.

EDITOR'S ANALYSIS: The Lanham Act was passed in 1946. It allows a seller to register a trademark and to prohibit his or her competitors from using it. The policy behind the use of trademarks is that they help customers easily identify a brand they associate with quality. Trademarks allow consumers to identify the source of the product, or the brand, immediately. In *Qualitex*, it was clear that consumers of dry cleaning press pads had come to associate green-gold press pads as Qualitex products. Therefore, the color met the legal requirements for a trademark and could be registered as such.

QUICKNOTES
LANHAM ACT - name of the Trademark Act of 1946 which governs federal law regarding trademarks.

NOTES:

TRAFFIX DEVICES, INC. v. MARKETING DISPLAYS, INC.
Manufacturer (D) v. Holder of expired utility patent (P)
532 U.S. 23 (2001).

NATURE OF CASE: Appeal from reversal of summary judgment for defendant in trade dress infringement action.

FACT SUMMARY: Marketing Displays, Inc. (MDI) (P), which held expired utility patents for a "dual-spring design" mechanism, claimed that TrafFix Devices, Inc. (TrafFix) (D), infringed MDI's (P) trade dress in its dual-spring design product.

CONCISE RULE OF LAW: An expired utility patent forecloses the possibility of the patentee's claiming trade dress protection in the product's functional design.

FACTS: Marketing Displays, Inc. (MDI) (P), held expired utility patents for a "dual-spring design" mechanism that keeps temporary road and other outdoor signs upright in adverse wind conditions. MDI (P) claimed that its sign stands were recognizable to buyers and users because the patented design was visible near the sign stand's base. After MDI's (P) patents expired and TrafFix Devices, Inc. (TrafFix) (D) began marketing sign stands with a dual-spring mechanism copied from MDI's (P) design, MDI (P) brought suit under the Trademark Act of 1946 for, *inter alia,* trade dress infringement. The District Court granted TrafFix's (D) motion for summary judgment, holding that no reasonable trier of fact could determine that MDI (P) had established secondary meaning in its alleged trade dress, *i.e.,* consumers did not associate the dual-spring design's look with MDI (P); and, as an independent reason, that there could be no trade dress protection for the design because it was functional. The Court of Appeals reversed, and the U.S. Supreme Court granted certiorari to resolve a conflict among the Circuits.

ISSUE: Does an expired utility patent foreclose the possibility of the patentee's claiming trade dress protection in the product's design?

HOLDING AND DECISION: (Kennedy, J.) Yes. An expired utility patent forecloses the possibility of the patentee's claiming trade dress protection in the product's design. Trade dress can be protected under federal law, but the person asserting such protection in an infringement action must prove that the matter sought to be protected is not functional. Trade dress protection must subsist with the recognition that in many instances there is no prohibition against copying goods and products. An expired utility patent has vital significance in resolving a trade dress claim, because a utility patent is strong evidence that the features claimed as trade dress are functional. Here, the principal advance claimed in the expired utility patents was the dual-spring design, which is an essential feature of the claimed trade dress MDI (P) seeks to protect. However, MDI (P) cannot carry the burden of overcoming the strong evidentiary inference of functionality based on the disclosure of the dual-spring design in the claims of the expired patents. The springs are necessary to the device's operation, and they would have been covered by the claims of the expired patents even though they look different from the embodiment revealed in those patents. The rationale for the rule that the disclosure of a feature in a utility patent's claims constitutes strong evidence of functionality is well illustrated in this case; statements in the expired patent applications demonstrate the functionality of the design. In reversing the summary judgment against MDI (P), the Court of Appeals gave insufficient weight to the importance of the expired utility patents, and their evidentiary significance, in establishing the device's functionality. The error was likely caused by its misinterpretation of trade dress principles in other respects. In general terms, a product feature is functional, and cannot serve as a trademark, if it is essential to the use or purpose of the article or if it affects the cost or quality of the article. This Court has expanded on that meaning, observing that a functional feature is one the exclusive use of which would put competitors at a significant non-reputation-related disadvantage. This Court has allowed trade dress protection to inherently distinctive product features on the assumption that they were not functional. Here, however, beyond serving the purpose of informing consumers that the sign stands are made by MDI (P), the design provides a unique and useful mechanism to resist the wind's force. Functionality having been established, whether the design has acquired secondary meaning need not be considered, nor is it necessary to speculate about other design possibilities. Reversed and remanded.

EDITOR'S ANALYSIS: Basic to the Court of Appeals' ruling was its observation that it took "little imagination to conceive of a hidden dual-spring mechanism or a tri or quad-spring mechanism that might avoid infringing [MDI's (P)] trade dress." The Court of Appeals explained that "[i]f TrafFix or another competitor chooses to use [MDI's (P)] dual-spring design, then it will have to find *some other way* to set its sign apart to avoid infringing [MDI's (P)] trade dress." It was not sufficient, according to the Court of Appeals, that allowing exclusive use of a particular feature such as the dual-spring design in the guise of trade dress would hinder competition somewhat. Rather, the Court of Appeals ruled that exclusive use of a feature must put competitors at a significant non-reputation-related disadvantage before trade dress protection is denied on functionality grounds. However, as the U.S. Supreme Court noted, the burden of proving nonfunctionality is on the party asserting trade dress, and here, MDI (P) could not meet that burden.

QUICKNOTES

TRADE DRESS - The overall image of, or impression created by, a product that a court may enforce as a trademark if it determines that such image has acquired secondary meaning and that the public recognizes it as an indication of source.

DIAMOND v. CHAKRABARTY

Acting commissioner of patents and trademarks (P) v.
Microbiologist (D)
447 U.S. 303 (1980).

NATURE OF CASE: Certiorari review of patentability of living organisms.

FACT SUMMARY: Chakrabarty (D) discovered a bacterium that can break down multiple components of crude oil. He filed a patent claim on the bacterium itself. The patent examiner rejected his claim. Chakrabarty (D) appealed the decision to the Patent Office Board of Appeals, and the Board affirmed the examiner's decision. The Court of Customs and Patent Appeals reversed that decision, and the Acting Commissioner of Patents and Trademarks (P) filed a petition for certiorari and the writ was granted.

CONCISE RULE OF LAW: A mirco-organism that is not naturally occurring and is the product of manufacture is patentable subject matter.

FACTS: Chakrabarty (D) discovered a method of developing a bacterium that could break down multiple components of crude oil. Chakrabarty (D) filed a patent claim for the process of developing the bacterium, for an inoculum comprised of a carrier material and the bacterium, and for the bacterium itself. The patent examiner allowed the first two claims but rejected the patent claim for the bacterium itself. The basis for the rejection of the claim for the bacterium was that it was a living organism and, therefore, not patentable subject matter. Chakrabarty (D) appealed the examiner's decision to the Patent Office Board of Appeals. The decision was upheld but reversed by the Court of Customs and Patent Appeals. The Acting Commissioner of Patents and Trademarks (P) petitioned for certiorari review to resolve the issue. The writ was granted.

ISSUE: Does a micro-organism constitute a "manufacture" or "composition of matter" such that it can be the subject matter of a patent?

HOLDING AND DECISION: (Burger, C.J.) Yes. Congress intends a broad interpretation of the term "manufacture" in the context of the statute governing patentable subject matter (35 U.S.C. section 101). The term is interpreted as having the same meaning it is given in the dictionary: "The production of articles for use from raw or prepared materials by giving to these materials new forms, qualities, properties, or combinations, whether by hand-labor or machinery." This allows for a very broad reading of the statute. Notwithstanding this broad construction, laws of nature and physical phenomena are not considered patentable subject matter. The petitioner (P) argues that the micro-organism in question is not patentable subject matter because it is a living organism precluded from patenting by the 1930 Plant Patent Act.

The Court rejects this argument because the relevant distinction made by Congress, in passing the Plant Patent Acts, was not between living and inanimate things but between products of nature and products of human ingenuity. In this case, Chakrabarty (D) applied for a patent for a product of his own ingenuity. The micro-organism in question does not occur naturally. Petitioner's (P) final argument is that micro-organisms are not patentable until Congress expressly authorizes patent protection for such organisms. Petitioner (P) contends that Congress could not have foreseen this type of technology when it enacted the statute at issue. The Court disagrees, believing that a finding that unforeseen inventions are not protected frustrates the purpose of patent law, which is to promote progress and ingenuity. The Court therefore rejects petitioner's (P) arguments and finds that the micro-organism in question is patentable subject matter. Affirmed.

EDITOR'S ANALYSIS: Naturally occurring organisms and plants are not patentable subject matter. As this case illustrates, however, when an organism is created through human ingenuity, it becomes patentable subject matter. The public policy behind intellectual property law is to promote human productivity and progress. This case underscores the fact that patent laws are designed to protect human ingenuity and scientific advances.

QUICKNOTES

35 U.S.C. § 101 - Whoever invents a new and useful process, machine, or composition of matter may obtain a patent.

NOTES:

MOORE v. REGENTS OF THE UNIVERSITY OF CALIFORNIA

Patient (P) v. Physician (D) and powers of hospital (D)
793 P.2d 479, *cert. denied*, 499 U.S. 936 (1991).

NATURE OF CASE: Review of conversion cause of action.

FACT SUMMARY: Moore (P), whose cells, unbeknownst to him, had been used in medical research, contended that the cells had been converted.

CONCISE RULE OF LAW: Unauthorized use of human tissue in medical research does not constitute a conversion.

FACTS: Golde (D), a physician associated with UCLA's School of Medicine, treated Moore (P) for a rare form of cancer, hairy-cell leukemia. Golde (D) realized that Moore's (P) tissues had certain unique qualities and commenced research thereon. He later developed certain tissue products whose potential economic value was great. Moore (P) later brought an action alleging that he had not consented to research on his tissues and that the tissues had been converted.

ISSUE: Does unauthorized use of human tissue in medical research constitute a conversion?

HOLDING AND DECISION: (Panelli, J.) No. Unauthorized use of human tissue in medical research does not constitute a conversion. Conversion is interference with a right of ownership or possession. One's giving up his tissue to a physician clearly has no possessory interest, so the question is whether he retains title thereto. This court concludes that he does not. Laws governing tissues tend to relate to public policy goals, not the general law of personal property. Also, California's Health and Safety Code § 7054.4 requires that human tissue and byproducts be disposed of by internment or incineration, which is certainly inconsistent with retention of title by the donor. In light of this, the rule must be that the donor of tissue does not retain title thereto. Finally, such a rule would increase the risk of liability for researchers and possibly hinder new medical research. Affirmed in part, reversed in part, remanded.

CONCURRENCE: (Arabian, J.) The majority opinion reaches the correct result but does not address the moral component of the case. As Justice Mosk correctly recognizes in his dissent, our society "acknowledges a profound ethical imperative to respect the human body as the physical and temporal expression of the unique human persona." His conclusion, however, that Moore (P) is entitled to compensation for conversion of his body tissue, is unpersuasive; Justice Mosk illuminates the problem, but does not offer a satisfactory solution. The issue is whether it would uplift or degrade the unique human persona to treat human tissue as a fungible article of commerce, and whether it would advance or impede the human condition, spiritually or scientifically, by

placing the force of law behind Moore's (P) claim. The answers to these questions are not merely ones of tort law susceptible to judicial resolution. These issues are not for the courts to decide, and must be left to the legislature, the proper deliberative forum for such complex questions of law and morality.

CONCURRENCE AND DISSENT: (Broussard, J.) If the doctor wrongfully withheld material information as to the intended use of the tissue, he committed a conversion.

DISSENT: (Mosk, J.) Research with human tissue that results in significant economic gain for the researcher and none for the patient offends the mores of our society by treating the human body as a commodity. To allow the researchers alone to profit would be unjust. The patient deserves a fair share for contributing the raw materials.

EDITOR'S ANALYSIS: As the court here noted in passing, it is often quite hard to apply laws that arose in ancient times to the types of controversies that can arise in the modern era. At common law, conversion was a remedy appropriate when two parties each claimed a chattel, such as a horse. This situation is light-years removed from the issues here, yet the rules of law applied were the same.

QUICKNOTES

CONVERSION - The act of depriving an owner of his property without permission or justification.

NOTES:

NEWMAN v. SATHYAVAGLSWARAN
Parents (P) v. Coroner (D)
287 F.3d 786 (9th Cir. 2002).

NATURE OF CASE: Appeal from dismissal of claim of taking of property.

FACT SUMMARY: Parents (P) whose deceased children's corneas were removed by a coroner (D) without notice or consent brought suit alleging a taking of their property without due process of law.

CONCISE RULE OF LAW: The exclusive right of next of kin to possess the bodies of their deceased family members creates a property interest, the deprivation of which must be accorded due process of law under the Fourteenth Amendment.

FACTS: The Los Angeles County Coroner's office (D) removed the corneas of children without notice or consent of their parents (P). Such removal was authorized by state statute. The parents (P) brought suit pursuant to 42 U.S.C. § 1983 alleging a taking of their property without due process of law in violation of the U.S. Constitution's Fourteenth Amendment.

ISSUE: Does the exclusive right of next of kin to possess the bodies of their deceased family members creates a property interest, the deprivation of which must be accorded due process of law under the Fourteenth Amendment?

HOLDING AND DECISION: (Fisher, J.) Yes. The exclusive right of next of kin to possess the bodies of their deceased family members creates a property interest, the deprivation of which must be accorded due process of law under the Fourteenth Amendment. The Fourteenth Amendment prohibits states from depriving any person of property without due process. Here there is no issue that the removal of the corneas of deceased children constituted a deprivation under color of state law, so the only issue is whether the corneas constituted property of the parents (P). The property interests protected by procedural due process extend well beyond real estate, chattels, or money, and are created by existing rules or understandings that stem from an independent source, such as state law. Thus, the first step in the analysis must be to analyze the history of rules and understandings of our country respecting the possession and protection of the bodies of the dead. Duties to protect the dignity of the human body after death date back to the Roman Empire, but were not included in English common law until 1840. Therefore, many American courts adopted the earlier common law holding that a dead body is not the subject of property right. The duty to bury the body stemmed not from property rights but from a "universal right of sepulture." Toward the end of the 19th century, as the demand by medical science increased, courts began to recognize an exclusive right of next of kin to possess and

control the disposition of their dead relatives' bodies. Thus a *quasi* property right in the bodies of the dead was recognized. In 1899, the California Supreme Court recognized such rights of possession, control and disposition, and these were eventually codified in California's Health and Safety Code. With the advent of successful transplants, states, including California, adopted the Uniform Anatomical Gift Act (UAGA), which grants next of kin the right to transfer the parts of bodies in their possession to others for medical or research purposes. Such right, however is limited, and may not be exercised for consideration. The increasing demand for transplanted organs prompted some states, including California, to pass "presumed consent" laws that allow the taking and transfer of body parts by a coroner without the consent of next of kin as long as no objection to the removal is known. This was the statute (California Government Code § 27491.47) under which the coroner (D) in this case proceeded. That statute also provides that the coroner acting under the statute is not subject to civil or criminal liability for the removal of corneal eye tissue. Property is defined as "the group of rights inhering in the citizen's relation to the physical thing, as the right to possess, use and dispose of it...." Some courts have recognized that the common law right of next of kin to possess the body for burial purposes and to bring a claim against others who disturb the body, along with the statutory right in the UAGA to control the disposition of the body, are sufficient to create in next of kin a property interest in the corneas of their deceased relatives that could not be taken without due process of law. Other courts, however, have not recognized the constitutional dimension of such *quasi* property rights. Those courts that do recognize the constitutional dimension of such rights are correct. Here, under the common law, the parents (P) had the exclusive right to possess, control, dispose and prevent the violation of the corneas and other parts of the bodies of their deceased children. Under the UAGA, they had the right to transfer body parts and to refuse such transfer. These rights are all components of the group of rights by which property is defined. Therefore, the parents (P) had property interests in the corneas of their deceased children protected by the Due Process Clause. This holding is not affected by California's labeling of such rights as "*quasi* property" rights, as federal constitutional law determines whether those rights rise to the level of constitutionally protected rights. Nor does the fact that California prohibits the trade of body parts for profit mean that the next of kin lack a property interest in them; a physical item may be property even though it has no economic or market value. Moreover, the statute under which the coroner (D) operated allowed removal only if the coroner (D) had no knowledge of

Continued on next page.

objection, thus implicitly acknowledging the ongoing property interest of the parents (P). The statute removed the requirement of notice and consent, but a state may not evade due process analysis by defining property by the procedures provided for its deprivation. Reversed and remanded.

DISSENT: (Fernandez, J.) It has always been the case in California that absent a statute there is no property in a dead body. To the extent that any right exists, it is, in general, merely a right to possession that exists solely for the limited purpose of determining who shall have custody for burial. California's statutory scheme does not confer a property right on anyone; if anything, it imposes a duty more than a right. Such a limited right hardly looks like the kind of interest the Constitution was designed to protect. All California has done is given next of kin enough of right to fulfill their duty of properly disposing of a loved one's body. And such a right is itself limited with respect to corneal tissue, as there is no correlative duty imposed.

EDITOR'S ANALYSIS: In states that have rejected corneal eye tissue as property of next of kin, *e.g.*, Florida and Georgia, the courts have weighed the public health interest in cornea donation and the "infinitesimally small intrusion" of corneal removal. In this case, however, the court, only after determining that next of kin have a property interest in the corneal tissue of their deceased relative, indicated that it was remanding the case for proceedings in which the government's justification for its deprivation of parents' interests may be fully scrutinized. Thus, on remand, some of the potential issues will be whether California's statute is constitutional, and whether the state effected a taking without just compensation to the parents (P).

NOTES:

CHAPTER 5*
ESTATES IN LAND AND FUTURE INTERESTS IN THE UNITED STATES TODAY

QUICK REFERENCE RULES OF LAW

1. **The Defeasible Fee Simple: Controlling Land Use and Behavior by Threat of Forfeiture.** The language in a deed will not be construed to constitute a condition subsequent unless the intention of the parties to create such a restriction upon the title is clearly manifested. (Station Associates, Inc. v. Dare County)

2. **The Defeasible Fee Simple: Controlling Land Use and Behavior by Threat of Forfeiture.** A deed containing a condition subsequent will be strictly construed to confine the determination of intent to the face of the deed. (Red Hill Outing Club v. Hammond)

3. **The Defeasible Fee Simple: Controlling Land Use and Behavior by Threat of Forfeiture.** When the purpose of taking a future interest is to permit the holder of the present interest to use the property in a manner violating the conditions under which the property was conveyed, the violation of those conditions is imminent and the taking is compensable. (City of Palm Springs v. Living Desert Reserve)

4. **Life Estates.** A deed subject to a life estate in a third person validly creates that life estate. (Nelson v. Parker)

5. **Life Estates.** The intention of the testator is the pole star in the construction of a will and that intention must be ascertained from the entire will. (In re Estate of Kinert v. Pennsylvania Department of Revenue)

6. **Life Estates.** A life tenant must make ordinary repairs to avoid waste. (In re Estate of Jackson)

7. **Life Estates.** Failure to pay real estate taxes may give rise to a cause of action in waste. (Hausmann v. Hausmann)

8. **Vested Remainders Subject to Partial Divestment.** The interest created in the grantor of a common law fee tail estate is a vested reversion which is fully descendible, devisable, and alienable *inter vivos*. (Long v. Long)

9. **The Rules Against Perpetuities and Other Doctrines That Destroy Future Interests.** A person's will should be enforced so as to avoid clearly unintended consequences. (In re Estate of Anderson)

10. **The Rules Against Perpetuities and Other Doctrines That Destroy Future Interests.** Options to purchase commercial property are not exempt from the prohibition on remote vesting under New York's Rule against Perpetuities. (Symphony Space, Inc. v. Pergola Properties, Inc.)

*There are no cases in Chapter 4.

STATION ASSOCIATES, INC. v. DARE COUNTY
Heirs (P) v. Grantee (D)
N.C. Sup. Ct., 513 S.E.2d 789 (1999).

NATURE OF CASE: Appeal from reversal of judgment for defendant in title action.

FACT SUMMARY: The district court's conclusion that Dare County (D) had title to property in fee simple absolute was reversed on appeal.

CONCISE RULE OF LAW: The language in a deed will not be construed to constitute a condition subsequent unless the intention of the parties to create such a restriction upon the title is clearly manifested.

FACTS: A deed granted coastal land to the United States for construction of a life-saving station in 1897. The Coast Guard later took over operation of the station and then later abandoned it. The United States then quitclaimed its interest in the property to Dare County (D). The heirs of the original grantor sold an ownership interest in the land to Station Associates (P) and instituted this action against Dare County (D). The trial court granted judgment on the pleadings to Dare County (D) but the court of appeals reversed, finding that the United States had been granted only a fee simple determinable with a possibility of reverter and not a fee simple absolute. Dare County (D) appealed.

ISSUE: Will the language in a deed be construed to constitute a condition subsequent only if the intention of the parties to create such a restriction upon the title is clearly manifested?

HOLDING AND DECISION: (Parker, J.) Yes. The language in a deed will not be construed to constitute a condition subsequent unless the intention of the parties to create such a restriction upon the title is clearly manifested. A mere expression of the purpose for which the property is to be used without provision for forfeiture or reentry is insufficient to create an estate on condition. The deed in the case at bar contained no language of reversion or termination and an unqualified fee simple absolute passed. Reversed and remanded.

EDITOR'S ANALYSIS: Courts will construe a deed to convey an estate on condition where the deed contained express and unambiguous language of reversion or termination. In this deed there was no provision that the estate would automatically terminate upon the happening of a certain event. Thus a fee simple absolute, not a defeasible fee, was created.

RED HILL OUTING CLUB v. HAMMOND
Grantee (P) v. Grantor (D)
N.H. Sup. Ct., 82 Cal. Rptr. 2d 859, 722 A.2d 501 (1998).

NATURE OF CASE: Appeal from declaratory judgment for plaintiff in land dispute.

FACT SUMMARY: The trial court found that Red Hill (P) had not substantially breached a condition in the deed granted by Hammond (D) conveying a ski slope.

CONCISE RULE OF LAW: A deed containing a condition subsequent will be strictly construed to confine the determination of intent to the face of the deed.

FACTS: When Hammond (D) deeded some land to the Red Hill Outing Club (P) for nominal consideration, a condition was included that the land be used as a public ski slope and that Hammond (D) had the right to re-enter and take possession if Red Hill (P) failed to provide skiing facilities for two consecutive years. When Hammond (D) filed a notice of re-entry and possession, Red Hill (P) instituted these proceedings for a declaratory judgment regarding the rights of the parties. The trial court found that Red Hill (P) had not substantially breached the condition because it had remained in existence and continued to offer use of the hill as a ski slope, despite declining use. Hammond (D) appealed, claiming that the court should have construed the condition subsequent by determining the parties' intent in light of circumstances at the time of conveyance.

ISSUE: Will a deed containing a condition subsequent be strictly construed to confine the determination of intent to the face of the deed?

HOLDING AND DECISION: (Horton, J.) Yes. A deed containing a condition subsequent will be strictly construed to confine the determination of intent to the face of the deed. Condition subsequents are viewed with disfavor because of their potential to cause a forfeiture of land. The rule of strict construction resolves all ambiguities against forfeiture. The trial court did not err in construing Red Hill's (P) obligation as limited to maintaining and making the hill available as a ski area. It was not required to import meanings not apparent on the face of the deed when it determined the parties' intent. Affirmed.

EDITOR'S ANALYSIS: Hammond (D) had argued that Red Hills (P) had agreed to provide a tow rope and ski instruction. But the court applied the rule of strict construction, limiting the condition subsequent to the express words of the deed. Other jurisdictions have made similar rulings because a forfeiture is a considered to be a drastic remedy to be avoided if at all possible.

QUICKNOTES

CONDITION SUBSEQUENT - Potential future occurrence that extinguishes a party's obligation to perform pursuant to the contract.

DECLARATORY JUDGMENT - An adjudication by the courts which grants not relief but is binding over the legal status of the parties involved in the dispute.

DEED - A signed writing transferring title to real property from one person to another.

FORFEITURE - The loss of a right or interest as a penalty for failing to fulfill an obligation.

NOTES:

CITY OF PALM SPRINGS v. LIVING DESERT RESERVE

Grantee (P) v. Holder of reversionary interest (D)
Cal. Ct. App., 82 Cal. Rptr. 2d 859, review denied (1999).

NATURE OF CASE: Appeal from judgment for plaintiff in land dispute.

FACT SUMMARY: The City of Palm Springs (P) wanted to use land that had been granted for use as a desert wildlife preserve to expand the municipal golf course.

CONCISE RULE OF LAW: When the purpose of taking a future interest is to permit the holder of the present interest to use the property in a manner violating the conditions under which the property was conveyed, the violation of those conditions is imminent and the taking is compensable.

FACTS: When land was granted to the City of Palm Springs (P) for use as a desert wildlife preserve, the deed stated that if the land were not so used, it would revert to the Living Desert Reserve (D). When the City of Palm Springs (P) wanted to use the land to expand its golf course, it successfully filed a complaint in eminent domain. Living Desert (D) recorded a notice of breach of condition subsequent and cross-complained to quiet title, claiming that its reversionary interest was compensable. The trial court held that the reversionary interest was not a compensable interest and entered judgment in favor of Palm Springs (P). The Living Desert Reserve (D) appealed.

ISSUE: When the purpose of taking a future interest is to permit the holder of the present interest to use the property in a manner violating the conditions under which the property was conveyed, is the violation of those conditions imminent and is the taking compensable?

HOLDING AND DECISION: (McKinster, J.) Yes. When the purpose of taking a future interest is to permit the holder of the present interest to use the property in a manner violating the conditions under which the property was conveyed, the violation of those conditions is imminent and the taking is compensable. The deed must be construed as granting to the City of Palm Springs (P) a fee simple subject to a condition subsequent, and a power of termination to the Living Desert Reserve (D). The general rule denying compensation to a holder of a reversionary interest does not apply if the reversion is likely to occur within a reasonably short time. In this case, a violation of the use restriction was reasonably imminent and the Living Desert's (D) power of termination was therefore compensable. That portion of the judgment ruling in favor of Palm Springs (P) on its complaint for eminent domain is reversed. Affirmed in part, reversed in part.

EDITOR'S ANALYSIS: The conveyance at issue here was from a charitable trust. The general rule is that the owner of a defeasible fee receives all the condemnation proceeds. The court applied an objective test to determine whether the violation of the condition in the deed was imminent.

QUICKNOTES

CONDITION SUBSEQUENT - Potential future occurrence that extinguishes a party's obligation to perform pursuant to the contract.

DEFEASIBLE FEE SIMPLE ESTATE - A fee simple interest in land that is subject to being terminated upon the happening of a future event.

EMINENT DOMAIN - The governmental power to take private property for public use so long as just compensation is paid therefore.

REVERSIONARY INTEREST - An interest retained by a grantor of property in the land transferred, which is created when the owner conveys less of an interest than he or she owns and which returns to the grantor upon the termination of the conveyed estate.

TAKING - A governmental action that substantially deprives an owner of the use and enjoyment of his or her property, requiring compensation.

NOTES:

NELSON v. PARKER
Grantee (P) v. Holder of life estate (D)
Ind. Sup. Ct., 687 N.E.2d 187 (1997).

NATURE OF CASE: Appeal from summary judgment for defendant.

FACT SUMMARY: The district court ruled that a life estate had been created for Parker (D) and Nelson (P) appealed.

CONCISE RULE OF LAW: A deed subject to a life estate in a third person validly creates that life estate.

FACTS: Nelson (P) claimed that his deceased father's deed conveying property to him did not effectively grant Parker (D), his father's roommate for fourteen years before his death, a life estate. When Nelson (P) tried to evict Parker (D), the court held that the father had intended to create a life estate and granted Parker's (D) motion for summary judgment. Nelson (P) appealed, claiming that at common law a grantor could not create an interest in a third person in a deed.

ISSUE: Does a deed subject to a life estate in a third person validly create that life estate?

HOLDING AND DECISION: (Boehm, J.) Yes. A deed subject to a life estate in a third person validly creates that life estate. The common law rule serves no practical purpose today. Public policy does not require adherence to a vestige of ancient conveyancing law with only pernicious effects. Affirmed.

EDITOR'S ANALYSIS: The court here discussed the public policy of promoting settled rules. But it held that settled rules may have to be changed at times. In this case, there were no advantages in retaining an archaic rule which served to destroy an intended interest in land.

QUICKNOTES

DEED - A signed writing transferring title to real property from one person to another.

LIFE ESTATE - An interest in land measured by the life of the tenant or a third party.

NOTES:

IN RE ESTATE OF KINERT v. PENNSYLVANIA DEPARTMENT OF REVENUE

Estate (P) v. State Tax Department (D)
Pa. Cmmw. Ct., 693 A.2d 643 (1996).

NATURE OF CASE: Appeal from judgment for plaintiff in will dispute.

FACT SUMMARY: The district court held that a bequest in a will only granted a license and not a life estate in property subject to taxation.

CONCISE RULE OF LAW: The intention of the testator is the pole star in the construction of a will and that intention must be ascertained from the entire will.

FACTS: When the Estate of Kinert (P) claimed that two foster children had only been granted a license to live in the deceased's house under the terms of her will, The Pennsylvania Department of Revenue (D) disagreed. When the Estate (P) filed its first and final accounting, Pa. (D) objected, and claimed that a taxable life estate had been created in the foster children. The Orphan's Court determined that a license had been created and Pennsylvania (D) appealed.

ISSUE: Is the intention of the testator the pole star in the construction of a will and must that intention be ascertained from the entire will?

HOLDING AND DECISION: (McGinley, J.) Yes. The intention of the testator is the pole star in the construction of a will and that intention must be ascertained from the entire will. Here, the decedent clearly intended to devise a life estate in the property to her foster sons. This conclusion is reinforced by the use of the word "devise" in the will. Reversed and remanded.

DISSENT: (Friedman, J.) The will includes a provision that the right to continue to live in the house will terminate if both foster children vacate the premises for a period of sixty days. Thus they do not have a life estate but merely a license to occupy the premises.

EDITOR'S ANALYSIS: A license usually only means that someone has permission to do something. A license would not confer a right to exercise exclusive possession and enjoyment of property. The modern trend is to consider a license an interest in property.

QUICKNOTES

BEQUEST - A transfer of property that is accomplished by means of a testamentary instrument.

DEVISE - The conferring of a gift of real or personal property by means of a testamentary instrument.

LICENSE - A right that is granted to a person allowing him or her to conduct an activity that without such permission he or she could not lawfully do, and which is unassignable and revocable at the will of the licensor.

LIFE ESTATE - An interest in land measured by the life of the tenant or a third party.

WILL - An instrument setting forth the distribution to be made of an individual's estate upon his death; since a will is not effective until the death of its maker, it is revocable during his life.

NOTES:

IN RE ESTATE OF JACKSON
Residuary beneficiaries (P) v. Estate (D)
S.D. Sup. Ct., 508 N.W.2d 374 (1993).

NATURE OF CASE: Appeal from probate court order.

FACT SUMMARY: The probate court found that insurance proceeds used to repair decedent's house should have been given to the estate, and not to the residuary beneficiaries.

CONCISE RULE OF LAW: A life tenant must make ordinary repairs to avoid waste.

FACTS: When a hail storm damaged the decedent's house, in which she retained a life estate, insurance funds were used to make the necessary repairs. Since she died before the insurance proceeds were distributed, the residuary beneficiaries (P) received the proceeds. The probate court later ruled that the estate (D) should have received the funds. The residuary beneficiaries (P) filed a claim against the estate (D) for the necessary repairs made and appealed, claiming that, as a life tenant, decedent had an obligation to repair the house.

ISSUE: Must a life tenant make ordinary repairs to avoid waste?

HOLDING AND DECISION: (Per curiam) Yes. A life tenant must make ordinary repairs to avoid waste. Since the house was damaged during her life estate, the decedent had an obligation to make necessary repairs. After her death, her estate was responsible for meeting that obligation. Reversed.

EDITOR'S ANALYSIS: The court here held that repairs made following a hail storm were "ordinary." A life tenant would not be required to make "extraordinary" repairs that were not her fault. The law tries to be fair to both the present and the future interest holders.

QUICKNOTES
LIFE ESTATE - An interest in land measured by the life of the tenant or a third party.

RESIDUARY BENEFICIARIES - Person specified pursuant to will to receive the portion of the estate remaining following distribution of the assets and the payment of costs.

WASTE - The mistreatment of another's property by someone in lawful possession.

HAUSMANN v. HAUSMANN
Remainderman (P) v. Life tenant (D)
Ill. App. Ct., 596 N.E.2d 216 (1992).

NATURE OF CASE: Appeal from judgment for plaintiff in suit alleging waste.

FACT SUMMARY: The trial court awarded compensatory and punitive damages to Charles Hausman (P), a remainderman, when George Hausman (D), a life tenant, committed waste.

CONCISE RULE OF LAW: Failure to pay real estate taxes may give rise to a cause of action in waste.

FACTS: Charles Hausman (P) alleged that his uncle, George Hausman (D), had committed waste by failing to pay real estate taxes on property in which Charles (P) held a remainder interest. The trial court awarded Charles (P) compensatory and punitive damages and George (D) appealed, claiming that failure to pay real estate taxes did not equal waste.

ISSUE: May failure to pay real estate taxes give rise to a cause of action in waste?

HOLDING AND DECISION: (Chapman, J.) Yes. Failure to pay real estate taxes may give rise to a cause of action in waste. When George (D) failed in his duty to pay the taxes, Charles (P) was compelled to act to avoid possible divestment. Charles (P) must be compensated for charges incurred when he redeemed the property by paying the taxes due. Affirmed.

EDITOR'S ANALYSIS: The court here noted that in other jurisdictions failure to pay real estate taxes could lead to an action in waste. In Illinois the issue had never been raised before. But Illinois law did require a life tenant to pay real estate taxes assessed against the land during his life tenancy.

QUICKNOTES
COMPENSATORY DAMAGES - Measure of damages necessary to compensate victim for actual injuries suffered.

LIFE ESTATE - An interest in land measured by the life of the tenant or a third party.

PUNITIVE DAMAGES - Damages exceeding the actual injury suffered for the purposes of punishment, deterrence and comfort to plaintiff.

REMAINDER - An interest in land that remains after the termination of the immediately preceding estate.

WASTE - The mistreatment of another's property by someone in lawful possession.

LONG v. LONG
Heir (P) v. Heir (D)
Ohio Sup. Ct., 343 N.E.2d 100 (1976).

NATURE OF CASE: Appeal from will contest.

FACT SUMMARY: The heirs to property disagreed on the proper distribution of a fee tail estate.

CONCISE RULE OF LAW: The interest created in the grantor of a common law fee tail estate is a vested reversion which is fully descendible, devisable, and alienable *inter vivos*.

FACTS: When Long (P) claimed that he inherited after the creation by deed of a fee tail estate, Long (D) claimed that the interest remaining in the grantor of a fee tails was a possibility of reverter that could not descend to an heir until the donee in tail died without issue.

ISSUE: Is the interest created in the grantor of a common law fee tail estate a vested reversion which is fully descendible, devisable and alienable *inter vivos*?

HOLDING AND DECISION: (Corrigan, J.) Yes. The interest created in the grantor of a common law fee tail estate is a vested reversion which is fully descendible, devisable and alienable *inter vivos*. The series of conveyances begun by Long's son (D) were effective to convey property. Reversed.

EDITOR'S ANALYSIS: The court here discussed the history of the fee tail. The language necessary for a fee tail to result is: "To A and the heirs of his body." All states have either abolished or altered the fee tail by statute.

QUICKNOTES

DEED - A signed writing transferring title to real property from one person to another.

FEE TAIL - A limitation in either a deed or will limiting succession of property to a grantee and the heirs of his body.

INTER VIVOS - Between living persons.

POSSIBILITY OF REVERTER - A type of reversionary interest referring to an interest in land that remains in the grantor until the happening of a condition precedent.

REVERSION - An interest retained by a grantor of property in the land transferred, which is created when the owner conveys less of an interest than he or she owns and which returns to the grantor upon the termination of the conveyed estate.

IN RE ESTATE OF ANDERSON
Remainderman (P) v. Estate (D)
Miss. Sup. Ct., 541 So.2d 423 (1989).

NATURE OF CASE: Appeal from declaratory judgment upholding trust.

FACT SUMMARY: The trial court applied the wait and see doctrine to save an educational trust.

CONCISE RULE OF LAW: A person's will should be enforced so as to avoid clearly unintended consequences.

FACTS: Where a will created an educational trust to be shared by all descendents of the testator's parents, the Chancery Court upheld the trust despite the claims of the testator's nephew, Howard Davis (P), that the bequest in trust violated the Rule against Perpetuities. Davis (P) appealed.

ISSUE: Should a person's will be enforced so as to avoid clearly unintended consequences?

HOLDING AND DECISION: (Robertson, J.) Yes. A person's will should be enforced so as to avoid clearly unintended consequences. By applying the wait and see doctrine, we can now say that the interests of all contingent remainders will vest or fail less than twenty-one years from today. Affirmed as modified and remanded.

EDITOR'S ANALYSIS: The court here discussed at length the modern application of the Rule Against Perpetuities. Under the "wait and see" doctrine, the validity of an interest is not judged by what might happen, but rather by what actually did happen. In this case, the court said it had waited and seen, and that Howard Davis (P) was alive and the contingent remainders would vest within twenty-years as of the date of these court proceedings, so the Rule would not be violated.

QUICKNOTES

CONTINGENT REMAINDER - A remainder limited to a person not in being, not certain or ascertained, or so limited to a certain person that his right to the state depends upon some contingent event in the future.

DECLARATORY JUDGMENT - An adjudication by the courts which grants not relief but is binding over the legal status of the parties involved in the dispute.

RULE AGAINST PERPETUITIES - The doctrine that a future interest that is incapable of vesting within twenty-one years of lives in being at the time it is created is immediately void.

SYMPHONY SPACE, INC. v. PERGOLA PROPERTIES, INC.
Lessee (P) v. Owner (D)
N.Y. Ct. App., 88 N.Y.2d 466, 669 N.E.2d 799 (1996).

NATURE OF CASE: Appeal from declaratory judgment.

FACT SUMMARY: Pergola (D) sought to exercise an option in a commercial lease to purchase property occupied by Symphony (P).

CONCISE RULE OF LAW: Options to purchase commercial property are not exempt from the prohibition on remote vesting under New York's Rule against Perpetuities.

FACTS: Symphony (P), a nonprofit group devoted to the arts, rented a two-story building from Broadwest. The two entered into a transaction whereby Broadwest sold the building to Symphony (P) for the below-market price of $10,010 and leased back the commercial property for $1 a year. Symphony (P) also granted Broadwest an option to repurchase the building. In 1981, Broadwest sold and assigned its interest under the lease, option, mortgage and mortgage note to Pergola (D) for $4.8 million. Pergola (D) began a cooperation conversion of a portion of the property. Pergola (D) served Symphony (P) with notice that it was exercising the option clause due to Symphony's (P) alleged default on the mortgage note. Symphony (P) initiated this declaratory judgment proceeding and the trial court granted Symphony's (P) motion, concluding that the Rule against Perpetuities (EPTL 9-1.1[b]) applied to the commercial option in the parties' agreement, that the option violated the Rule and that Symphony (P) was entitled to exercise its right to redeem the mortgage. The Appellate Division affirmed and certified the following question to this court, "Was the order of the Supreme Court, as affirmed by this court, properly made?"

ISSUE: Are options to purchase commercial property exempt from the prohibition on remote vesting under New York's Rule against Perpetuities?

HOLDING AND DECISION: (Kaye, C.J.) No. Options to purchase commercial property are not exempt from the prohibition on remote vesting under New York's Rule against Perpetuities. The rule states that, "No interest is good unless it must vest, if at all, not later than twenty-one years after some life in being at the creation of the interest." Pergola (D) offers three arguments for upholding the option. First, the statutory prohibition against remote vesting does not apply to commercial options. It is well settled in New York that the rule against remote vesting applies to options. Since the common law rule prohibition applies to both commercial and noncommercial options, then EPTL 9-1.1(b) also applies to both. This option agreement is precisely the type of control over the future disposition of the property that the state law sought to prevent. The option grants the holder the absolute power to purchase the property at his whim and at a price far below market value. Second, Pergola (D) argues that the option here cannot be exercised beyond the statutory period. Pergola (D) claims that only the possible closing dates fall outside the permissible time frame. Where parties to a transaction are corporations and no measuring lives are stated in the instruments, the perpetuities period is simply 21 years. Third, Pergola (D) argues the court to adopt a "wait and see" approach to the Rule, meaning that an interest is valid if it actually vests during the perpetuities period. Here the option would survive under this approach since it was exercised within the 21-year limitation. This court, however, has long refused to adopt a wait and see approach to determine whether a perpetuities violation in fact occurs. Thus, the option agreement is invalid under EPTL 9-1.1(b). Affirmed.

EDITOR'S ANALYSIS: Defendants also argued that the contract should be rescinded due to mutual mistake of fact on the basis that neither party realized the option violated the Rule against Perpetuities. The court concludes that such mistake was simply a misunderstanding as to the applicable law and thus did not require undoing the transaction.

QUICKNOTES

OPTION - A contract pursuant to which a seller agrees that property will be available for the buyer to purchase at a specified price and within a certain time period.

RULE AGAINST PERPETUITIES - The doctrine that a future interest that is incapable of vesting within twenty-one years of lives in being at the time it is created is immediately void.

NOTES:

CHAPTER 6
LANDLORD-TENANT

QUICK REFERENCE RULES OF LAW

1. **Duty to Deliver Possession.** The extent of a landlord's implied agreement with his lessee is that he has good title by which he can give an unencumbered lease for the term demised; so, if at the time of commencement of the term, possession is held by a trespassing holdover, the landlord is under no duty to oust him. (Teitelbaum v. Direct Realty Co.)

2. **Duty to Protect Tenant's Quiet Enjoyment: Constructive Eviction.** Where a landlord permits conduct of third persons which substantially impairs the right of quiet enjoyment of other tenants, it is a constructive eviction. (Blackett v. Olanoff)

3. **Duty to Protect Tenant's Quiet Enjoyment: Constructive Eviction.** (1) A landlord's breach of its covenant to repair does not constitute constructive eviction where the landlord's breach does not render the premises untenantable. (2) The mutually dependent covenants rule, rather than the common law's independent covenants rule, applies to commercial leases. (Wesson v. Leone Enterprises, Inc.)

4. **Condition of the Premises: The Warrant of Habitability.** The modern urban tenant seeks more from a lease than the outdated common-law conveyance of an interest in land, rather, he seeks a well-known package of goods and services; and, modern housing regulations imply into every lease a warranty of habitability, the breach of which by the landlord will justify a suspension of the tenant's covenant to pay rent. (Javins v. First National Realty Corp.)

5. **Landlord's Tort Liability.** The proprietor of a hotel cannot be held strictly liable under a products liability theory in tort for injuries to guests caused by defects in the premises. (Peterson v. Superior Court)

6. **Continuing Issues in Substandard Rental Housing: Lead Paint.** No liability attaches for injuries resulting from a dangerous condition unless the landlord had actual or constructive notice of the condition. (Gore v. People's Savings Bank)

7. **Duty to Preserve the Premises.** Where an alteration is essential to the proper use of the premises and increases its value, it may be made by a tenant if a prudent owner of the property would be likely to make it in view of the conditions existing on or in the neighborhood of the affected land. (Sigsbee Holding Corp. v. Canavan)

8. **Duty to Operate.** A lease agreement containing a provision for free assignability by the tenant does not bind the tenant to continue its business on the premises throughout the term of the lease. (Piggly Wiggly Southern, Inc. v. Heard)

9. **Duty to Pay Rent.** The accidental destruction of the leased premises excuses the parties from further performance of their obligations under a lease agreement. (Albert M. Greenfield & Co. v. Kolea)

10. **Recovery of Possession.** Ownership or a right of possession to the property is not a defense to an action for forcible entry. Any unauthorized opening of a closed door is a breaking open of the door sufficient to constitute forcible entry. A person who obtains possession to property by a forcible entry does not have the right to retain possession. In the absence of provisions in a lease for enforcement of lien granted by the lease, equitable action would be necessary to make the lien operative. (Jordan v. Talbot)

11. **Recovery of Possession.** An affirmative cause of action for retaliatory eviction is available to a tenant when the tenant exercises a right related to the tenancy. (Murphy v. Smallridge)

12. **Monetary Damages.** A landlord must show he made a reasonable good faith effort to mitigate his damages upon a tenant's abandonment by attempting to rent the premises to a third party for the remainder of the lease period. (Lefrak v. Lambert)

13. **Monetary Damages.** A landlord may recover the balance of rent payments called for under a lease after the premises are abandoned by the tenant (Lefrak v. Lambert)

14. **Monetary Damages.** An acceleration clause is valid if it reasonably approximates the anticipated or actual loss suffered. (Aurora Business Park Associates v. Michael Albert, Inc.)

15. **Liability for Rent and other Covenants.** An assignee who takes possession under an assignment without an express assumption of the obligation of the lease is not bound by the contractual obligations of the lease. (Kelly v. Tri-Cities Broadcasting, Inc.)

16. **Liability for Rent and Other Covenants.** The right of reentry is a reversionary interest that qualifies a transfer of rights under a lease as a sublease, not an assignment. (American Community Stores Corp. v. Newman)

17. **Power to Assign or Sublet.** If a lease contains a silent consent clause requiring that the tenant obtain the landlord's consent in order to assign or sublease, such consent may not be unreasonably withheld. (Julian v. Christopher)

TEITELBAUM v. DIRECT REALTY CO.
Lessor (P) v. Lessee (D)
Nassau County Sup. Ct., 172 Misc. 48, 13 N.Y.S. 2d 886 (1939).

NATURE OF CASE: Action to recover damages for failure to provide premises under a lease.

FACT SUMMARY: Direct Realty (D) executed a lease with Teitelbaum (P), but was unable to deliver possession of the premises on time because of a wrongful holdover by a prior tenant.

CONCISE RULE OF LAW: The extent of a landlord's implied agreement with his lessee is that he has good title by which he can give an unencumbered lease for the term demised; so, if at the time of commencement of the term, possession is held by a trespassing holdover, the landlord is under no duty to oust him.

FACTS: Direct Realty Co. (D) executed a lease with Teitelbaum (P) for certain commercial premises. Teitelbaum (P) had gotten out of a lease with another landlord so he could take possession of the premises in July and open up business in August. On July 1, however, the Fergangs, who had occupied the Direct Realty (D) premises as tenants up to that date, refused to move out. (They claimed a right of renewal under their lease, but subsequently defaulted in proceedings by Direct Realty (D) to oust them.) They did not move out, in fact, until January of the following year. Teitelbaum (P) sued to recover damages (consideration paid to be released from the other lease, *etc.*) for Direct Realty's (D) failure to oust the holdovers from the premises by the time of the commencement of the term. Direct Realty (D) moves for a dismissal of the complaint.

ISSUE: Does a landlord owe a duty to remove all wrongful holdovers and trespassers from his promises before commencement of the term of a lease?

HOLDING AND DECISION: (Lockwood, J.) No. The extent of a landlord's implied responsibility to his lessee is that he has good title by which he can give an unencumbered lease for the term demised; so, if at the time of commencement of the term, possession is held by a trespassing holdover, the landlord is under no duty to oust him. As such, the failure to do so does not render a landlord liable for damages. It is true that if the holdover tenant does by the authority of the landlord (prior "effective" lease, etc.), such landlord will be held for resultant damage to a lessee. Here, however, such is not the case. The Fergangs, by defaulting, admitted that they wrongfully held over, that they were trespassers. As such, Direct Realty (D) more than met its responsibilities to Teitelbaum (P) when it commenced the action to which the Fergang's defaulted. Direct Realty (D) had no duty to break. The complaint must be dismissed.

EDITOR'S ANALYSIS: A landlord merely covenants that a lessee will have a legal right to possession and quiet enjoyment of his premises. This is the overwhelming American rule although a minority of states do follow the English rule. In England, the landlord also implicitly covenants to deliver possession of the promises to the lessee at the commencement of the lease.

QUICKNOTES
COVENANT - A written promise to do, or to refrain from doing, a particular activity.

HOLDOVER TENANT - A tenancy that arises upon the expiration of a lawful tenancy and the tenant remains in possession of the property.

TRESPASS - Unlawful interference with, or damage to, the real or personal property of another.

NOTES:

BLACKETT v. OLANOFF
Landlord (P) v. Tenants (D)
371 Mass. 714, 358 N.E.2d 817 (1977).

NATURE OF CASE: Action for rent due and owing.

FACT SUMMARY: Tenants (D) alleged that Blackett (P), the landlord, had breached his covenant of quiet enjoyment as a defense to an action for rent.

CONCISE RULE OF LAW: Where a landlord permits conduct of third persons which substantially impairs the right of quiet enjoyment of other tenants, it is a constructive eviction.

FACTS: Olanoff (D) and other tenants vacated an apartment building owned by Blackett (P) and others. Blackett (P) sued for rent due and owing. The tenants (D) alleged that their right to quiet enjoyment had been substantially impaired by the landlords (P). Blackett (P) had rented nearby property as a bar. The noise from the bar was often very loud and significantly disturbed the apartment tenants. Blackett (P) periodically warned the bar tenants to keep the noise down as they were obligated to do under the lease. The noise would be abated for a while, but it always became loud again. The tenants (D) finally vacated the apartments and Blackett (P) sued for rent. The court found that the tenants' right to quiet enjoyment had been substantially interfered with and that this constituted a constructive eviction which was a defense to an action for rent. Blackett (P) appealed, alleging that there could be no constructive eviction where the landlord had not, by his actions, caused the breach of the covenant.

ISSUE: Can a constructive eviction be found where the landlord permits a third party to substantially impair the rights of other tenants?

HOLDING AND DECISION: (Wilkins, J.) Yes. Normally, there must be some action by the landlord himself which causes the constructive eviction. Intent to deprive the tenants of their rights is not required. Where the landlord permits an activity to continue, which he can control, which causes significant impairment of the rights of other tenants, this constitutes a breach of the landlord's covenants. Here, Blackett (P) permitted a bar next to a residential apartment. Blackett (P) had the power to control the noise in the bar under the terms of its lease. Blackett (P) knew that the noise from the bar was disturbing tenants and failed to correct the matter. Under these circumstances, a constructive eviction may be found. Affirmed.

EDITOR'S ANALYSIS: Other examples of nonconduct by the landlord which have been held to constitute constructive eviction are: failure to supply adequate light, heat, *etc. Burt, Inc. v. Seven Grand Corp.*, 340 Mass. 124 (1959); authorization by the landlord for a tenant to obstruct the view, light and air of another tenant to a substantial extent. *Case v. Minot*, 158 Mass. 577 (1893); and a defective boiler causing excessive soot and smoke for a long period of time. *Westland Housing Corp. v. Scott*, 312 Mass. 375 (1942).

NOTES:

WESSON v. LEONE ENTERPRISES, INC.

Landlord (P) v. Tenant (D)

Mass. Sup. Ct., 437 Mass. 708, 774 N.E.2d 611 (2002).

NATURE OF CASE: Appeal from judgment of constructive eviction and application of the dependent covenants rule to a commercial lease.

FACT SUMMARY: Leone Enterprises, Inc. (the tenant) (D) vacated the leased premises before the end of the commercial lease, claiming constructive eviction based on a perennially leaky roof. Wesson (P), the landlord, sued for breach of contract and damage to the premises.

CONCISE RULE OF LAW: (1) A landlord's breach of its covenant to repair does not constitute constructive eviction where the landlord's breach does not render the premises untenantable. (2) The mutually dependent covenants rule, rather than the common law's independent covenants rule, applies to commercial leases.

FACTS: In March 1988, Leone Enterprises, Inc. (the tenant) (D), a high-tech printing enterprise, entered a five-year commercial lease with Wesson (P), the landlord. In 1991, the third year of the lease, the tenant (D) complained about a leaky roof on several occasions, despite Wesson's (P) repeated attempts to have the leaks in the roof fixed. After complaining about the leaks for about seven months, the tenant (D) gave one-month's notice to Wesson (P) that it would be vacating the premises by the end of 1991, well before the end of the lease, based on the leaky roof and lack of heat. The tenant (D) paid rent in full through the end of 1991. Wesson (P) sued for breach of contract and damage to the premises, and the tenant (D) counterclaimed for constructive eviction and deceptive business practices. The trial judge, finding the tenant's (D) testimony credible and that the roof was in a state of disrepair, ruled that the tenant (D) had been constructively evicted and was therefore relieved of its obligation to pay rent. Alternatively, the trial judge held that the tenant (D) could have lawfully withheld the rent under the dependent covenants rule, because Wesson (P) had failed to provide a "dry space," a service "essential" to the lease. The state's supreme court transferred the case to itself on its own motion.

ISSUE: (1) Does a landlord's breach of its covenant to repair constitute constructive eviction where the landlord's breach does not render the premises untenantable? (2) Does the mutually dependent covenants rule, rather than the common law's independent covenants rule, apply to commercial leases?

HOLDING AND DECISION: (Cordy, J.) (1) No. A landlord's breach of its covenant to repair does not constitute constructive eviction where the landlord's breach does not render the premises untenantable. Here, the evidence showed that Wesson (P) had the obligation to maintain the roof. Where there is a breach of the covenant of quiet enjoyment, a tenant may raise constructive eviction as a defense to an action to recover rent. Thus, the issue is whether Wesson' (P) conduct amounted to the breach of the covenant of quiet enjoyment. However, not every act or failure to act on the landlord's part that causes disruption to a tenant rises to the level of a constructive eviction. Conduct that does not render the premises untenantable does not rise to the level of a constructive eviction. Here, there was insufficient evidence that Wesson's (P) failure to fix the leaks caused work stoppages, missed or delayed coustomer deliveries, or otherwise prevented the tenant (D) from carrying on its business. Therefore, Wesson's (P) failures did not make the premises untenantable, and did not constitute to a constructive eviction, even though it did make the tenant's (D) operation less convenient and more expensive. (2) Yes. The mutually dependent covenants rule, rather than the common law's independent covenants rule, applies to commercial leases. At common law, covenants in leases were considered "independent" so that the lessee was relieved from performance of his covenants only by actual or constructive eviction. This was based on the theory of a lease as a conveyance of an interest in realty. This apparent unfairness was balanced under the same doctrine by the landlord's inability to recover possession of the property, even if the tenant did not pay rent. This "equilibrium" was lost with the enactment of dispossession statutes that permitted landlords to repossess their property if the tenant failed to pay rent, even if the landlord breached express covenants with the lease. Accordingly, the independent covenants rule was eventually abandoned in the context of residential leases, which are regarded as contracts between the landlord and tenant for the possession of property. The move away from the independent covenants rule was also a consumer-protection response. However, there are significant differences between commercial leases and residential leases. Because the reality is that a commercial lease no longer is a conveyance of property, but is a contract intended to secure the right to occupy improvements to the land rather than the land itself, and which usually contemplates a continuing flow of necessary services from landlord to tenant, the rule of mutually dependent covenants supplants the independent covenant rule as regards commercial leases. Thus, the landlord's failure to abide by the terms of the lease in connection with the condition of the leased premises allows the tenant to terminate the lease. Under this rule—the requirements of which are different from the requirements necessary to demonstrate a constructive eviction—it is sufficient for the tenant to show the landlord's failure, after notice, to perform a promise that was a significant inducement for

Continued on next page.

entering the lease. This includes a promise that constitutes a substantial benefit understood at the time the lease was entered to be significant to the purpose thereof. Here, that substantial benefit was the provision of a dry space. In other cases, it might have little to do with the condition of the premises. Thus, all the requirement of the rule have been met, and the tenant (D) was entitled to terminate the lease and recover relocation costs. Affirmed.

EDITOR'S ANALYSIS: A landlord's failure to provide a service that is essential to the use and enjoyment of the demised premises (*e.g.*, heat, electricity) may qualify as a constructive eviction. However, courts usually refuse to find a constructive eviction when other tenants, but not the landlord, cause the disturbance that interferes with the implied covenant of quiet enjoyment. Although the tenant (D) in this case claimed that Wesson (P) failed to provide heat, this issue was not discussed by the court.

NOTES:

JAVINS v. FIRST NATIONAL REALTY CORP.
Tenant (P) v. Landloord (D)
428 F.2d 1071 (D.C. Cir. 1970).

NATURE OF CASE: Action to recover rent.

FACT SUMMARY: Javins (D) refused to pay his April rent to First National Realty Corp. (D) because of the approximately 1,500 housing code violations existing in the leased premises.

CONCISE RULE OF LAW: The modern urban tenant seeks more from a lease than the outdated common-law conveyance of an interest in land, rather, he seeks a well-known package of goods and services; and, modern housing regulations imply into every lease a warranty of habitability, the breach of which by the landlord will justify a suspension of the tenant's covenant to pay rent.

FACTS: Javins (D) and others are tenants of First National Realty Corp. (P). First National (P) filed an action to regain possession of the leased premises for failure to pay rent. Javins (D) et al. admit not paying rent for April; but, contend that they were relieved from doing so (equitably) by the approximately 1,500 housing code violations which exist in their premises. The trial court, however, refused their offer of proof of the alleged violations and gave judgment for First National (P). Javins (D) appeals, contending that the offer of proof was improperly denied since the housing code violations would relieve him of his duty to pay rent.

ISSUE: Is a tenant precluded from asserting housing code violations as a defense to his rent liability by the common-law concept of a lease as a mere conveyance of an interest in land in which warranties as to habitability exist?

HOLDING AND DECISION: (Wright, J.) No. The modern urban tenant seeks more from a lease than the outdated common-law conveyance of an interest in land, rather, he seeks a well-known package of goods and services; and, modern housing regulations imply into every lease a warranty of habitability, the breach of which by the landlord will justify a suspension of the tenant's covenant to pay rent. This implied warranty, further, is coextensive with the scope of the housing regulations. The common-law rule that, as a conveyance of an interest in land (not a contract), a lease placed no duty to repair on the landlord. The feudal conditions which gave rise to this rule no longer exist, and it is the duty of the court to reappraise old rules to keep them up to date. Three situations mandate such a change: (1) the old factual assumptions of feudalism are obviously no longer valid; (2) considerable authority in other areas of the law (*e.g.,* consumer protection) have placed implied duties upon sellers that their goods are fit for the purpose sold; and (3) the shortages inherent in the modern housing market give a landlord too great a bargaining advantage to believe that the market mechanism

(competition) can effectively assure quality housing. Modern contract law has long recognized the concept of implied warranties to cover situations in which buyers, relying upon the skill and honesty of their sellers, assume certain facts (such as compliance with housing regulations) not mentioned expressly in their contracts because "they . . . supposed it was unnecessary to speak of (them) because the law provided for them." Such is the case with housing code violations and leases. As a result, the court finds that every lease contains an implied warranty of habitability to the extent of relevant housing regulations. The breach of this warranty relieves a tenant of his duty to pay rent under the lease. As such, the 1,500 violations alleged here must be considered by the court in determining Javins' (D) rent liability. The decision must be reversed. On remand, the trier of fact must determine (1) whether the alleged violations existed during the period for which past-due rent is claimed; and (2) what portion, if any, of the tenant's obligation to pay rent was suspended by the landlord's breach. The action for possession, thereupon, may only be maintained by the landlord if the tenant refuses to pay whatever remaining increment of rent is found to be owed over and above the suspended part.

EDITOR'S ANALYSIS: This case points up the clear trend of authority that every lease contains an implied warranty of habitability (Wisconsin, Hawaii and California have also recently approved such). In *Javins, supra,* it is found to be coextensive with the housing code of the particular jurisdiction. Other jurisdictions find it to exist independently, with housing code violations mere evidence on the issue of the extent to which a landlord has permitted premises to become uninhabitable. The basis for relief of rent liability comes from the contract concept of mutually dependent covenants. Under this concept, the covenants made by one party are dependent upon the covenants of the other. Breach by one party of a contractual covenant justifies breach by the other. In traditional real property conveyances, however, covenants are not mutually dependent. As a result, only by viewing a lease as a contract may a tenant be relieved of his covenant to pay rent by his landlord's breach of the above-described implied warranty of habitability. Of course, at common law, a lease contained no such warranty. A lease was a mere sale (of an interest in land) and the doctrine of caveat emptor implied that the buyer-tenant take the promises as they were and as they would be for the term of the lease (since that was all he had bargained for or bought). So, Javins really establishes two doctrines for leases. (1) That they are contracts with mutually dependent covenants, and (2) that an implied warranty of habitability is one such mutually dependent covenant.

PETERSON v. SUPERIOR COURT
Injured guest (P) v. Court (D)
Sup. Ct. of Calif. 10 Cal. 4th 1185, 899 P.2d 905 (1995).

NATURE OF CASE: Appeal from issuance of peremptory writ of mandate directing trial court to permit strict liability theory in personal injury action.

FACT SUMMARY: Peterson (P) sued proprietors of the Palm Springs Marquis Motel (D) on a theory of strict liability for injuries sustained when she slipped and fell in the bathtub.

CONCISE RULE OF LAW: The proprietor of a hotel cannot be held strictly liable under a products liability theory in tort for injuries to guests caused by defects in the premises.

FACTS: Peterson (P), a guest at the Palm Springs Marquis Motel (D), slipped in the bathtub while taking a shower, sustaining serious head injuries. Peterson (P) filed suits against the owners of the hotel (D), the operator of the hotel (D), and the manufacturer of the bathtub (D). In addition to a cause of action for negligence, Peterson (P) brought a cause of action for strict liability in tort, asserting that the bathtub was so slippery and smooth that it was defective. Prior to trial, the operator of the hotel (D) filed a motion in limine to preclude Peterson (P) from bringing the strict liability action. The trial court granted the motion, but the court of appeal overruled and issued a peremptory writ to allow Peterson (P) to proceed on her strict liability claim. The California Supreme Court granted review to determine whether a hotel proprietor or a residential landlord can be held strictly liable in tort for injuries caused by defects in the premises.

ISSUE: Can the proprietor of a hotel be held strictly liable under a products liability theory in tort for injuries to guests caused by defects in the premises?

HOLDING AND DECISION: (George, J.) No. The proprietor of a hotel cannot be held strictly liable under a products liability theory in tort for injuries to guests caused by defects in the premises. A hotel owner differs significantly from a manufacturer or retailer of a product, and it would be unfair as a matter of principle, as well as from an economic standpoint, to hold the owner strictly liable. Although a tenant injured by a defect in the premises may bring a negligence action if the hotel owner breached its duty to exercise reasonable care, a tenant cannot reasonably expect that a proprietor would have eliminated in a rented dwelling defects of which the proprietor was unaware and which would not have been disclosed by a reasonable inspection. These principles apply to residential landlords as well. Therefore, *Becker v. IRM Corp.*, 38 Cal.3d 454 (1985), is overruled. Remanded.

EDITOR'S ANALYSIS: Almost every state that has examined this issue has similarly refused to extend liability to landlords under strict liability for injuries caused by defects in leased premises. An injured party may still bring a strict liability case against the manufacturer of the product, or a negligence action against the proprietor or landlord, so a guilty party is by no means absolved of responsibility. Similar cases have arisen involving condominium associations; courts have generally held them to a standard similar to that applied to landlords and hotel proprietors.

QUICKNOTES
NEGLIGENCE - Conduct falling below the standard of care that a reasonable person would demonstrate under similar conditions.

PRODUCT LIABILITY - The legal liability of manufacturers and sellers for damages and injuries suffered by buyers, users, and even bystanders because of defects in goods purchased.

WARRANTY OF HABITABILITY - An implied warranty owed by a landlord to a tenant to provide leased premises in properly maintained in a habitable condition prior to leasing the premises and during the duration of the lease.

NOTES:

GORE v. PEOPLE'S SAVINGS BANK

Remainderman (P) v. Life tenant (D)

Conn. Sup. Ct., 235 Conn. 360, 665 A.2d 1341 (1995).

NOTES:

NATURE OF CASE: Review of reversal of denial of motion to set aside verdict.

FACT SUMMARY: The trial court granted People's (D) motion for a directed verdict when Gore (P) alleged that People's Savings Bank (D) was strictly liable for damage caused by his son's exposure to lead-based paint in the Bank's (D) building.

CONCISE RULE OF LAW: No liability attaches for injuries resulting from a dangerous condition unless the landlord had actual or constructive notice of the condition.

FACTS: Gore (P) alleged that his landlord, People's Savings Bank (D), was strictly liable for damages under a state statute when his son was injured as a result of exposure to lead-based paint in his apartment. The jury found for the Bank's (D) and Gore's (P) motion to set aside the verdict was denied. On appeal, the denial was reversed and People's (D) moved to certify for appeal. The Connecticut Supreme Court granted certiorari.

ISSUE: May liability attach for injuries resulting from a dangerous condition if the landlord did not have actual or constructive notice of the condition?

HOLDING AND DECISION: (Katz, A.J.) No. No liability attaches for injuries resulting from a dangerous condition unless the landlord had actual or constructive notice of the condition. The violation of the state statute constituted negligence per se but did not impose strict liability. Notice is necessary for a claim of to succeed. Reversed and remanded.

EDITOR'S ANALYSIS: An earlier case held that a tenant could not be evicted for withholding rent when an apertment had excessive levels of lead paint. In that case, there was no need for notice to the landlord. Federal statutes have also been enacted to regulate lead paint problems.

QUICKNOTES

CONSTRUCTIVE NOTICE - Knowledge of a fact that is imputed to an individual who was under a duty to inquire and who could have learned of the fact through the exercise of reasonable prudence.

NEGLIGENCE PER SE - Conduct amounting to negligence as a matter of law because it is either so contrary to ordinary prudence or it is in violation of statute.

STRICT LIABILITY - Liability for all injuries proximately caused by a party's conducting of certain inherently dangerous activities without regard to negligence or fault.

SIGSBEE HOLDING CORP. v. CANAVAN
N.Y. Civ. Ct., Bronx County, 39 Misc. 2d 465, 240 N.Y.S. 2d 900 (1963).

NATURE OF CASE: Action to evict.

FACT SUMMARY: While Sigsbee Holding Corp's (P) tenant, Canavan (D), replaced old used cabinets with new ones, Sigsbee (P) contends this constituted waste.

CONCISE RULE OF LAW: Where an alteration is essential to the proper use of the premises and increases its value, it may be made by a tenant if a prudent owner of the property would be likely to make it in view of the conditions existing on or in the neighborhood of the affected land.

FACTS: Canavan (D) is a tenant of Sigsbee Holding Corp. (P). As such, he replaced some old used cabinets with new ones. Sigsbee (P) contends that this constituted waste and a violation of a substantial obligation of the tenancy. The old cabinets hung on only two nails, and there was a hole in the ceiling above with an exposed BX cable.

ISSUE: Does a tenant's replacing of old cabinets with new ones constitute waste?

HOLDING AND DECISION: (Wachtel, J.) No. The common-law rule which prohibits material and substantial alterations has been changed by the legislature. Now where an alteration is essential to the proper use of the premises and increases its value, it may be made by a tenant if a prudent owner of the property would be likely to make it in view of the conditions existing on or in the neighborhood of the affected land. Where a tenant removes a landlord's sink, stove or refrigerator and replaces them with his own without the landlord's consent, he does not violate a substantial obligation of the tenancy. Likewise, in the absence of a specific covenant in a lease prohibiting the use of washing machines without the landlord's consent, the use of a movable washing machine which is not permanently attached does not constitute a violation of a substantial obligation of the tenancy. The real inquiry in all cases involving alterations made by the tenant is whether there has been damage done which injures the reversion. In this case there was no proof that Canavan's (D) alterations involved an injury to the reversion. The alterations were made in the course of Canavan's (D) proper use and enjoyment of the promises, and enhanced their value. Nor was there any proof that the alterations were a substantial and permanent change in the nature and character of the property. Petition dismissed.

EDITOR'S ANALYSIS: Likewise, the installation of air conditioning units which are not attached to the property does not constitute waste. Generally, a tenant may, when it is good husbandry and necessary to the enjoyment of his use, clear off timber and prepare land for cultivation, and sell the timber so cut. But he cannot cut timber merely to sell. Also, a tenant may use mines which have already been opened, but he will commit waste if he opens up new mines or quarries on the demised promises and takes rock, oil, minerals, *etc.* from them.

NOTES:

PIGGLY WIGGLY SOUTHERN, INC. v. HEARD
Lessee (D) v. Lessor (P)
Ga. Sup. Ct., 261 Ga. 503, 405 S. E. 2d 478 (1991).

NATURE OF CASE: Review of judgment for plaintiff for breach of a commercial lease.

FACT SUMMARY: The trial court held that a shopping center lease included both express and implied continued use covenants, but Piggly Wiggly (D) claimed that the lease did not require continuous operation of the premises.

CONCISE RULE OF LAW: A lease agreement containing a provision for free assignability by the tenant does not bind the tenant to continue its business on the premises throughout the term of the lease.

FACTS: Piggly Wiggly (D) drafted a lease for a shopping center supermarket that Heard (P) constructed. When Piggly Wiggly (D) closed its store and vacated the premises, Piggly Wiggly (D) continued paying the base rent but refused to sublease the vacant store. Heard (P) sued for damages. When the district court held that the lease contained an express and implied covenant of continued operation and the appeals court agreed, the Georgia Supreme Court granted certiorari. Piggly Wiggly (D) claimed that the lease agreement did not contain an express or an implied covenant of continuous operation.

ISSUE: Does a lease agreement containing a provision for free assignability by the tenant not bind the tenant to continue its business on the premises throughout the term of the lease?

HOLDING AND DECISION: (Hunt, J.) Yes. A lease agreement containing a provision for free assignability by the tenant does not bind the tenant to continue its business on the premises throughout the term of the lease. The lease agreement did not include any provision implying a covenant of continuous operation. The existence of a substantial base rent also suggested the absence of an implied covenant of continuous operation. Reversed and remanded.

DISSENT: (Benham, J.) Construing the lease most strongly against Piggly Wiggly (D) as the drafter of the lease, I conclude that the lease contained an express covenant that Piggly Wiggly (D) would continue business operations during the entire duration of the lease.

EDITOR'S ANALYSIS: The court here considered the base rent as a factor pointing to the absence of a covenant. The lease agreement also included a percentage rental provision. The tenant was required to pay a percentage of its revenues as rent, in addition to the base rent.

QUICKNOTES

BREACH OF CONTRACT - Unlawful failure by a party to perform its obligations pursuant to contract.

DAMAGES - Monetary compensation that may be awarded by the court to a party who has sustained injury or loss to his or her person, property or rights due to another party's unlawful act, omission or negligence.

IMPLIED COVENANT - A promise inferred by law from a document as a whole and the circumstances surrounding its implementation.

LEASE - An agreement or contract which creates a relationship between a landlord and tenant (real property) or lessor and lessee (real or personal property).

NOTES:

ALBERT M. GREENFIELD & CO., INC. v. KOLEA
Lessor (P) v. Lessee (D)
475 Pa. 351, 380 A.2d 758 (1977).

NATURE OF CASE: Appeal from award of damages for broach of loose agreements.

FACT SUMMARY: After a fire had accidentally destroyed the leased promises, Albert M. Greenfield & Co., Inc. (P) (Greenfield), the lessor, sought to enforce the lease agreement against Kolea (D), the lessee.

CONCISE RULE OF LAW: The accidental destruction of the leased premises excuses the parties from further performance of their obligations under a lease agreement.

FACTS: On March 20, 1971, Kolea (D) executed two agreements to lease two buildings for a term of two years, beginning May 1, 1971. On May 1, 1972, an accidental fire completely destroyed the building covered by one of the leases. On the following day, barricades were placed around the perimeter of the premises covered by both leases. Kolea (D) then refused to pay rent under either of the leases. Greenfield (P) sued Kolea (D) for breach of the two lease agreements and was granted judgment for $7,200.00.

ISSUE: Does the accidental destruction of the leased premises excuse the parties from further performance of their obligations under a lease agreement?

HOLDING AND DECISION: (Manderino, J.) Yes. The accidental destruction of a building by fire excuses the parties from further performance of their obligations under a lease agreement. The traditional rule provided that in the absence of a lease agreement to the contrary, a tenant was not relieved from the obligation to pay rent despite the total destruction of the leased premises. Two exceptions to this rule have been widely recognized. Where only a portion of a building is leased, total destruction of the building relieves the tenant of the obligation to pay rent. The second exception provides that impossibility or impracticability of performance arising from the accidental destruction of the leased property ends all contractual obligations relating to the property destroyed. Here, it is more equitable for Greenfield (P), the lessor, to assume the risk of accidental loss of the leased premises. Reversed and remanded.

CONCURRENCE: (Roberts, J.) The unexpressed intent of the parties to allocate risks is irrelevant, because the Restatement, Second, Property, allocates the risk of loss in these circumstances to the lessor.

CONCURRENCE: (Nix, J.) The common law rule that an accidental fire which totally destroys a building is no defense to a claim for rent is clearly inappropriate in our present society.

EDITOR'S ANALYSIS: As contract law is increasingly applied in the landlord-tenant context, the doctrine of frustration of purpose is being invoked with increasing regularity. This approach recognizes that in situations such as those presented by this case, the parties have bargained for the existence of a building, rather than for the possession of the soil on which the building was located.

QUICKNOTES
LEASE AGREEMENT – An agreement pursuant to which the owner of an interest in property relinquishes the right to possession to another for a specified consideration and for a definite time period.

NOTES:

JORDAN v. TALBOT
Tenant (P) v. Landlord (D)
Cal. Sup. Ct., 55 Cal. 2d 597, 361 P.2d 20 (1961).

NATURE OF CASE: Action for forcible entry and detainer and conversion.

FACT SUMMARY: When Jordan (P) was behind in her rental payments, Talbot (D), her lessor, entered her apartment, removed her furniture and refused to allow her to re-enter. Her lease gave Talbot (P) the right of re-entry upon the breach of any of its conditions.

CONCISE RULE OF LAW: Ownership or a right of possession to the property is not a defense to an action for forcible entry. Any unauthorized opening of a closed door is a breaking open of the door sufficient to constitute forcible entry. A person who obtains possession to property by a forcible entry does not have the right to retain possession. In the absence of provisions in a lease for enforcement of lion granted by the lease, equitable action would be necessary to make the lien operative.

FACTS: Jordan (P) was a tenant in Talbot's (D) apartment house. Her lease gave Talbot (D) a right of re-entry upon the breach of any of its conditions and a lien upon all personal effects, furniture and baggage in Jordan's (P) premises to secure the rent. When Jordan (P) had become two months behind in her rent, Talbot (D) without her consent, and during her absence, unlocked the door of her apartment, entered and removed her furniture to a warehouse, and refused to allow her to re-occupy the apartment.

ISSUE: Where a lease grants a landlord a right of re-entry upon the breach of any of its conditions and a lien upon the tenant's personal property, has a landlord who enters the tenant's premises by unlocking the door, and removes his/her belongings, committed forcible entry?

HOLDING AND DECISION: (Traynor, J.) Yes. Ownership or a lien upon the tenant's personal property is not a defense to an action for forcible entry. Absent a voluntary surrender of the premises by the tenant, the landlord could enforce his right of re-entry only by judicial process, not by self-help. Since a lessor may summarily obtain possession of real property within three days, he has a sufficient remedy, and self-help is not necessary. Further, a provision in a lease expressly permitting forcible entry would be void as contrary to the public policy. Any unauthorized opening of a closed door is a breaking open of the door sufficient to constitute forcible entry. It is not necessary that there have been any physical damage to the premises or actual violence. Also, a forcible entry is completed if, after a peaceable entry, the tenant is excluded from possession by force or threats of violence. A person who obtains possession to property by a

forcible entry does not have the right to retain possession. Such detention is unlawful and constitutes forcible detainer. In the absence of provisions in a lease for enforcement of a lien granted by the lease, equitable action would be necessary to make the lien operative. In this case Talbot (D) entered Jordan's (P) apartment without her consent. His lien and the right of re-entry granted by the lease did not give him the right to enter her apartment. Such unauthorized entry constituted forcible entry, even though there was no actual violence accompanying it. Jordan (P) was restrained from re-entering her apartment by threats of violence (Talbot's [D] employee told her, "Get the hell out of here. You're out."). This constitutes a second basis for the finding of a forcible entry. Moreover, Talbot's (D) detention of the premises by force constituted forcible detainer. Lastly, Talbot (D) did not convert Jordan's (P) goods. Talbot (D) stored most of the items removed from Jordan's (P) apartment in a warehouse in Jordan's (P) name, and those that could not be easily moved were stored in the Talbot's (D) basement and held for Jordan (P). Talbot (D) did not use any of Jordan's (P) belongings or make any claim of ownership to them. Mere removal of another's property and storing it in the owner's name without any exercise of dominion or control over it is not a conversion, but may amount to intermeddling or interference with the use of the property for which an action in trespass or case may lie. Here, therefore, Jordan (P) is entitled only to actual damages for any impairment of the property or loss of its use. Furthermore, Jordan (P), knowing that the property was being held in storage for her, had a duty to minimize damages by retrieving the property as soon as she could, provided she had adequate funds to do so. The verdict for conversion was unsupported as a matter of law by the evidence. New trial affirmed.

EDITOR'S ANALYSIS: The object of the law of forcible entry and detainer is to prevent the disturbance of the public peace by the forcible assertion of a private right. Regardless of who has the right to possession, orderly procedure and preservation of the peace require that the actual possession shall not be disturbed except by legal process. Because of the importance of public peace, a tenant's rights under the laws of forcible entry and detainer cannot be contracted away, as demonstrated by this case, where Talbot's (D) right of re-entry and his lien on personal property in Jordan's (P) apartment did not justify his entry, even though not violent, into the apartment. The dissenting Justice believes that where entry is authorized by contract and is made by means of a key only, without any actual force or violence, there has not been a forcible entry. The refusal

Continued on next page.

of the majority to sustain Talbot's (D) contract rights appears, he feels, to constitute state action impairing the obligation of a contract in violation of the United States and California constitutions.

_____

QUICKNOTES

FORCIBLE ENTRY - The entry onto real property of another through the use of violence in order to oust that person from possession.

LIEN - A claim against the property of another in order to secure the payment of a debt.

POSSESSION - The holding of property with the right of disposition.

NOTES:

MURPHY v. SMALLRIDGE
Lessees (P) v. Lessors (D)
W. Va. Sup. Ct., 468 S.E.2d 167 (1996).

NATURE OF CASE: Appeal from dismissal of affirmative cause of action for retaliatory eviction for failure to state a claim.

FACT SUMMARY: After lessees (P) reported unlawful dumping of trash on their leased premises to state authorities, lessors (D) terminated the lease. Lessees (P) brought an action for retaliatory eviction.

CONCISE RULE OF LAW: An affirmative cause of action for retaliatory eviction is available to a tenant when the tenant exercises a right related to the tenancy.

FACTS: Lessors (D) and lessees (P) entered into a lease that provided that lessors (D) could terminate the lease at any time with thirty days written notice. The lease also provided that the lessees (P) had to keep the premises neat and clean. The lessees (P) informed the lessors (D) on multiple occasions that it became impossible for them to comply with this lease term because one of the lessor's (D) agents, Smallridge (D), was dumping trash in the yard of the leased premises. After the lessors (D) failed to respond to requests that they stop dumping, the lessees (P) anonymously reported the dumping to state authorities, who inspected and notified the lessors (D) that the dumping was illegal. The day after the lessors (D) were so notified, they notified the lessees (P) that they had 30 days to vacate the premises. The lessees (P) vacated and filed suit for retaliatory eviction. The trial court dismissed the complaint for failure to state a cause of action, and the states highest court granted review.

ISSUE: Is an affirmative cause of action for retaliatory eviction available to a tenant when the tenant exercises a right related to the tenancy?

HOLDING AND DECISION: (Cleckley, J.) Yes. An affirmative cause of action for retaliatory eviction is available to a tenant when the tenant exercises a right related to the tenancy. Ordinarily, retaliatory eviction is offered as a defense to an eviction proceeding, and reflects public policy that protects a tenant when the tenant asserts certain legal rights related to the tenancy. The issue of whether a tenant may bring an affirmative cause of action for retaliatory eviction when the tenant exercises a right related to the tenancy is one of first impression in this state. Based on the law of other states, which have recognized that there is no rational basis for allowing retaliatory eviction as a substantive defense but not as an affirmative action, such an affirmative cause of action is recognized for retaliatory eviction that results from a tenant's exercise of rights incidental to the tenancy. To permit only a defense of retaliatory eviction would benefit a landlord whose unknowing tenant vacates, after notice, unaware of his rights to a defense of retaliatory eviction. It would also be unfair and unreasonable to require a tenant, subject to a retaliatory rent increase, to wait and raise the matter as a defense only, after he is confronted with an unlawful detainer action and a possible lien on his personal property. Here, the tenants' (P) report of their landlords' (D) dumping was incidental to their tenancy on the leased premises. Reversed.

EDITOR'S ANALYSIS: The court also held that a residential tenant does not have to continue living on leased premises to preserve a cause of action for retaliatory eviction. The court reasoned that since in retaliatory eviction cases a tenant typically has notified authorities of housing code violations, it would be contrary to public policy and common sense to rule that tenants must live in potentially dangerous conditions to retain a cause of action for retaliatory eviction. Some jurisdictions go further and provide security of tenure by permitting eviction of residential tenants only for good cause.

QUICKNOTES

RETALIATORY EVICTION - The removal of a tenant from possession of property due to the tenant's complaints or other conduct to which the landlord is opposed.

NOTES:

LEFRAK v. LAMBERT

Lessor (P) v. Lessee (D)

N.Y. Civ. Ct., Queens County, 89 Misc. 2d 197, 390 N.Y.S. 2d 959 (1976).

NATURE OF CASE: Action for damages for breach of a lease.

FACT SUMMARY: Lefrak (P) sued to recover the balance due on a three-year lease after Lambert (D) abandoned the premises.

CONCISE RULE OF LAW: A landlord must show he made a reasonable good faith effort to mitigate his damages upon a tenant's abandonment by attempting to rent the premises to a third party for the remainder of the lease period.

FACTS: Lefrak (P) owned a 5,000 unit apartment complex in New York. He leased one unit to Lambert (D) under a three-year lease. Lambert (D) paid a security deposit equalling two months' rent, and occupied the apartment from September 1973 to November 1974, when he abandoned possession while two months behind in rent. The apartment remained unrented for 17 months. Lefrak (P) sued to recover the balance of the rent due under the lease, $4,552, plus $910 for legal fees. Although denying a duty to mitigate damages, Lefrak (P) presented evidence that a five-member staff worked full time during the period of vacancy screening potential tenants and advertising the availability of units. No evidence was presented showing efforts exclusively aimed at renting Lambert's (D) apartment. Lambert (D) contended he would pay what was fair and did not deny liability.

ISSUE: Does a landlord have a duty to mitigate his damages by asserting a good faith effort to rent abandoned apartments?

HOLDING AND DECISION: (Posner, J.) Yes. A landlord must show he made a reasonable good faith effort to mitigate his damages upon a tenant's abandonment by attempting to rent the premises for the remainder of the lease period. The modern trend is to apply contract principles to lease agreements, and the duty to mitigate damages is a long standing precept of contract law. In this case, Lefrak (P) failed to show that a good faith effort had been made to rent Lambert's apartment. The 17 months of vacancy was clearly unreasonable given the size of the complex. As a result, a reasonable period of three months vacancy will be inferred. Therefore, three-months' rent will be added to the two months Lambert (D) was behind, and the security deposit will be subtracted to arrive at damages of $743. Legal fees will be $148.

EDITOR'S ANALYSIS: The preface to the opinion of the Court in this case belies the underlying predisposition of Judge Posner to find for Lambert (D). It is clear that he felt it would be inequitable for an apartment owner with Lefrak's resources to be allowed to recover against a man of simple means like Lambert (D). This led him to abandon the traditional rule that there is no duty to mitigate. On appeal, this case was modified, yet the court did not decide whether a duty to mitigate existed as it found Lefrak (P) had made a good faith effort to rent the apartment.

QUICKNOTES

DUTY TO MITIGATE - The general rule that a person who is wronged must act reasonably to avoid or limit losses or precluded from recovering damages that could reasonably could have been avoided.

NOTES:

LEFRAK v. LAMBERT
Lessor (P) v. Lessee (D)
93 Misc. 2d 632, 403 N.Y.S.2d 397 (1978).

NATURE OF CASE: Appeal from award of damages for abandonment of a tenancy.

FACT SUMMARY: The trial court held Lefrak (P) could not recover for the rent due on the full lease after Lambert's (D) abandonment because it found he had not made a good faith effort to mitigate his damages.

CONCISE RULE OF LAW: A landlord may recover the balance of rent payments called for under a lease after the premises are abandoned by the tenant.

FACTS: Lefrak (P) leased an apartment to Lambert (D) for three years. Prior to the termination date of the lease, Lambert (D) abandoned the tenancy while two months behind in rent. Lefrak (P) maintained a full time staff which sought to fill vacancies in the apartment complex through advertising available units and screening applicants. Despite these efforts, the apartment remained vacant for 17 months. Lefrak (P) sued to recover the full rent due under the lease and attorney's fees. The trial court held that Lefrak (P) had failed to make a good faith effort to mitigate his damages by renting the apartment and limited the recovery to three-months' rent. Lefrak (P) appealed.

ISSUE: May a landlord recover for the rent due on the balance of a lease period upon the tenant's abandonment of the tenancy?

HOLDING AND DECISION: (Per curiam) Yes. A landlord may recover the balance of rent payments due on a lease upon the tenant's abandonment of the tenancy. Whether or not a duty exists in the landlord to mitigate his damages, in this case Lefrak (P) demonstrated he made a good faith effort to rent the apartment, and therefore was entitled to recover the full amount of the lease. Reversed.

EDITOR'S ANALYSIS: The majority rule holds that a landlord has no duty to mitigate damages upon a tenant's abandonment. The rationale for this is that under this rule, a lease is considered a conveyance rather than a contract. The tenant is considered to have purchased the leasehold, and the landlord is under no duty to resell it for him.

NOTES:

QUICKNOTES

DUTY TO MITIGATE - The general rule that a person who is wronged must act reasonably to avoid or limit losses or precluded from recovering damages that could reasonably could have been avoided.

AURORA BUSINESS PARK ASSOCIATES v. MICHAEL ALBERT, INC.

Lessor (P) v. Lessee (D)

Iowa Sup. Ct., 548 N.W.2d 153 (1996).

NATURE OF CASE: Review of judgment for landlord for breach of lease.

FACT SUMMARY: The trial court upheld an acceleration clause in a lease as a valid liquidated damages provision.

CONCISE RULE OF LAW: An acceleration clause is valid if it reasonably approximates the anticipated or actual loss suffered.

FACTS: Aurora Business Park Associates (P) leased office and warehouse space to Michael Albert, Inc. (D). When Albert (D) broke the lease, Aurora (P) retook possession but could not relet the property. When Aurora (P) sued to recover past unpaid rent and future rent due on the lease, the court found that an acceleration clause in the lease was a valid liquidated damages provision and awarded damages. On appeal, the future accelerated rent payments were reduced to present value. The Iowa Supreme Court granted certiorari.

ISSUE: Is an acceleration clause valid if it reasonably approximates the anticipated or actual loss suffered?

HOLDING AND DECISION: (Andreasen, J.) Yes. An acceleration clause is valid if it reasonably approximates the anticipated or actual loss suffered. If the landlord goes back into possession and relets the premises, he must give the tenant credit for the rents received. The acceleration clause reasonably approximated the anticipated or actual loss that Aurora (P) suffered and was properly upheld. The judgment should be off set for rents actually received when the premises were relet during the remainder of the lease. Affirmed as modified, and remanded.

EDITOR'S ANALYSIS: In this case the renter vacated the premises before the acceleration clause was triggered. The liquidated damages clause placed the plaintiff in the position he would have been in had the defendant performed the entire lease. On remand the trial court was to determine whether the property had been relet and credit Albert (D) for any rents rents received.

QUICKNOTES

ACCELERATION CLAUSE - A contract provision that upon the happening of a specified event an interest will immediately vest.

LEASE - An agreement or contract which creates a relationship between a landlord and tenant (real property) or lessor and lessee (real or personal property).

LIQUIDATED DAMAGES - An amount of money specified in a contract representing the damages owed in the event of breach.

NOTES:

KELLY v. TRI-CITIES BROADCASTING, INC.
Lessor (P) v. Lessee (D)
Cal. App. Ct., 147 Cal.App. 3d 666 (1983).

NATURE OF CASE: Review of order to arbitrate and order confirming arbitrator's award.

FACT SUMMARY: The arbitrator found that the lessee, Tri-Cities (D), had assumed the lease when it acquired the radio station leasing the land, but Tri-Cities (D) appealed.

CONCISE RULE OF LAW: An assignee who takes possession under an assignment without an express assumption of the obligation of the lease is not bound by the contractual obligations of the lease.

FACTS: Kelly (P) agreed to lease his land for twenty years to a radio station for placement of a radio tower. When the radio station was sold to Tri-Cities (D) ten years later, a new transmitter site was found and the leased premises were abandoned. Tri-Cities (D) did not read the lease and had not expressly assumed the lease. The lease agreement expressly provided for arbitration of disputes. Kelly (P) sued for the remaining rent on the lease and filed a petition to compel arbitration. The arbitrator found that Tri-Cities (D) had assumed the lease. Tri-Cities (D) appealed.

ISSUE: Is an assignee who takes possession under an assignment without an express assumption of the obligation of the lease bound by the contractual obligations of the lease?

HOLDING AND DECISION: (Staniforth, Acting P.J.) No. An assignee who takes possession under an assignment without an express assumption of the obligation of the lease is not bound by the contractual obligations of the lease. As long as the assignee remains in possession he is required to pay the rent and other expenses as stipulated in the lease. A lease has a dual character – it is both a conveyance of an estate and a contract between the lessee and the lessor. Unless the assignee specifically assumes all of the contractual obligations incident to the lease, his relationship with the landlord is based only on privity of estate. The covenant to arbitrate is binding upon a nonassuming assignee only as to matters arising during the term or period that the assignee was bound by privity of estate. Reversed and remanded.

EDITOR'S ANALYSIS: The court noted that the problem here was the lessee's insolvency. The lessee's agreement to pay rent is a covenant that runs with the land. A covenant to pay rent is upheld because it touches and concerns the land.

QUICKNOTES

ARBITRATION - An agreement to have a dispute heard and decided by a neutral third party, rather than through legal proceedings.

NOTES:

AMERICAN COMMUNITY STORES CORP. v. NEWMAN
Lessee (P) v. Lessor (D)
232 Neb. 434, 441 N.W.2d 154 (1989).

NATURE OF CASE: Appeal of summary judgment.

FACT SUMMARY: American Community Stores Corp. (P) (hereinafter, ACS) held leases on grocery store buildings. ACS (P) sought a determination as to whether or not it had violated the terms of its lease, and defendants counterclaimed for possession based on illegal assignments of the lease. The court granted summary judgment to ACS (P).

CONCISE RULE OF LAW: The right of reentry is a reversionary interest that qualifies a transfer of rights under a lease as a sublease, not an assignment.

FACTS: ACS (P) leased buildings to house its grocery stores. The leases prohibited assignments without permission of the landlord. When ACS (P) experienced financial difficulty and had to close down three stores, it assigned the leases and then submitted the assignments to the trustees for the landlord (D). The landlord informed ACS (P) that it did not consent to the assignment of the leases and that if it did not hear from ACS (P) within two weeks, ACS (P) should be on notice of default. ACS (P) responded to the letter by changing the terms of the assignments so that there was a right of reentry two days before the lease periods ended. ACS (P) contended that the agreements were now subleases, not assignments. ACS (P) brought suit to determine whether or not it had violated the terms of the lease. Both parties cross-filed for summary judgment. The court found in favor of ACS (P). The landlord appealed.

ISSUE: Is the right of reentry a sufficient interest in land to change what would have been considered an assignment into a sublease?

HOLDING AND DECISION: (Hastings, C.J.) Yes. The distinction between an assignment and a sublease is that, in an assignment, the leaseholder conveys the balance of his interest in the property entirely to another individual. A transfer of land is considered a sublease when the interest transferred is shorter than the balance of the term of the original lease and is on materially different terms than the original lease. In general, the reversionary interest retained by the original leaseholder need not be for an extended period of time for the agreement to be considered a sublease rather than an assignment. In this case, ACS (P) reserved a right of reentry for condition broken. In addition, ACS (P) was to resume its lease two days prior to the end of the tenancy under the original lease. Accordingly, the court found that ACS (P) reserved a sufficient reversionary interest in the land to render its agreements subleases, rather than assignments. We affirm the trial court's decision and grant summary judgment to ACS (P).

EDITOR'S ANALYSIS: This case represents a minority opinion with respect to the distinction between subleases and assignments. Most courts have found that the power of termination does not amount to the retention of an estate and, therefore, does not transform an assignment into a sublease.

QUICKNOTES
RIGHT OF REENTRY - An interest in property reserved in the conveyance of a fee that gives the holder the right to resume possession of property upon the happening of a condition subsequent.

SUBLEASE - A transaction in which a tenant or lessee conveys an interest in the leased premises that is less than his own or retains a reversionary interest.

NOTES:

JULIAN v. CHRISTOPHER
Lessee (D) v. Lessor (P)
Md. App. Ct., 320 Md. 1, 575 A.2d 735 (1990).

NATURE OF CASE: Appeal from judgment for plaintiff in lease dispute.

FACT SUMMARY: The trial court found that the landlord could withhold consent for a sublease for any reason, and the tenant appealed.

CONCISE RULE OF LAW: If a lease contains a silent consent clause requiring that the tenant obtain the landlord's consent in order to assign or sublease, such consent may not be unreasonably withheld.

FACTS: The landlord, Christopher (P), told the tenant, Julian (D), that he would not agree to sublease the apartment above his business unless Julian (D) agreed to pay more rent. When Julian (D) permitted the sublessee to move in, Christopher (P) filed an action requesting repossession of the premises. When the district court ruled in Christopher's (P) favor, Julian (D) appealed.

ISSUE: If a lease contains a silent consent clause requiring that the tenant obtain the landlord's consent in order to assign or sublease, may such consent be unreasonably withheld?

HOLDING AND DECISION: (Chasanow, J.) No. If a lease contains a silent consent clause requiring that the tenant obtain the landlord's consent in order to assign or sublease, such consent may not be unreasonably withheld. The rule that a landlord could withhold permission for a good reason, a bad reason, or no reason at all should be modified in light of changes in the Restatement (Second) of Property. The modern trend is to impose a standard of reasonableness on a landlord unless the lease expressly states otherwise. Reversed and remanded.

EDITOR'S ANALYSIS: Some states have changed the rule by statute. In California the statute requires a reasonableness standard only in commercial leases. Another reason for the change is to uphold the lessee's right to freely alienate the leasehold.

Q\UICKNOTES

ASSIGNMENT - A transaction in which a party conveys his or her entire interest in property to another.

LEASE - An agreement or contract which creates a relationship between a landlord and tenant (real property) or lessor and lessee (real or personal property).

SUBLEASE - A transaction in which a tenant or lessee conveys an interest in the leased premises that is less than his own or retains a reversionary interest.

NOTES:

77

7

CHAPTER 7
CONCURRENT ESTATES AND MARITAL PROPERTY

QUICK REFERENCE RULES OF LAW

1. **Problems with Sharing Possession.** An ouster must amount to exclusive possession of the entire jointly held property. (Martin v. Martin)

2. **Problems with Sharing Possession.** A cotenant has an equal right of possession with all other cotenants. (Yakavonis v. Tilton)

3. **Problems with Sharing Possession.** Partition by sales are employed only where partition in kind is unworkable. (Delfino v. Vealencis)

4. **Joint Tenancy with Right of Survivorship: Creation and Severance.** When a deed uses the words "joint tenants" a joint tenancy is established. (Downing v. Downing)

5. **Joint Tenancy with Right of Survivorship: Creation and Severance.** An execution of a mortgage by one joint tenant does not operate to terminate the joint tenancy and sever his interest. The mortgage is a charge of lien upon his interest as a joint tenant only and therefore upon his death, his interest having ceased to exist, the lien of the mortgage terminates. (People v. Nogarr)

6. **Joint Tenancy with Right of Survivorship: Creation and Severance.** A joint tenant may unilaterally transfer his interest and terminate the estate. (Smolen v. Smolen)

7. **Rights of One Spouse's Creditors to Reach Marital Property.** Tenancy-by-the-entirety property may not be reached by the separate creditors of either spouse. (Sawada v. Endo)

8. **Rights of One Spouse's Creditors to Reach Marital Property.** The victim of a tort may execute a judgment against the tortfeasor's interest in community real property. (Keene v. Edie)

9. **Rights of One Spouse's Creditors to Reach Marital Property.** Creditors of one joint tenant may reach that joint tenant's interest and force partition in kind or by sale only if the interest of the other person will not be prejudiced thereby. (Harris v. Crowder)

10. **Marital Property Available for Division on Divorce.** An advanced degree is properly classified as an expectancy rather than a presently existing property interest. (Simmons v. Simmons)

11. **Marital Property Available for Division on Divorce.** The concept of equitable restitution would constitute a lifetime estate in the paying spouse's earnings that had no necessary relationship to the receiving spouse's actual contribution or needs. (Martinez v. Martinez)

12. **Marital Property Available for Division on Divorce.** The nature and extent of the contribution by the spouse seeking equitable distribution, rather than the nature of the other spouse's career, should determine whether it is marital property. (Elkus v. Elkus)

13. **Marital Property Available for Division on Divorce.** Pre-embryos are not either persons or property. (Davis v. Davis)

MARTIN v. MARTIN
Cotenant (P) v. Cotenant (D)
Ky. App. Ct., 878 S.W.2d 30 (1994).

NATURE OF CASE: Appeal from judgment in an accounting proceedings.

FACT SUMMARY: The trial court held that the Martins (P) had to pay rent to the Martins (D) who owned the property as cotenants with them.

CONCISE RULE OF LAW: An ouster must amount to exclusive possession of the entire jointly held property.

FACTS: The Martins (P) owned an undivided one-eighth interest in property and the Martins (D) owned a life estate in the rest of the property, with the remainder to the Martins (P). The Martins (P) alleged that they were entitled to a portion of the net rent the Martins (D) collected on their portion of the land which they had developed as a mobile home park, and sought an accounting. The court held that the Martins (P) had to pay rent because they lived on one of the mobile home lots. The Martins (P) appealed, claiming that their occupancy of one mobile home lot did not constitute an ouster.

ISSUE: Must an ouster amount to exclusive possession of the entire jointly held property?

HOLDING AND DECISION: (Johnstone, J.) Yes. An ouster must amount to exclusive possession of the entire jointly held property. The Martins' (P) occupancy of one of four lots (P) did not amount to an ouster. Each cotenant has a right to possess the whole. A cotenant is not liable to pay rent absent an ouster or agreement to pay. Reversed and remanded.

EDITOR'S ANALYSIS: The general rule is that an occupying tenant must account for outside rental income. The occupying tenant may offset maintenance expenses. The rent is usually fixed at the reasonable value of the occupancy.

QUICKNOTES
ACCOUNTING - The evaluation of assets for the purpose of assigning relative interests.

LIFE ESTATE - An interest in land measured by the life of the tenant or a third party.

OUSTER - The unlawful dispossession of a party lawfully entitled to possession of real property.

TENANCY IN COMMON - An interest in property held by two or more people, each with equal right to its use and possession, interests may be partitioned, sold, conveyed, or devised.

YAKAVONIS v. TILTON
Nonoccupying cotenant (P) v. Occupying tenant (D)
Wash. App. Ct., 968 P.2d 908 (1998).

NATURE OF CASE: Appeal from accounting.

FACT SUMMARY: Yakavonis (P) claimed he was entitled to rental value of property he held as tenant in common with Tilton (D).

CONCISE RULE OF LAW: A cotenant has an equal right of possession with all other cotenants.

FACTS: During their nine-year relationship, Tilton (D) quitclaimed a one half interest in a house to Yakavonis (P). After they split up, Tilton (D) moved into the house and Yakavonis (P) filed to partition the property in 1992. Tilton (D) was liable to Yakavonis (P) for rent after the ouster and Yakavonis (P) alleged that he was permitted to offset Tilton's (D) claim to apportion the property-related expenses with the rental value received. Tilton (D) claimed that there was no ouster until Tilton (D) was no longer willing to let Yakavonis (P) rent or occupy his share of the house in 1997. The court ruled in 1994 that ouster had occurred, but Tilton (D) claimed that ouster required a wrongful affirmative act by her and appealed.

ISSUE: Does a cotenant have an equal right of possession with all other cotenants?

HOLDING AND DECISION: (Coleman, J.) Yes. A cotenant has an equal right of possession with all other cotenants. An occupying tenant cannot be required to compensate nonoccupying tenants for a right she already has. Both case precedent and the attributes of real property ownership prevent the use of rental value to offset expenses while the occupying tenant's actions are not hostile to the nonoccupying cotenant's interests. The trial court correctly refused to charge Tilton (D) for rental value of the property during that time. The correct date of the ouster was in 1994 when the court quieted title. Affirmed and remanded.

EDITOR'S ANALYSIS: The court here found there was conflicting case precedent on the issue of the use of rental value as an offset. Since the latest authority in the state controlled, Washington now followed the majority rule. Earlier case precedents were to the contrary.

QUICKNOTES
ACCOUNTING - The evaluation of assets for the purpose of assigning relative interests.

OUSTER - The unlawful dispossession of a party lawfully entitled to possession of real property.

PARTITION - The division of property held by co-owners, granting each sole ownership of his or her share.

DELFINO v. VEALENCIS
Tenant in common (P) v. Tenant in common (D)
Conn. Sup. Ct., 436 A.2d 27 (1980).

NATURE OF CASE: Appeal from judicially ordered partition by sale.

FACT SUMMARY: The trial court held the rights of the parties would best be protected by a partition by sale rather than a partition in kind.

CONCISE RULE OF LAW: Partition by sales are employed only where partition in kind is unworkable.

FACTS: The Delfinos (P) owned an undivided 99/144 interest in land, in which Vealencis (D) owned an undivided 45/144 interest. The property was held as a tenancy in common. Delfino (P) wanted to develop residential housing on the tract and sought a partition by sale. Vealencis (D) defended, contending the court should order partition in kind. She used her portion of the property for her dwelling and for the operation of a rubbish removal business. The court held the partition in kind was not feasible, and ordered a partition by sale. Vealencis (D) appealed, contending the property, rectangular in shape and having only three co-tenants, could easily be subjected to partition in kind.

ISSUE: Are partition by sales employed only where partition in kind is unworkable?

HOLDING AND DECISION: (Healey, J.) Yes. Partition by sales are employed only where partition in kind is unavailable. Partition by sales should be employed only in extraordinary circumstances, as the forced sale of a party's interest should be avoided. In this case, the limited number of competing interests and the relative ease of division make partition in kind very workable. Reversed.

EDITOR'S ANALYSIS: The court rejected the proposition that the property could not be used jointly. The trial court had found that the use for residential property was mutually exclusive with use as a rubbish removal business. The shape of the property allowed for easy partition.

QUICKNOTES
JOINT TENANCY - An interest in property whereby a single interest is owned by two or more persons and created by a single instrument; joint tenants possess equal interests in the use of the entire property and the last survivor is entitled to absolute ownership.

PARTITION - The division of property held by co-owners, granting each sole ownership of his or her share.

DOWNING v. DOWNING
Joint tenant (P) v. Estate (D)
Md. Ct. App., 606 A.2d 208 (1992).

NATURE OF CASE: Appeal from interpretation of a deed.

FACT SUMMARY: The trial court ruled that no joint tenancy had ever come into being when property was conveyed to a straw man.

CONCISE RULE OF LAW: When a deed uses the words "joint tenants" a joint tenancy is established.

FACTS: Mrs. Downing had conveyed property to a straw man who immediately reconveyed it to her son John Downing (P) and herself as joint tenants. When Mrs. Downing died, her estate (D) successfully argued that no joint tenancy had ever been established because the right of survivorship was not spelled out in the deed. Downing (P) appealed.

ISSUE: When a deed uses the words "joint tenants," is a joint tenancy established?

HOLDING AND DECISION: (Chasanow, J.) Yes. When a deed uses the words "joint tenants" a joint tenancy is established. A mortgage executed by all joint tenants does not destroy the joint tenancy. Reversed and remanded.

EDITOR'S ANALYSIS: If the deed had said "as joint tenants with the right of survivorship" there would have been no question as to creation of the joint tenancy. Likewise the words, "as joint tenants and not tenants in common" would have been equally effective. The joint tenants here had later granted a mortgage on the property which did not sever the joint tenancy.

QUICKNOTES
JOINT TENANCY - An interest in property whereby a single interest is owned by two or more persons and created by a single instrument; joint tenants possess equal interests in the use of the entire property and the last survivor is entitled to absolute ownership.

MORTGAGE - An interest in land created by a written instrument providing security for the payment of a debt or the performance of a duty.

RIGHT OF SURVIVORSHIP - Between two or more persons, such as in a joint tenancy relationship, the right to the property of a deceased passes to the survivor.

TENANCY IN COMMON - An interest in property held by two or more people, each with equal right to its use and possession, interests may be partitioned, sold, conveyed, or devised.

PEOPLE v. NOGARR
Wife (P) v. Parents-in-law (D)
Cal. Ct. of App., 330 P. 2d 858, 67 A.L.R.2d 992 (1958).

NATURE OF CASE: Action to determine rights of mortgage holder to condemnation proceeds.

FACT SUMMARY: During his lifetime, husband mortgaged property he held in joint tenancy with his wife.

CONCISE RULE OF LAW: An execution of a mortgage by one joint tenant does not operate to terminate the joint tenancy and sever his interest. The mortgage is a charge of lien upon his interest as a joint tenant only and therefore upon his death, his interest having ceased to exist, the lien of the mortgage terminates.

FACTS: Elaine and Calvert Wilson, husband and wife, purchased property as joint tenants. After they separated, husband mortgaged the property to his parents. Elaine did not have knowledge of or give her consent to the execution of this mortgage. Calvert then died, and the State of California commenced an action to condemn the property. The parents claimed that their mortgage should be satisfied from the proceeds of the condemnation award.

ISSUE: Is a mortgage upon real property executed by one of two joint tenants enforceable after the death of that joint tenant?

HOLDING AND DECISION: (Nourse, J.) No. Since the mortgage did not operate to transfer the legal title, or entitle the mortgagees to possession, the estate in joint tenancy was not severed. Elaine had a right of survivorship, and upon Calvert's death she became the sole owner of the property. Calvert's interest, upon which the mortgage was based, expired upon his death. It is illogical and unjust to allow one joint tenant to mortgage his interest and obtain the value of one-half of the joint tenancy property, and to retain his right to all the property upon his cotenant's death, yet by the same reasoning deny to the cotenant her full right to the property should the mortgagor die first. Reversed.

EDITOR'S ANALYSIS: The remedy for the parents, the mortgagees here, is to enforce the lien and mortgage by foreclosure and sale prior to the death of the mortgagor and, thus, sever the joint tenancy. In this event, Elaine and Calvert would have become simply tenants in common. A tenant in common does not have a right to survivorship (receiving all the property upon the death of a cotenant) as does a joint tenant.

QUICKNOTES
FORECLOSURE SALE - Termination of an interest in property, usually initiated by a lienholder upon failure to tender mortgage payments, resulting in the sale of the property in order to satisfy the debt.

MORTGAGE - An interest in land created by a written instrument providing security for the payment of a debt or the performance of a duty.

SMOLEN v. SMOLEN
Widow (P) v. Estate (D)
Nev. Sup. Ct., 956 P.2d 128 (1998).

NATURE OF CASE: Appeal from order canceling deed.

FACT SUMMARY: The trial court held that a joint tenancy had not been destroyed when one joint tenant had conveyed his interest in the property.

CONCISE RULE OF LAW: A joint tenant may unilaterally transfer his interest and terminate the estate.

FACTS: When Mr. Smolen became ill, the Smolens divorced and Mrs. Smolen (P) later obtained temporary legal guardianship over him without his knowledge or consent. When Mrs. Smolen (P) placed him in a group home against his wishes, Mr. Smolen contacted a nephew (D) who was an attorney who helped him revoke the temporary guardianship and set up a trust with the nephew as sole beneficiary. Mr. Smolen also executed a deed transferring his interest in the house to the trust. After his death, Mrs. Smolen (P) successfully moved to cancel the deed to the trust because it violated the divorce decree which specifically preserved the joint tenancy. The nephew (D) appealed.

ISSUE: May a joint tenant unilaterally transfer his interest and terminate the estate?

HOLDING AND DECISION: (Per curiam) Yes. A joint tenant may unilaterally transfer his interest and terminate the estate. Decedent severed the joint tenancy when he conveyed his interest in the house to the new trust. Reversed and remanded.

EDITOR'S ANALYSIS: The court here found that the district court's order canceling the deed was incorrect. The common law rule is that a joint tenant has the power to transfer his interest. Such a transfer works to sever the joint tenancy and change it to a tenancy in common.

QUICKNOTES
DEED - A signed writing transferring title to real property from one person to another.

JOINT TENANCY - An interest in property whereby a single interest is owned by two or more persons and created by a single instrument; joint tenants possess equal interests in the use of the entire property and the last survivor is entitled to absolute ownership.

RIGHT OF SURVIVORSHIP - Between two or more persons, such as in a joint tenancy relationship, the right to the property of a deceased passes to the survivor.

TENANCY IN COMMON - An interest in property held by two or more people, each with equal right to its use and possession, interests may be partitioned, sold, conveyed, or devised.

SAWADA v. ENDO

Judgment creditor (P) v. Judgment debtor (D)
Hawaii Sup. Ct., 561 P.2d 1291 (1977).

NATURE OF CASE: Action to set aside conveyance of real property.

FACT SUMMARY: Endo (D) and his wife conveyed tenancy-by-the-entirety property to their son after Endo (D) had been sued.

CONCISE RULE OF LAW: Tenancy-by-the-entirety property may not be reached by the separate creditors of either spouse.

FACTS: Endo (D), who had no liability insurance, severely injured Helen (P) and Masako Sawada (P). Suits for personal injuries were filed against Endo (D). Endo's (D) only real asset was real property held as a tenant by the entirety with his wife. This was conveyed to their son, for no consideration, shortly after the Sawadas (P) had filed suit. Endo (D) and his wife continued to live on the land even though they had not reserved an estate in it. The Sawadas (P) each recovered a judgment against Endo (D), but were unable to satisfy it. The Sawadas (P) subsequently brought an action to set aside the conveyance of Endo's (D) property to the son, alleging that it was fraudulent. Endo's (D) wife had died prior to the action. Endo (D) alleged that the conveyance could not be deemed fraudulent because the separate creditor of either spouse may not reach property held as tenants by the entirety.

ISSUE: May the separate creditor of either spouse reach property held in tenancy by the entirety?

HOLDING AND DECISION: (Menor, J.) No. While this is a question of first impression, and there are four separate views, we hold that the separate creditors of either spouse cannot reach property held as a tenancy by the entirety. The other views are that: (1) the creditor may reach the entire property subject to the wife's contingent right of survivorship if the husband is the debtor; (2) the creditor may reach the property subject only to the other spouse's right of survivorship; and (3) the right of survivorship may be levied upon. Tenancy-by-the-entirety property is generally the family residence and public policy considerations of promoting family solidarity, as well as stare decisis, favor the result reached herein. Since the Sawadas (P) could not have reached the property, the conveyance to the son was not fraudulent. Dismissed.

DISSENT: (Kidwell, J.) Under the Married Women's Act there is equality between the spouses. I would, on this basis, choose to allow creditors of either spouse to reach their right of survivorship.

EDITOR'S ANALYSIS: In *Hurd v. Hughes*, 12 Del. Ch. at 193, the court stated in support of its decision not to allow creditors of one spouse to reach tenancy-by-the-entirety property, "But creditors are not entitled to special consideration. If the debt arose prior to the creation of the estate, the property was not a basis of credit, and if the debt arose subsequently, the creditor presumably had notice of the characteristics of the estate which limited his right to reach the property."

QUICKNOTES

CONVEYANCE - The transfer of property, or title to property, from one party to another party.

RIGHT OF SURVIVORSHIP - Between two or more persons, such as in a joint tenancy relationship, the right to the property of a deceased passes to the survivor.

TENANCY BY THE ENTIRETY - The ownership of property by a husband and wife whereby they hold undivided interests in the property with right of survivorship.

NOTES:

KEENE v. EDIE

Judgment creditor (P) v. Tortfeasor (D)
Wash. Sup. Ct., 935 P.2d 588 (1997).

NATURE OF CASE: Appeal from judgment for plaintiff.

FACT SUMMARY: The trial court consolidated two cases dealing with execution of a judgment against a married tortfeasor.

CONCISE RULE OF LAW: The victim of a tort may execute a judgment against the tortfeasor's interest in community real property.

FACTS: Keene (P) alleged that Edie (D) had molested her as a child and successfully sued him. When Edie's (D) separate and community property were insufficient to satisfy the judgment, a sheriff's sale of the property was ordered. Edie (D) appealed and the court of appeals reversed.

ISSUE: May the victim of a tort execute a judgment against the tortfeasor's interest in community real property?

HOLDING AND DECISION: (Alexander, J.) Yes. The victim of a tort may execute a judgment against the tortfeasor's interest in community real property. Public policy and the absence of any statutory exemption for community property lead to the conclusion that a judgment creditor can execute against the tortfeasor's interest in community property. Reversed and remanded.

EDITOR'S ANALYSIS: The court here extended a rule that had been applied to community personal property. Expansion of the rule permits judgment creditors to execute against real property as well.

QUICKNOTES

COMMUNITY PROPERTY - Property owned jointly by both spouses during a marriage, and which both spouses have equal rights of control over.

JUDGMENT CREDITOR - A creditor who has obtained an enforceable judgment against a debtor and who may collect on that debt once the debtor has been given notice of the action.

SEPARATE PROPERTY - Property that is owned by one spouse prior to the marriage, or any income derived therefrom, and any property that is received by one spouse pursuant to a gift, devise, bequest or descent.

TORTFEASOR - Party that commits a tort or wrongful act.

HARRIS v. CROWDER

Creditor (P) v. Joint tenant (D)
322 S.E.2d 854, 51, ALR 4th 893 (1984).

NATURE OF CASE: Certified question regarding joint tenants.

FACT SUMMARY: The trial court certified a question whether a judgment lien creditor can force a sale of jointly held property where his judgment is against only one of the joint owners.

CONCISE RULE OF LAW: Creditors of one joint tenant may reach that joint tenant's interest and force partition in kind or by sale only if the interest of the other person will not be prejudiced thereby.

FACTS: When Harris (P) tried to enforce a judgment against Mr. Crowder (D) and force a sale of property he held as joint tenant with right of survivorship with his wife, the court certified on his own motion a question to the Supreme Court of Appeals of West Virginia. The question was whether the Circuit Court should grant the wife's motion to dismiss when one of the husband's judgment lien creditors seeks a judicial sale of the jointly owned property.

ISSUE: May creditors of one joint tenant reach that joint tenant's interest and force partition in kind or by sale only if the interest of the other person will not be prejudiced thereby?

HOLDING AND DECISION: (Neely, J.) Yes. Creditors of one joint tenant may reach that joint tenant's interest and force partition in kind or by sale only if the interest of the other person will not be prejudiced thereby. The certified question cannot be answered with a simple yes or no. Public policy and equity demand that the court must look closely at the issue of prejudice to the nondebtor spouse. There should be a fairly strong presumption that business property may be reached in a creditor's suit. This case must be remanded for further inquiry on the question of prejudice. Affirmed and remanded.

EDITOR'S ANALYSIS: The court here described the historical development of joint tenancies. It discussed tenancies by the entireties where the right of survivorship cannot be destroyed involuntarily by a creditor.

QUICKNOTES

JOINT TENANCY - An interest in property whereby a single interest is owned by two or more persons and created by a single instrument; joint tenants possess equal interests in the use of the entire property and the last survivor is entitled to absolute ownership.

JUDGMENT CREDITOR - A creditor who has obtained an enforceable judgment against a debtor and who may collect on that debt once the debtor has been given notice of the action.

SIMMONS v. SIMMONS
Husband (P) v. Wife (D)
Conn. Sup. Ct., 708 A.2d 949 (1998).

NATURE OF CASE: Appeal from marital property distribution.

FACT SUMMARY: The trial court decided that Mr. Simmons' (P) medical degree was not property subject to equitable distribution and Ms. Simmons (D) appealed.

CONCISE RULE OF LAW: An advanced degree is properly classified as an expectancy rather than a presently existing property interest.

FACTS: After completing medical school, Mr. Simmons (P) sued for dissolution of marriage. Ms. Simmons (D) alleged that Simmons' (P) medical degree was property subject to equitable distribution. The trial court disagreed and denied alimony. Ms. Simmons (D) appealed.

ISSUE: Is an advanced degree properly classified as an expectancy rather than a presently existing property interest?

HOLDING AND DECISION: (Callahan, C.J.) Yes. An advanced degree is properly classified as an expectancy rather than a presently existing property interest. Sound public policy would dictate an award of alimony in this case since Ms. Simmons (D) had become the sole source of support of the family in order to help Mr. Simmons (P) complete his degree. The trial court abused its discretion in not awarding alimony. Affirmed in part, reversed in part, and remanded.

EDITOR'S ANALYSIS: The court here found that it was not necessary to consider an advanced degree to be property to avoid injustice. There are other ways to equitably distribute the marital estate. In this case the wife was twenty years older than the husband and the court considered her age as a factor as well in awarding alimony.

NOTES:

QUICKNOTES

ALIMONY - Allowances (usually monetary) which husband or wife by court order pays other spouse for maintenance while they are separated, or after they are divorced (permanent alimony), or temporarily, pending a suit for divorce (*pendente lite*).

DISSOLUTION - The termination of a marriage.

EQUITABLE DISTRIBUTION - The means by which a court distributes all assets acquired during a marriage by the spouses equitably upon dissolution.

MARTINEZ v. MARTINEZ
Wife (P) v. Husband (D)
Utah Sup. Ct., 818 P.2d 538 (1991).

NATURE OF CASE: Review of order granting equitable restitution as well as alimony.

FACT SUMMARY: The court created a new type of remedy in divorce cases called equitable restitution which it awarded in addition to alimony, child support and property.

CONCISE RULE OF LAW: The concept of equitable restitution would constitute a lifetime estate in the paying spouse's earnings that had no necessary relationship to the receiving spouse's actual contribution or needs.

FACTS: Mrs. Martinez (P) sued for divorce after her husband (D) had finished medical school. Martinez (P) alleged that she had made substantial sacrifices to help her husband (D) in his career. The court refused to consider the husband's medical degree as a property interest but awarded alimony, child support and property to Martinez (P). The court of appeals fashioned a new remedy called equitable restitution to reflect the husband's increased earning power. The Supreme Court of Utah granted certiorari.

ISSUE: Would the concept of equitable restitution constitute a lifetime estate in the paying spouse's earnings that had no necessary relationship to the receiving spouse's actual contribution or needs?

HOLDING AND DECISION: (Stewart, J.) Yes. The concept of equitable restitution would constitute a lifetime estate in the paying spouse's earnings that had no necessary relationship to the receiving spouse's actual contribution or needs. Such an award is virtually indistinguishable from valuing Mr. Martinez's (D) medical degree as property. A person's personal attributes and talents are not subject to monetary valuation. The court of appeals erred in designing an award of equitable distribution. Reversed and remanded.

DISSENT: (Durham, J.) If the court is to reject the principles of equitable restitution, it must also fashion a new and more flexible theory of alimony. First, there is insufficient tangible property to compensate the spouse who has been investing in the marital community when the marriage ends before the "investment" has paid off. In such situations, child support cannot be used to compensate a former spouse for the value of what that spouse invested without return as a result of the termination of the marriage. Finally, alimony as currently understood is also inadequate to make such compensation, since alimony is limited to maintaining the parties' standard of living as enjoyed during the marriage. This is inadequate because the "investor" spouse has made tangible and intangible sacrifices to postpone improvements in the standard of living during the marriage for the long-

term benefit of the marital community. When the marriage ends, the nonholder of the degree suffers a very real loss. The court must address the requirements of equity and justice to compensate in some way for that loss. One doctrine that would produce such equitable balancing is equitable restitution. Such an approach assesses loss, not need, as has traditionally been the case in the theory of alimony. This approach also is a "reliance measure" of loss, as opposed to the traditional contract measure of expectation. This, however, is only one approach of several that might be used. The point is that the majority opinion does not fashion a realistic remedy for what is a realistic loss; the legal status quo is unacceptable and must change so the disadvantaged spouse does not suffer the full cost of his or her decision to support the advantaged spouse, and so the advantaged spouse does not walk away from the marriage with all the major financial gain.

EDITOR'S ANALYSIS: The court here gave three reasons why the new remedy was wrong. First, it assumed that a marriage was like a commercial venture. Second, such an award would be very speculative. Third, it tried to create a property interest out of the husband's education.

QUICKNOTES

ALIMONY - Allowances (usually monetary) which husband or wife by court order pays other spouse for maintenance while they are separated, or after they are divorced (permanent alimony), or temporarily, pending a suit for divorce (pendente lite).

ELKUS v. ELKUS
Wife (P) v. Husband (D)
N.Y. Sup. Ct., 167 A.D.2d 134, 572 N.Y.S.2d 901 (1991).

NATURE OF CASE: Appeal from order dividing marital property.

FACT SUMMARY: The trial court held that Frederica von Stade Elkus' (P) career and celebrity status were not marital property.

CONCISE RULE OF LAW: The nature and extent of the contribution by the spouse seeking equitable distribution, rather than the nature of the other spouse's career, should determine whether it is marital property.

FACTS: Ms. Elkus (P) alleged that her fame and success could not be considered marital property for purposes of equitable distribution. Mr. Elkus (D) alleged that he had made sacrifices and had contributed to Elkus' (P) success and should be awarded equitable distribution of this property. Ms. Elkus (P) argued that because her success and celebrity status were not licensed (akin to a doctor's license), they could not be considered entities to be owned like a business. When the court ruled that the enhanced value of Ms. Elkus' (P) career was not marital property, Mr. Elkus (D) appealed.

ISSUE: Should the nature and extent of the contribution by the spouse seeking equitable distribution, rather than the nature of the other spouse's career, determine whether it is marital property?

HOLDING AND DECISION: (Rosenberger, J.) Yes. The nature and extent of the contribution by the spouse seeking equitable distribution, rather than the nature of the other spouse's career, should determine whether it is marital property. The fact that Elkus' (P) career did not require a license had no bearing on the fact that Elkus' (D) efforts and contributions constituted marital property. Reversed and remanded.

EDITOR'S ANALYSIS: The court here found that Elkus' (P) career increased in value in part due to the contributions of her husband. Potential future earnings are hard to calculate. The lack of any established business practices in this area were also an issue.

QUICKNOTES
EQUITABLE DISTRIBUTION - The means by which a court distributes all assets acquired during a marriage by the spouses equitably upon dissolution.

MARITAL PROPERTY - Property accumulated by a married couple during the term of their marriage.

DAVIS v. DAVIS
Husband (P) v. Wife (D)
Tenn. Sup. Ct., 842 S.W.2d 588 (1992).

NATURE OF CASE: Review of dissolution order.

FACT SUMMARY: The trial court decided that frozen embryos were human beings and gave custody to Ms. Davis (D), but the court of appeals ordered joint custody.

CONCISE RULE OF LAW: Pre-embryos are not either persons or property.

FACTS: Mr. Davis (P) sued for divorce after trying in vitro fertilization. Ms. Davis (D) sought custody of the frozen embryos so she could later have them transferred to her own uterus and have children. The trial court found that the frozen embryos were human beings and awarded custody to Ms. Davis (D). The court of appeals reversed, holding that Davis (P) had a constitutional right not to beget a child, and Davis (D) sought review. The Tennessee Supreme Court granted certiorari.

ISSUE: Are pre-embryos either persons or property?

HOLDING AND DECISION: (Daughtrey, J.) No. Pre-embryos are not either persons or property. Mr. Davis (P) and Ms. Davis (D) have a property-like interest since they have decision-making authority concerning disposition of the embryos. The right of procreation is a vital part of an individual's right to privacy. When balancing the interests of the parties, Mr. Davis' (P) right to avoid parenthood is more significant than Ms. Davis' (D) interest in possibly donating the embryos to another couple. Affirmed.

EDITOR'S ANALYSIS: In this case the couple had no prior agreement about the embryos. The preferences of the progenitors are to be considered first by a court. In the absence of an agreement, the relative interests of the parties should be weighed.

QUICKNOTES
RIGHT TO PRIVACY - The violation of an individual's right to be protected against unwarranted interference in his personal affairs, falling into one of four categories: (1) appropriating the individual's likeness or name for commercial benefit; (2) intrusion into the individual's seclusion; (3) public disclosure of private facts regarding the individual; and (4) disclosure of facts placing the individual in a false light.

CHAPTER 8
LIFETIME GIFTS THAT ARE NOT IN TRUST

QUICK REFERENCE RULES OF LAW

1. **Donative Intent and Formalities Required When No Deed or Gift is Used.** In order to transfer property by gift, there must be either a deed or instrument of gift, or an actual delivery of the thing to the donee. (Irons v. Smallpiece)

2. **Donative Intent and Formalities Required When No Deed or Gift is Used.** A gift *inter vivos* may be made in apprehension of death as long as the donor intends that the gift shall remain the donee's no matter whether he lives or dies. (Newell v. National Bank of Norwich)

3. **Donative Intent and Formalities Required When No Deed or Gift is Used.** To establish that gifts were *causa mortis* it must be shown that at the time of the alleged gift the decedent: (1) intended to make a gift; (2) apprehended death; (3) the gift was delivered; and (4) death actually occurred. (In re Estate of Smith)

4. **Donative Intent and Formalities Required When No Deed or Gift is Used.** Mere delivery of a check is an unenforceable promise to make a gift. (Woo v. Smart) *A check — promise*

5. **Donative Intent and Delivery When an Instrument of Transfer is Used.** A gift of personal property can be made by delivering the subject of the gift to a third person who will deliver the gift to the donee upon the death of the donor. (Innes v. Potter) *Agent*

6. **Donative Intent and Delivery When an Instrument of Transfer is Used.** A valid *inter vivos* gift of chattel may be made where the donor reserves a life estate and the donee never has physical possession until the donor's death. (Gruen v. Gruen)

IRONS v. SMALLPIECE
Son of deceased (P) v. Executrix (D)
King's Bench, 106 English Reports 467 (1819).

NATURE OF CASE: Action in trover for claim to personal property.

FACT SUMMARY: Irons (P) claimed that his father had promised to give him two colts which had passed to Smallpiece (D), the father's executrix, upon the father's death 12 months after his making the promise of the gift. Father never gave Irons (P) physical possession of the colts.

CONCISE RULE OF LAW: In order to transfer property by gift, there must be either a deed or instrument of gift, or an actual delivery of the thing to the donee.

FACTS: One year before his death, Irons' (P) father promised to give to Irons (P) two colts. Father kept physical possession of the colts up until his death. As the colts remained in father's possession at the time of his death, they passed to Smallpiece (D), father's executrix and residuary legatee. Smallpiece (D) refused to turn over the colts to Irons (P). Six months before the father died, Irons (P) and the father agreed that Irons (P) would pay the price for hay for the colts. However, no hay was furnished until a few days before the father's death.

ISSUE: Did the father's failure to give up physical possession of the items of the gift defeat the gift?

HOLDING AND DECISION: (Abbott, C.J.) Yes. In order to transfer property by gift, there must be either a deed or instrument of gift, or an actual delivery of the thing to the donee. There must be an actual change of possession or physical evidence of a change of possession.

CONCURRENCE: (Holroyd, J.) The court is correct that for the gift to have been effective, there would have had to have been a corresponding change in possession. If Irons (P) could make out a case that he was chargeable for the hay provided for the colts, then the father's possession could be attributed to Irons (P). However, no hay was delivered for a very long time after Irons (P) and his father entered their agreement about the hay, so that when it was finally delivered, it was not done so pursuant to the agreement. Therefore, possession did not transfer to the son.

EDITOR'S ANALYSIS: A verbal gift is not completed until the donor gives and the donee accepts delivery. The donee, after the act, has *prima facie* evidence in favor of the gift. Physical delivery makes significant to the donor his act of gift. Physical delivery is an unequivocal act to the witnesses of it. Other forms of gift or grant of a chattel are by deed and by sales contract where the parties intend for the property to pass before delivery.

90

NEWELL v. NATIONAL BANK OF NORWICH

Friend of decedent (P) v. Executor of estate (P)

N.Y. Sup. Ct., App. Div., 212 N.Y.S. 158 (1925).

NATURE OF CASE: Action to reclaim a gift of personal property.

FACT SUMMARY: Upon what appeared to be his deathbed, Reynolds, Bank's (D) testator, gave Newell (P), his closest friend, a diamond ring. As Reynolds recovered, Newell (P) returned the ring, but Reynolds insisted it was Newell's (P) and consented to wear it again only if it was understood the ring was Newell's (P). Upon Reynolds' death, the Bank (D), executor of Reynolds' estate, refused to recognize the gift.

CONCISE RULE OF LAW: A gift *inter vivos* may be made in apprehension of death as long as the donor intends that the gift shall remain the donee's no matter whether he lives or dies.

FACTS: Reynolds, Bank's (D) testator, on what appeared to be his deathbed, gave Newell (P), his closest and most intimate friend, a diamond ring. Reynolds recovered and lived another four years. After his recovery, Newell (P) insisted that Reynolds take back the ring, but he refused and would only agree to again wear the ring if it was understood that the ring remained Newell's (P), and that it would be returned to Newell (P) upon Reynolds' death. Reynolds remained in possession of the ring until his death. Reynolds' executor, Bank (D) refused to return the ring to Newell (P).

ISSUE: Can a gift *inter vivos* be made upon one's deathbed?

HOLDING AND DECISION: (Cochrane, P.J.) Yes. The circumstances surrounding the gift indicate that Reynolds, during his illness, gave the gift of the ring to Newell (P) irrespective of whether he lived or died, although, at the time, Reynolds was in apprehension of death. Whether a gift is made *inter vivos* or *causa mortis* is not the fact alone that the donor expects to die, but whether the donor intended the gift to take effect presently, irrevocably, and unconditionally, whether he lives or dies. Reynolds' refusal to accept the ring after his recovery reflected his mental attitude at the time of his illness when he delivered the ring to Newell (P), although insufficient in itself to constitute a gift as Reynolds retained possession of the gift. If Reynolds' purpose was to give Newell (P) the ring no matter whether he lived or died, then absolute title vested in Newell (P). Reynolds' subsequent use and possession was merely as bailee. Affirmed.

EDITOR'S ANALYSIS: A gift *inter vivos* is made when the donor intends upon his giving physical possession of the gift to the donee for the donee to have present, irrevocable, and unconditional ownership whether the donor lives or dies. A gift *causa mortis* is made in fear or present apprehension of death.

The donor intends that the donee shall retain the gift only if the donor dies. Should the donor not die, the gift is ineffective, and the item of gift is returned to the donor. Accordingly, it can be understood that even though the donor may be in present apprehension of death, he can still intend for the donee to retain the gift permanently.

QUICKNOTES

BAILEE - Person holding property in trust for another party.

INTER VIVOS - Between living persons.

NOTES:

IN RE ESTATE OF SMITH
Wife (P) v. Girlfriend (D)
Pa. Super. Ct., 694 A.2d 1099 (1997).

NATURE OF CASE: Appeal from judgment for defendant in suit for conversion.

FACT SUMMARY: The trial court found that checks were gifts *causa mortis* and were not converted.

CONCISE RULE OF LAW: To establish that gifts were *causa mortis* it must be shown that at the time of the alleged gift the decedent: (1) intended to make a gift; (2) apprehended death; (3) the gift was delivered; and (4) death actually occurred.

FACTS: Decedent left checks for his girlfriend (D) and her sister, his sister, and his niece (D) prior to committing suicide. After his death, his wife (P), who was administratrix of his estate, sued them for conversion and restitution. The court held that the checks were valid gifts *causa mortis* and the wife (P) appealed.

ISSUE: To establish that gifts were *causa mortis*, must it be shown that at the time of the alleged gift the decedent intended to make a gift, apprehended death, the gift was delivered, and death actually occurred?

HOLDING AND DECISION: (Del Sole, J.) Yes. To establish that gifts were *causa mortis*, it must be shown that at the time of the alleged gift the decedent: (1) intended to make a gift; (2) apprehended death; (3) the gift was delivered; and (4) death actually occurred. It is not necessary that the decedent actually say that he knows or thinks that he is going to die. The lower court was correct in refusing to revoke the checks. Affirmed.

CONCURRENCE AND DISSENT: (Cirillo, Pres.J.Emer.) The intended suicide of the donor is not a peril or disease which can serve as a foundation for a gift *causa mortis*. Other jurisdictions have ruled that gifts made in contemplation of suicide are against public policy and therefore invalid.

EDITOR'S ANALYSIS: Some states still have *mortmain* statutes. Such statutes invalidate testamentary gifts to charities made within six months before death. The theory is based on the notion that impending death impaired the decedent's judgment.

QUICKNOTES
CONVERSION - The act of depriving an owner of his property without permission or justification.

GIFT CAUSA MORITS - A gift made contingent on the donor's anticipated death.

RESTITUTION - The return or restoration of what the defendant has gained in a transaction to prevent the unjust enrichment of the defendant.

WOO v. SMART
Donee (D) v. Estate (P)
Va. Sup. Ct., 442 S.E.2d 690 (1994).

NATURE OF CASE: Appeal from judgment for plaintiff in declaratory judgment.

FACT SUMMARY: The trial court found that checks that had not been cashed were not valid gifts *causa mortis*.

CONCISE RULE OF LAW: Mere delivery of a check is an unenforceable promise to make a gift.

FACTS: Decedent left several checks to Woo (D), his girlfriend, several days before he died of a heart attack. The administrator of the estate (P) sought a declaratory judgment that the checks were not valid gifts. The trial court found that there was no gift because delivery of the checks didn't effect a present transfer of money. Woo (D) appealed.

ISSUE: Is mere delivery of a check an unenforceable promise to make a gift?

HOLDING AND DECISION: (Compton, J.) Yes. Mere delivery of a check is an unenforceable promise to make a gift. Delivery does not place the gift beyond the donor's power of revocation. Under the Uniform Commercial Code, delivery of a check does not effect a present transfer. The bank is not liable until the check is paid. Since no money was actually delivered, no money can be claimed by the donee as a gift *causa mortis*. Affirmed.

EDITOR'S ANALYSIS: There is a split among courts as to whether delivery of a check is a valid gift. Some states find that because the donor can stop payment on a check, no gift was actually made by delivery. Other states imply a constructive delivery of the funds in the account.

QUICKNOTES
DECLARATORY JUDGMENT - An adjudication by the courts which grants not relief but is binding over the legal status of the parties involved in the dispute.

DELIVERY - The transfer of title or possession of property.

GIFT - A transfer of property to another person that is voluntary and which lacks consideration.

GIFT CAUSA MORITS - A gift made contingent on the donor's anticipated death.

INNES v. POTTER
Minn. Sup. Ct., 153 N.W. 604, 3 A.L.R. 896 (1915).

NATURE OF CASE: Action by administrator to recover personal property for the estate.

FACT SUMMARY: Potter, deceased, endorsed a stock certificate in favor of his daughter, Potter (D), but gave it to a third person to deliver to his daughter upon his death.

CONCISE RULE OF LAW: A gift of personal property can be made by delivering the subject of the gift to a third person who will deliver the gift to the donee upon the death of the donor.

FACTS: Potter, a man of advanced years (and deceased at the time of this action), desired to give his daughter a gift of 1,000 shares in his company. He endorsed the certificate and gave it along with a writing to Casey, his business associate. The writing instructed Casey to hold the certificate for Potter (D) until the older Potter's death when Casey was to deliver the certificate by registered mail. Casey delivered as instructed. Innes (P), the administrator of Potter's estate, seeks to recover the 1,000 shares, alleging the gift to be invalid and testamentary in character.

ISSUE: Can an effective gift of personal property be made where the donor gives the subject of gift to a third person to deliver it to the donee upon the death of the donor?

HOLDING AND DECISION: (Hallam, J.) Yes. The deceased relinquished all control over the stock and all rights in it; he intended to give and gave the stock to Potter (D); and intended for the gift to take effect upon delivery to Casey. Beneficial enjoyment by the donee was delayed until the death of the donor. Such has been the rule for gifts of real property, and the court sees no reason for a distinction between a gift of real property and a gift of personal property. Delivery of the gift was made to a third person and some interest vested upon delivery. As a present interest was transferred and the donor relinquished all control in the gift, an effective, irrevocable gift *inter vivos* was made. Judgement for defendant affirmed.

EDITOR'S ANALYSIS: Historically, there was no question as to the effectiveness of a gift of the nature of the one here as to real property. As real property could not be consumed, it could be held without it being lost. The trend in equity was away from any distinction between the gift in real property and personal property. The court here simply said there was no distinction of merit. The gift was inter vivos. The gift could not be *causa mortis* for the obvious reason that the donor was not ill or in any peril of death. The gift was not made in contemplation of death. As intent to transfer a present interest in the gift was found, an effective gift *inter vivos* was uphold.

GRUEN v. GRUEN
Deceased man's son (P) v. Deceased man's wife (D)
N.Y. Ct. of A.P., 496 N.E.2d 869, 83 A.L.R. 4th 955 (1986)

NATURE OF CASE: Appeal from an enforcement of an inter vivos gift.

FACT SUMMARY: Gruen (D) contended her husband could not make a valid inter vivos gift to his son and still retain present exclusive possession of the property for his life.

CONCISE RULE OF LAW: A valid *inter vivos* gift of chattel may be made where the donor reserves a life estate and the donee never has physical possession until the donor's death.

FACTS: Gruen (P) received a letter from his father indicating the latter wished to make a gift of a painting, but that he wished to use it for his life. Gruen (P) never took possession of the painting. After his father's death, he requested the painting from his stepmother, who refused. Gruen (P) sued contending a valid inter vivos gift had been made. His stepmother defended, contending no valid gift could be made if the donor retained a life estate and no physical delivery was made during life. The trial court held against Gruen (P) while the appellate court reversed. Gruen (D) appealed.

ISSUE: May a valid *inter vivos* gift of chattel be made where the donor reserves a life estate and the donee does not take physical possession?

HOLDING AND DECISION: (Simons, J.) Yes. A valid *inter vivos* gift of chattel may be made where the donor reserves a life estate and the donee never takes physical possession until after the donor's death. In this case, donative intent was established constructively through the document of transfer, the letter. Acceptance is implied because the painting had value. Thus, a valid gift was made. Affirmed.

EDITOR'S ANALYSIS: Various estates in chattel can be created just as various estates in land are created. The property in this case happened to be personal rather than real, yet the creation of a remainder interest was valid. It is clear the elder Gruen intended to make a current transfer of such interest, while retaining a possessory interest.

CHAPTER 9
THE MODERN REAL ESTATE TRANSACTION

QUICK REFERENCE RULES OF LAW

1. **The Lawyer's Professional Responsibility.** Failure to make full disclosure of a conflict of interest subjects an attorney to sanctions. (In re Conduct of Baer)

2. **Brokers.** A seller of real estate has no obligation to pay a commission to his broker unless a sale by the seller to a buyer procured by the broker is actually consummated. (Tristram's Landing, Inc. v. Wait)

3. **Ground Rules.** A clause in a sales contract permitting the buyer to terminate if he is unable to procure certain conditions creates an implied obligation on the part of the buyer to attempt to procure those conditions. (Sechrest v. Safiol)

4. **Marketable Title.** Where the purchaser in an action for rescission has shown that the record title is held by a person other than the seller, the seller has the burden of establishing his title by adverse possession. (Conklin v. Davi)

5. **Equitable Conversation/ Risk of Loss.** Where a contract places the risk of loss on the vendor, the purchaser may recover the down payment. (Bryant v. Willison Real Estate Co.)

6. **Quality of the Property.** Where a condition which has been created by the seller materially impairs the value of the contract and is peculiarly within the knowledge of the seller or unlikely to be discovered by a prudent purchaser exercising due care with respect to the subject transaction, nondisclosure constitutes a basis for rescission as a matter of equity. (Stambovsky v. Ackley)

7. **Delivery.** A deed left with a bank with unequivocal instructions to deliver the deed, which is delivered pursuant to those instructions, is validly delivered. (Chandler v. Chandler)

8. **Covenants for Title.** The violation of a subdivision ordinance breaches a covenant against encumbrances only where the violation already exists at the time of the conveyance. (Seymour v. Evans)

9. **The Mortgage.** A contingent remainder is an ownership interest sufficient to require notice of a foreclosure. (Williams v. Kimes)

10. **Record Notice.** An instrument executed by an owner which is recorded before acquisition or after relinquishment of title is outside the chain of title. (Ryczkowski v. Chelsea Title & Guaranty Co.)

11. **Record Notice.** If a purchaser, upon examining the registry, finds a conveyance from the owner of the land to his grantor, which gives the grantor a perfect record title, the purchaser is entitled to rely upon such title and is not required to search the records further to see if there has been any prior unrecorded deed of the original owner. (Morse v. Curtis)

12. **Record Notice.** A purchaser of a lot which formed part of a larger tract is not charged with notice of restrictive covenants contained in a prior deed from the same grantor to any other lot or parcel of the same general tract, even though the deed is recorded and by its terms applies to all other lots. (Buffalo Academy of the Sacred Heart v. Boehm Bros.)

13. **Inquiry Notice.** If the owner of two or more lots, which are situated so as to bear a relation to each other, sells one with restrictions which are of benefit to the land retained, during the period of restraint, the owner of the lot or lots retained can do nothing forbidden to the owner of the lot sold. This is the doctrine of reciprocal negative easements. (Sanborn v. McLean)

14. **When a Person is a Purchaser.** Where one creditor holds a mortgage that is granted on the same day a judgment is handed down against the debtor in favor of a second creditor, but the second creditor does not record the judgment until after the mortgage is recorded, the first creditor's mortgage is supported by legal consideration so that the first creditor is a purchaser entitled to priority. (Manufacturers and Traders Trust Co. v. First National Bank)

15. **Bona Fide Purchasers of Personal Property.** Where goods are sold by a person who is not the owner thereof, and who does not sell them under the authority or with the consent of the owner, the buyer acquires no better title to the goods than the seller had, unless the owner of the goods is, by his conduct, precluded from denying the seller's authority to sell. (Sherer-Gillette Co. v. Long)

16. **The Torrens System.** A purchaser of registered land who has actual notice of an unregistered lease for more than seven years takes subject to the lease. (Killam v. March)

17. **Title Insurance.** (1) A statutory provision that requires governmental consent to an owner's intended use of property does not, for title insurance purposes, constitute an encumbrance on or defect in the title to the property or render title to the property unmarketable. (2) A claim against a title insurer based on negligence in notifying an insured of matters discovered in a title search voluntarily assumed outside the policy is not barred by an integration clause in a title insurance policy. (Somerset Savings Bank v. Chicago Title Insurance Co.)

IN RE CONDUCT OF BAER
State Bar (P) v. Attorney (D)
Ore. Sup. Ct., 298 Or. 29, 688 P.2d 1324 (1984).

NOTES:

NATURE OF CASE: Appeal from State Bar Disciplinary Review.

FACT SUMMARY: The Oregon State Bar Board recommended a public reprimand of an attorney who failed to make a full disclosure when he had a conflict of interest.

CONCISE RULE OF LAW: Failure to make full disclosure of a conflict of interest subjects an attorney to sanctions.

FACTS: Baer (D) represented both his wife and the sellers in negotiations to buy a house. Baer (D) did not explain to the sellers that he was not representing them and did not explain to them that they needed independent legal advice. Baer (D) also acted as escrow agent and later filed suit on behalf of his wife asking for rescission of the purchase agreement. The sellers then hired another attorney and charged Baer (D) with violations of the State Bar Disciplinary Rules. The Trial Board found Baer (D) guilty and recommended a public reprimand and that he take the legal ethics exam. The Disciplinary Review Board recommended a 30-day suspension and the exam. Baer (D) appealed.

ISSUE: May failure to make full disclosure of a conflict of interest subject an attorney to sanctions?

HOLDING AND DECISION: (Per curiam) Yes. Failure to make full disclosure of a conflict of interest subjects an attorney to sanctions. A conflict of interest existed when Baer (D) undertook the representation of both sides in the real estate transaction. He did not explain the conflict of interest in sufficient detail and so did not make full disclosure. Baer (D) is suspended from the practice of law for not less than sixty days. Affirmed.

EDITOR'S ANALYSIS: The rule is that both parties have to consent to dual representation after full disclosure. Some state case law precludes dual representation in real estate transactions. Other cases have held that dual representation is not permitted only in complex commercial real estate transactions.

QUICKNOTES

CONFLICT OF INTEREST - Refers to ethical problems that arise, or may be anticipated to arise, between an attorney and his client if the interests of the attorney, another client or a third party conflict with those of the present client.

SANCTIONS - A penalty imposed in order to ensure compliance with a statute or regulation.

TRISTRAM'S LANDING, INC. v. WAIT

Real estate brokers (P) v. Property owner (D)

367 Mass. 622, 327 N.E.2d 727 (1975).

NATURE OF CASE: Action to recover a brokerage commission.

FACT SUMMARY: Tristram's Landing (P), real estate brokers, located a buyer for Wait's (D) property. When no sale was consummated, Wait (D) refused to pay a commission to Tristram's Landing (P).

CONCISE RULE OF LAW: A seller of real estate has no obligation to pay a commission to his broker unless a sale by the seller to a buyer procured by the broker is actually consummated.

FACTS: Tristram's Landing, Inc. (P), real estate brokers in Nantucket, had previously acted as rental agent for Wait (D) when Wait (D) decided to sell her property. Van Der Wolk (P), one of Tristram's Landing's (P) professional brokers, received permission to act as her broker. No mention was made of any commission, although Wait (D) knew that a 5% brokerage commission was standard in Nantucket. Wait (D) did not tell Van Der Wolk (P) that Tristram's Landing (P) could act as exclusive broker for her. The property was offered for sale at $110,000, and Van Der Wolk (P) located a prospective buyer, Louise Cashman, who made a written offer of $100,000. Cashman ultimately accepted Wait's (D) counter-offer of "$105,000 with an October 1st closing," which counter-offer had been transmitted through Tristram's Landing (P). On September 22, Wait (D) signed a 15-day extension of the closing date, but Cashman did not sign the extension. Wait (D) eventually appeared for closing on October 1st, but Cashman was not present and later refused to go through with the purchase. Wait (D) took no action against Cashman to compel performance of the sale contract. Van Der Wolk (P) later presented Wait (D) with a bill for $5,250, which sum represented the amount allegedly owed him as a commission. When Wait (D) refused payment, Tristram's Landing (P) filed suit, alleging that the purchase and sale agreement had provided for a commission and that Van Der Wolk (P) had earned it by securing a purchaser who was willing,and able to buy Wait's (D) property at the specified price. The trial court agreed but Wait (D) appealed, arguing that no commission was due since Cashman had not actually completed the purchase.

ISSUE: Must a brokerage commission be paid it the broker locates an acceptable buyer for the seller's property but the agreement of sale subsequently entered into between the buyer and seller is never carried out?

HOLDING AND DECISION: (Tauro, C.J.) No. A seller of real estate has no obligation to pay a commission to his broker unless a sale by the seller to a buyer procured by the broker is actually consummated. Traditionally a commission is owed once the buyer locates a ready, able and willing buyer, acceptable to the seller, even if a sale to that buyer is never completed. In this case, however, the purchase and sale agreement stated that the commission would be paid "on the said sale," which must be construed as meaning only if the sale was actually consummated. The rule that a sale must actually occur before a commission becomes due represents the view of a growing minority of states. It derives from the New Jersey case of *Ellsworth Dobbs, Inc. v. Johnson.* That case realized that, in practice, both seller and broker expect the latter's commission to be paid out of the proceeds of the sale. If the sale fails to materialize, the seller should not have the burden of paying the commission, especially since he may be without the funds to do so. Thus, the judgment in favor of Tristram's Landing must be reversed.

EDITOR'S ANALYSIS: The rule of *Tristram's Landing, Inc v. Wait* represents, as the court acknowledges, the minority view. The rule has the advantage of protecting the seller, presumably the less wealthy of the two, from liability to the broker. However, in many cases it will be the breaching buyer who is legally responsible for the fact that the sale was not consummated. In such a circumstance, the seller would clearly have a right to sue for specific performance of the contract, while the broker would have, at best, a tenuous cause of action against the buyer based on a third party beneficiary theory. Thus, the Wait rule casts the burden of the loss on the party who stands the least chance of forcing it to be borne by the party whose conduct caused it.

NOTES:

SECHREST v. SAFIOL

Seller (D) v. Buyer (P)

383 Mass. 568, 419 N.E.2d 1384 (Mass. 1981).

NATURE OF CASE: Action for return of a deposit.

FACT SUMMARY: Sechrest (D) claimed he was entitled to keep a deposit paid by Safiol (P) when Safiol (P) breached the sales contract.

CONCISE RULE OF LAW: A clause in a sales contract permitting the buyer to terminate if he is unable to procure certain conditions creates an implied obligation on the part of the buyer to attempt to procure those conditions.

FACTS: Sechrest (D) contracted to sell a parcel of property to Safiol (P) and Safiol (P) paid a deposit of $3,800. The contract provided that Safiol's (P) obligation to purchase was conditioned on his obtaining the necessary permits for construction from the proper public authorities. After successfully requesting three separate extensions for the date of performance, Safiol (P) notified Sechrest (D) that he had not obtained the necessary permits and was thus terminating the contract. He sought the return of his deposit. Sechrest (D) refused, contending that Safiol (P) had breached his good faith obligation to attempt to secure the necessary permits, and thus Sechrest (D) was entitled to keep the deposit as damages. The trial court found no such obligation on Safiol's (P) part and ordered Sechrest (D) to return the money. Sechrest (D) appealed.

ISSUE: Does a clause in a sales contract permitting the buyer to terminate it he is unable to procure certain conditions create an implied good faith obligation on the part of the buyer to attempt to procure those conditions?

HOLDING AND DECISION: (Hennessey, C.J.) Yes. Although the contract provision, when read literally, creates no obligation of good faith performance on the part of the buyer, such a literal interpretation must be rejected. Otherwise, the provision would operate to give the buyer an option to purchase without any requirement to act affirmatively. This was clearly not the intent of the parties. Instead, they sought to allow the buyer to terminate only if he was unable to obtain the necessary construction permits from the proper authorities. Accordingly, an implied obligation arose on Safiol's (P) part to make a good faith attempt to secure the permits. Since the evidence shows that he breached his good faith obligation by failing to act, Sechrest (D) is entitled to retain the $3,800 deposit as damages. Reversed.

EDITOR'S ANALYSIS: As the principal case holds, a buyer under such a contract is only obligated to make a good faith effort to procure the contract conditions. He is not required to act unreasonably or spend a disproportionate amount of money in doing so. Thus, in *Livoli v. Stoneman*, 332 Mass. 473 (1955), the buyer was not held to have breached a sales contract where he had failed to secure approval of a subdivision plan due to unanticipated prohibitive costs. The buyer had acted reasonably in that case and was not required to secure approval of his plan "at all costs."

NOTES:

CONKLIN v. DAVI

Property seller (P) v. Repudiating buyer (D)

N.J. Sup. Ct., 76 N.J. 468, 388 A.2d 598 (1978).

NATURE OF CASE: Appeal from rescission of contract for purchase of property.

FACT SUMMARY: Davi (D) sought rescission of contract to purchase property from Conklin (P), charging that Conklin (P) failed to deliver marketable title.

CONCISE RULE OF LAW: Where the purchaser in an action for rescission has shown that the record title is held by a person other than the seller, the seller has the burden of establishing his title by adverse possession.

FACTS: Conklin (P) contracted to sell a parcel of property to Davi (D). Title to the property was to be both marketable and insurable. Davi (D), upon learning that part of the property to be conveyed was obtained by adverse possession, refused to go through with the sale. Davi (D) contended that property obtained by adverse possession could not be conveyed by marketable title. Conklin (P) sued for specific performance and Davi (D) counter-claimed for rescission. Before trial began, Conklin (P) dropped his specific performance claim and the sole action was Davi's (D) suit for rescission. At the end of Davi's (D) case, the trial court granted Conklin's (P) motion for judgment. The appellate division reversed and entered judgment for Davi (D).

ISSUE: In an action for rescission of a land sales contract where the purchaser has established that the record title is held by someone other than the seller, does the seller have the burden of proving his title by adverse possession?

HOLDING AND DECISION: (Mountain, J.) Yes. A warranty of marketable and insurable title does not require that the title conveyed be flawless. Title obtained by adverse possession may still be marketable. However, the seller has the burden of establishing that such a title exists. Once the burden is met, the court must then decide whether a likelihood exists that adverse claimants would challenge the title to the property and whether they would succeed if such a challenge were made. If the court finds the likelihood of a successful challenge to be minimal, then the title to the property may be deemed marketable. Thus, in the instant case, the trial court erred in failing to require Conklin (P) to meet his burden of proving title by adverse possession. Although the appellate division was correct in reversing the trial court's judgment, it, too, erred by entering judgment rather than remanding to the lower court for further findings. Reversed and remanded.

EDITOR'S ANALYSIS: The main concern in a situation such as that presented in *Conklin*, is that the buyer be able to protect himself from future adverse claimants to his title. Thus the seller must clearly prove his title by adverse possession. He may be required to furnish written evidence or such other evidence which can later be utilized by the purchaser in defense of his title. *Messer-Johnson Realty Co. v. Security Savings & Loan Co.*, 208 Ala. 541. If the seller cannot establish adverse possession, he may be permitted to file suit to quiet title against adverse claimants, known or unknown. However, in the latter case, problems of jurisdiction and due process may arise.

QUICKNOTES

ADVERSE POSSESSION - A means of acquiring title to real property by remaining in actual, open, continuous, exclusive possession of property for the statutory period.

MARKETABLE TITLE - Title that, although not perfect, would be acceptable to a reasonably well-informed buyer exercising ordinary business prudence.

QUIET TITLE - Equitable action to resolve conflicting claims to an interest in real property.

RESCISSION - The canceling of an agreement and the return of the parties to their positions prior to the formation of the contract.

SPECIFIC PERFORMANCE - An equitable remedy whereby the court requires the parties to perform their obligations pursuant to a contract.

NOTES:

BRYANT v. WILLISON REAL ESTATE CO.
Purchasers (P) v. Vendors (D)
W.Va. Sup. Ct. App., 350 S.E.2d 748 (1986).

NATURE OF CASE: Appeal from judgment for defendant in action for rescission of real estate contract.

FACT SUMMARY: The trial court awarded damages for third-party property loss on purchasers of real estate before closing.

CONCISE RULE OF LAW: Where a contract places the risk of loss on the vendor, the purchaser may recover the down payment.

FACTS: Bryant (P) contracted to buy real estate from Willison (D). When a water line broke before delivery of the deed, Willison (D) refused to make necessary repairs. Bryant (P) then sued for rescission of the contract and return of the down payment. The trial court held that Bryant (P) must bear the risk of loss under the doctrine of equitable conversion. Bryant (P) appealed, alleging that the contract assigned the risk of loss to Willison (D).

ISSUE: Where a contract places the risk of loss on the vendor, may the purchaser recover the down payment?

HOLDING AND DECISION: (Miller, C.J.) Yes. Where a contract places the risk of loss on the vendor, the purchaser may recover the down payment. If the contract allocates the risk of loss, then the doctrine of equitable conversion does not apply. Reversed and remanded.

EDITOR'S ANALYSIS: Equitable conversion provides that the risk of loss is on a purchaser where a contract is executory. That is because the purchaser is deemed to hold equitable title. Modern law permits the risk of loss to be assigned in the contract.

NOTES:

QUICKNOTES

EQUITABLE TITLE - Interest in property that is not recognized in a court of law but that is protected in equity.

RISK OF LOSS - Liability for damage to or loss of property that is the subject matter of a contract for sale.

STAMBOVSKY v. ACKLEY
Buyer (P) v. Seller (D)
N.Y. Sup. Ct. App. Div., 169 A.D.2d 254, 572 N.Y.S.2d 672 (1991).

NATURE OF CASE: Suit for rescission of contract.

FACT SUMMARY: Plaintiff sought to rescind a contract to purchase defendant's house on the basis that it was widely reputed to be possessed by poltergeists.

CONCISE RULE OF LAW: Where a condition which has been created by the seller materially impairs the value of the contract and is peculiarly within the knowledge of the seller or unlikely to be discovered by a prudent purchaser exercising due care with respect to the subject transaction, nondisclosure constitutes a basis for rescission as a matter of equity.

FACTS: Plaintiff sought to rescind a contract to buy defendant's house on the basis that it was reputed to be haunted by poltergeists, reportedly seen by defendant and members of her family for the last 9 years. The supreme court dismissed for failure to state a remedy at law.

ISSUE: Where a condition which has been created by the seller materially impairs the value of the contract and is peculiarly within the knowledge of the seller or unlikely to be discovered by a prudent purchaser exercising due care with respect to the subject transaction, does nondisclosure constitute a basis for rescission as a matter of equity?

HOLDING AND DECISION: (Rubin, J.) Yes. Where a condition which has been created by the seller materially impairs the value of the contract and is peculiarly within the knowledge of the seller or unlikely to be discovered by a prudent purchaser exercising due care with respect to the subject transaction, nondisclosure constitutes a basis for rescission as a matter of equity. While I agree with the supreme court that the real estate broker is under no duty to disclose to a potential buyer the haunted reputation of the premises, equity permits the buyer to seek rescission of the contract and recovery of his down payment. New York law fails to recognize any remedy for damages incurred as a result of a seller's mere silence, applying the strict rule of *caveat emptor.* That rule imposes no duty upon the vendor of real property to disclose any information concerning the condition of the premises, unless there is a confidential or fiduciary relationship between the parties or some conduct on the part of the seller which constitutes active concealment or partial disclosure. *Caveat emptor*, however, does not render every act of nondisclosure immune from redress. Rather, the doctrine requires that a buyer act prudently to assess the fitness and value of his purchase and bars the purchaser who fails to exercise due care from seeking the equitable remedy of rescission. For purposes of the instant motion to dismiss, the plaintiff is entitled to every favorable inference which may be drawn from the pleadings. While here he met his obligations to inspect the premises and conduct a title search, such actions would not reveal the presence of poltergeists or the property's haunted reputation in the community. Thus, there are no sound policy reasons to deny plaintiff relief for failure to discover a state of affairs which the most prudent purchaser would not be expected to contemplate. The case law dealing with the duty of a vendor of real property to disclose information to the buyer is distinguishable from this case. Here the defendant seller deliberately fostered the public belief that her home was haunted. Where as here the seller not only takes advantage of the seller's ignorance but has created and perpetuated a condition about which he is unlikely to inquire, enforcement of the contract offends equity. Judgment modified.

DISSENT: (Smith, J.) Here there is no allegation that defendant deceived the plaintiff, nor has plaintiff alleged the existence of a confidential or fiduciary relationship giving rise to a duty to disclose.

EDITOR'S ANALYSIS: The court noted that something more than "mere concealment" is necessary to overcome the general rule of *caveat emptor.* Short of affirmative misrepresentation, courts have held that where a seller has undertaken to disclose a portion of information affecting the subject property, he is then under a duty to make full disclosure.

QUICKNOTES
NONDISCLOSURE - The failure to communicate certain facts to another person.

NOTES:

CHANDLER v. CHANDLER
Sibling (P) v. Sibling (D)
Ala. Sup. Ct., 409 So. 2d 780 (1982).

NATURE OF CASE: Appeal from finding of a valid delivery of a deed.

FACT SUMMARY: Siblings (P) of J.P. (D) contested the delivery of a deed conveying property to J.P. (D).

CONCISE RULE OF LAW: A deed left with a bank with unequivocal instructions to deliver the deed, which is delivered pursuant to those instructions, is validly delivered.

FACTS: J.W. and Maggie Chandler executed a deed purportedly conveying to Maggie an undivided one-half interest in 270 acres for life, reserving unto J.W. an undivided one-half interest for life, with right of survivorship for the lifetime of the survivor, and with remainder in fee simple to their son, J.P. (D). Both parents eventually died. J.P.'s (D) siblings (P) brought an action seeking to set aside the deed on grounds of, *inter alia*, no legal delivery. The deed was not transferred directly to J.P. (D), but rather was transferred (by J.W.) to a bank vault and instructions were left to the bank, both orally as well as on a note, that the deed was to be delivered to J.P. (D) upon J.W.'s death. J.W. had the right to pick up the deed any time he desired to. The service the bank provided was "safekeeping." The trial court held that the delivery of the deed was valid. The state's highest court granted review.

ISSUE: Is a deed left with a bank with unequivocal instructions to deliver the deed, which is delivered pursuant to those instructions, validly delivered?

HOLDING AND DECISION: (Jones, J.) Yes. A deed left with a bank with unequivocal instructions to deliver the deed, which is delivered pursuant to those instructions, is validly delivered. The issue is whether J.W., at the time he delivered the deed to the bank, possessed the requisite intent to relinquish control over the deed and have it take effect as a present conveyance. Given that J.W. never sought to retrieve the deed, although he could do so under the bank's policy, the trial court did not err in concluding that the deed was validly delivered, since the totality of the circumstances indicates that he, as grantor, intended to surrender control of the deed. A grantor's intention is a fact to be determined from all the circumstances at the time. Central to this holding is that J.W. gave express, unequivocal instructions to the bank (third party) for delivery of the deed to the named grantee upon a certain future event—his death. Also determinative was the absence of words or conduct reserving J.W.'s right of revocation. Accordingly, there is ample evidence of completed delivery, fully executed. Affirmed.

DISSENT: (Trobert, C.J.) The majority misapplies the law to the facts of this case. For the delivery to be complete, the grantor must completely divest himself of any control over the title. As long as he reserves to himself the *"locus poenitentiae"*, whether by express reservation or by not placing the deed beyond his control, then as a matter of law he has not foregone his right of revocation. Here, J.W. retained control over the deed, as he could retrieve it from the bank whenever he wanted to. Thus, as a matter of law, his right of revocation was not gone. This is akin to leaving the deed in a safety deposit box, in which case there would have been no doubt that delivery would not have been complete.

EDITOR'S ANALYSIS: The court also held that the trial court was warranted under the evidence in finding the requisite delivery as between the grantors and the life tenants without reference to any issue of delivery as between the grantors and the remaindermen. However, the court noted that it only addressed the issue of delivery as between the grantor (J.W.) and the grantee (J.P.) (D). It is not atypical for grantors to deliver a deed to a third party with instructions to transfer the deed to the grantee upon the grantor's death. Even though the grantee does not receive the benefit of the property at the time of the delivery to the third party, courts usually hold that such deliveries are valid as long as the grantor has parted with control over the deed.

QUICKNOTES
LOCUS POENITENTIAE - The time period within which a party may withdraw from an agreement or transaction before he is bound thereby.

NOTES:

SEYMOUR v. EVANS
Seller (D) v. Buyer (P)
Miss. Sup. Ct., 608 So.2d 1141 (1992).

NATURE OF CASE: Appeal from judgment for plaintiffs in action to set aside a deed.

FACT SUMMARY: The Evans (P) had a warranty deed set aside when they successfully alleged that the seller's implied warranties were violated because the conveyance conflicted with zoning restrictions.

CONCISE RULE OF LAW: The violation of a subdivision ordinance breaches a covenant against encumbrances only where the violation already exists at the time of the conveyance.

FACTS: Seymour (P) conveyed land to the Evans (D). When the Evans (D) couldn't get a building permit because the conveyance dividing the property violated the local subdivision ordinances, they sued Seymour (D) to rescind the contract and recover their purchase payments. Seymour (D) appealed, alleging that the deed was valid and did not give rise to a breach of implied covenants.

ISSUE: Does the violation of a subdivision ordinance breach a covenant against encumbrances only where the violation already exists at the time of the conveyance?

HOLDING AND DECISION: (McRae, J.) Yes. The violation of a subdivision ordinance breaches a covenant against encumbrances only where the violation already exists at the time of the conveyance. The ordinances allegedly violated regulate actions which are merely *malum prohibitum*, not *malum in se.* Reversed and remanded.

EDITOR'S ANALYSIS: The existence of zoning violations is not a violation of the covenant against encumbrances. There was no violation of the covenant of quiet enjoyment since the owner held good title and the right to possession. The conveyances gave rise to the violations, the violations did not exist at the time of the conveyance.

QUICKNOTES

COVENANT AGAINST ENCUMBRANCES - A guarantee in a contract that the interest in property being conveyed is unencumbered.

COVENANT OF QUIET ENJOYMENT - A promise contained in a lease or a deed that the tenant or grantee will enjoy unimpaired use of the property.

COVENANT OF SEISIN - A promise that the conveyor of property has the lawful right to convey the interest he is attempting to transfer.

IMPLIED WARRANTY - An implied promise made by one party to a contract that the other party may rely on a fact, relieving that party from the obligation of determining whether the fact is true and indemnifying the other party from liability if that fact is shown to be false.

NOTES:

WILLIAMS v. KIMES

Remainderman (P) v. Buyer (D)
Mo. Sup. Ct., 949 S.W.2d 899 (1997).

NATURE OF CASE: Review of probate dispute.

FACT SUMMARY: The trial court ruled that Williams (P) and other holders of contingent remainders did not have to be notified of a power of sale foreclosure.

CONCISE RULE OF LAW: A contingent remainder is an ownership interest sufficient to require notice of a foreclosure.

FACTS: Williams (P) held a contingent remainder to real property which the life tenant mortgaged. Williams (P) did not receive actual notice of the foreclosure sale and sued. The Kimeses (D) successfully claimed that constructive notice through weekly newspaper publication was sufficient, and Williams (P) appealed.

ISSUE: Is a contingent remainder an ownership interest sufficient to require notice of a foreclosure?

HOLDING AND DECISION: (Benton, J.) Yes. A contingent remainder is an ownership interest sufficient to require notice of a foreclosure. The holder of a recorded contingent remainder is an owner entitled to notice of a power of sale foreclosure. A buyer at a statutory sale takes subject to the interests of those who were entitled to notice but did not receive it. Reversed and remanded.

EDITOR'S ANALYSIS: The court here held that the presumptive heirs' interest was not extinguished by the foreclosure sale. The Kimeses (D) purchased only the decedent's life estate. The heirs were not required to file a request for notice.

QUICKNOTES

CONTINGENT REMAINDER - A remainder limited to a person not in being, not certain or ascertained, or so limited to a certain person that his right to the state depends upon some contingent event in the future.

FORECLOSURE - An action to recover the amount due on a mortgage of real property where the owner has failed to pay their debt, terminating the owner's interest in the property which must then be sold to satisfy the debt.

LIFE ESTATE - An interest in land measured by the life of the tenant or a third party.

RYCZKOWSKI v. CHELSEA TITLE & GUARANTY CO.

Record owners (P) v. Title insurance company
Nev. Sup. Ct., 85 Nev. 37, 449 P.2d 261 (1969).

NATURE OF CASE: Review of judgment for defendant in action against title company.

FACT SUMMARY: The trial court held that an easement which was recorded and had been granted by a predecessor in interest before the sale of the land was recorded was a "wild" document not covered by a title insurance policy.

CONCISE RULE OF LAW: An instrument executed by an owner which is recorded before acquisition or after relinquishment of title is outside the chain of title.

FACTS: A power line easement was recorded but the contract for the land sale was never recorded. Title then passed to new owners. When Chelsea Title (D) was hired to insure title to the land, the power line easement did not appear in the chain of title. Ryczkowski (P) sued Chelsea (D) for failure to list the recorded easement as an encumbrance upon his title. The trial court entered judgment for Chelsea (D) and Ryczkowski (P) appealed.

ISSUE: Is an instrument executed by an owner which is recorded before acquisition or after relinquishment of title outside the chain of title?

HOLDING AND DECISION: (Thompson, J.) Yes. An instrument executed by an owner which is recorded before acquisition or after relinquishment of title is outside the chain of title. Chelsea (D), as the title searcher, was not liable for failing to discover such an instrument. Affirmed.

EDITOR'S ANALYSIS: Instruments which have been properly recorded and can be discovered by a reasonable search of records are said to be within the chain of title. One is deemed to have record notice of such instruments. There is no record notice of instruments outside the chain of title, however.

QUICKNOTES

CHAIN OF TITLE - Successive transfers of particular property.

EASEMENT - The right to utilize a portion of another's real property for a specific use.

RECORD TITLE - Title to real property that is recorded in the public land records.

TITLE SEARCH - An examination of records of title documents in order to ascertain whether title to a particular property is defective.

MORSE v. CURTIS

Mortgagee (P) v. Subsequent mortgagee (D)
Mass. Sup. Jud. Ct., 140 Mass. 112, 2 N.E. 929 (1885).

NATURE OF CASE: Writ of entry.

FACT SUMMARY: Curtis (D) received a mortgage on certain land from Clark by assignment. Although his assignor had notice of an earlier mortgage on the land to Morse (P), Curtis (D) had no actual notice of that mortgage.

CONCISE RULE OF LAW: If a purchaser, upon examining the registry, finds a conveyance from the owner of the land to his grantor, which gives the grantor a perfect record title, the purchaser is entitled to rely upon such title and is not required to search the records further to see if there has been any prior unrecorded deed of the original owner.

FACTS: On August 8, 1872, Hall mortgaged certain land to Morse (P). On September 7, 1875, Hall mortgaged the land to Clark, who had notice of the earlier mortgage. This mortgage was recorded on January 31, 1876. The earlier mortgage was recorded on September 8, 1876. On October 4, 1881, Clark assigned his mortgage to Curtis (D), who had no actual notice of the mortgage to Morse (P).

ISSUE: If a purchaser examines the registry and finds a conveyance which gives his grantor a perfect record title, is the purchaser required to search further to see if there has been any prior unrecorded deed of the original owner?

HOLDING AND DECISION: (Morton, C.J.) No. The earliest registry laws provided that no conveyance of land was good and effectual in law against anyone but the grantor or grantors and their heirs, unless the deed had been properly recorded. An exception to this rule was adopted, and it was held that a prior unrecorded deed would be valid against a second purchaser who took his deed with a knowledge of the prior deed. The basis for this exception was that it was a fraud for a second purchaser to take a deed if he had knowledge of the prior deed. In this case, Curtis (D) had no actual knowledge of Morse's (P) prior mortgage. However, Morse (P) contends that he had constructive notice, because Morse's (P) mortgage was recorded before the assignment. The court feels that the better rule is that where a purchaser has examined the registry and found a conveyance to his grantor which gives him a perfect record title, the purchaser is entitled to rely upon such record title. He is not required to search the records afterwards in order to see if there has been any prior unrecorded deed of the original owner. Hence, in this case once Curtis (D) found record of Hall's mortgage to Clark, he was not required to search further to discover the Morse (P) mortgage which was recorded after the Clark mortgage.

EDITOR'S ANALYSIS: Only recordable documents will give record notice when placed on the land records. Local statutes must be examined to ascertain what documents are recordable. The principal exclusion from the requirement of recording is a short-term lease. An instrument that purports to be a deed but which has not been executed with the formalities required by law, such as a deed which has not been acknowledged, may not be a recordable document. Placing such a deed on record will not provide record notice in regard to it.

QUICKNOTES

CONVEYANCE - The transfer of property, or title to property, from one party to another party.

NOTES:

BUFFALO ACADEMY OF THE
SACRED HEART v. BOEHM BROS.
Conveyor of property (P) v. Creditor (D)
N.Y. Ct. of App., 267 N.Y. 242, 196 N.E. 42 (1935).

NATURE OF CASE: Submission of a controversy pursuant to civil practice act.

FACT SUMMARY: Buffalo Academy of the Sacred Heart (P) agreed to convey certain land to Boehm Bros. (B) to satisfy a debt. Boehm Bros. (B) refused to accept on the ground that the title was unmarketable because of building restrictions of the subdivision where the lots were situated.

CONCISE RULE OF LAW: A purchaser of a lot which formed part of a larger tract is not charged with notice of restrictive covenants contained in a prior deed from the same grantor to any other lot or parcel of the same general tract, even though the deed is recorded and by its terms applies to all other lots.

FACTS: Buffalo Academy of the Sacred Heart (P) agreed to discharge a debt to Boehm Bros. (D) by conveying to Boehm Bros. (D) good and marketable title to certain realty. Buffalo (P) agreed that if the title proved unmarketable, it would pay Boehm Bros. (D) $60,000 in cash. Buffalo (P) executed a deed to the property. Boehm Bros. (D) refused to accept on the ground that the title is unmarketable. Boehm Bros. (D) contends that the title is unmarketable because the subdivision in which the property is located is subject to a uniform building plan which restricts use of it to residential purposes. Boehm Bros. (D) contends it is also unmarketable because of Buffalo's (P) covenants in a deed to Kendal. In the deed Buffalo (P) agreed to not sell gasoline or erect filling stations on the remaining lots.

ISSUE: (1) Is there a uniform building plan which restricts the use of the property so as to render the title unmarketable? (2) Does a covenant to a grantee by a grantor of subdivision lots that he will not sell gasoline or erect filling stations on the remaining lots render title to the remaining lots unmarketable?

HOLDING AND DECISION: (Finch, J.) (1) No. The court decided that there was no uniform building plan restricting use of the property to residential purposes. It based its decision on the following: No restriction plan was indicated in the maps filed; none of the deeds contained covenants by Buffalo (P) that the remainder of the tract would be subject to restriction; and Buffalo (P) made restrictions only when he thought them necessary, but did not follow a fixed plan of restricting use of the lots. (2) No. The court decided that Buffalo's (P) covenant not to build filling stations on the remaining lots did not render the title unmarketable. In reaching its decision the court first looked to the deed which contained the covenant. The deed did not expressly make Buffalo's (P) covenant run with the land. Buffalo (P) did not

agree that his grantees would not sell gasoline or erect filling stations on the remaining lots. Applying the rules that restrictive covenants must always be construed strictly against those seeking to enforce them and that a land owner is only bound by restrictions appearing in his deed, the title is marketable, since no restrictions are mentioned in Boehm Bros.' (D) deed. Lastly, a purchaser of a lot which forms part of a larger tract is not charged with notice of restrictive covenants contained in a prior deed from the same grantor to any other lot of the same tract, even though the deed is recorded and by its terms applies to all other lots. In the absence of exceptional circumstances, a purchaser takes notice from the record only of encumbrances in his direct chain of title. Reversed.

EDITOR'S ANALYSIS: Some states have followed the opposing rule that the recording of a deed containing, restriction covenants by a common grantor gives notice of the restrictions to all subsequent grantees. This case demonstrates recording problems that arise in relation to subdivisions which involve multiple transfers out of a common grantor with various covenants in the deeds that are designed to restrict not only the land conveyed, but also the land retained by the common grantor.

QUICKNOTES
COMMON GRANTOR - Mutual conveyor of property.

DEED - A signed writing transferring title to real property from one person to another.

RESTRICTIVE COVENANT - A promise contained in a deed to limit the uses to which the property will be made.

NOTES:

SANBORN v. McLEAN

Adjoining property owner (P) v. Adjoining property owner (D)
Mich. Sup. Ct., 233 Mich. 227, 206 N.W. 496 (1925).

NATURE OF CASE: Action to enjoin erection of gasoline filling station.

FACT SUMMARY: Sanborn (P) and McClean (D) trace the titles to their adjoining lots to the proprietor of the subdivision. Residences are built on all the surrounding lots. Sanborn (P) objected to McClean's (D) erection of a gas station on her lot.

CONCISE RULE OF LAW: If the owner of two or more lots, which are situated so as to bear a relation to each other, sells one with restrictions which are of benefit to the land retained, during the period of restraint, the owner of the lot or lots retained can do nothing forbidden to the owner of the lot sold. This is the doctrine of reciprocal negative easements.

FACTS: On December 28, 1892, McLaughlin, who was then owner of the lots on Collingwood Avenue, deeded four of the lots with the restriction that only residences would be built on the lots. On July 24, 1893, McLaughlin conveyed several more lots with the same restriction. Sanborn (P) traces title to McLaughlin. McClean's (D) title runs back to a deed dated September 7, 1893, which does not contain the restrictions. No buildings other than residences have been erected on any of the lots of the subdivision.

ISSUE: (1) If the owner of two or more lots, which are situated so as to bear a relation to each other, sells one with restrictions which are of benefit to the land retained, during the period of restraint, can the owner of the lot or lots retained do anything forbidden to the owner of the lot sold? (2) Is a reciprocal negative easement personal to owners?

HOLDING AND DECISION: (Wiest, J.) (1) No. The doctrine of reciprocal negative easements makes restrictions which are of benefit to the land retained mutual so that the owner can do nothing upon the land he has retained that is forbidden to the owner of the lot sold. In this case McLaughlin deeded lots with the restriction that only residences he built on them. Such restrictions were imposed for the benefit of the lands retained by McLaughlin to carry out the scheme of a residential district, and a restrictive negative easement attached to the lots retained. Since his was one of the lots retained in the December 1892 and July 1893 deeds, a reciprocal negative easement attached to the lot which later became McClean's (D). (2) No. Reciprocal negative easements are not personal to owners but are operative upon use of the land by any owner having actual or constructive notice thereof. In this case the reciprocal negative easement attached to McClean's (D) lot may now be enforced by Sanborn (P) provided McClean (D) had constructive knowledge of the easement at the time of purchase. At the time of purchase McClean (D) had an abstract of title showing the subdivision and that his lot had 97 companion lots. He could not avoid noticing the strictly uniform residence character of the companion lots, and the least inquiry would have revealed the fact that his lot was subject to a reciprocal negative easement. The injunction is granted.

EDITOR'S ANALYSIS: Reciprocal negative easements must start with common owners. They cannot arise and fasten upon one lot by reason of other lot owners conforming to a general plan. Such easements are never retroactive, and as demonstrated here, they pass their benefits and carry their obligations to all purchasers of land provided the purchaser has constructive notice of the easement.

QUICKNOTES

RECIPROCAL NEGATIVE EASEMENTS - An implied covenant that arises when a common grantor conveys property and fails to contain a restriction placed on prior conveyances, pursuant to a general development scheme, to the present one and the grantee has either actual or constructive notice of such restrictions.

NOTES:

MANUFACTURERS AND TRADERS TRUST CO. v. FIRST NATIONAL BANK

Creditor (D) v. Creditor (P)

Fla. Dist. Ct. of App., 113 So. 2d 869 (1959).

NATURE OF CASE: Appeal from ruling that a mortgage was supported by adequate consideration in foreclosure action.

FACT SUMMARY: First National Bank (plaintiff) (P) obtained from the Schinstocks a note secured by a mortgage on the same day that Manufacturers and Traders Trust Co. (appellant) (D) obtained a federal judgment against the Schinstocks. Plaintiff (P) had no knowledge of the judgment and recorded its mortgage before appellant (D) recorded its judgment. The appellant (D) claimed that the mortgage was not supported by legal consideration.

CONCISE RULE OF LAW: Where one creditor holds a mortgage that is granted on the same day a judgment is handed down against the debtor in favor of a second creditor, but the second creditor does not record the judgment until after the mortgage is recorded, the first creditor's mortgage is supported by legal consideration so that the first creditor is a purchaser entitled to priority.

FACTS: The Schinstocks borrowed $25,000 from First National Bank (plaintiff) (P). On August 20, 1957, the Schinstocks executed to plaintiff (P) a renewal note for $25,000 secured by a second mortgage on their property. This note provided that all sums due under the note were "due and payable on or before ninety (90) days from the date thereof." During this time, Manufacturers and Traders Trust Co. (appellant) (D) obtained a federal judgment against the Schinstocks, also on August 20, 1957. The plaintiff's (P) mortgage was recorded on August 23, 1957, but the appellant's (D) judgment was not recorded until August 28, 1957. There was no evidence that plaintiff (P) had actual or constructive notice of appellant's (D) judgment lien. Plaintiff (P) sued to foreclose on its mortgage, and the chancery court ruled that the plaintiff's (P) mortgage was supported by adequate consideration. The court of appeals granted review.

ISSUE: Where one creditor holds a mortgage that is granted on the same day a judgment is handed down against the debtor in favor of a second creditor, but the second creditor does not record the judgment until after the mortgage is recorded, is the first creditor's mortgage supported by legal consideration so that the first creditor is a purchaser entitled to priority?

HOLDING AND DECISION: (Allen, C.J.) Yes. Where one creditor holds a mortgage that is granted on the same day a judgment is handed down against the debtor in favor of a second creditor, but the second creditor does not record the judgment until after the mortgage is recorded, the first creditor's mortgage is supported by legal consideration so that the first creditor is a

purchaser entitled to priority. The issue of whether a mortgagee is a purchaser depends on whether he parted with anything valuable, surrendered an existing right, incurred a fixed liability, or submitted to loss or detriment, contemporaneously with the execution of the mortgage. Here, there was a definite period of forebearance stated at the time the mortgage and note were executed (90 days). Consequently, it is apparent that the consideration for the giving of the second mortgage was the extension of time for the payment of the pre-existing debt—a detriment of the plaintiff (P) and a benefit to the Schinstocks. Such a consideration was a valuable one and sufficient to support the mortgage. Nonetheless, appellant (D) contends that because there is no evidence that there was an express agreement to extend time for payment of the pre-existing debt made at the same time the note and mortgage were executed, plaintiff's (P) mortgage should not be given priority. This argument is rejected because the legal efficacy of accepting a note for a pre-existing debt is to postpone the original due date and extend the time of payment for the specified period set forth in the note. This rule is predicated on the principle that in case of a mere agreement to extend the time of payment, without consideration, there is no binding agreement. Affirmed.

EDITOR'S ANALYSIS: The issue in this case was essentially whether plaintiff (P) was a purchaser; the court held it was. Some jurisdictions protect only purchasers against prior unrecorded interests, whereas others protect both purchasers and creditors (those who provide debtor credit and subsequently obtain a judgment lien on the property after debtor defaults on the loan).

QUICKNOTES

CONSIDERATION - Value given by one party in exchange for performance, or a promise to perform, by another party.

JUDGMENT LIEN - Lien filed by a judgment creditor against the property of a judgment debtor pursuant to a judgment rendered in a civil case.

PRIORITY - The relative preference of different claims to specific property.

SHERER-GILLETTE CO. v. LONG
Seller (P) v. Bona fide purchaser (D)
Ill. Sup. Ct., 318 Ill. 432, 149 N.E. 225 (1925).

NATURE OF CASE: Action of replevin for a display counter.

FACT SUMMARY: Long (D) purchased a display counter from Taylor, not knowing that the title to it was held by the Sherer-Gillette Company.

CONCISE RULE OF LAW: Where goods are sold by a person who is not the owner thereof, and who does not sell them under the authority or with the consent of the owner, the buyer acquires no better title to the goods than the seller had, unless the owner of the goods is, by his conduct, precluded from denying the seller's authority to sell.

FACTS: The Sherer-Gillette Company (P) sold a display counter to Taylor on a conditional sales contract. It was to retain title to the counter until the contract was paid. Two days later, Taylor sold the counter to Long (D) without telling him of the title reservation. Long (D) paid one hundred dollars for the counter. The Sherer-Gillette Company (P) brought an action of replevin against Long (D) to recover the counter. The municipal court entered judgment in favor of appellant; the Appellate Court reversed.

ISSUE: Is a bona fide purchaser for value protected against an undisclosed reservation of title?

HOLDING AND DECISION: (Thompson, J.) No. A bona fide purchaser for value is not protected against an undisclosed reservation of title. Section 23 of the state's uniform sales act states that "where goods are sold by a person who is not the owner thereof, and who does not sell them under the authority or with the consent of the owner, the buyer acquires no better title to the goods than the seller had, unless the owner of the goods is by his conduct precluded from denying the seller's authority to sell." This is in keeping with the overwhelming weight of authority in place before the uniform sales act was passed, but represents a departure from the law in this state at the time that statute was enacted. In this state, prior to the enactment of the uniform legislation, an undisclosed reservation of title on a conditional sales contract was considered a constructive fraud on an innocent third-party purchaser because the conditional vendee had been given, through possession of the property, the indicia of ownership. Section 23 provides, in keeping with settled principles of estoppel, that the owner of the goods may by his conduct be estopped from denying the seller's authority to sell the property. The law of estoppel requires that the estopped party make by act or word a representation that the person asserting the estoppel has relied on to his detriment. Here, Sherer-Gillett (P) did not make any representation that Long (D) relied on to his detriment, nor did it clothe Taylor with indicia of ownership. Giving someone possession by itself does not clothe that person with indicia of ownership, because owners must frequently entrust others with their possession, as in the case of lessees, bailees, agents, or servants. Thus, while possession is one indicator of possession, it is not conclusive. Here, there is no basis for finding estoppel of Sherer-Gillett (P) under the uniform act, especially since the court must take the act as written, and should give its words their natural and common meaning. Affirmed.

EDITOR'S ANALYSIS: Two conflicting public policies are represented in this case. First, how can innocent third parties be protected in similar situations? Secondly, if all conditional sales contracts had to be perfected by filing, the cost in time, money and manpower would be staggering. The Uniform Commercial Code has attempted to take an approach in between the two extremes presented in this case. U.C.C. 9-301(1)(c) gives the bona fide purchaser for value, without notice, superior title to the unperfected security holder if the transaction involved goods, instruments, documents and chattel paper and was not a bulk transfer or made in the ordinary course of business. U.C.C. 9-301(1)(d) gives the bona fide purchaser for value, without notice, superior title in the case of accounts and intangibles. The secured party has ten days to file after the debtor receives possession of the property (U.C.C. 9-301[2]) if he is to protect himself against an immediate reconveyance by the debtor (as was the situation in this case). U.C.C. 9-302 presents numerous exceptions to this filing requirement. The most notable are where possession is retained by the secured party and a purchase money security interest in consumer goods other than motor vehicles or fixtures is involved. Long (D) might have prevailed under the Uniform Commercial Code if he could have shown that the display counter was not a consumer good (or was a fixture) or was not bought in the normal course of business. He would have to further prove that the Sherer-Gillette Company had not perfected their security interest within ten days of delivering the counter to Taylor.

QUICKNOTES

REPLEVIN - An action to recover personal property wrongfully taken.

KILLAM v. MARCH
Purchaser of property (P) v. Prior lease holder (D)
Mass. Sup. Jud. Ct., 316 Mass. 646, 55 N.E.2d 945 (1944).

NATURE OF CASE: Bill in equity brought to remove Cloud from title.

FACT SUMMARY: March (D) leased a garage and driveway from Killam's (P) predecessor in title for a 25-year period in 1938. The lease was recorded but not registered. In 1941, Killam (P) bought the property and acquired a certificate of title which did not mention the lease.

CONCISE RULE OF LAW: A purchaser of registered land who has actual notice of an unregistered lease for more than seven years takes subject to the lease.

FACTS: In 1941, Killam (P) purchased a parcel of registered land and became holder of a certificate of title. The certificate noted that the land was subject to a mortgage and to sewer assessments. On Killam's (P) land there is a driveway leading to a garage, which March (D) has been using since Killam (P) acquired title. March (D) claims the right to use these premises by virtue of a deed dated 1938, given to them by Killam's (P) predecessor in title for a 25-year term. The lease was recorded but not registered. The lower court found that Killam (P) had actual notice of the lease prior to their purchasing the property.

ISSUE: Does one purchasing registered land take subject to an unregistered lease if he has actual notice of it?

HOLDING AND DECISION: (Spalding, J.) Yes. General Laws C. 185 provide a system for the registration of land titles and contains provisions relative to transfers of land. Section 46 of the act states that subsequent purchasers of registered land taking a certificate of title for value and in good faith shall hold the land free from all encumbrances except those noted in the certificate. Section 51 states that no deed, mortgage or other voluntary instrument, except a will and a lease for a term not exceeding seven years shall be an effective conveyance unless it is registered. Section 57 does not mention good faith. Section 71 requires that leases for more than seven years be registered. This seems to point to the conclusion that no one can claim a leasehold interest for more than seven years in registered land where the lease has not been registered. However, in construing General Laws C. 185, well-settled principles of statutory construction must be kept in mind. Various sections of a statute must, if reasonably possible, be interpreted so as to be harmonious and not contradictory, and the legislative intention must be ascertained in light of the common law and previous statutes. The recording acts prior to General Laws C. 185 reveal that a purchaser acquiring title with actual notice of a prior deed takes subject to it. The basis of this rule is that a party with such notice could not take a deed without fraud. The same provision as to leases is found in the early statutes and has been retained in General Laws C. 183. The court decides that General Laws C. 185 construed against this background does not give certificate holders an indefeasible title as against interests of which they had actual notice. Any other construction would ignore the provision of § 46 that one acquires registered land free from unregistered encumbrances if he is a purchaser in good faith. In this case, since it was found that Killam (P) did have actual notice of March's (D) unregistered lease for 25 years, Killam took subject to March's (D) lease. Dismissal affirmed.

EDITOR'S ANALYSIS: A transfer of registered land to a bona fide purchaser conveys an indefeasible title, but the acts protect only the bona fide purchaser. A transferee who takes with knowledge that his transferor acquired title by fraud or a purchaser who buys registered land with notice of the fact that it is in litigation is not a purchaser in good faith. Likewise, as demonstrated here, a purchaser of registered land takes subject to an unregistered lease which he had actual notice of. However, the rights of a subsequent purchaser or lessee whose lease is duly registered and who does not know of a prior unregistered lease will prevail over the former lessee's.

NOTES:

SOMERSET SAVINGS BANK v. CHICAGO TITLE INSURANCE CO.

Insured (P) v. Title insurer (D)

Mass. Sup. Ct., 649 N.E.2d 1123 (1995).

NATURE OF CASE: Appeal from affirmance of summary judgment for defendant in action for breach of contract and negligence.

FACT SUMMARY: Somerset Savings Bank (P), which was insured under a title insurance policy issued by Chicago Title Insurance Co. (D), claimed that defendant was negligent and breached its contract of insurance by failing to inform plaintiff that approval by the Executive Office of Transportation and Construction (EOTC) would be necessary as a condition of obtaining a building permit.

CONCISE RULE OF LAW: (1) A statutory provision that requires governmental consent to an owner's intended use of property does not, for title insurance purposes, constitute an encumbrance on or defect in the title to the property or render title to the property unmarketable. (2) A claim against a title insurer based on negligence in notifying an insured of matters discovered in a title search voluntarily assumed outside the policy is not barred by an integration clause in a title insurance policy.

FACTS: Somerset Savings Bank (P) agreed to finance a $9.5 million site acquisition and construction project in the town of Revere. It obtained a title insurance policy in the face amount of $9.5 million issued by Chicago Title Insurance Co. (D). Revere issued a building permit to construct the project, but the state's attorney general requested a halt to the construction. Because all or part of the property had been owned by the Boston and Maine Railroad, the Executive Office of Transportation and Construction (EOTC) would have to give its consent to the issuance of any building permits. The policy excluded from coverage governmental regulation, including building and zoning ordinances and laws. The policy also contained an integration clause that limited claims to the provisions of the policy. Plaintiff made claim under the policy, and the defendant denied coverage on the ground that the effect of the statute requiring EOTC approval was not an insured risk and that it did not have any obligations or duties to the plaintiff beyond those specified in the policy. Plaintiff sued for breach of contract, negligence, and negligent misrepresentation. Defendant moved for summary judgment on all claims, which the trial court granted. The intermediate appeals court limited its review to whether the policy exclusions applied, and the state's highest court granted review.

ISSUE: (1) Does a statutory provision that requires governmental consent to an owner's intended use of property, for title insurance purposes, constitute an encumbrance on or defect in the title to the property or render title to the property unmarketable? (2) Is a claim against a title insurer based on negligence in notifying an insured of matters discovered in a title search voluntarily assumed outside the policy barred by an integration clause in a title insurance policy?

HOLDING AND DECISION: (Lynch, J.) (1) No. A statutory provision that requires governmental consent to an owner's intended use of property does not, for title insurance purposes, constitute an encumbrance on or defect in the title to the property or render title to the property unmarketable. It is well established that building or zoning laws are not encumbrances or defect affecting title to property. Such restrictions are concerned with the use of the land, but do not affect title to it. Also, there is a difference between economic lack of marketability, and title marketability, which relates to defects affecting legally recognized rights and incidents of ownership. Title insurance provides no protection for governmentally imposed impediments on the use of the land or for impairments to the value of the land. Thus, the statutory requirement of EOTC approval prior to the issuance of a building permit does not affect the owner's title to the property and does not give rise to coverage under the policy. Summary judgment was appropriately granted on the breach of contract claim. (2) No. A claim against a title insurer based on negligence in notifying an insured of matters discovered in a title search voluntarily assumed outside the policy is not barred by an integration clause in a title insurance policy. The trial court ruled that the defendant had no duty to disclose the prior use of the property as a railroad right-of-way or the applicability of the statute requiring EOTC approval. It also found that defendant had not voluntarily assumed such a duty. Here, however, summary judgment was inappropriate because there is a factual dispute as to whether the defendant voluntarily assumed a duty to inform the plaintiff of these matters. In general, a title insurer has no duty to search for or to disclose to the insured any reasonably discoverable information that would affect the insured's decision to proceed with the purchase. However, if the title insurer agrees to conduct a search and to provide the insured with an abstract of title, it may expose itself to liability for negligence as a title searcher, in addition to any liability under the policy. Here, the plaintiff offered evidence that the defendant's advertising claimed knowledge of local laws and practices, which could be fairly interpreted as an assurance that all matters recorded at the registry that might influence the decision to buy the property would be called to the insured's attention. Also, the language in the policy's integration clause would not obviate liability for the

Continued on next page.

insurance company's negligence as a title searcher because the conditions in a title insurance policy are dictated by the insurance company to the insured. Therefore, it must be determined whether the clause exculpating the defendant from loss arising from its own negligence is unfair or unconscionable. Such analysis requires balancing the freedom of contract against possible harm to the public resulting from such exculpation. Based on public policy considerations, and the relative lack of bargaining power of an insured, negligence in conducting a title search voluntarily assumed outside the policy is not barred by the integration clause. Summary judgment on the negligence claims is reversed.

EDITOR'S ANALYSIS: The court also held that Chicago Title (D) had no contractual obligation to examine, review, or analyze the title to the premises and to notify the plaintiff of any facts regarding title. This was because the title insurance company was not employed to examine the title, but to issue a policy to insure against existing defects and encumbrances on the title. However, as the court's opinion relating to the negligence claims shows, there was the possibility that Chicago Title voluntarily assumed such duties—a question for a trier of fact.

QUICKNOTES

NEGLIGENCE - Conduct falling below the standard of care that a reasonable person would demonstrate under similar conditions.

NOTES:

CHAPTER 10
PROTECTION AGAINST DISCRIMINATION IN
HOUSING

QUICK REFERENCE RULES OF LAW

1. **Protection Under the Federal Constitution.** The Equal Protection Clause of the Fourteenth Amendment prohibits judicial enforcement by state courts of restrictive covenants based on race or color. (Shelley v. Kraemer)

2. **Protection Under the Civil Rights Act of 1866 and the Federal Fair Housing Act.** (1) The Act of Congress, 42 U.S.C.A. § 1982, bars all racial discrimination, private as well as public, in the sale or rental of property. (2) That statute, thus construed, is a valid exercise of the power of Congress to enforce the Thirteenth Amendment. (Jones v. Alfred H. Mayer Co.)

3. **Discrimination Against the Handicapped.** A restrictive covenant limiting the use of a residence to single-family occupancy does not prohibit the use of the residence a a group home. (Hill v. Community of Damien of Molokai)

4. **Discrimination Against the Handicapped.** Once a landlord elects to participate in the Section 8 certificate program, it may not thereafter refuse a prospective tenant on the ground that he is a Section 8 certificate holder. (Salute v. Stratford Greens)

5. **Discrimination on the Basis of Familial Status.** FHA § 3607 requires the following to meet the 55 and older exemption for older persons: (1) the facility has significant facilities and services specifically designed to meet the physical and social needs of older persons; 2) at least 80% of the units are occupied by persons age 55 or older; and 3) the housing facility complies with HUD rules and regulations for verification of occupancy. (Simovits v. Chanticleer Condominium Ass'n)

6. **Discrimination on the Basis of Marial Status and Sexual Orientation.** The right to free exercise does not relieve an individual of the obligation to comply with a valid and neutral law of general applicability on the ground that the law proscribes (or prescribes) conduct that the religion either proscribes or prescribes. (Smith v. Fair Employment and Housing Commission)

7. **Discrimination on the Basis of Marial Status.** Homosexuals are protected from arbitrary discrimination in rental housing by the Unruh Civil Rights Act. (Hubert v. Williams)

SHELLEY v. KRAEMER
Property owners (D) v. Neighbors (P)
334 U.S. 1 (1948).

NATURE OF CASE: On writ of certiorari in action to enjoin a sale of property.

FACT SUMMARY: The Kraemers (P) sought to oust the Shelleys (D), Negroes, from their recently purchased property on the grounds that it was subject to a racially restrictive covenant.

CONCISE RULE OF LAW: The Equal Protection Clause of the Fourteenth Amendment prohibits judicial enforcement by state courts of restrictive covenants based on race or color.

FACTS: In 1945, the Shelleys (D), Negroes, purchased property which, unknown to them, was subject to a racially restrictive covenant signed in 1911 for a 50-year period by the majority of property owners on the block. The Kraemers (P), also owners of property subject to the covenant, sued in the state court to restrain the Shelleys (D) from taking possession and to revest the title in others. The state court denied relief on the grounds that the covenant had never been finalized. However, the Missouri Supreme Court reversed. The U.S. Supreme Court granted the Shelley's (D) certiorari. They argued that the Equal Protection Clause of the Fourteenth Amendment prevented the judicial enforcement by state courts of racially restrictive covenants.

ISSUE: Does the Equal Protection Clause of the Fourteenth Amendment prohibit judicial enforcement by state courts of racially restrictive covenants?

HOLDING AND DECISION: (Vinson, C.J.) Yes. The Equal Protection Clause of the Fourteenth Amendment prohibits judicial enforcement by state courts of racially restrictive covenants. Equality in the enjoyment of property rights was clearly among the civil rights intended to be protected from discriminatory state action by the framers of the Fourteenth Amendment. And although past cases have struck down such discrimination when enacted by state legislatures or city councils, it may not be said that such discrimination, as in the instant case, may escape on the grounds that it was only an agreement between private individuals. Indeed, were it no more than that, no violation would exist, However, in this case state action is clearly present by reason of the active intervention of the state court to enforce the covenant. As early as 1880, in *Ex Parte Virginia*, this Court found state action in violation of the Fourteenth Amendment when a state judge restricted jury service to whites. Nor is the amendment ineffective simply because this action was taken according to the state's common law policy. We hold that in granting judicial enforcement of these restrictive covenants, the state has denied the Shelleys (D) equal protection of the laws. Reversed.

EDITOR'S ANALYSIS: In the 1961 case of *Burton v. Wilmington Parking Authority*, a state agency had built and owned a parking garage, and rented space in the garage to a private restaurant. The Supreme Court held that the restaurant's exclusion of blacks from service amounted to state action under the Fourteenth Amendment. The test announced was that of significant state involvement in private discrimination.

QUICKNOTES

EQUAL PROTECTION - A constitutional guarantee that no person shall be denied the same protection of the laws enjoyed by other persons in life circumstances.

RESTRICTIVE COVENANT - A promise contained in a deed to limit the uses to which the property will be made.

STATE ACTION - Actions brought pursuant to the Fourteenth Amendment claiming that the government violated the plaintiff's civil rights.

NOTES:

JONES v. ALFRED H. MAYER CO.
Negro home buyer (P) v. Seller (D)
392 U.S. 409 (1968).

NATURE OF CASE: On writ of certiorari in an action for injunctive relief.

FACT SUMMARY: Mayer (D) refused to sell a home to Jones (P) allegedly for the sole reason that Jones (P) was a Negro.

CONCISE RULE OF LAW: (1) The Act of Congress, 42 U.S.C.A. § 1982, bars all racial discrimination, private as well as public, in the sale or rental of property. (2) That statute, thus construed, is a valid exercise of the power of Congress to enforce the Thirteenth Amendment.

FACTS: The Joneses (P) filed a complaint in the federal district court alleging that Mayer (D) had refused to sell them a home for the sole reason that Joseph Jones (P) was a Negro. They sought an injunction under an Act of Congress, 42 U.S.C.A. § 1982, which provides that all citizens shall enjoy the same right in every state, as is enjoyed by the citizens thereof, to hold and convey property. The district court dismissed the complaint. The court of appeals affirmed, concluding that § 1982 applied only to state—not private—action. The U.S. Supreme Court granted certiorari. Mayer (D) pointed out that § 1982 was originally part of § 1 of the 1866 Civil Rights Act and, as such, was intended to forbid only discriminatory governmental action—not private action. Also, Mayer (D) claimed, Congress lacked the power under the Constitution to prohibit private racial discrimination in the sale and rental of property.

ISSUE: (1) Does the Act of Congress, 42 U.S.C.A. § 1982, bar all racial discrimination, private as well as public, in the sale or rental of property? (2) Is § 1982, thus construed, a valid exercise of the power of Congress to enforce the Thirteenth Amendment?

HOLDING AND DECISION: (Stewart, J.) (1) Yes. The Act of Congress, 42 U.S.C.A. § 1982, bars all racial discrimination, private as well as public, in the sale or rental of property. Although in 1948, this Court, in *Hurt v. Hodge*, applied § 1982 to forbid private racially discriminatory housing covenants, still, that case did not reach the instant issue, but rather involved governmental action since those wrongful covenants had been enforced by the courts. However, we believe that the plain language of § 1982 forbids private action since it prohibits denying to any citizen "the same right" to purchase and lease property "as is enjoyed by white citizens." But to exclude Negroes from property on the public market is clearly a denial of such rights. Next, as Mayer (D) noted, § 1982, in its original form, was part of § 1 of the 1866 Civil Rights Act. But we note that, although § 2 of that Act provided fines and prison for those violating § 1, it was nevertheless drafted so as to exempt private violations from these penalties.

This would have been nonsensical if § 1 dealt only with governmental violations. (2) Yes. Section 1982, thus construed, is a valid exercise of the power of Congress to enforce the Thirteenth Amendment. The amendment not only eliminates badges of slavery, but also grants Congress the power to enforce the article by appropriate legislation. This includes legislation reaching the conduct of private individuals. Reversed.

EDITOR'S ANALYSIS: The "Badges of Slavery" theory is limited to congressional regulation. That is to say, the Supreme Court has not held that the Thirteenth Amendment forbids, of its own force, all private racial discrimination. Thus, in the absence of a congressional law, private racial discrimination is not reached by the Thirteenth Amendment. Additionally, Congress' power to prohibit private racial discrimination is probably limited, at some point, by a right of privacy.

QUICKNOTES

42 U.S.C. § 1982 - "All citizens of the United States shall have the same right in every state at territory, as is enjoyed by white citizens thereof to inherit, purchase, lease, sell, hold, and convey real and personal property."

NOTES:

HILL v. COMMUNITY OF DAMIEN OF MOLOKAI
Neighbors (P) v. Group home (D)
121 N.M. 353, 911 P.2d 861 (1996).

NATURE OF CASE: Review of order enforcing restrictive covenant upon real estate.

FACT SUMMARY: Local residents contended that Community of Damien of Molokai (D) violated a covenant limiting use to a single-family residence on premises it occupied by operating a group home for persons with AIDS.

CONCISE RULE OF LAW: A restrictive covenant limiting the use of a residence to single-family occupancy does not prohibit the use of the residence as a group home.

FACTS: A certain real estate development contained, on all homes in the development, a restrictive covenant that mandated use of the homes as single-family dwellings exclusively. Community of Damien of Molokai (D) began operating at the property a group home for persons with AIDS. Hill (P) and other neighbors (P) brought suit to enforce the covenant. The trial court entered an order enforcing the covenant, and the Community (D) appealed.

ISSUE: Does a restrictive covenant limiting the use of a residence to single-family occupancy prohibit the use of the residence as a group home?

HOLDING AND DECISION: (Frost, J.) No. A restrictive covenant limiting the use of a residence to single-family occupancy does not prohibit the use of the residence as a group home. There are two reasons why such a covenant does not create the limitation advanced by Hill (P). First, this court does not accept the notion that a use as a single-family residence solely means occupancy by persons related by blood or by law. The local zoning law defines "family" as, among other things, "any group of not more than five unrelated persons living together in a dwelling." Moreover, federal policy favors including small group homes as "families," as the federal government has expressed a strong policy toward breaking down barriers preventing persons with disabilities from living together, and including a small group of persons with similar disabilities living together advances this policy. The second reason why the covenant must fail in this instance is that the interpretation advanced here violates the Fair Housing Act. Section 3604(f)(1) prohibits discrimination in housing against those with disabilities; HIV infection has been classified as a disability, so the covenant here, if applied to the Community (D), would violate the Fair Housing Act (FHA). For these reasons, this court finds that the covenant does not apply as against the Community (D). Reversed.

EDITOR'S ANALYSIS: Restrictive covenants such as the one at issue here are fairly common around the nation. Because of this, there has been a good deal of litigation regarding what exactly constitutes a family. As the current opinion shows, courts have deviated considerably from the traditional notions of a family in deciding these types of cases.

QUICKNOTES

FAIR HOUSING ACT 42 U.S.C. § 3601 - Prohibits housing discrimination on the basis of familial status.

INJUNCTION - A court order requiring a person to do or prohibiting that person from doing a specific act.

RESTRICTIVE COVENANT - A promise contained in a deed to limit the uses to which the property will be made.

ZONING ORDINANCE - A statute that divides land into defined areas and which regulates the form and use of buildings and structures within those areas.

NOTES:

SALUTE v. STRATFORD GREENS

Disabled person (P) v. Rental apartment (D)

888 F. Supp. 17 (E.D.N.Y. 1995).

NATURE OF CASE: Class action suit.

FACT SUMMARY: Salute (P) and Long Island Housing Services brought a purported class action alleging Stratford's (D) refusal to rent Salute (P) an apartment in the Stratford Greens (D) complex on account of his disability constituted a violation of the Fair Housing Act.

CONCISE RULE OF LAW: Once a landlord elects to participate in the Section 8 certificate program, it may not thereafter refuse a prospective tenant on the ground that he is a Section 8 certificate holder.

FACTS: Salute (P) and Long Island Housing Services brought a purported class action alleging that Stratford's (D) refusal to rent Salute (P) an apartment in the Stratford Greens (D) complex on account of his disability constituted a violation of the Fair Housing Act. Due to his disability, Salute (P) applied for and received a "section 8" certificate which entitled him to a 70% subsidy by the federal government towards any rent falling within the fair market guidelines. Salute (P) claims Stratford (D) rejected him as a tenant on account of his participation in the program. Since he was unable to find suitable housing within the proscribed period, he was forced to give up his certificate. The complaint was amended to add as a plaintiff Kravette (P), who was also a participant in the Section 8 program. Stratford (D) denied her application as well on the basis of her participation in the program.

ISSUE: Once a landlord elects to participate in the Section 8 certificate program, may it thereafter refuse a prospective tenant on the ground that he is a Section 8 certificate holder?

HOLDING AND DECISION: (Gleeson, D.J.) No. Once a landlord elects to participate in the Section 8 certificate program, it may not thereafter refuse a prospective tenant on the ground that he is a Section 8 certificate holder. Kravette (P) contends that Stratford (D) violated 42 U.S.C. § 1437f(t)(1)(A) when they refused to rent her a one-bedroom unit because of her status as a Section 8 participant. That provision makes it illegal for a housing owner who has entered into a contract for housing assistance payments on behalf of a tenant to refuse to lease any available dwelling unit on account of his status as a Section 8 certificate holder. While the apartment dwelling currently has two such tenants, defendants contend that the only circumstances in which this occurred involved existing tenants who became indigent while already living in the complex. Defendants further contend that their acceptance of these certificates was an act of compassion, not an election to become a Section 8 complex, and seek an exception to that effect. Defendants have cited no authority for such an exception. Such an exemption from the statute is a matter for the legislature and not the courts. Defendants are ordered to rent to Kravette (P) a one-bedroom unit.

EDITOR'S ANALYSIS: The Americans with Disabilities Act of 1990 provides additional protections for persons with disabilities. That statute requires landlords of existing public places to remove barriers to access where such removal is "readily achievable."

QUICKNOTES

FAIR HOUSING ACT 42 U.S.C. § 3601 - Prohibits housing discrimination on the basis of familial status.

NOTES:

SIMOVITS v. CHANTICLEER CONDOMINIUM ASS'N

Condominium owners (P) v. Association (D)

933 F. Supp. 1394 (N.D. Ill. 1996).

NATURE OF CASE: Suit for damages.

FACT SUMMARY: The Simovits (P) brought suit against Chanticleer (D) seeking damages as a result of the diminishment in value of their condominium allegedly as the result of a negative covenant prohibiting persons 18 and under from residing in its dwelling units without prior association approval.

CONCISE RULE OF LAW: FHA § 3607 requires the following to meet the 55 and older exemption for older persons: (1) the facility has significant facilities and services specifically designed to meet the physical and social needs of older persons; (2) at least 80% of the units are occupied by persons age 55 or older; and (3) the housing facility complies with HUD rules and regulations for verification of occupancy.

FACTS: The Simovits (P) owned a condominium in Chanticleer. The association has a restrictive covenant stating that no minor children under the age of 18 may reside in any unit purchased after the effective date of the covenant without prior approval. The Simovits (P) attempted to sell their condominium several times and were unable to do so on account of the covenant. They finally entered a deal to sell their apartment to a young couple after the association agreed to waive the covenant. They allege that as a result they lost numerous opportunities to sell their condominium at a higher price and brought suit for damages.

ISSUE: Does FHA § 3607 require the following to meet the 55 and older exemption for older persons: (1) the facility has significant facilities and services specifically designed to meet the physical and social needs of older persons; (2) at least 80% of the units are occupied by persons age 55 or older; and (3) the housing facility comply with HUD rules and regulations for verification of occupancy?

HOLDING AND DECISION: (Keys, U.S. Magistrate J.) Yes. FHA § 3607 requires the following to meet the 55 and older exemption for older persons: (1) the facility has significant facilities and services specifically designed to meet the physical and social needs of older persons; (2) at least 80% of the units are occupied by persons age 55 or older; and (3) the housing facility comply with HUD rules and regulations for verification of occupancy. The issue regarding the association's liability turns on whether Chanticleer (D) meets the exemption for housing for older persons in § 3607(b)(2) of the FHA. This includes a category of housing for persons 55 years or older. Prior to December 1995 the FHA required the following to meet the 55 and older exemption: (1) the facility has significant facilities and services

specifically designed to meet the physical and social needs of older persons; (2) at least 80% of the units are occupied by persons age 55 or older; and (3) the complex publishes and adheres to policies demonstrating an intent to provide housing for persons 55 or over. On December 28, 1995 Congress eliminated the significant facilities and services requirement and added the requirement that the housing facility comply with HUD rules and regulations for verification of occupancy. The defendant must meet all the requirements and bears the burden of proof. Here the association failed to show that since 1985, 80 percent of the dwellings have had at least one person 55 years of age or older in residence. Moreover, it conceded that it does not publish and adhere to policies or procedures demonstrating an intent to provide housing for such persons. The FHA provides that if a defendant has engaged in a discriminatory housing practice, the court may award plaintiff actual and punitive damages as the court deems appropriate and a permanent or temporary injunction. The court agrees with plaintiffs that the covenant had a negative effect on the value of their property, but not in the amount of $30,000 as claimed by plaintiff's expert. The Simovits (P) are entitled to the difference between the amount at which they sold their property and what they could have reasonably realized but for the covenant. They are also entitled to the sum they incurred as a result of additional mortgage obligations created by the delay in selling the condominium on account of the covenant. Section 3613(c)(1) also provides for an award of punitive damages where a defendant shows a reckless disregard for the plaintiff's rights. The record here demonstrates an overwhelming disregard for the plaintiff's rights. A $10,000 award constitutes reasonable punitive damages in this case. Last, section 3613(c)(1) also authorizes the court to order injunctive relief. The testimony shows that the association had no intention of discontinuing the enforcement of the covenant unless enjoined. The association is liable for discrimination on the basis of familial status under the FHA.

EDITOR'S ANALYSIS: The threshold issue in this case was whether the Simovits (P) lacked standing because they themselves were not the victims of discrimination on the basis of familial status. The court determined that the Simovits (P) satisfied the statute's permissive standing requirements on account of the financial losses incurred as a result of the covenant's enforcement.

QUICKNOTES

HUD - Federal agency: Department of Housing and Urban Development

NEGATIVE COVENANT - A written promise to refrain from doing a particular activity.

SMITH v. FAIR EMPLOYMENT AND HOUSING COMMISSION
Landlord (D) v. Government Agency (P)
Ca. Sup. Ct., 913 P.2d 909 (1996).

NATURE OF CASE: Complaints alleging violation of federal law.

FACT SUMMARY: An unmarried couple filed complaints with the California Fair Employment and Housing (FEHC) against Smith, the owner of a rental building, for her refusal to lease them an apartment on the basis that they were unmarried.

CONCISE RULE OF LAW: The right to free exercise does not relieve an individual of the obligation to comply with a valid and neutral law of general applicability on the ground that the law proscribes (or prescribes) conduct that the religion either proscribes or prescribes.

FACTS: Smith owns and leases four rental units. She is a Christian who refused to rent to unmarried couples. When Randall and Phillips inquired about leasing an apartment, she told them she did not rent to unmarried couples and asked if they were married. They lied and when they later disclosed the truth, Smith stated that she could not rent to them and returned their deposit. The couple filed complaints with the FEHC and the commission issued a decision in favor of the couple. Smith sought review of the commission's decision. The court of appeal reversed.

ISSUE: Does the right to free exercise relieve an individual of the obligation to comply with a valid and neutral law of general applicability on the ground that the law proscribes (or prescribes) conduct that the religion either proscribes or prescribes?

HOLDING AND DECISION: (Werdegar, J.) No. The right to free exercise does not relieve an individual of the obligation to comply with a valid and neutral law of general applicability on the ground that the law proscribes (or prescribes) conduct that the religion either proscribes or prescribes. Smith argued that the statutory ban on marital status discrimination does not include unmarried cohabiting couples. This argument lacks merit. The usual and ordinary meaning of the term means that a landlord may not ask a couple whether they are married or refuse to rent to them because they are unmarried. The FEHC has interpreted Government Code § 12955 as protecting unmarried couples since its enactment in 1980. While responsibility for interpreting statutes lies with the court, a commission's interpretation of the law is entitled to consideration since the agency is charged with the statute's administration. Nothing in the legislative history contradicts the established interpretation. Having concluded that Smith violated the FEHA it must next be determined whether the state is required to exempt her from that law to avoid burdening her exercise of religious freedom. The Supreme Court of Alaska has rejected such an exemption. Such a claim must be considered under three areas of law: the First Amendment, the Religious Freedom Restoration Act (RFRA), and Article I, section 4 of the California Constitution. The First Amendment does not support Smith's claim. The right to free exercise does not relieve an individual of the obligation to comply with a valid and neutral law of general applicability on the ground that the law proscribes (or prescribes) conduct that the religion either proscribes or prescribes. The statutory prohibition against discrimination on the basis of marital status is such a law. It is generally applicable in that it prohibits discrimination without respect to motivation and neutral in that its object is to prohibit discrimination irrespective of reason. RFRA provides that the government shall not substantially burden a person's exercise of religion even if the burden results from a rule of general applicability, except where the government demonstrates that such application of the burden is in furtherance of a compelling government interest and is the least restrictive means of furthering that interest. Read together, RFRA, the decisions interpreting RFRA, and the decisions interpreting free exercise prior to Employment Division v. Smith require the following analysis for cases in which a neutral, generally applicable law is claimed to burden the exercise of religion: (1) the burden must fall on a religious belief rather than on a philosophy or way of life; (2) the burdened belief must be sincere; (3) the plaintiff must show the burden is substantial; and (4) if all the above are true, the government must demonstrate the application of the burden to the person furthers a compelling governmental interest and is the least restrictive means of furthering that interest. The religious practice burdened here is not the renting of apartments, but Smith's practice of not committing the sin she believes inheres in renting to unmarried cohabitants. The fact that the burden is indirect is irrelevant; such is the case with most laws of general applicability. The fact that Smith's beliefs are religious and sincere is not in question. The parties disagree with respect to whether section 12955 substantially burdens Smith's exercise of religion by forbidding her to discriminate against unmarried cohabitants. Under RFRA, unless the challenged law imposes a substantial burden, the government need not demonstrate a compelling interest or show that it is the least restrictive means of furthering that interest. Several factors are to be considered in deciding whether a burden is substantial: (1) whether one can avoid it without violating his beliefs; (2) whether it can be described as simply making religious exercise more expensive; and (3) whether the granting of an accommodation would detrimentally affect the rights of third parties. Smith's (D) religion does not require her to rent

Continued on next page.

apartments, nor is investment in rental apartments her only available means of income. She can avoid the burden on her religious exercise without violating her beliefs or threatening her income source. The burden here is not a law directed against religious exercise, but a generally applicable law that makes such exercise more expensive. Last, to grant the accommodation would impair the rights of third parties wishing to rent such apartment units. Last, California courts have construed article 1, section 4 as affording the same protection for religious exercise as the federal constitution. Affirmed in part, reversed in part.

EDITOR'S ANALYSIS: Prior to RFRA, under Employment Division v. Smith courts took a case-by-case approach as to what constituted a substantial burden and failed to provide a generally applicable definition. In Sherbert v. Verner, the court first held that unemployment compensation benefits could not be denied to a person who quit a job for religious reasons. The court stated the general rule what "where the state conditions receipt of an important benefit upon conduct proscribed by a religious faith, or where it denies such benefit because of conduct mandated by religious belief, thereby putting substantial pressure on an adherent to modify his behavior and to violate his beliefs, a burden upon religion exists." The court distinguished the present matter from unemployment-compensation cases generally in that the landlord here could avoid the conflict without threat to her livelihood and that in granting the landlord an accommodation would infringe upon the rights of third parties.

NOTES:

HUBERT v. WILLIAMS
Lessee (P) v. Lessor(D)
Cal. App. Dept. Super. Ct. (1982).

NATURE OF CASE: Appeal from dismissal of action alleging housing discrimination.

FACT SUMMARY: When Hubert (P) alleged that his landlord Williams (D) discriminated against him and his lesbian attendant, the trial court granted Williams' (D) demurrer.

CONCISE RULE OF LAW: Homosexuals are protected from arbitrary discrimination in rental housing by the Unruh Civil Rights Act.

FACTS: Hubert (P) was a quadriplegic who had hired a lesbian to be his attendant. When his landlord Williams (D) evicted them from his apartment, Hubert (P) filed suit, claiming that Williams (D) had violated state law by discriminating against homosexuals. The trial court granted Williams' (D) demurrer and Hubert (P) appealed.

ISSUE: Are homosexuals protected from arbitrary discrimination in rental housing by the Unruh Civil Rights Act?

HOLDING AND DECISION: (Bernstein, J.) Yes. Homosexuals are protected from arbitrary discrimination in rental housing by the Unruh Civil Rights Act. Homosexuals are a class protected under the Act. Landlords may not refuse to rent an apartment solely because of a person's sexual preference. Reversed and remanded.

EDITOR'S ANALYSIS: The court here extended the protection of the Unruh Act, California's Civil Rights Act, to homosexuals as a group. The court relied on precedent holding that landlords may not refuse to rent to families solely because the family includes minor children. The Unruh Act prohibits all forms of discrimination by business establishments. The term "business establishment" has been construed to include rental housing.

QUICKNOTES
UNRUH CIVIL RIGHTS ACT - Cal. Civil. Code § 51, 52. - prohibits discrimination by all business establishments.

11

CHAPTER 11
NUISANCE

QUICK REFERENCE RULES OF LAW

1. **Nuisance:** *Sic Utere Tuo Ut Alienum Non Laedas.* A nuisance is a condition that materially interferes with the enjoyment of another's premises or materially impairs their use by people of ordinary sensibilities. (Clark v. Wambold)

2. **Nuisance:** *Sic Utere Tuo Ut Alienum Non Laedas.* Detriment to health need not be proved to show a private nuisance. (Mitchell v. Hines)

3. **Nuisance:** *Sic Utere Tuo Ut Alienum Non Laedas.* Although the rule in New York is that a nuisance will be enjoined even when there is a marked disparity shown in economic consequence between the effect of the injunction and the effect of the nuisance, an injunction should not be applied if the result is to close down a plant. Permanent damages may be awarded as an alternative. (Boomer v. Atlantic Cement Co.)

4. **Nuisance:** *Sic Utere Tuo Ut Alienum Non Laedas.* Although the operation of a business, lawful in the first instance, which becomes a nuisance by reason of a nearby residential area, may be enjoined in an action brought by the developer of the residential area, the developer must indemnify the business for a reasonable amount of the cost of moving or shutting down. (Spur Industries, Inc. v. Del E. Webb Development Co.)

5. **Nuisance:** *Sic Utere Tuo Ut Alienum Non Laedas.* An action brought by a landowner claiming unreasonable obstruction of his access to sunlight is maintainable under private nuisance law. (Prah v. Maretti)

6. **Nuisance:** *Sic Utere Tuo Ut Alienum Non Laedas.* (1) Property owners state a claim for either public or private nuisance that will support an injunction where they allege that they are routinely subjected to adult nudity and sexual activity on defendant's land and that defendant knows about such activity by third parties and fails to exercise reasonable care to prevent it. (2) A government agency has discretionary immunity from liability for monetary damages for its actions or inactions in abating a nuisance where its response in whether or how to deal with the nuisance is discretionary. (3) A claim of inverse condemnation based on failure to abate a nuisance cannot be sustained where the nuisance does not deprive a plaintiff of all feasible private uses of his property or render the property valueless. (Mark v. State Department of Fish and Wildlife)

CLARK v. WAMBOLD
Neighbor (P) v. Pig farmer (D)
Wis. Sup. Ct., 165 Wis. 70, 160 N.W. 1039 (1917).

NATURE OF CASE: Appeal from dismissal of complaint for nuisance.

FACT SUMMARY: The trial court found that Wambold's (D) pigpens were reasonably clean and did not constitute a nuisance.

CONCISE RULE OF LAW: A nuisance is a condition that materially interferes with the enjoyment of another's premises or materially impairs their use by people of ordinary sensibilities.

FACTS: Clark (P) alleged that his use of a lakeside summer residence was impaired because his neighbor Wambold (D) had a pig farm and the odors interfered with Clark's (P) enjoyment of his property. When Clark's (P) action for nuisance was dimissed by the trial court, he appealed.

ISSUE: Is a nuisance a condition that materially interferes with the enjoyment of another's premises or materially impairs their use by people of ordinary sensibilities?

HOLDING AND DECISION: (Winslow, C.J.) Yes. A nuisance is a condition that materially interferes with the enjoyment of another's premises or materially impairs their use by people of ordinary sensibilities. In this case Wambold (D) maintained his pig pens in a reasonably clean condition and his use of his land was lawful and reasonable. The odors did not materially interfere with Clark's (P) enjoyment of his neighboring property. In the spirit of good neighborliness, however, it would be a good idea and would not be very difficult for Wambold (D) to move some of his pig pens to another part of his land to avoid causing discomfort to his neighbor Clark (P). Affirmed.

EDITOR'S ANALYSIS: The court here added a short homily to its holding affirming dismissal of the case. It gently chided the defendant for not trying to get along with his neighbor. The court said that the golden rule could be applied in this case to avoid further bad feelings between the neighbors.

QUICKNOTES
NUISANCE - An unlawful use of property that interferes with the lawful use of another's property.

MITCHELL v. HINES
Neighbors (P) v. Pig farmer (D)
Mich. Sup. Ct., 305 Mich. 296, 9 N.W.2d 547 (1943).

NATURE OF CASE: Appeal from injunction against nuisance.

FACT SUMMARY: The trial court enjoined Hines (D) from operating a large-scale piggery next to a residential area.

CONCISE RULE OF LAW: Detriment to health need not be proved to show a private nuisance.

FACTS: Mitchell and others (P) alleged that Hines' (D) piggery had become a nuisance because it had grown in size and the odors coming from the garbage the pigs fed on diminished the property value and enjoyment of their residences. The court issued an injunction against Hines' (D) use of the land as a piggery and Hines (D) appealed.

ISSUE: Must detriment to health be proved to show a private nuisance?

HOLDING AND DECISION: (North, J.) No. Detriment to health need not be proved to show a private nuisance. The increased size of the piggery and the condition of the fields through the continued dumping of garbage created such foul odors that this nuisance suit resulted. Tests did not show any satisfactory means of carrying on a large-scale, garbage-feeding piggery without causing a nuisance. Affirmed.

EDITOR'S ANALYSIS: The court noted that courts hesitate to bar the operation of a lawful business. But in this case the odors were unbearable and there was no other way to raise pigs. So the injunction was affirmed.

QUICKNOTES
INJUNCTION - A court order requiring a person to do or prohibiting that person from doing a specific act.

PRIVATE NUISANCE - An unlawful use of property interfering with the enjoyment of the private rights of an individual or a small number of persons.

BOOMER v. ATLANTIC CEMENT CO.
Land owners (P) v. Cement plant (D)
N.Y. Ct. of App., 26 N.Y.2d 219, 257 N.E.2d 870, 309 N.Y.S.2d 312 (1970).

NATURE OF CASE: Action to enjoin maintenance of nuisance and for damages.

FACT SUMMARY: Trial court refused to issue an injunction which would close down a large cement plant, but awarded temporary damages instead.

CONCISE RULE OF LAW: Although the rule in New York is that a nuisance will be enjoined even when there is a marked disparity shown in economic consequence between the effect of the injunction and the effect of the nuisance, an injunction should not be applied if the result is to close down a plant. Permanent damages may be awarded as an alternative.

FACTS: A group of land owners (P), complaining of injury to their property from dirt, smoke, and vibration emanating from a neighboring cement plant (D), brought an action to enjoin the continued operation of the plant and for damages. The trial court held that the plant constituted a nuisance, found substantial damage but, because an injunction would shut down the plant's operation, refused to issue one. Temporary damages were awarded the group of land owners (P) instead.

ISSUE: Where the issuance of an injunction to enjoin the maintenance of a business would shut down a business, may permanent damages be issued as an alternative?

HOLDING AND DECISION: (Bergan, J.) Yes. Damages may be awarded as an alternative to an injunction in nuisance cases. Another alternative would be to grant the injunction but postpone its effect to a specified future date to give opportunity for technical advances to permit the company (D) to eliminate the nuisance. However, there is no assurance that any significant technical improvement would occur. Moreover, the problem is universal, and can only be solved by an industry-wide effort. Permanent damages would themselves be a spur to conduct more research. Future owners of this land would not be able to recover additional damages, since the award is to the land. Reversed.

DISSENT: (Jasen, J.) The majority approach is licensing a continuing wrong. Furthermore, permanent damages alleviate the need for more research, and decrease incentive.

EDITOR'S ANALYSIS: The reasoning advanced here has been carried one step further by other courts. In *Pennsylvania Coal Co. v. Sanderson*, 113 Pa. St. 126, 6 A. 453 (1886), a suit for damages was frowned upon by the Supreme Court which said, "To encourage the development of the great natural resources of a country, trifling inconveniences to particular persons must sometimes give way to the necessities of a great community."

QUICKNOTES
NUISANCE - An unlawful use of property that interferes with the lawful use of another's property.

NOTES:

SPUR INDUSTRIES, INC. v. DEL E. WEBB DEVELOPMENT
Feedlot operator (D) v. Developer (P)
Ariz. Sup. Ct., 108 Ariz. 178, 494 P.2d. 700 (1972).

NATURE OF CASE: Action by developer to enjoin operation of a business as a public nuisance.

FACT SUMMARY: Del Webb (P), developer of Sun City, a residential community which sprang up in a rural area near Spur's (D) cattle feedlot, sought an injunction against Spur (D) on the ground that as a breeder of flies the feedlot constituted a public nuisance.

CONCISE RULE OF LAW: Although the operation of a business, lawful in the first instance, which becomes a nuisance by reason of a nearby residential area, may be enjoined in an action brought by the developer of the residential area, the developer must indemnify the business for a reasonable amount of the cost of moving or shutting down.

FACTS: Spur Industries, Inc. (D) maintained a cattle feedlot in an area which had long been devoted to farming. Del Webb (P) began to develop Sun City, a retirement community, originally some distance from Spur (D). However, the development progressed rapidly and expanded, coming within 500 feet of Spur (D). Complaining that the Spur (D) feeding operation was a public nuisance because of the flies and the odor which were being blown over Sun City, Del Webb (P) sought a permanent injunction against Spur's (D) continued operations. State law defined a public nuisance as including "any condition or place in populous areas which constitutes a breeding place" for disease-carrying "flies, rodents, mosquitos, and other insects..." The trial court, finding that some of the citizens of Sun City were unable to enjoy the outdoor living which Del Webb (P) had advertised, and that prospective purchasers were being discouraged, issued the injunction, but denied any compensatory relief for Spur (D) who appealed.

ISSUE: (1) May a residential tract bring an action to abate a business as a public nuisance if the business was in the area first? (2) If an injunction is issued, must the developer of the tract indemnify the business?

HOLDING AND DECISION: [Judge not stated in casebook excerpt.] (1) Yes. Under the doctrine of "coming to the nuisance," courts of equity held that a residential landowner may not have relief if he knowingly came into a neighborhood reserved for industrial or agricultural endeavors and has been damaged thereby. The reasoning behind this rule is that a party cannot justly call upon the law to make the place suitable for his residence which was not so when he selected it. However, under our state statute, a business which is not per se a public nuisance may become such by being carried on at a place where the health, comfort, or convenience of a populous neighborhood is affected. Were Del Webb (P) the only injured party, "coming to the nuisance" would be a bar to the relief sought by it. However, since the residents of Sun City are being injured as well, Spur (D) must move, not because of any wrongdoing on its part, but because of the court's concern for the health and safety of the public. (2) Yes. It does not seem harsh to require a developer, who has taken advantage of the lesser land values in a rural area, as well as the availability of large tracts of land on which to build and develop a new town or city in the area, to indemnify those who are forced to leave as a result. Del Webb (P) must therefore compensate Spur (D) for a reasonable amount of the cost of moving or shutting down. Affirmed in part, reversed in part. Remanded.

EDITOR'S ANALYSIS: Most courts have held that ordinarily plaintiff who purchases land next to a nuisance is not barred from bringing an action by the "coming to the nuisance" doctrine. However, where the equities between the two parties are fairly evenly balanced, the doctrine may be invoked and given controlling weight. The instant case perhaps represents a new trend in balancing the equities by looking to the compensation accorded the defendant were the plaintiff to prevail, and discarding the "coming to the nuisance" doctrine. Note, however, that "public nuisance" is specifically defined by statute in Arizona.

QUICKNOTES
INDEMNIFY - Securing against potential injury; compensation for injury suffered.

NOTES:

PRAH v. MARETTI
Neighbor (P) v. Neighbor (D)
Wisc. Sup. Ct., 108 Wis.2d 223, 321 N.W.2d 182 (1982).

NATURE OF CASE: Action to enjoin construction of a residence and seeking damages.

FACT SUMMARY: Plaintiff, owner of a solar-heated residence, brought suit against his neighbor, claiming that his proposed construction of a residence interfered with his access to an unobstructed path for sunlight across the neighbor's property, seeking injunctive relief and damages.

CONCISE RULE OF LAW: An action brought by a landowner claiming unreasonable obstruction of his access to sunlight is maintainable under private nuisance law.

FACTS: Plaintiff, owner of a solar-heated residence, brought suit against his neighbor (D), claiming that defendant's proposed construction of a residence interfered with his access to an unobstructed path for sunlight across the neighbor's property, seeking injunctive relief and damages. The circuit court denied plaintiff's motion for injunctive relief and entered summary judgment in favor of defendant.

ISSUE: Is an action brought by a landowner claiming unreasonable obstruction of his access to sunlight maintainable under private nuisance law?

HOLDING AND DECISION: (Abrahamson, J.) Yes. An action brought by a landowner claiming unreasonable obstruction of his access to sunlight is maintainable under private nuisance law. First it must be determined whether the complaint states a claim for relief based on common law private nuisance. When a landowner's use of his or her property unreasonably interferes with another's enjoyment of his or her property, such use constitutes a private nuisance. The Restatement (Second) of Torts § 821D defines private nuisance as "a nontrespassory invasion of another's interest in the private use and enjoyment of land." Although defendant's obstruction of plaintiff's access to sunlight appears to fall within this definition, defendant claims he has a right to develop his property in accordance with statutes, ordinances and covenants without regard to whether he blocks his neighbor's access to sunlight. While courts have declined to recognize easements to light and air across adjacent property, many jurisdictions protect landowners from malicious obstructions of access to light under the common law private nuisance doctrine. This jurisdiction has recognized "spite fences" as an actionable private nuisance. The policy considerations which limited broader protection for a landowner's access to sunlight are now obsolete. Thus, recognition of a nuisance claim for unreasonable obstruction of access to sunlight will not prevent land development or unduly hinder the use of adjoining land. The dispositive question is whether the conduct complained of is unreasonable. Here the plaintiff has stated a claim for relief. Reversed and remanded.

DISSENT: (Callow, J.) A landowner has the right to use his property within the limits of ordinances, statutes and restrictions of record. The facts of this case do not give rise to a cause of action for private nuisance.

EDITOR'S ANALYSIS: American courts have not been as receptive as English courts in recognizing a landowner's right to access of sunlight. At English common law, a landowner could acquire such right through express agreement or the doctrine of "ancient lights." The doctrine of ancient lights permitted a landowner to continue to receive unobstructed access to sunlight across adjacent property, if the landowner had previously received such sunlight for a prescribed time period. While American courts honor express easements for access to sunlight, they will not find that such easements are created or acquired by prescription or implication.

QUICKNOTES
MALICE - The intention to commit an unlawful act without justification or excuse.

PRIVATE NUISANCE - An unlawful use of property interfering with the enjoyment of the private rights of an individual or a small number of persons.

NOTES:

MARK v. STATE DEPARTMENT OF FISH AND WILDLIFE

Property owners (P) v. State agency (D)

Ore. Ct. App., 974 P.2d 716 (1999).

NATURE OF CASE: Appeal from dismissal for failure to state a claim in an action for nuisance and an injunction.

FACT SUMMARY: Mark (plaintiffs) (P) asserted that public nudity occurring on a state wildlife preserve (D) adjacent to their property was a public and private nuisance and sought damages as well as an injunction against the nudity.

CONCISE RULE OF LAW: (1) Property owners state a claim for either public or private nuisance that will support an injunction where they allege that they are routinely subjected to adult nudity and sexual activity on defendant's land and that defendant knows about such activity by third parties and fails to exercise reasonable care to prevent it. (2) A government agency has discretionary immunity from liability for monetary damages for its actions or inactions in abating a nuisance where its response in whether and how to deal with the nuisance is discretionary. (3) A claim of inverse condemnation based on failure to abate a nuisance cannot be sustained where the nuisance does not deprive a plaintiff of all feasible private uses of his property or render the property valueless.

FACTS: Mark (plaintiffs) (P) owned and lived on property surrounded by a state wildlife preserve. The portion of the wildlife area near where they lived—a public beach on a river—was a popular location for extensive public nudity. They also contended that users of the wildlife area paraded naked throughout the year all over the wildlife area, including the roads and bushes, and on, around, and in view of plaintiffs' and others' private residences. They claimed they and their families and guests, and visitors to the area, were forced to witness repeated instances of adult nudity and repeated acts of sexuality, depravity, illegality and lewdness, and that they could not enjoy the full use of their property out of reluctance to expose themselves to such conditions, and because they feared for their safety due to their proximity to the nude beach activities. Plaintiffs (P) brought suit asserting that the nudity constituted a private and public nuisance, and sought to enjoin the state, through its Division of State Lands and Department of Fish and Wildlife (D), from allowing public nudity in the wildlife area. They also sought compensation for the effects of the nudity on their land, and asserted inverse condemnation for the significantly lowered value of their property. They argued that defendant, to whom they repeatedly complained about the nudity and other conditions on the wildlife area, had a duty and authority to control the activities of the public in the wildlife area so as not to constitute a nuisance, but failed to do so, and that defendant was not even adequately implementing a management plan for controlling this problem. The trial court dismissed the complaint for failure to state a claim.

In particular, the trial court dismissed the nuisance claims on the ground that defendant's actions came within the discretionary function exception to a public body's liability in tort. After the trial court's decision, the state supreme court held that such an exception did not apply to claims for an injunction because such an action does not involve potential monetary liability. The court of appeals granted review.

ISSUE: (1) Do property owners state a claim for either public or private nuisance that will support an injunction where they allege that they are routinely subjected to adult nudity and sexual activity on defendant's land and that defendant knows about such activity by third parties and fails to exercise reasonable care to prevent it? (2) Does a government agency have discretionary immunity from liability for monetary damages for its actions or inactions in abating a nuisance where its response in whether and how to deal with the nuisance is discretionary? (3) Can a claim of inverse condemnation based on failure to abate a nuisance be sustained where the nuisance does not deprive a plaintiff of all feasible private uses of his property or render the property valueless?

HOLDING AND DECISION: (Warren, P.J.) (1) Yes. Property owners state a claim for either public or private nuisance that will support an injunction where they allege that they are routinely subjected to adult nudity and sexual activity on defendant's land and that defendant knows about such activity by third parties and fails to exercise reasonable care to prevent it. A public nuisance is the invasion of a right that is common to all members of the public. Because the primary responsibility for preventing public nuisances is with the public authorities, a private action against a public nuisance must prove that the plaintiff suffered an injury distinct from the injury that the public as a whole has suffered. A private nuisance is an unreasonable non-tresspassory interference with another's private use and enjoyment of land. The right to recover is in the person whose land is harmed. Undesired exposure to sexual activity is a traditional ground for finding either a public or private nuisance. However, there is no precedent that nudity in itself, with no clear sexual component, constitutes a nuisance. Public nudity is not illegal unless it occurs with the intent to arouse sexual desire. But merely because an activity is otherwise legal, does not mean that it does not constitute a nuisance. The question is a factual one as to the effect the activity has on an ordinary person. Here, plaintiffs' allegations support a finding that the nudity constitutes a nuisance. Because plaintiffs also claim they have been exposed to sexual activity, they make

Continued on next page.

out a claim for public nuisance. Because of the proximity of their land to the intrusive nudity and sexual activity, those things have affected their property or their enjoyment of it, and therefore, their injury is different in kind from that of the public at large, so that they may sue for enjoinment of such activity. The same facts would also support a finding that the intrusive activity impaired plaintiffs' use and enjoyment of their land, which would constitute a private nuisance for which they could seek damages or an injunction. Nonetheless, the analysis does not stop there. The question becomes whether a court can hold defendants responsible for the acts of third parties when those third parties' actions on defendant's land may constitute a nuisance. Under the Restatement (Second) of Torts § 838 (1979), which is followed in this state, to be liable for the acts of third parties that create a nuisance on their land, defendant must both (1) know that the activity is being carried on and will involve an unreasonable risk of causing the nuisance, and (2) must consent to the activity or fail to exercise reasonable care to prevent it. Here, defendant has authority to control the behavior of members of the public who congregate in the wildlife area and has failed to do so, and has even failed to adequately implement a management plan intended to control the activity complained of so that it will not rise to the level of a nuisance. Therefore, plaintiffs have stated claims for private and public nuisance and may pursue their injunction claims. (2) Yes. A government agency has discretionary immunity from liability for monetary damages for its actions or inactions in abating a nuisance where its response in whether and how to deal with the nuisance is discretionary. Defendant has discretionary immunity from damages because its actions or inactions are not required by statute, and whether to adopt rules dealing specifically with nudity require the exercise of independent policy judgment, and discretion about whether to regulate nudity and, if so, how to regulate it. The trial court correctly dismissed plaintiffs' claims to the extent they sought monetary damages. (3) No. A claim of inverse condemnation based on failure to abate a nuisance cannot be sustained where the nuisance does not deprive a plaintiff of all feasible private uses of his property or render the property valueless. The issue is whether, as a matter of fact, the governmental activity has resulted "in so substantial an interference with use and enjoyment of one's land as to amount to a taking of private property for public use." A nuisance would have to be so aggravated as to amount to a complete ouster or deprivation of the beneficial use of property. Here, the nudity did not deprive plaintiffs of all feasible private uses of their property. Their land is not unusable. Although the property has allegedly lost value, it is not alleged that it is valueless. Because plaintiffs are currently using the property for a residence, they are necessarily receiving some economic benefit from it. Therefore, the trial court correctly dismissed their claims for inverse condemnation. Reversed and remanded.

DISSENT: (Edmonds, J.) I disagree. I would permit a damage claim for nuisance under the circumstances alleged.

EDITOR'S ANALYSIS: On remand, the trial court ruled that the presence of nudity on the public beach and the Department of Fish and Wildlife's (D) failure to regulate or exercise control over that use constituted a private nuisance, and, accordingly, issued an injunction that required the Department (D) to abate the nuisance. This decision was affirmed on appeal.

NOTES:

12

CHAPTER 12
SERVITUDES AND COMMON INTEREST COMMUNITIES

QUICK REFERENCE RULES OF LAW

1. **Easement or Fee?** A deed that conveys a right-of-way and land, the purpose of which is specified in the deed, conveys an easement only. (Brown v. The Penn Central Corporation)

2. **Easement or License?** (1) A warranty deed that uses the word "grant" and specific words of inheritance, and that does not withhold rights of revocation, creates an easement rather than a license. (2) A condition subsequent is not created unless an intention to create such a condition is clearly expressed. (Stratis v. Doyle)

3. **Easement or License?** (1) Regardless of the designation of a document, a document purporting to create an easement that is executed by holders of only an equitable interest in property, for nominal consideration, for a limited purpose, that does not use words of succession and that does not specify the duration of the privilege, creates only a license. (2) A permissive use under a revocable license does not become hostile by a mere transfer or conveyance of the licensor's interest in the land. (3) A license does not become irrevocable by estoppel where consideration paid for the license is nominal and sums expended on the use do not exceed the value received from the use. (Cooper v. Boise Church of Christ)

4. **Creation by Estoppel.** When a licensee makes valuable improvements on the basis of a promise, the licensor will not be permitted to revoke the license. (Mund v. English)

5. **Implied on the Basis of Prior Use.** Whether there is an implied easement on certain property will be inferred from the intentions of the parties, and such inference will be drawn from the circumstances under which the conveyance was made. Parties to a conveyance will be assumed to know and to contemplate the continuance of reasonably necessary uses which have so altered the premises as to make them apparent upon reasonably prudent investigation. (Van Sandt v. Royster)

6. **Implied on the Basis of Necessity.** An easement by strict necessity should benefit the dominant estate for any lawful and reasonable use. (Morrell v. Rice)

7. **Creation by Prescription.** An easement by prescription is created by a use that is made pursuant to the terms of an intended but imperfectly created servitude. (Paxson v. Glovitz)

8. **Creation by Dedication, Condemnation, and Other Forced Sales.** Courts will not enjoin truly minimal encroachments. (Goulding v. Cook)

9. **Creating Easements for Third Parties.** A grantor cannot create an easement over land that he does not own. (Estate of Thomson v. Wade)

10. **Location, Relocation, and Use of Easements.** An easement may not be relocated on the application of the owner of the servient estate. (Davis v. Bruk)

11. **Location, Relocation, and Use of Easements.** In the absence of an intent otherwise, a landowner can relocate a right of way easement so long as he bears the expense of the relocation and the change does not frustrate the parties' intent or purpose in creating the right of way or significantly lessen its utility. (Lewis v. Young)

12. **Use of Easement for Non-Dominant Land.** If an easement is appurtenant to a particular parcel of land, any extension thereof to other parcels is a misuse of the easement. (Brown v. Voss)

25. **Design Controls.** Restrictive covenants requiring approval by an architectural committee are enforceable so long as the committee's decision is not arbitrary or capricious. (Rhue v. Cheyenne Homes, Inc.)

26. **Covenants Restricting Household Occupants and Personal Freedoms.** Common interest development use restrictions contained in a project's recorded declaration are enforceable unless unreasonable. (Nahrstedt v. Lakeside Village Condominium Ass'n, Inc.)

27. **Changed Conditions.** Restrictive covenants may not be removed on the application of the developer, where purchasers have relied on the restrictions, and where there is no change in the character of the neighborhood. (Rick v. West)

28. **Amendment.** (1) A modification clause of a subdivision's covenants that permits changes or modifications to the covenants permits the addition of an entirely new covenant where the effect of the new covenant is not unreasonable or unduly burdensome on the lot owners. (2) Even in the absence of an express covenant mandating payment of assessments, a homeowners association that is a common interest community has the implied power to levy assessments against lot owners in a subdivision to raise the funds necessary to maintain the common areas of the subdivision. (Evergreen Highlands Association v. West)

29. **Termination.** A county that acquires title in a tax foreclosure sale takes title subject to servitudes. (Westwood Homeowners Ass'n v. Lane County)

BROWN v. THE PENN CENTRAL CORPORATION

Property owners (P) v. Railroad (D)

Ind. Sup. Ct., 510 N.E.2d 641 (1987).

NATURE OF CASE: Appeal from affirmance of judgment in quiet title action holding that land was vested in defendant in fee simple.

FACT SUMMARY: Penn Central Corporation (Penn Central) (D) was a successor to railroads that were deeded a railroad right-of-way and land for depot and railroad purposes. Penn Central (D) abandoned the right-of-way, and property owners (P) of land contiguous to the right-of-way and to the depot and railroad property brought suit to quiet title in these lands in themselves.

CONCISE RULE OF LAW: A deed that conveys a right-of-way and land, the purpose of which is specified in the deed, conveys an easement only.

FACTS: Penn Central Corporation (Penn Central) (D) was a successor to several railroads. A deed to these railroads conveyed a right-of-way and land for "Depot and Rail Road purposes." The deed was a form prepared by the railroads for use in acquiring right-of-ways, and the description of the land to be used was handwritten, whereas the remainder of the deed was preprinted. Penn Central (D) abandoned its right-of-way, but continued to collect rent from tenants on the depot and railroad property. Property owners (P) of land contiguous to the right-of-way and to the depot and railroad property brought suit to quiet title in these lands in themselves. The trial court held that the railroad had received nothing more than an easement in the right-of-way, but had received the depot and railroad property in fee simple. The court of appeals affirmed, and the state's supreme court granted review.

ISSUE: Does a deed that conveys a right-of-way and land, the purpose of which is specified in the deed, convey an easement only?

HOLDING AND DECISION: (Pivarnik, J.) Yes. A deed that conveys a right-of-way and land, the purpose of which is specified in the deed, conveys an easement only. The resolution of this case turns on deed construction, the aim of which is to determine the intent of the parties. When a railroad prepares a conveyance form, it is responsible for the printed word, and so the deed here is construed in the light most favorable to the grantors. A deed that conveys a right generally conveys only an easement. The general rule is that a conveyance to a railroad of land, without additional language as to the use or purpose to which the land is to be put, or in other ways limiting the estate conveyed, is to be construed as passing an estate in fee. However, if such a conveyance contains a reference to a right-of-way, it is generally construed as conveying only an easement. Here, the deed had such additional language that indicated the purpose to which the land was to be put, and included reference to a right-of-way. Therefore, the deed falls within the general rule and must be construed as conveying only an easement in the depot and railroad property. The court of appeals was wrong when it found that the deed was ambiguous, and that the parties intended to create a hybrid deed that conveyed both a right-of-way and a fee in a separate strip of land. Rather the deed granted a right-of-way that included the strip of land for depot and railroad use. This conclusion is supported by the state's public policy in favor of finding easements as opposed to conveyances in fee simple. Accordingly, Penn Central's (D) right-of-way was an easement that was extinguished when it abandoned the right-of-way. Reversed.

EDITOR'S ANALYSIS: The issue of whether railroads were granted easements or conveyances in fee simple is not an academic one. As railroads have scaled back service and abandoned tracks all over the country, substantial litigation has ensued. Whereas many courts agree with the reasoning of the court in this case, some have found that notwithstanding the use of the words "right-of-way," deeds conveyed fee simple interests.

QUICKNOTES

EASEMENT - The right to utilize a portion of another's real property for a specific use.

FEE SIMPLE - An estate in land characterized by ownership of the entire property for an unlimited duration and by absolute power over distribution.

NOTES:

STRATIS v. DOYLE

Grantee's successor (P) v. Grantor (D)
N.Y. App. Div., 575 N.Y.S.2d 400 (1991).

NATURE OF CASE: Appeal from summary judgment for plaintiffs in action for interference with the use of a right-of-way.

FACT SUMMARY: Doyle (D) granted Abbatiello a right-of-way, and then sold some of the property over which the right-of-way was to run. Abbatiello's successors-in-interest, Stratis (P), claimed Doyle (D) improperly interfered with their use of the right-of-way.

CONCISE RULE OF LAW: (1) A warranty deed that uses the word "grant" and specific words of inheritance, and that does not withhold rights of revocation, creates an easement rather than a license. (2) A condition subsequent is not created unless an intention to create such a condition is clearly expressed.

FACTS: Doyle (D) granted in a warranty deed to Abbatiello a right-of-way across his property for the purpose of constructing a driveway. The deed also provided that Abbatiello agree to construct and maintain the driveway in a good, workmanlike manner. Then Doyle (D) sold some of the property over which the right-of-way was to run to Dennenbaum Thereafter, Stratis (P) obtained Abbatiello's property and commenced an action alleging that Doyle (D) improperly interfered with their use of the right-of-way they claimed to have obtained upon purchasing Abbatiello's property. Doyle (D) answered that the right-of-way was merely a license, and that, in any event, a condition subsequent requiring construction and maintenance of the driveway had failed, resulting in a forfeiture of the right-of-way. The trial court granted summary judgment for Stratis (P), and the appellate division granted review.

ISSUE: (1) Does a warranty deed that uses the word "grant" and specific words of inheritance, and that does not withhold rights of revocation, create an easement rather than a license? (2) Is a condition subsequent created if an intention to create such a condition is not clearly expressed?

HOLDING AND DECISION: (Mahoney, P.J.) (1) Yes. A warranty deed that uses the word "grant" and specific words of inheritance, and that does not withhold rights of revocation, creates an easement rather than a license. The interest here was created by a warranty deed, suggesting a transfer of an interest in real property. The use of the word "grant" suggests that an easement was intended. Specific words of inheritance are used, and no rights of revocation are withheld. Therefore, the grant created an easement rather than a license. (2) No. A condition subsequent is not created unless an intention to create such a condition is clearly expressed. Conditions subsequent are disfavored and are

not found to exist unless the intention to create them is clearly expressed. Here, nothing in the deed expresses such an intention. Also, Doyle (D) did not retain any expressed or implied reversionary interest or a right of reentry. Taking these facts together leads to the conclusion that the deed contains only a covenant requiring construction and maintenance of a driveway and not a condition subsequent.

EDITOR'S ANALYSIS: The difference between a covenant and a condition subsequent is that if a covenantor breaches a covenant, the covenantee is entitled to damages or injunctive relief. However, if a property owner breaches a condition subsequent, the property owner forfeits the property to the beneficiary of the condition—the person who holds the power of entry or power of termination. Here, there was no beneficiary with such power, a fact that added weight to the court's conclusion that the deed created a covenant.

QUICKNOTES

COVENANT - A written promise to do, or to refrain from doing, a particular activity.

EASEMENT - The right to utilize a portion of another's real property for a specific use.

LICENSE - A right that is granted to a person allowing him or her to conduct an activity that without such permission he or she could not lawfully do, and which is unassignable and revocable at the will of the licensor.

WARRANTY DEED - A deed that guarantees that the conveyor possesses the title that he purports to convey.

NOTES:

COOPER v. BOISE CHURCH OF CHRIST

Property owner (P) v. Grantee of right to use property (D)
Idaho Sup. Ct., 524 P.2d 173 (1974).

NATURE OF CASE: Appeal from judgment quieting title to property in plaintiff.

FACT SUMMARY: Cooper (P) claimed the Boise Church of Christ (the "church") (D) had no interest in property that she owned, and she sought to have the church remove its sign from the property.

CONCISE RULE OF LAW: (1) Regardless of the designation of a document, a document purporting to create an easement that is executed by holders of only an equitable interest in property, for nominal consideration, for a limited purpose, that does not use words of succession and that does not specify the duration of the privilege, creates only a license. (2) A permissive use under a revocable license does not become hostile by a mere transfer or conveyance of the licensor's interest in the land. (3) A license does not become irrevocable by estoppel where consideration paid for the license is nominal and sums expended on the use do not exceed the value received from the use.

FACTS: The Adams held an equitable interest in property, with a contract for the property held in escrow. In a document labeled "Electric Sign Easement" they purported to convey an easement to the Boise Church of Christ (the "church") (D) that would allow the church to erect a sign on the property. Pursuant to this grant, the church (D) erected a large electric sign on the property. Several years later, Cooper (P) became the record title owner of the property. She brought a quiet title action to compel the church (D) to remove the sign. The trial court held that the church (D) had no interest in the property and enjoined the church and its successors from claiming any interest in the property. The state's highest court granted review.

ISSUE: (1) Regardless of the designation of a document, does a document purporting to create an easement that is executed by holders of only an equitable interest in property, for nominal consideration, for a limited purpose, that does not use words of succession and that does not specify the duration of the privilege create only a license? (2) Does a permissive use under a revocable license become hostile by a mere transfer or conveyance of the licensor's interest in the land? (3) Does a license become irrevocable by estoppel where consideration paid for the license is nominal and sums expended on the use do not exceed the value received from the use?

HOLDING AND DECISION: (Shepard, C.J.) (1) Yes. Regardless of the designation of a document, a document purporting to create an easement that is executed by holders of only an equitable interest in property, for nominal consideration, for a limited

purpose, that does not use words of succession and that does not specify the duration of the privilege creates only a license. This issue is a mixed question of law and fact as to the extent of the interest conveyed by the Adamses. Here, the Adamses owned only an equitable interest in the property and therefore had no power to grant an easement binding on the conditional vendors. The consideration paid ($1) was nominal, and the right given was only for the limited purpose of advertising church services and the location of the church building. No words of succession were used, and the duration of the privilege was not specified. The document also did not guarantee non-default by the Adamses in performing their obligations before they could obtain record title. The church also did not assume any obligations to facilitate the Adamses' acquisition of record title. The dimensions of the sign was not specified, nor was there any obligation to maintain a clear space so the sign could be seen from the highway. Taking all these fact together, the trial court did not err in deciding that the parties intended to create only a license, regardless of the designation of the document. (2) No. A permissive use under a revocable license does not become hostile by a mere transfer or conveyance of the licensor's interest in the land. Here, the church (D) alternatively claims it acquired a permanent easement by prescription. A revocable license may continue by implication even after the transfer or conveyance of the licensor's interest in the land, where the new owner makes no objection to the use and the grantee's use is not inconsistent with the rights of the grantee or transferee. Here, there was no evidence that the church (D) changed its stance in the maintenance of the sign from a permissive to a hostile use. Therefore, the trial court correctly rejected the church's (D) claim of a prescriptive easement; the church (D) began and continued its maintenance of the sign under a license. (3) No. A license does not become irrevocable by estoppel where consideration paid for the license is nominal and sums expended on the use do not exceed the value received from the use. The church (D) contends that even if it had been granted only a license, that such license became irrevocable owing to the expenditures made by the church in erecting and maintaining the sign. However, no estoppel can arise where there is no injury. Here, the consideration paid ($1) was nominal, and from the time the sign was erected to the time Cooper (P) challenged its use, the church (D) spent less on the sign than the value it received from it. Therefore, Cooper (P) was not barred by the doctrine of equitable estoppel from quieting title to the property. Affirmed.

Continued on next page.

EDITOR'S ANALYSIS: Contrary to statements made by the court in this decision, licenses are often said to be revoked when the land is transferred. It is true, however, that the landowner is free to revoke the license at any time (absent an agreement to the contrary or estoppel), but, until the license is revoked, use by the licensee is permissive. And, as this case highlights, something more than a change of ownership is required to convert a permissive use to a hostile use.

QUICKNOTES

ESTOPPEL - An equitable doctrine precluding a party from asserting a right to the detriment of another who justifiably relied on the conduct.

LICENSE - A right that is granted to aperson allowing him or her to conduct an activity that without such permission he or she could not lawfully do, and which is unassignable and revocable at the will of the licensor.

PRESCRIPTIVE EASEMENT - A manner of acquiring an easement in another's property by continuous and uninterrupted use in satisfaction of the statutory requirements of adverse possession.

NOTES:

MUND v. ENGLISH
Children (P) v. Parent (D)
Or. Ct. App., 684 P.2d 1248 (1984).

NATURE OF CASE: Appeal from judgment for defendant in suit for declaratory judgment and specific performance.

FACT SUMMARY: Mund (P) claimed that English (D) had granted them a permanent and irrevocable license to use a well they had built together.

CONCISE RULE OF LAW: When a licensee makes valuable improvements on the basis of a promise, the licensor will not be permitted to revoke the license.

FACTS: Mund (P) and their mother, English (D), purchased adjoining land and drilled a well on English's (D) property. Pipes and equipment were installed so both parties received water from the one well. When disagreements arose as to rights to the well and water, Mund (P) sought declaratory judgment and specific performance. The court found for English (D) and Mund (P) appealed.

ISSUE: When a licensee makes valuable improvements on the basis of a promise, will the licensor be permitted to revoke the license?

HOLDING AND DECISION: (Rossman, J.) No. When a licensee makes valuable improvements on the basis of a promise, the licensor will not be permitted to revoke the license. An irrevocable license does not depend upon proof of the agreement of the parties, but arises by operation of law to prevent an injustice. Mund (P) obtained a loan and constructed a residence on the property, and the well on English's (D) property was the only source of domestic water. The improvements Mund (P) made clearly show their reliance on a permanent agreement. The law will not permit English to claim she can withdraw the license to use the well. Reversed and remanded.

EDITOR'S ANALYSIS: The court here did not require proof that the parties had agreed to an irrevocable license. Rather it relied on the equitable principle of quasi-contract. An implied-in-law contract is also referred to as a quasi-contract.

QUICKNOTES

DECLARATORY JUDGMENT - An adjudication by the courts which grants not relief but is binding over the legal status of the parties involved in the dispute.

LICENSE - A right that is granted to a person allowing him or her to conduct an activity that without such permission he or she could not lawfully do, and which is unassignable and revocable at the will of the licensor.

QUASI-CONTRACT - An implied contract created by law to prevent unjust enrichment.

SPECIFIC PERFORMANCE - An equitable remedy whereby the court requires the parties to perform their obligations pursuant to a contract.

NOTES:

VAN SANDT v. ROYSTER

Property owner (P) v. Grantees of right to use property (D)
Kan. Super. Ct., 83 P.2d 698 (1938).

NATURE OF CASE: Action to enjoin Royster (D) and Gray (D) from using an underground sewer drain across Van Sandt's (P) property.

FACT SUMMARY: Van Sandt (P) found his cellar flooded with sewage and discovered for the first time the existence of a sewer drain across his property. Royster (D) and Gray (D) refused to stop using the drain.

CONCISE RULE OF LAW: Whether there is an implied easement on certain property will be inferred from the intentions of the parties, and such inference will be drawn from the circumstances under which the conveyance was made. Parties to a conveyance will be assumed to know and to contemplate the continuance of reasonably necessary uses which have so altered the premises as to make them apparent upon reasonably prudent investigation.

FACTS: Bailey owned three adjoining lots numbered 4, 20, and 19. In 1904, a private lateral drain was built running from the house on Lot 4 across Lots 20 and 19. Bailey conveyed Lot 20 to Murphy by a general warranty deed without exceptions or reservations in 1904. Title passed to Royster (D). In 1904, Bailey also conveyed Lot 19 to Jones by a general warranty deed without exceptions or reservations. Jones conveyed part of Lot 19 to Reynolds, who in 1924 conveyed to Van Sandt (P). Gray (D) succeeded title to Lot 4. In 1936, Van Sandt (P) discovered his basement flooded with sewage and filth. Upon investigation, he discovered for the first time the existence of a sewer drain running on, across, and through his property. Royster (D) and Gray (D) refuse to stop using the sewer. Van Sandt (P) argues that no easement has been created on his land, and even assuming there was an easement created, he took the land free from the burden of the easement because he was a bona fide purchaser, without notice.

ISSUE: Can a purchaser be charged with notice of a prior necessary use so as to create an implied easement where the use was not visible, but a reasonable inspection would have made the use apparent?

HOLDING AND DECISION: (Allen, J.) Yes. When one utilizes part of his land for the benefit of another, a quasi easement exists. The part of the land being benefitted is referred to as the quasi dominant tenement, and the part being utilized is referred to as the *quasi servient* tenement. If the owner of land, one part of which is subject to a *quasi* easement, conveys the *quasi* dominant tenement, an easement corresponding to such *quasi* easement is vested in the grantee, provided such *quasi* easement is apparent and continuous. An implied easement, in favor of either the grantor or the grantee, arises as an inference of the intentions of the parties. This inference is drawn from the circumstances under which the conveyance is made. Factors to consider include whether the claimant is the grantee or grantor, the terms of the conveyance, the consideration given, the extent of necessity of the easement and the extent to which the use, which is the subject of the easement, was or might have been known to the parties. Parties to a conveyance will be assumed to know and to contemplate the continuance of reasonably necessary uses which have so altered the premises as to make them apparent upon reasonably prudent investigation. The degree of necessity required to imply an easement in favor of the grantor is greater than that required in the case of the grantee. But where land may be used without an easement, but cannot be used without disproportionate effort and expense, an easement may be implied in favor of either the grantor or grantee on the basis of necessity alone. In this case, the trial court found that Jones was aware of the sewer at the time he purchased Lot 19. It further found that the easement was necessary to the comfortable enjoyment of the grantor's, Bailey, land. Van Sandt (P) cannot claim that he purchased without notice. He inspected the property at the time of purchase, and knew the house was equipped with modern plumbing which had to drain into a sewer. The majority view is that appearance and visibility of easements is not synonymous, and the fact that the pipe, sewer or drain is hidden underground does not make it non-apparent. Here the easement was apparent within this meaning, and Van Sandt (P) is charged with notice of its existence. Affirmed.

EDITOR'S ANALYSIS: The law does not favor implied easements since they are in derogation of the rule that written instruments speak for themselves. They also retard building and improvements, and violate the policy of recording acts. The implication of easements is based on the theory that when one conveys property he includes or intends to include in the conveyance whatever is necessary for its beneficial use and enjoyment and to retain whatever is necessary for the use and enjoyment of the land retained. In view of the rule that a conveyance is to be construed most strongly against the grantor, an easement in favor of the grantee will be implied more readily than one in favor of the grantor.

QUICKNOTES

CONVEYANCE - The transfer of property, or title to property, from one party to another party.

QUASI SERVIENT TENEMENT - Property that is burdened in some aspect for the benefit of a dominant estate.

MORRELL v. RICE
Easement holders (P) v. Neighbors (D)
Me. Sup. Jud. Ct., 622 A.2d 1156 (1993).

NATURE OF CASE: Appeal from judgment for plaintiffs in action to establish an easement.

FACT SUMMARY: The trial court found that the Morrells (P) had an easement by necessity over the Rices' (D) land, but only for single-family use.

CONCISE RULE OF LAW: An easement by strict necessity should benefit the dominant estate for any lawful and reasonable use.

FACTS: The Morrells (P) successfully alleged that they had an easement by necessity over adjoining land owned by Rice (D). On appeal, Rice (P) alleged that there was no easement by necessity because there was no unity of title and there was alternate access to the Morrell's (P) land. The Morrells (P) also appealed, claiming that the court erred in restricting the use of the easement to serve only a single-family residence.

ISSUE: Should an easement by strict necessity benefit the dominant estate for any lawful and reasonable use?

HOLDING AND DECISION: (Clifford, J.) Yes. An easement by strict necessity should benefit the dominant estate for any lawful and reasonable use. The scope of use of the easement is not determined solely in reference to the time of its creation, but should be defined with respect to the reasonable enjoyment of the land and all lawful uses to which it may be put. In the absence of any proof that underground utilities would pose an undue burden, the court did not err in concluding that the right to install such utilities was included in the easement. Judgment modified to delete the restriction on use of the easement to a single-family residence. Affirmed as modified.

EDITOR'S ANALYSIS: The court held that since there was no evidence that the only lawful use of the Morrell's (P) house would be for one single-family home, the judgment should be modified. Nor was any evidence introduced on the extent of the burden on the Rice (D) land should the Morrell (P) land be used by more than one family. Whether such uses would pose an undue burden in the future will have to be decided at that time.

QUICKNOTES

DOMINANT ESTATE - Property whose owners benefit from the use of another's property.

EASEMENT BY NECESSITY - An easement that arises by operation of law without which the owner of the benefited property is deprived of the use and enjoyment of his property.

UNDUE BURDEN - Unlawfully oppressive or troublesome.

NOTES:

PAXSON v. GLOVITZ

Property owner (P) v. Adjoining property owner (D)
Ariz. Ct. App., 50 P.3d 420 (2002) (as amended, 2003).

NATURE OF CASE: Appeal from grant of summary judgment to defendant in prescriptive easement action.

FACT SUMMARY: Paxson (P) claimed she had a prescriptive easement to use a driveway that extended onto Glovitz's (D) land.

CONCISE RULE OF LAW: An easement by prescription is created by a use that is made pursuant to the terms of an intended but imperfectly created servitude.

FACTS: Paxson (P) and Glovitz (D) owned adjoining parcels of residential property. A twenty-foot driveway ran across the two properties, with ten feet on either side of the boundary line. Previous landowners, the Murphys and Baker, had intended to create an easement in 1979, but no written grant was ever produced or recorded. Intervening owners of the two parcels treated the driveway as an easement, and both Paxson (P) and Glovitz (D) were informed, respectively, by those who sold them their property, that the driveway was for use by neighbors and the public, and they knew the driveway extended onto the property adjacent to theirs. In 2000, Glovitz (D) began to construct a fence along his property line where the driveway ran, and Paxson (P) filed an action to obtain an easement by prescription for the ten-foot portion of the driveway extending onto Glovitz's (D) land. The trial court granted Glovitz (D) summary judgment, and Govitz (D) moved for attorneys' fees, which were granted. The court of appeals granted review.

ISSUE: Is an easement by prescription created by a use that is made pursuant to the terms of an intended but imperfectly created servitude?

HOLDING AND DECISION: (Ehrlich, J.) Yes. An easement by prescription is created by a use that is made pursuant to the terms of an intended but imperfectly created servitude. The principles underlying the Restatement: Servitudes § 2.16 relating to prescriptive easements, and the underlying principles of adverse possession, govern the resolution of this case. To gain a prescriptive easement, a person must establish that the land in question was actually and visibly used for ten years, that the use began and continued under a claim of right, and that the use was hostile to the title of the true owner. Here, the only disputed issue is whether the creation of the easement was adverse or permissive. Glovitz (D) argues the use was permissive because it was made by agreement. Paxson (P) counters that it was adverse because it was imperfectly created and, therefore, inaugurated a use adverse to the owners' title. Glovitz's (D) argument runs counter to the original landowners' intent to permanently relinquish their exclusive rights to their land in favor of adverse

rights to use the driveway. An oral or parol grant of title to real property, when coupled with possession, gives rise to the beginning of an adverse possession. The Restatement also provides that an easement by prescription may be created by a use that is made pursuant to the terms of an intended, but imperfectly created, servitude. Here, this is exactly what happened: the predecessors in title to Paxson (P) and Glovitz (D) attempted to create an easement, but failed to perfect their intention by failing to comply with the necessary procedures. Therefore, an easement by prescription had been established before Glovitz (D) bought the property. The resolution of this matter in favor of Paxson (P) serves to reverse the attorneys' fees awarded to Glovitz (D). Reversed.

EDITOR'S ANALYSIS: The court also noted that Glovitz (D) contended that Paxson (P) had improperly expanded the scope of the easement by using it in ways allegedly different from its historical uses—a contention that Paxson (P) disputed. The court observed that such a factual dispute could not be resolved by summary judgment, and that, in any event, the appropriate remedy for an unreasonable use of an easement is to seek injunctive relief to limit the use, plus damages if warranted.

QUICKNOTES

ADVERSE POSSESSION - A means of acquiring title to real property by remaining in actual, open, continuous, exclusive possession of property for the statutory period.

EASEMENT BY PRESCRIPTION - A manner of acquiring an easement in another's property by continuous and uninterrupted use in satisaction of the statutory requirements of adverse possession.

NOTES:

GOULDING v. COOK
Landowners (P) v. Neighbors (D)
Mass. Sup. Jud. Ct., 661 N.E.2d 1322 (1996).

NATURE OF CASE: Appeal from grant of easement to defendants.

FACT SUMMARY: The Gouldings (P) sought a preliminary injunction against the Cooks' (D) use of their land for their septic system.

CONCISE RULE OF LAW: Courts will not enjoin truly minimal encroachments.

FACTS: When the Cooks' (D) cesspool malfunctioned they tried to negotiate with their neighbors, the Gouldings (P), over the use of some of their land to install a new septic system. When the Gouldings' (P) suit for preliminary injunction against the Cooks' (D) trespass on their land was denied, the Cooks (D) entered on the land and installed the septic system. The court granted the Cooks (D) an easement over the Gouldings' (P) land for maintenance of the system at a negotiated price. The Gouldings (P) appealed and the court of appeals affirmed. The Massachusetts Supreme Judicial Court granted certiorari.

ISSUE: Will courts enjoin truly minimal encroachments?

HOLDING AND DECISION: (Fried, J.) No. Courts will not enjoin truly minimal encroachments, especially when the burden on a defendant would be very great. Here the Cooks (D) were seeking to install a potentially permanent, possibly malodorously malfunctioning septic system encroaching on a spatially significant portion of the Gouldings' (P) lot. A permanent physical occupation amounting to a transfer of a traditional estate in land is not a minor encroachment. The Cooks (D) must remove the septic system and pay damages. Vacated and remanded.

EDITOR'S ANALYSIS: The court here called the lower court's action granting an easement "enforced good neighborliness." The Cooks (D) had been warned that their claim to the land was sharply in dispute. They proceeded at their own peril.

QUICKNOTES

EASEMENT - The right to utilize a portion of another's real property for a specific use.

PRELIMINARY INJUNCTION - A judicial mandate issued to require or restrain a party from certain conduct; used to preserve a trial's subject matter or to prevent threatened injury.

TRESPASS - Unlawful interference with, or damage to, the real or personal property of another.

ESTATE OF THOMSON v. WADE
Landowner (P) v. Neighbor (D)
N.Y. Ct. of App., 509 N.E.2d 309 (1987).

NATURE OF CASE: Appeal from judgment for defendant in declaratory judgment action.

FACT SUMMARY: The trial court held that no express easement had been created when the grantor had reserved a right of way over the land being conveyed.

CONCISE RULE OF LAW: A grantor cannot create an easement over land that he does not own.

FACTS: The original owner conveyed two adjacent lots and failed to convey an express easement appurtenant over Wade's (D) parcel for the benefit of Thomson's (P) land. When Wade's (D) parcel was reconveyed, the grantor excepted and reserved a right of way over Wade's (D) land to himself and to Thomson's (P) predecessor-in-interest. Wade's (D) unimproved inland lot was adjacent to Thomson's (P) riverfront land on which a motel had been built(P), and Thomson (P) sought declaratory judgment that she held valid title to an express easement over Wade's (D) land. The court held that no express easement existed and Thomson (P) appealed.

ISSUE: May a grantor create an easement over land that he does not own?

HOLDING AND DECISION: (Per curiam) No. A grantor cannot create an easement over land that he does not own. Having already conveyed the parcel, the grantor could not reserve in the deed to Wade's (D) predecessor-in-interest an easement appurtenant for the benefit of Thomson's (P) predecessor-in-interest. Affirmed.

EDITOR'S ANALYSIS: The court applied the "stranger to the deed" rule. The rule states that a deed with a reservation by the grantor in favor of a third party does not create a valid interest in favor of the third party. The minority view is that such an interest can be created if it was clearly the intent of the grantor to do so.

QUICKNOTES

DEED - A signed writing transferring title to real property from one person to another.

EASEMENT APPURTENANT - A burden attached to real property that either benefits or burdens the owner's right to utilize that property.

DAVIS v. BRUK
Owner of dominent estate (P) v. Owner of servient estate (D)
Me. Sup. Ct., 411 A.2d 660 (1980).

NOTES:

NATURE OF CASE: Appeal of order affecting an easement across certain property.

FACT SUMMARY: Bruk (D) wished to relocate an easement running across her property, despite objections from the owners of the dominant estate.

CONCISE RULE OF LAW: An easement may not be relocated on the application of the owner of the servient estate.

FACTS: Davis (P) and others owned certain property adjacent to that of Bruk (D). Bruk's (D) property was subject to a right of way easement appurtenant to Davis' (P) property. Davis (P) filed an action to enjoin Bruk (D) from obstructing the access road across her property. Bruk (D) counterclaimed by petitioning for an order relocating the easement, The court approved Bruk's (D) proposal, and Davis (P) appealed.

ISSUE: May an easement be relocated on the application of the owner of the servient estate?

HOLDING AND DECISION: (Dufresne, Active Ret'd.J.) No. An easement may not be relocated on the application of the owner of the servient estate. The general rule is that once the location of an expressly deeded easement is established, it may be changed only by agreement of the owners of both the dominant and servient estates, or by some provision in the creating instrument permitting such a change. No authority exits for a court ordering such a change on the unilateral application of only one of the estates. To so permit, even if a showing of need is made, would create great uncertainty in land ownership and in the real estate market, and this court will not condone such a rule. Here, since the owners of the dominant estate will not agree to the change, it will not be allowed. Reversed.

EDITOR'S ANALYSIS: The rule stated here is fairly universal. A few jurisdictions have carved out necessity exceptions allowing the owner of a servient estate to change an easement. For the most part, however, the policy considerations enumerated by this court have prevented most jurisdictions from recognizing any exception to the general rule.

QUICKNOTES

DOMINANT ESTATE - Property whose owners benefit from the use of another's property.

EASEMENT - The right to utilize a portion of another's real property for a specific use.

SERVIENT ESTATE - Property that is burdened in some aspect for the benefit of a dominant estate.

LEWIS v. YOUNG

Owner of dominant estate (P) v. Owner of servient estate (D)

N.Y. Ct. of App., 705 N.E.2d 649 (1998).

NATURE OF CASE: Action to quiet title in an easement and seeking a permanent injunction.

FACT SUMMARY: Lewis (P) brought suit against the Youngs (D), owners of an adjoining parcel of land, seeking to quiet title in an easement running through their land, which the Youngs (D) moved in order to make certain improvements on the property.

CONCISE RULE OF LAW: In the absence of an intent otherwise, a landowner can relocate a right-of-way easement so long as he bears the expense of the relocation and the change does not frustrate the parties' intent or purpose in creating the right-of-way or significantly lessen its utility.

FACTS: Lewis (P) and Young (D) owned adjoining parcels of land both formerly owned by the Browns. The Browns divided their plot into three parcels, a four-acre tract they retained for themselves and two smaller tracts, which they sold. Neither parcel had direct access to the roadway, therefore both deeds granted rights of way over the Brown's property. The Youngs (D) subsequently purchased the property with the intent of substantially improving it. In the midst of such construction, Lewis (P) obtained title to the adjoining tract. Lewis's (P) attorney informed the Youngs (D) by letter that his client would agree to relocation of the driveway if they would agree to certain renovations. Mrs. Young (D) stated that they agreed to perform such renovations when their home was completed, but were delayed by Mr. Young's death and by poor weather. A second letter was sent demanding that the driveway be improved as agreed within ten days or Lewis (P) would put the driveway back in its original location, through the Youngs' (D) tennis court. Lewis (P) finally filed suit seeking a declaration of the parties' rights regarding the easement and a permanent injunction compelling removal of the tennis court and the return of the driveway to its original location. The supreme court granted Lewis's (P) motion for partial summary judgment, holding that Lewis (P) had an easement that the Youngs (D) had no right to move. The court granted Lewis's (P) request for an order compelling Young (D) to return the driveway to its original location. The appellate division affirmed. Mrs. Young (D) appealed.

ISSUE: In the absence of an intent otherwise, may a landowner relocate a right-of-way easement so long as he bears the expense of the relocation and the change does not frustrate the parties' intent or purpose in creating the right-of-way or significantly lessen its utility?

HOLDING AND DECISION: (Kaye, C.J.) Yes. In the absence of an intent otherwise, a landowner can relocate a right-of-way easement so long as he bears the expense of the relocation and the change does not frustrate the parties' intent or purpose in creating the right-of-way or significantly lessen its utility. The general rule is that when the intent in granting an easement is to afford ingress and egress, it is the right of passage, and not any right to a physical passageway itself, that is granted to the easement holder. In the absence of an intent otherwise, a landowner burdened by an express easement of egress and ingress may make any changes to the area so long as the holder's right of passage is not impaired. Allowing the landowner the authority to alter the right-of-way balances the landowner's right to use and enjoy his property against the easement holder's right of ingress and egress. While other jurisdictions have required consent to the relocation of easements, the lower courts in New York have not required such prior permission. The concerns in giving a landowner the unilateral right to relocate a right-of-way easement are adequately addressed by the limitation that a landowner may not unilaterally change a right-of-way if that change impairs enjoyment of the easement holder's rights. Thus a balancing test must be invoked as to relocation of a defined right-of-way. In the absence of an intent otherwise, a landowner can move the right-of-way so long as he bears the expense of the relocation and the change does not frustrate the parties' intent or purpose in creating the right-of-way and does not significantly lessen the utility of the right-of-way. Here the language of the grant does not demonstrate an intent to preclude the landowner's right to relocate the right-of-way. Reversed.

EDITOR'S ANALYSIS: An express easement is construed in accordance with the parties' intent. The court first looks to the express words used in the instrument creating the easement. Even where the express language of the grant does not show an intent to restrict the landowner's right to relocate the easement, the court must consider the circumstances surrounding the conveyance, including the parties' conduct.

BROWN v. VOSS

Owner of easement (P) v. Servient estate (D)
Wash. Sup. Ct., 715 P.2d 514 (1986).

NATURE OF CASE: Appeal from reversal of denial of defendant's request for an injunction.

FACT SUMMARY: The trial court found that the Browns (P) had made no unreasonable use of their private road easement over Voss's (D) land and granted the Browns (P) the right to use the easement for access to two parcels where they were building a new home.

CONCISE RULE OF LAW: If an easement is appurtenant to a particular parcel of land, any extension thereof to other parcels is a misuse of the easement.

FACTS: Brown (P) used an easement over Voss's (D) land to access two parcels of land where he was constructing a single family home, but the easement had been granted only for access to the one parcel. When Voss (D) obstructed the road, Brown (P) sued for removal of the obstructions and for an injunction against Voss's (D) interference with his use of the easement and damages. Voss (D) counterclaimed for damages and an injunction against Brown's (P) using the easement other than for the one parcel. The court denied Voss's (D) request for an injunction and granted Brown (P) the use of the easement. The court of appeals reversed and remanded for entry of an order enjoining the use of the easement to gain access to the other parcel. Brown (P) appealed.

ISSUE: If an easement is appurtenant to a particular parcel of land, is an extension to other parcels a misuse of the easement?

HOLDING AND DECISION: (Brachtenbach, J.) Yes. If an easement is appurtenant to a particular parcel of land, any extension thereof to other parcels is a misuse of the easement. The trial court acted within its discretion in denying Voss's (D) request for an injunction based upon the equities of the case. Affirmed.

DISSENT: (Dore, J.) Although the majority correctly found that an extension of this easement to nondominant property is a misuse of the easement, it nonetheless did not grant the owners of the servient estate, the Vosses (D), injunctive relief. The Browns' (P) continued use of the easement to benefit the nondominant parcel would constitute a continuing trespass for which damages would be hard to assess. In such a case, injunctive relief should be granted.

EDITOR'S ANALYSIS: The court here applied the ordinary default rule that limits the scope of an appurtenant easement to the original dominant estate. The Browns (P) had bought an adjoining parcel after purchasing the parcel which included the easement and they wanted to build a home straddling both parcels. The trial court made findings that there was no increase in the burden on the subservient estate from the use of the easement to access the new parcel.

QUICKNOTES

BURDEN - Oppressive or troublesome; the duty of a party to introduce evidence to support a fact that is in dispute in an action.

DOMINANT ESTATE - Property whose owners benefit from the use of another's property.

EASEMENT - The right to utilize a portion of another's real property for a specific use.

INJUNCTION - A remedy imposed by the court ordering a party to cease the conduct of a specific activity.

SERVIENT ESTATE - Property that is burdened in some aspect for the benefit of a dominant estate.

NOTES:

CITY OF PASADENA v. CALIFORNIA-MICHIGAN LAND & WATER CO.

Easement grantee (P) v. Competitor (D)

Cal. Sup. Ct., in bank, 110 P.2d 983 (1941).

NATURE OF CASE: Appeal from denial of injunction in action for exclusive easement.

FACT SUMMARY: The City of Pasadena (P) sought to enjoin the use by the California-Michigan Land & Water Co. (D)—its competitor in the provision of water—of easements granted to plaintiff for laying water mains and connections.

CONCISE RULE OF LAW: An exclusive easement is not created by a grant of easement that is granted for a limited purpose and that does not expressly indicate that it is exclusive.

FACTS: The City of Pasadena (P) and the California-Michigan Land & Water Co. (D) are competing vendors of water service in an unincorporated area. Defendant installed water mains and connections in five-foot easements that had previously been granted to plaintiff and that were partially occupied by water mains and connections. The grants given to plaintiff described the easements as follows: "Easements for the purpose of installing and maintaining water mains and connections thereto . . . all of said easements being five feet in width." Plaintiff claimed these were grants of exclusive easements that left the owners of the servient tenements no power to grant similar easements to defendant in the same strips of land. Plaintiff also contended that defendant's installations substantially interfered with plaintiff's present partial occupation of the land and with its possible future use of the land, and thus sought to enjoin the defendant's use of the easements.

ISSUE: Is an exclusive easement created by a grant of easement that is granted for a limited purpose and that does not expressly indicate that it is exclusive?

HOLDING AND DECISION: (Gibson, C.J.) No. An exclusive easement is not created by a grant of easement that is granted for a limited purpose and that does not expressly indicate that it is exclusive. The language of the easement grants eliminates the possibility that the easements created thereby were exclusive. There was no language in the grant that indicated such an intent. Also, prior easements in the same land were in effect at the time the easements were granted. Furthermore, an exclusive easement is an unusual interest in land that is practically tantamount to a conveyance of the fee. No intention to convey such a complete interest can be imputed to the owners of the servient tenement in the absence of a clear indication to do so. The general rule is that the grantor may make any use of the land that does not interfere unreasonably with the easement, and it is unnecessary for him to make any reservation to protect this interest. Since the grantor retains the right to use the land reasonably himself, he retains also the power to transfer these rights to a third person, such as defendant. Therefore, the issue becomes whether the servient owner could have made such use as made by defendant. The question is whether such use was reasonable, a question of fact decided by the trial court, which held that such use did not unreasonably interfere with plaintiff's easement. Plaintiff, however, argues that a different rule should apply, namely that because these easements specify the location and width of the easement, the easement holder has the right to occupy it to the full width if it ever desires to do so. Therefore, plaintiff argues, any use of the strip for laying other water pipes should be held to an unreasonable interference as a matter of law. However, plaintiff relies on cases that apply to surface right-of-ways. There is a significant difference between such right-of-ways and easements for laying water pipe because with surface right-of-ways, the location and width do clearly and completely define the entire easement, whereas with easements for laying underground pipe, there are important factors to be considered in addition to the location and width—such as depth, number and size of the pipes, and the right to shift the pipes at will. Thus, the extent of the burden which the parties intend to impose on the servient tenement is not definitely fixed by mere specification of width and location. The very general language used in the grants in this case cannot be given the effect of legally determining the complete burden intended. Moreover, the easements were granted for a limited purpose of securing domestic water for the owners, not for protecting plaintiff from competition. Accordingly, the granting of the second easement to the defendant did not interfere with plaintiff's prior easement as a matter of law. This does not mean, however, that at some point in the future, plaintiff will not be able to fully use the easement granted to it. At that point, it is possible that defendant's pipes will unreasonably interfere with plaintiff's reasonable use of its prior easement, and that plaintiff's paramount right will prevail. But that is not the case now. Affirmed.

EDITOR'S ANALYSIS: The basic rule of exclusive easements is that the easement holder is entitled to use the servient estate as reasonably necessary for the convenient enjoyment of the easement and that the holder of the servient estate is entitled to make any use that does not unreasonably interfere with enjoyment of the easement.

QUICKNOTES

SERVIENT ESTATE - Property that is burdened in some aspect for the benefit of a dominant estate.

FAIRBROTHER v. ADAMS
Grantor of rights (P) v. Grantee of rights (D)
Vt. Sup. Ct., 378 A.2d 102 (1977).

NATURE OF CASE: Appeal from judgment for plaintiff in an action interpreting a grant of rights.

FACT SUMMARY: The Fairbrothers (P) claimed that language in a deed pursuant to which they conveyed to the Adamses (D) "the hunting and fishing rights on the other lands of the Fairbrother farm" created purely personal, non-exclusive rights.

CONCISE RULE OF LAW: A deed that grants "the hunting and fishing rights . . . on . . . other lands . . ." creates an exclusive, assignable profit *à prendre* in those other lands.

FACTS: The Fairbrothers (P) conveyed to the Adamses (D) a parcel of land of approximately three acres. The warranty deed contained the following language: "There is also conveyed herewith the hunting and fishing rights on the other lands of the Fairbrother farm." This raised issues as to whether the deed conveyed exclusive hunting and fishing rights; the scope of those rights; whether those rights were personal only or were alienable and assignable; and if so, what parts of the entire Fairbrother (P) farm was subject to them.

ISSUE: Does a deed that grants "the hunting and fishing rights . . . on . . . other lands . . ." create an exclusive, assignable profit *à prendre* in those other lands?

HOLDING AND DECISION: (Billings, J.) Yes. A deed that grants "the hunting and fishing rights . . . on . . . other lands . . ." creates an exclusive, assignable profit *à prendre* in those other lands. There is no dispute that the grant of hunting and fishing rights by a deed conveyance creates a profit *à prendre*, which is an interest in land. Here, what constitutes the "other lands" of the Fairbrother (P) farm is to be determined by what land the deed described and in what towns the land is located in the recorded reference deed. Here, the rights are exclusive because of the deed's use of the definite article "the," which implies exclusivity. The rights here are also alienable and assignable, not merely personal. Because profits *à prendre* may be granted separately from the freehold of the land, they imply inheritance and assignability unless expressly reserved. The language of the *habendum* clause does not need to be repeated in every paragraph of the deed to have effect. Here, the deed was clear and unambiguous. Vacated and remanded.

EDITOR'S ANALYSIS: The modern view is that partial assignments of benefits in gross are permissible so long as the resulting use does not burden the estate beyond what was originally contemplated. Thus, theoretically, the Adamses (D) in this case could partially assign their profit and retain part of it, as long as the burden placed on the Fairbrother (P) farm was not increased unreasonably.

QUICKNOTES

DEED - A signed writing transferring title to real property from one person to another.

HABENDUM CLAUSE - A clause contained in a deed that specifies the parties to the transaction and defines the interest in land to be conveyed.

PROFIT Á PRENDRE - The right to take something (such as minerals, gas, etc.) from another's land.

NOTES:

CENTRAL OREGON FABRICATORS, INC. v. HUDSPETH
Remainderman (P) v. Life tenant (D)
Ore. Appeals. Ct., 977 P.2d 416 (1999).

NATURE OF CASE: Appeal from quiet title action extinguishing a profit *à prendre*.

FACT SUMMARY: The trial court extinguished a profit à prendre that gave Hudspeth (D) the right to hunt and fish on Central Oregon's (P) property.

CONCISE RULE OF LAW: A party claiming abandonment of property must show both nonuse and a specific act of abandonment.

FACTS: Central Oregon (P) purchased land in 1964 from Hudspeth's (D) business but Hudspeth (D) and his family were granted rights to hunt and fish on the property. Hudspeth (D) and his family never exercised their rights to hunt or fish on the property or were prevented from doing so when they tried. Central Oregon (P) developed the property for tourists and began charging hunters fees for hunting trips on the property. When Hudspeth (D) began assigning its rights and planning to sell memberships to hunt on the property, Central Oregon (P) filed suit to quiet title and for declaratory judgment that the Hudspeths (D) had abandoned their rights and that the rights were strictly personal. The trial court found that the Hudspeths (D) had abandoned the property or that their rights had been extinguished by adverse possession. The Hudspeths (D) appealed.

ISSUE: Must a party claiming abandonment of property show both nonuse and a specific act of abandonment?

HOLDING AND DECISION: (Haselton, J.) Yes. A party claiming abandonment of property must show both nonuse and a specific act of abandonment. The intent to abandon must be clear and unequivocal and must be accompanied by some specific act of abandonment. In this case the Hudspeths' (D) passivity or acquiescence was insufficient to demonstrate an intent to abandon. The Hudspeths (D) never verbally or by conduct expressed an intent to abandon. Reversed and remanded in part; affirmed in part.

EDITOR'S ANALYSIS: The court also found that the trial court erred in granted relief on the basis of adverse possession. The Hudspeths (D) also were entitled to assign their rights. But they could only assign the rights to natural persons.

QUICKNOTES

ABANDONMENT - The voluntary relinquishment of a right without the intent of reclaiming it.

ADVERSE POSSESSION - A means of acquiring title to real property by remaining in actual, open, continuous, exclusive possession of property for the statutory period.

ASSIGNMENT - A transaction in which a party conveys his or her entire interest in property to another.

DEED - A signed writing transferring title to real property from one person to another.

NOTES:

RUNYON v. PALEY
Property owners (P) v. Condominium builder (D)
N.C. Sup. Ct., 416 S.E.2d 177 (1992).

NATURE OF CASE: Action to enforce restrictive covenants.

FACT SUMMARY: Runyon (P) and Williams (P) contend that Paley's (D) property is subject to restrictive covenants that prohibit the construction of condominiums.

CONCISE RULE OF LAW: In order to enforce a restrictive covenant on the theory of equitable servitude, it must be shown: (1) that the covenant touches and concerns the land, (2) that the original covenanting parties intended the covenant to bind the person against whom enforcement is sought and to benefit the person seeking to enforce the covenant, and (3) notice of the covenant is contained in a chain of title instrument.

FACTS: Gaskins owned a four-acre tract of land. By various deeds, Gaskins conveyed out several lots, which were eventually developed for residential use. Gaskins conveyed a strip of land to the Runyons (P). Gaskins later conveyed another parcel of land to the Brughs. Included in the Brughs' deed of conveyance was a restrictive covenant restricting use to residential purposes only and prohibiting business, commercial, and apartment house use of the land. The covenant was to run with the land indefinitely. Gaskins lived on a separate parcel of land which bordered the Brughs property. Gaskins continued to live on the property until her death. Williams (P) then acquired the Gaskins property. Thereafter, the Paleys (D) acquired the Brughs' property and began constructing condominium units. The Runyons (P) and Williams (P) brought a suit, seeking to enjoin the Paleys (D) from using the property in a manner inconsistent with the restrictive covenants in the Brughs deed. They alleged that the restrictive covenants were placed on the Brughs property for the benefit of Gaskins and neighboring property owners, including the Runyons (P). The Paleys (D) moved to dismiss the lawsuit. The trial court granted the Paleys' (D) motion to dismiss for failure to state a claim upon which relief could be granted. The court of appeals affirmed.

ISSUE: In order to enforce a restrictive covenant as an equitable servitude, must touch and concern, intent, and notice be shown?

HOLDING AND DECISION: (Meyer, J.) Yes. In order to enforce a restrictive covenant on the theory of equitable servitude, it must be shown (1) that the covenant touches and concerns the land, (2) that the original covenanting parties intended the covenant to bind the person against whom enforcement is sought and to benefit the person seeking to enforce the covenant, and (3) notice of the covenant is contained in a chain of title instrument. The right to restrict the use of the Paleys' (D) property would affect the Runyons' (P) ownership interests in their property. Therefore, the covenants touch and concern the land at law and in equity. Furthermore, the Runyons (P) purchased their property prior to the creation of the restrictive covenants at issue here, and thus cannot be said to be successors in interest to any property retained by Gaskins that was intended to be benefitted by the covenants. There is no evidence that the original covenanting parties intended that the Runyons (P) have its benefit. Lastly, a restrictive covenant is not enforceable at law or in equity against a subsequent purchaser of property burdened by the covenant unless notice of the covenant is contained in an instrument in his chain of title. The Runyons (P) have not made a sufficient showing so as to charge the Paleys (D) with notice of the existence of any restriction that may have inured or was intended to inure to their benefit. While the records in the Paleys' (D) chain of title unambiguously provide notice of the restrictive covenants, they do not in any way suggest any right of enforcement in favor of the Runyons (P), either personally or as owners of any land. The Runyons (P) did not record Gaskins' conveyance to them until fifteen or sixteen years after the Brughs recorded their deed of conveyance which included the restrictive covenants. Thus, the deed from Gaskins to the Runyons (P) provided no notice to the Paleys (D) that the Runyons (P) claimed any interest in adjacent land that may have been benefitted by the restrictive covenants. Therefore, the Runyons (P) have not proferred sufficient evidence to show that they have standing to enforce the restrictive covenants, either personally or as owners of any land intended to be benefitted by the restrictions. Affirmed in part concerning the dismissal of the Runyons' claim; reversed in part concerning the dismissal of Williams' claim.

EDITOR'S ANALYSIS: Treating a covenant as an equitable servitude rather than a real covenant has the added advantage of eliminating the privity requirement, vertical and horizontal. However, courts will not ordinarily give damages as a remedy for breach of an equitable servitude; the traditional equitable remedy is injunctive relief.

QUICKNOTES

CONVEYANCE - The transfer of property, or title to property, from one party to another party.

DEED - A signed writing transferring title to real property from one person to another.

EQUITABLE SERVITUDE - Land use restriction enforceable in equity.

PRIVITY - Commonality of rights or interests between parties.

RESTRICTIVE COVENANT - A promise contained in a deed to limit the uses to which the property will be made.

SONOMA DEVELOPMENT, INC. v. MILLER

Successor in interest (D) v. Successor in interest (P)

Va. Sup. Ct., 515 S.E.2d 577 (1999).

NATURE OF CASE: Appeal from summary judgment and injunction for plaintiffs in action to enforce a covenant.

FACT SUMMARY: The Millers (P) claimed that Sonoma Development, Inc. (Sonoma) (D) violated a setback requirement contained in a covenant. Sonoma (D) countered that there was no horizontal privity between the original covenanting parties to support the covenant.

CONCISE RULE OF LAW: A party is not limited to a single document to establish horizontal privity between original covenanting parties that supports a real covenant.

FACTS: The Schaers owned two adjacent lots. One lot (Lot 38) had a house on it, and the other (Lot 39) was vacant. The house on Lot 38 physically encroached on the southern boundary line of Lot 39 by 0.1 feet at the northeast corner of the house and by 0.2 feet at the northwest corner. The Millers (P) purchased Lot 38 from the Schaers, and as part of the transaction, required the Schaers to provide a deed restriction on Lot 39 prohibiting the use of a common wall with Lot 38 and requiring a sufficient easement to facilitate maintenance of the portion of the house that encroached on Lot 39. Accordingly, the Schaers executed a "Declaration of Restriction" that required that no improvement of any kind could be constructed on Lot 39 within three feet of the north wall of the existing house on Lot 38. Although the Schaers were designated as the "Grantor" in the declaration, the document did not name any entity or individual as the "Grantee." On the same day, the Schaers also executed a "Declaration of Easement," in which they granted an easement on Lot 39 for the benefit of Lot 38 for the purpose of permitting necessary repairs and maintenance to be reasonably made to the northern wall of the house. This document also did not name anyone as "Grantee," but it did state that the Schaers had agreed to sell Lot 38 to the Millers (P). In addition, both documents were recorded. The deed conveying Lot 38 to the Millers (P) stated that it was subject to recorded conditions, restrictions and easements. Subsequently, Sonoma Development, Inc. (Sonoma) (D) purchased Lot 39 and built a house on it. The Millers (P) brought suit because the Sonoma (D) house violated the three-foot setback requirement in the Declaration of Restriction. The trial court upheld the validity of the Declaration of Restriction and ordered Sonoma (D) to remove all improvements that were within three feet of the Miller's (P) residence. The state's supreme court granted review.

ISSUE: Is a party limited to a single document to establish horizontal privity between original covenanting parties that supports a real covenant?

HOLDING AND DECISION: (Kinser, J.) No. A party is not limited to a single document to establish horizontal privity between

original covenanting parties that supports a real covenant. In this state, there are two types of restrictive covenants: (1) common law covenants running with the land, and (2) equitable easements and equitable servitudes. The Millers (P) do not dispute that the second type of restrictive covenant is not at issue here. Therefore, the issue is whether the Declaration of Restriction created a valid common law restrictive covenant that runs with the land, also known as a "real covenant." To enforce a real covenant, a party must show (1) privity between the original parties to the covenant (horizontal privity); (2) privity between the original parties and their successors in interest (vertical privity); (3) an intent by the original parties that the benefits and burdens of the covenant would run with the land; (4) that the covenant touches and concerns the land; and (5) the covenant is in writing. Sonoma (D) contended that no horizontal privity existed between the original parties because the Declaration of Restriction did not name the Millers (P) as grantees. Thus, Sonoma (D) posits that horizontal privity must be demonstrated within the four corners of a single document. This position is rejected because in every situation it is not true that only one document can be examined to determine if such horizontal privity existed. To establish horizontal privity, the party seeking to enforce a real covenant must prove that the original covenanting parties made their covenant in connection with the conveyance of an estate in land from one of the parties to the other. Thus, horizontal privity can be satisfied when the transaction of which the promise is a part includes a transfer of an interest either in land or in the land burdened by the promise (Restatement of Property § 534(a)). Here, the transaction of which the covenant was a part started with the real estate contract between the Schaers and the Millers (P), and culminated with the deed conveying Lot 38 to the Millers (P). The Declaration of Restriction was part of this transaction, as it fulfilled the Schaers' obligation under the real estate contract, and was a part of a transaction that included the transfer of an interest in the land benefitted by the real covenant. Furthermore, an injunction was the appropriate form of relief on summary judgment because Sonoma (D) had notice of the Declaration of Restriction; when "parties, for valuable consideration, with their eyes open, contract that a particular thing shall not be done, all that a court of equity has to do is to say by way of injunction that which the parties have already said by way of covenant—that the thing shall not be done." Therefore, there was no need for the trial court to hear more evidence to enforce the Declaration of Restriction. Affirmed.

EDITOR'S ANALYSIS: Virginia is one of the few states that limits equitable servitudes to "general plan" covenants, *i.e.*, covenants imposed by a developer or subdivider on all lots in a subdivision to implement a general plan of development. Ordinarily, the Declaration of Restriction in this case would have been enforceable as an equitable servitude because the burden was negative, the benefit was appurtenant to the adjacent property owned by the Millers (P), and Sonoma (D) purchased with notice of the covenant.

SHALIMAR ASSOCIATION v. D.O.C. ENTERPRISES, LTD.
Homeowners (P) v. Golf course (D)
Ariz. Ct. App., 688 P.2d 682 (1984).

NATURE OF CASE: Appeal from judgment for plaintiffs in enforcement action.

FACT SUMMARY: The trial court found that D.O.C. Enterprises (D) was not a bona fide purchaser without notice and was therefore subject to an implied restriction limiting use of the property to a golf course.

CONCISE RULE OF LAW: A mere change in economic conditions rendering it unprofitable to continue a restrictive use is not alone sufficient to justify abrogating a restrictive covenant.

FACTS: Shalimar (P) was a group of homeowners in a residential land development area adjacent to a golf course. The developer later sold the golf course to D.O.C. Enterprises (D), and when D.O.C. (D) tried to develop the property for other uses, Shalimar (P) sued to enforce an implied restriction limiting the use of the land to a golf course. The court held that an implied covenant restricting the use of the property to a golf course arose from the sale of adjacent lots to the homeowners. That covenant was enforceable against subsequent purchasers who took their ownership with knowledge of the restriction. D.O.C. (D) appealed, alleging that economic frustration rendered the golf course restriction unenforceable.

ISSUE: Is a mere change in economic conditions rendering it unprofitable to continue a restrictive use alone sufficient to justify abrogating a restrictive covenant?

HOLDING AND DECISION: (Froeb, J.) No. A mere change in economic conditions rendering it unprofitable to continue a restrictive use is not alone sufficient to justify abrogating a restrictive covenant. Although changed circumstances may at times justify relief from restrictive covenants, such changes must frustrate and defeat the original purpose of the restrictions to warrant voiding them. If the original purpose of the covenant can still be realized, it will be enforced even though other uses might be more profitable. The trial court determined that the purpose of the golf course had not been defeated or frustrated by any change. Affirmed.

EDITOR'S ANALYSIS: The developer had orally promised all the homeowners that the golf course restriction would exist until the year 2000 and would be renewed for another twenty-five years if a majority of the owners agreed. The court here concluded that the purchasers were on inquiry notice of the restriction. Had they made a reasonable investigation they would have learned of the duration of the restriction.

NOTES:

NEPONSIT PROPERTY OWNERS' ASS'N., INC. v. EMIGRANT INDUSTRIAL SAVINGS BANK

Agent of property owner (P) v. Deed holder (D)

N.Y. Ct. of App., 15 N.E. 2d 793 (1938).

NATURE OF CASE: Action to foreclose a lien upon land.

FACT SUMMARY: Neponsit Property Owners (P) claim that Emigrant Bank's (D) deed to certain property conveyed such property subject to a covenant contained in the original deed which provided for the payment by all subsequent purchasers of an annual improvements charge.

CONCISE RULE OF LAW: A covenant in deed subjecting land to an annual charge for improvements to the surrounding residential tract is enforceable by the property owners' association against subsequent purchasers if: (1) grantor and grantee so intended; (2) it appears that the covenant is one touching or concerning the land; and (3) privity of estate is shown between the party claiming benefit of the covenant and the party under the burden of such covenant.

FACTS: Neponsit Property Owners' (P) assignor, Neponsit Realty Company, conveyed the land now owned by Emigrant Bank (D) to R. Deyer and wife by deed. That original deed contained a covenant providing: (1) that the conveyed land should be subject to an annual charge for improvements upon the entire residential tract then being developed; (2) that such charge should be a lien; (3) such charge should be payable by all subsequent purchasers to the company or its assigns, including a property owners' association which might thereafter be organized; and (4) such covenant runs with the land. Neponsit Property Owners (P) brought action based upon the above covenant to foreclose a lien upon the land which Emigrant Bank (D) now owns, having purchased it at a judicial sale. Emigrant Bank (D) appealed from an order denying their motion for judgment on the pleadings.

ISSUE: Does a covenant in the original deed subjecting land to an annual charge for improvements run with the land and create a lien which is enforceable against subsequent owners by Neponsit Property Owners (P)?

HOLDING AND DECISION: (Lehman, J.) Yes. A covenant will run with the land and will be enforceable against a subsequent purchaser if: (1) the grantor and grantee intend that the covenant run with the land; (2) the covenant touches or concerns the land with which it runs; (3) there is privity of estate between the party claiming benefit of the covenant and the party who rests under the burden of the covenant. In the instant case the grantor and grantee manifested their intent that the covenant run with the land by so stating in the original deed. The covenant touches or

concerns the land in substance if not in form, *i.e.*, the covenant alters the legal rights of ownership of the land, by providing that the burden of paying the cost of maintaining public improvements is inseparably attached to the land which enjoys the benefits of such improvements. The concept of privity of estate between parties usually requires that the party claiming benefit from the enforcement of a covenant own the property which benefits from such enforcement. Although Neponsit Property Owners (P), the corporation, does not own the property which would benefit from enforcement, the corporation is acting as the agent of property owners and should therefore be considered in privity in substance if not in form. Since the covenant complies with the legal requirements for one which runs with the land and is enforceable against subsequent purchasers, the order which denied Emigrant Bank's (D) motion for judgment on the pleadings is affirmed.

EDITOR'S ANALYSIS: It has been suggested that the technical requirements which determine the enforceability of covenants as to future parties, *e.g.*, Neponsit, might well be abandoned and that the intention of the covenanting parties be the sole criterion. This suggestion is supported by the following developments: (1) the benefit of a contract may now be assigned, or even created initially for the benefit of a third person; (2) recording systems, though imperfect, afford much protection to the purchaser of land against outstanding burdens of which he may be unaware. It should be noted, however, that the unrestricted enforcement of covenants may seriously impair the usefulness of land. A student reading this case should keep in mind that Neponsit, is not concerned with the enforcement of covenants between original covenanting parties. That question of enforceability is left to the contracts course.

QUICKNOTES

COVENANT - A written promise to do, or to refrain from doing, a particular activity.

LIEN - A claim against the property of another in order to secure the payment of a debt.

EAGLE ENTERPRISES, INC. v. GROSS
N.Y. Ct. App., 349 N.E.2d 816 (1976).

NATURE OF CASE: Appeal in an action for goods sold and delivered.

FACT SUMMARY: Both Eagle Enterprises (P) and Gross (D) succeeded to parcels of land burdened by covenants whereby Gross (D) had to pay for water to be supplied annually by Eagle (P).

CONCISE RULE OF LAW: An affirmative covenant will not run with the land unless it "touches and concerns" the land, nor will it run when the covenant either creates an undue restriction on alienation or a burden in perpetuity.

FACTS: Orchid Hill Realtors conveyed property in its subdivision to the Baums. The deed provided that Orchid Hill would provide the property with water for six months annually for which the Baums would pay $35. The deed expressly stated that this covenant would run with the land and bind all successive takers. Gross (D) succeeded to the Baums interest by a deed making no mention of the covenant to purchase water. Accordingly, Gross (D) refused to accept or pay for it, especially because he (D) had since constructed his own water supply. Eagle Enterprises (P), the successor to Orchid Hill, brought this action to collect the fee specified in the covenant. Although the lower courts ruled for Eagle (P), finding that the covenant "ran with the land," the appellate division reversed, holding that the covenant failed to "touch and concern" the land, was an undue restriction on alienation, and a burden in perpetuity. Eagle (P) appealed.

ISSUE: Will affirmative covenants run with the land when they fail to "touch and concern" the land, or when they either create an undue restraint on alienation or a burden in perpetuity?

HOLDING AND DECISION: (Gabrielli, J.) No. Affirmative covenants will not run with the land when they fail to "touch and concern" the land, or when they either create an undue restraint on alienation or a burden in perpetuity. But this covenant to supply water for six months fails to touch and concern the land since the record shows that no landowners would be deprived of water without it nor that the price of water would be prohibitive without this service. In fact, this obligation to receive water more closely resembles a contractual promise rather than an interest attaching to the property. Also, the covenant creates a burden in perpetuity to all future owners, regardless of how they choose to use the land. Affirmed.

EDITOR'S ANALYSIS: If the covenant affects the quality or value of the property, or has some impact an its use, it is said to touch and concern the land. There is no mechanical test for "touch and concern." The following are examples: (1) a promise restricting use of the land; (2) a promise to pay rent, taxes, or insurance; (3) a promise to repair, maintain, improve, or cultivate the land.

QUICKNOTES
AFFIRMATIVE COVENANT - A written promise to do a particular activity.

BURDEN - Oppressive or troublesome; the duty of a party to introduce evidence to support a fact that is in dispute in an action.

TOUCH AND CONCERN - The requirement, in order for a covenant to be binding upon successors, that the covenant enhance the use or value of the benefited party.

NOTES:

1515-1519 LAKEVIEW BOULEVARD CONDOMINIUM ASS'N v. APARTMENT SALES CORP.

Homeowners (P) v. Development company (D)

Wash. Sup. Ct., en banc, 43 P.3d 1233 (2002).

NATURE OF CASE: Appeal [from dismissal on summary judgment] in action to determine whether an exculpatory covenant in a recorded deed runs with the land.

FACT SUMMARY: The 1515-1519 Lakeview Boulevard Condominium Association (homeowners) (P) brought suit against the City of Seattle (city) (D) when their condominiums became uninhabitable as the result of a landslide, arguing that a covenant exculpating the city from liability for damages caused by soil movement did not run with the land.

CONCISE RULE OF LAW: (1) The abolition of sovereign immunity is not violated when a local government requires, as a condition of granting a building permit, an exculpatory covenant tailored to alleviate specific concerns unique to a particular project. (2) An exculpatory covenant recorded in a deed touches and concerns the land, and therefore runs with the land.

FACTS: Three condominiums of the 1515-1519 Lakeview Boulevard Condominium Association (homeowners) (P) became uninhabitable when the soil underlying the property gave way precipitously. The homeowners (P) brought suit against the City of Seattle (city) (D), arguing that the city (D) should not have permitted the condominiums to be built due to the latent risk of soil movement. Before allowing the construction of the condominiums, the city (D) imposed several conditions on the developer (D), including a covenant exculpating the city from liability for damages caused by soil movement. The covenant was properly recorded and the homeowners (P) had notice of it.

ISSUE: (1) Is the abolition of sovereign immunity violated when a local government requires, as a condition of granting a building permit, an exculpatory covenant tailored to alleviate specific concerns unique to a particular project? (2) Does an exculpatory covenant recorded in a deed touch and concern the land, and therefore run with the land?

HOLDING AND DECISION: (Chambers, J.) (1) No. The abolition of sovereign immunity is not violated when a local government requires, as a condition of granting a building permit, an exculpatory covenant tailored to alleviate specific concerns unique to a particular project. Exculpatory covenants do not categorically violate sovereign immunity. However, ordinances immunizing local governments for their own negligence are like blanket grants of immunity and will be invalidated. To encourage development on land that is marginal for development, a local government and a property owner may reach an arm's-length,

bargained-for agreement that may include waivers of liability for risks created by the proposed use of the property because of the unique characteristics of that particular property. Here, because the exculpatory language was tailored to the specific risks presented by the proposed development of the property and appropriately limited in scope to the danger of soil movement, it does not violate the abolition of sovereign immunity by functionally enacting blanket immunity. (2) Yes. An exculpatory covenant recorded in a deed touches and concerns the land, and, therefore, runs with the land. The homeowners (P) argue that exculpatory waivers do not run with the land, and, therefore, cannot bind successors in interest. Generally, there are five elements required for a covenant to run: (1) a promise that is enforceable between the original parties; (2) that touches and concerns; (3) that the parties intended to bind successors; (4) that is sought to be enforced by an original party or a successor, against the same; (5) who has notice of the covenant or has not given value. Here, the only disputed element is whether the covenant "touches and concerns" the land. Generally, a covenant touches and concerns if it is such as to benefit the grantor, lessor, grantee, or lessee, as the case may be, and must concern the occupation or enjoyment of the land. But it is an open issue whether a covenant warning of a risk and exculpating liability for that risk touches and concerns the land. The touches and concerns requirement, although relaxed for subdivisions, is still required for a covenant to run with the land in all other settings. Here, the covenant satisfies the touch and concern doctrine because the covenant burdens the use of the land, since the covenant is limited to the reasonable enjoyment of the land and limits rights normally associated with ownership. Further, few things touch and concern the land more than the soil itself. Therefore, the covenant runs with the land, and the city (D) is exculpated for losses that are not caused by the city's (D) own negligence arising from soil movement. Affirmed.

EDITOR'S ANALYSIS: The Restatement (Third) of Property has abolished "touch and concern" as an element of enforceable covenants. Instead, the Restatement provides that a servitude is valid unless it is illegal, unconstitutional, or violates public policy. The court in this case did not consider the Restatement approach because it was not timely raised.

KERLEY v. NU-WEST, INC.
Buyer (P) v. Seller (D)
Ariz. Ct. of App., 762 P.2d 631 (1988).

NATURE OF CASE: Appeal from summary judgment for defendant in rescission action.

FACT SUMMARY: Kerley (P) sought rescission of a land sale and consulting agreement alleging that it constituted an unreasonable restraint on the alienation of property.

CONCISE RULE OF LAW: Restraints on alienation are permissible under Arizona law if they are reasonably designed to attain or encourage accepted social or economic ends.

FACTS: Kerley (P) agreed to purchase land for development from Nu-West (D), subject to an express condition precedent that Kerley (P) agree to an Architectural Planning and Consulting Agreement. That Agreement called for the payment of ten percent of the gross sale price of all portions later sold and this obligation to pay was to constitute a covenant running with the land. When Kerley (P) sued Nu-West (D) for rescission he claimed that the Agreement was void because it was an unreasonable restraint on the alienation of property. The trial court held that the Agreement did not restrain alienation and granted Nu-West's (D) motion for summary judgment. Kerley (P) appealed.

ISSUE: Are restraints on alienation permissible under Arizona law if they are reasonably designed to attain or encourage accepted social or economic ends?

HOLDING AND DECISION: (Kleinschmidt, J.) Yes. Restraints on alienation are permissible under Arizona law if they are reasonably designed to attain or encourage accepted social or economic ends. The trial judge was correct in finding that the agreements on their face met this standard. The whole purpose of the agreements was to develop and sell land. It really does not matter whether we label the ten percent Kerley (P) was required to pay as payment for land or as payment for consulting services, or both. The parties had bargained for this share in Kerley's (P) profit. Affirmed.

EDITOR'S ANALYSIS: The court here also discussed Kerley's (P) allegations that the ten percent share constituted a quarter sale. A "quarter sale" is a transfer of a fee simple interest in land without retention of a reversionary interest but with the requirement that the buyer pay a portion of any subsequent sale price to the original seller. Such sales are impermissible because they discourage sales since the owner does not receive full value for the property.

QUICKNOTES

RESCISSION - The canceling of an agreement and the return of the parties to their positions prior to the formation of the contract.

NOTES:

WHITINSVILLE PLAZA, INC. v. KOTSEAS
Buyer (P) v. Seller (D)
Mass. Sup. Jud. Ct., 390 N.E.2d 243 (1979).

NATURE OF CASE: Review of dismissal of plaintiff's claims for violation of covenants.

FACT SUMMARY: The trial court dismissed Whitinsville Plaza's (P) claims for violation of real covenants and for interference with contractual relations on the basis of a rule that covenants against competition would not run with the land.

CONCISE RULE OF LAW: Reasonable covenants against competition may be considered to run with the land when they serve a purpose of facilitating orderly and harmonious development for commercial use.

FACTS: Whitinsville Plaza (P), a shopping center, was developed on land Kotseas (D) had sold to Whitinsville's (P) predecessor-in-interest. The deed included a covenant not to compete. When Kotseas (D) later leased his neighboring land to a drug store that would compete with Whitinsville (P), Whitinsville (P) sued for breach of the covenant. The trial court dismissed the complaint based on case precedent that covenants not to compete did not run with the land. Whitinsville (P) appealed.

ISSUE: May reasonable covenants against competition be considered to run with the land when they serve a purpose of facilitating orderly and harmonious development for commercial use?

HOLDING AND DECISION: (Quirico, J.) Yes. Reasonable covenants against competition may be considered to run with the land when they serve a purpose of facilitating orderly and harmonious development for commercial use. Massachusetts has been practically alone in its position that covenants not to compete do not run with the land to which they relate. Such covenants are only enforceable if reasonably limited in time and space and are consonant with the public interest. Where a covenant restrains an individual employee from competing with his employer, the covenant must be necessary for the employer's protection. These include unreasonableness in time, space or product line, or obstruction of the public interest, and raise an issue of fact to be resolved at a trial on the merits. It is often difficult to separate overall planning goals from a businessman's desire to be free from unlimited and ruinous competition by its neighbors. In this case, great unfairness would result if the covenant were not enforced since Kotseas (D) had agreed to it after arm's-length negotiations. Reversed and remanded.

EDITOR'S ANALYSIS: The court here reversed an earlier court decision. It overruled the earlier case because it felt the facts of this case warranted it. The court also said that the earlier rule may have really been based on the policy against monopolies, rather than on the law of real covenants.

NOTES:

DAVIDSON BROS., INC. v. D. KATZ & SONS, INC.
Seller (P) v. Buyer (D)
N.J. Super. Ct. App. Ct., 643 A.2d 642 (1994).

NATURE OF CASE: Appeal from judgment for defendant on remand.

FACT SUMMARY: On remand, the trial court applied a reasonable test and determined that a covenant prohibiting the use of certain property as a supermarket was unenforceable.

CONCISE RULE OF LAW: A covenant may be so contrary to the public interest that it is unreasonable and unenforceable.

FACTS: Davidson (P) sought to enjoin Katz (D) from operating a supermarket on land in a decaying inner-city area. The property had been sold subject to a covenant prohibiting such use for forty years. The court decided that the forty-year term was unreasonably long; that the covenant was unenforceable for public policy reasons. On remand, Davidson (P) sought only damages for lost profits and for the reduced value of its neighboring supermarket. The court held that the covenant imposed an unreasonable restraint of trade; that the covenant was contrary to the public interest; and that the evidence was not sufficient to determine whether Davidson (P) had sustained any damages. Davidson (P) appealed.

ISSUE: May a covenant be so contrary to the public interest that it is unreasonable and unenforceable?

HOLDING AND DECISION: (D'Annunzio, J.) Yes. A covenant may be so contrary to the public interest that it is unreasonable and unenforceable. New Jersey courts have consistently refused to enforce contracts that violate public policy. The rehabilitation of New Jersey's inner cities is a public policy often expressed in relevant legislation. In this case, if the covenant were enforced it would cause harm both to the residents of the area and to the government efforts to revitalize the area. Affirmed.

EDITOR'S ANALYSIS: The court here reviewed the history of the inner-city area in question. The lack of supermarkets in the area not only contributed to the blight and poverty, but also endangered the health of the residents. Barriers of location and transportation tighten the grip of hunger and poverty in such areas, according to Congressional studies.

QUICKNOTES
COVENANT - A written promise to do, or to refrain from doing, a particular activity.

DAMAGES - Monetary compensation that may be awarded by the court to a party who has sustained injury or loss to his or her person, property or rights due to another party's unlawful act, omission or negligence.

RHUE v. CHEYENNE HOMES, INC.
Homeowner (D) v. Subdivision (P)
Colo. Sup. Ct., 449 P.2d 361 (1969).

NATURE OF CASE: Appeal from plaintiff's injunction.

FACT SUMMARY: Rhue (D) claimed that a subdivision's restrictive covenants were unenforceable because they lacked specific standards.

CONCISE RULE OF LAW: Restrictive covenants requiring approval by an architectural committee are enforceable so long as the committee's decision is not arbitrary or capricious.

FACTS: Cheyenne Homes (P) alleged that the subdivision's restrictive covenant were violated when the Rhues (D) failed to submit their plans to the subdivision's architectural control committee. Cheyenne (P) also claimed that property values would depreciate if the Rhues (P) moved a thirty year old Spanish style house into a subdivision with only modern ranch style or split level homes. The court granted Cheyenne's (P) request for an injunction and the Rhues (D) appealed. The Rhues (D) claimed that the covenants lacked specific standards and were therefore unenforceable.

ISSUE: Are restrictive covenants requiring approval by an architectural committee enforceable so long as the committee's decision is not arbitrary or capricious?

HOLDING AND DECISION: (Pringle, J.) Yes. Restrictive covenants requiring approval by an architectural committee are enforceable so long as the committee's decision is not arbitrary or capricious. The committee's disapproval of the plans was reasonable and in good faith and in harmony with the covenant's purposes to protect property values. Affirmed.

EDITOR'S ANALYSIS: The court here found that design covenants were valid. Other courts have held that specific guidelines are necessary to enable a homeowner to determine whether his plans would be acceptable. In the past, lawsuits regarding satellite dishes and television antennas resulted from enforcement of similar design covenants.

QUICKNOTES
RESTRICTIVE COVENANT - A promise contained in a deed to limit the uses to which the property will be made.

NAHRSTEDT v. LAKESIDE VILLAGE CONDOMINIUM ASS'N, INC.

Condo owner (P) v. Homeowners' association (D)
Cal. Sup. Ct., 878 P.2d 1275 (1994).

NATURE OF CASE: Review of reversal of dismissal of claim for declaratory judgment and damages.

FACT SUMMARY: The trial court dismissed Nahrstedt's (P) complaint alleging that use restrictions forbidding the keeping of cats in her condominium were unreasonable, but the dismissal was reversed on appeal.

CONCISE RULE OF LAW: Common interest development use restrictions contained in a project's recorded declaration are enforceable unless unreasonable.

FACTS: Nahrstedt (P) bought a condominium and moved in with her three cats. When the Lakeside Village Condominium Association (D) learned of the cats' presence, it assessed fines against Nahrstedt (P) for violating a use restriction that the project's developer had included in the recorded declaration of the covenants, conditions and restrictions. Nahrstedt (P) sued for declaratory judgment and damages, alleging that the condominium use restrictions were unreasonable because they restricted the use of her unit. The trial court sustained Lakeside's (D) demurrer, but the court of appeals reversed. Lakeside (D) appealed.

ISSUE: Are common interest development use restrictions contained in a project's recorded declaration enforceable unless unreasonable?

HOLDING AND DECISION: (Kennard, J.) Yes. Common interest development use restrictions contained in a project's recorded declaration are enforceable unless unreasonable. Courts accord presumptive validity to recorded use restrictions to promote stability and predictability. When an association determines that a homeowner violated a use restriction, it must do so in good faith and not in an arbitrary or capricious manner. Here, Nahrstedt's (P) allegations, even if true, were insufficient to show that the pet restriction's harmful effects substantially outweighed its benefits to the condominium development as a whole or that it violated public policy. Affirmed.

DISSENT: (Arabian, J.) The pet restriction is patently arbitrary and unreasonable.

EDITOR'S ANALYSIS: The court here explained that giving deference to use restrictions protects the general expectations of all condominium owners. In a common interest development, individual property rights are subordinated to the collective judgment of the owners association. Each unit owner must give up a little freedom of choice when using facilities in common.

RICK v. WEST

Developer (P) v. Buyer (D)
N.Y. Sup. Ct., Westchester County, 228 N.Y.S. 2d 195 (1962).

NATURE OF CASE: Action for declaratory judgment to permit violation of restrictive covenants.

FACT SUMMARY: West (D) refused to permit Rick (P) to sell residential land to a hospital, in violation of restrictive covenants.

CONCISE RULE OF LAW: Restrictive covenants may not be removed on the application of the developer, where purchasers have relied on the restrictions, and where there is no change in the character of the neighborhood.

FACTS: Rick (P), the developer of a residential community, voluntarily imposed upon his 62 acres covenants which restricted them to residential use. West (D), relying upon these restrictions, bought a lot. Later, Rick (P) attempted to sell 15 acres of the subdivision to a hospital, and West (D) refused to consent to this violation of the restrictions. Rick contended that the sale should be allowed, because (1) the original covenants contained a clause providing for "exceptions in certain cases," and (2) substantial changes have occurred in the neighborhood, making the covenants unenforceable.

ISSUE: Can the developer violate restrictive covenants which he voluntarily imposed on his property?

HOLDING AND DECISION: (Hoyt, J.) No. Even though Rick (P) voluntarily imposed the restrictions on the lots in his subdivision, West (D) bought her lot in reliance on those restrictions. The character of the neighborhood had not changed significantly enough to warrant a violation of the covenant, and while certain exceptions may be allowed, the non-residential use of 15 acres does not constitute a permissible exception.

EDITOR'S ANALYSIS: The retention by a developer of the right to modify the restrictions as to any properties in the development has generally been held to negate the idea of a uniform plan or scheme in the subdivision. In such a case, even if the developer does not exercise this reserved right, one owner will be precluded from enforcing the restrictions against another owner.

QUICKNOTES

RESTRICTIVE COVENANT - A promise contained in a deed to limit the uses to which the property will be made.

EVERGREEN HIGHLANDS ASSOCIATION v. WEST

Homeowners association (D) v. Homeowner (P)
Colo. Sup. Ct., en banc, 73 P.3d 1 (2003).

NATURE OF CASE: Appeal from reversal of judgment that a homeowners association has authority to amend a subdivision's covenants to permit for mandatory assessments.

FACT SUMMARY: West (P) claimed that Evergreen Highlands Association (the "Association") (D), the homeowners association for the Evergreen Highlands Subdivision (Evergreen Highlands), did not have the power to amend its covenants to allow for assessments for maintaining common areas. The Association (D) counterclaimed that it had implied power to make such assessments.

CONCISE RULE OF LAW: (1) A modification clause of a subdivision's covenants that **permits changes or modifications to the covenants permits the addition of an entirely new covenant where the effect of the new covenant is not unreasonable or unduly burdensome on the lot owners. (2) Even in the absence of an express covenant mandating payment of assessments, a homeowners association that is a common interest community has the implied power to levy assessments against lot owners in a subdivision to raise the funds necessary to maintain the common areas of the subdivision.**

FACTS: Evergreen Highlands Association (the "Association") (D), the homeowners association for the Evergreen Highlands Subdivision (Evergreen Highlands) was incorporated to maintain the subdivision's common areas and facilities, enforce the subdivision's covenants, pay taxes on the common areas, and determine annual fees. Evergreen Highlands had a 22-acre park area open to all residents of the subdivision. Protective covenants for Evergreen Highlands did not require lot owners to be members of or pay dues to the Association (D), which had title to the park. Initially, the Association (D) relied on voluntary assessments from lot owners to pay for maintenance and improvements to the park. Article 13 of the original Evergreen Highlands covenants provided that a majority (75%) of lot owners could modify the covenants—"change or modify any one or more of said restrictions." Pursuant to the article, the required majority voted to add a new article that required all lot owners to be members of and pay assessments to the Association (D), and permitted the Association (D) to impose liens on the property of any owners who failed to pay their assessment. West (P) had purchased his lot when membership in the Association (D), and payment of assessments, was voluntary. He did not vote for the new article that made membership and assessments mandatory, and he refused to pay his lot assessment of $50 per year. When the Association (D) threatened to record a lien against his property, he filed suit

challenging the validity of the amendment. The Association (D) counterclaimed for a declaratory judgment that it had the implied power to collect assessments from all lot owners in the subdivision, and sought damages from West (P) for breach of the implied contract. The trial court ruled in favor of the Association (D) on the ground that the amendment was valid and binding. The intermediate court of appeals reversed, finding that the terms "change" or "modify" did not permit the addition of new covenants, but applied only to existing covenants. The state's highest court granted certiorari.

ISSUE: (1) Does a modification clause of a subdivision's covenants that permits changes or modifications to the covenants permit the addition of an entirely new covenant where the effect of the new covenant is not unreasonable or unduly burdensome on the lot owners? (2) Even in the absence of an express covenant mandating payment of assessments, does a homeowners association that is a common interest community have the implied power to levy assessments against lot owners in a subdivision to raise the funds necessary to maintain the common areas of the subdivision?

HOLDING AND DECISION: (Rice, J.) (1) Yes. A modification clause of a subdivision's covenants that permits changes or modifications to the covenants permits the addition of an entirely new covenant where the effect of the new covenant is not unreasonable or unduly burdensome on the lot owners. Some courts faced with nearly identical fact patterns have held that the modification clause does not permit the addition of a new covenant, whereas others have permitted the addition of a new covenant. The distinction between these cases does not turn on how narrowly or broadly the particular modification clause is written, but rather on the differing factual scenarios and severity of consequences that the cases present. In those cases where courts disallowed the amendment of the covenants, the impact on the objecting lot owner was far more substantial and unforeseeable than the impact of the amendment at issue in this case. Those cases that permitted amendments did so where the amendment's purpose was to impose mandatory assessments on lot owners for the purpose of maintaining common elements of a subdivision. That line of cases (the *Zito* line) is more applicable here. Moreover, the amendment in this case was changed according to the modification clause of the original Evergreen Highlands covenants, of which West (P) had notice when he purchased his property. Finally, at $50 per year, the mandatory assessment is neither unreasonable nor burdensome. To the

Continued on next page.

contrary, the existence of a well-maintained park immediately adjacent to West's (P) lot undoubtedly enhances his property value. The amendment was valid and binding on all lot owners in Evergreen Highlands. (2) Yes. Even in the absence of an express covenant mandating payment of assessments, a homeowners association that is a common interest community has the implied power to levy assessments against lot owners in a subdivision to raise the funds necessary to maintain the common areas of the subdivision. This is a question of first impression in this state. Most other jurisdictions hold that homeowners associations have the implied power to levy dues or assessments even in the absence of express authority. The latest version of the Restatement of Property (Servitudes) reflects this approach, but refers to "common-interest" communities. West (P) argues that the implied power to mandate assessments can only be imputed to such communities, which are defined as residential communities in which there exists a mandatory obligation or servitude imposed on individual owners to pay for common elements of the community. He therefore argues that because the original covenants did not impose such a servitude, Evergreen Highlands is not a common interest community. This argument is rejected because West (P) incorrectly assumes that the obligation or servitude had to be expressed in the covenants or in his deed. Instead, such obligation need only arise from the "declarations," which are defined as "any recorded instruments however denominated." The declarations in effect for Evergreen Highlands at the time West (P) bought his property included the covenants; a plat that noted the park would be conveyed to the Association (D); the Association's (D) articles of incorporation, which stated the Association's (D) purpose; and the deed whereby the developer quit-claimed his ownership in the park to the Association (D). These declarations were sufficient to create a common interest community by implication, and the Association (D) had the implicit power to levy assessments against lot owners for the purpose of maintaining and operating the common area. Reversed and remanded.

CONCURRENCE: (Coats, J.) The Evergreen Highlands covenants permitted the amendment, which is an express covenant permitting collection of assessments. Therefore, the court should not have reached the hypothetical question whether the Association (D) would have the implied power to collect assessments in the absence of such an express provision. Nor should the court have legislated a new category of common-interest community.

EDITOR'S ANALYSIS: The Restatement (Third) § 6.10(2) provides that amendments to covenants that do not apply uniformly to similar lots and amendments that treat members unfairly are not effective without approval of the members whose

interests would be adversely affected. Here, the court seems to conclude that the assessments were fair and treated all members of Evergreen Highlands alike. Had this not been the case, West's (P) action would have been significantly stronger.

QUICKNOTES

LIEN - A claim against the property of another in order to secure the payment of a debt.

WESTWOOD HOMEOWNERS ASS'N v. LANE COUNTY
Homeowners association (P) v. County owner (D)
Or. Sup. Ct., 864 P.2d 350 (1993).

NATURE OF CASE: Review of summary judgment for plaintiff.

FACT SUMMARY: Westwood Homeowners Association (P) filed an action to foreclose its lien against fifteen lots acquired by Lane County (D) as a result of the County's (D) failure to pay common maintenance fees.

CONCISE RULE OF LAW: A county that acquires title in a tax foreclosure sale takes title subject to servitudes.

FACTS: Lane County (D) foreclosed on fifteen lots in a planned unit development for nonpayment of real property taxes and acquired title to those lots. When Lane County (D) refused to pay common maintenance fees, Westwood Homeowners Association (P) filed an action to foreclose its lien against the fifteen lots for the unpaid assessments. Lane County (D) counterclaimed to quiet title or to extinguish the Association's (P) lien if it had not been extinguished by the tax foreclosure, arguing that the Association's (P) assessments created liens or encumbrances and that Lane County had acquired title free from any liens or encumbrances. The court granted the Association's (P) motion for summary judgment and the court of appeals affirmed. The Oregon Supreme Court granted Lane County's (D) petition for review.

ISSUE: Does a county that acquire title in a tax foreclosure sale take title subject to servitudes?

HOLDING AND DECISION: (Unis, J.) Yes. A county that acquires title in a tax foreclosure sale takes title subject to servitudes. There is no lien on the servient estate until the Association (P) exercises its power to make annual or special assessments. Servitudes are neither liens nor encumbrances as the term is used in the statute. Encumbrances relate to only claims for money or security interest in the servient estate. If a tax foreclosure extinguished servitudes of the dominant estate, it would arguably infringe on the constitutional rights of the owners of the dominant estate and on the rights of the other owners in the same subdivision. Affirmed.

EDITOR'S ANALYSIS: The court here considered public policy in reaching its decision. The expectations of the homeowners would be defeated by extinguishing the servitudes. The value of the entire subdivision would be seriously impaired if the burden of a covenant regarding the use of the land were extinguished by a tax sale.

QUICKNOTES
BURDEN - Oppressive or troublesome; the duty of a party to introduce evidence to support a fact that is in dispute in an action.

NOTES:

CHAPTER 13
EMINENT DOMAIN

QUICK REFERENCE RULES OF LAW

1. **"Public Purpose."** Redistribution of fees simple to correct deficiencies in the market is a rational exercise of the eminent domain power. (Hawaii Housing Authority v. Midkiff)

2. **Illustrative Cases of Claims of Inadequate Government Compensation for Condemnation.** It is the settled policy of Congress to limit the right to compensation for the taking of land to interest in the land taken. (Mitchell v. United States)

3. **Illustrative Cases of Claims of Inadequate Government Compensation for Condemnation.** The government as condemnor may not be required to compensate a condemnee for elements of value that the government has created or that it might have destroyed under the exercise of its authority other than the eminent domain power. (United States v. Fuller)

4. **Flyover.** Invasion of superadjacent airspace affects the use of the surface of the land itself. (Griggs v. Allegheny County)

5. **River Navigation and Flooding.** A permanent liability to intermittent but inevitably recurrent flooding is a partial taking of property. (Phelps v. Board of Supervisors of Muscatine)

6. **Restricting Pollution in Rivers and Streams.** A polluter has no absolute right to discharge industrial waste into a river. (United States v. 531.13 Acres of Land, Etc.)

7. **Condemnation of Restrictive Covenants and Affirmative Covenants to Pay.** Where the reduction in value of property is due to the construction of a highway and not to the breach of a covenant, no damages can be awarded. (Arkansas State Highway Commission v. McNeill)

8. **Condemnation of Restrictive Covenants and Affirmative Covenants to Pay.** The right of a private owner to receive an income stream from a monthly fee assessed against an owner of adjacent property pursuant to a covenant running with the land constitutes a property right compensable upon inverse condemnation by a public authority for use of that adjacent property in a public road improvement project. (Palm Beach County v. Cove Club Investors Ltd.)

HAWAII HOUSING AUTHORITY v. MIDKIFF
State agency (D) v. Landowners (P)
467 U.S. 229 (1984).

NATURE OF CASE: Appeal from injunction against enforcement of state legislation.

FACT SUMMARY: The Hawaii Land Reform Act of 1967 created a mechanism for redistribution of lands by condemnation of residential tracts and transferring ownership of the condemned fees simple to existing lessees.

CONCISE RULE OF LAW: Redistribution of fees simple to correct deficiencies in the market attributable to land oligopoly is a rational exercise of the eminent domain power.

FACTS: The Hawaii Housing Authority (HHA) (D) was authorized by the Hawaii Land Reform Act of 1967 to condemn residential tracts for resale to existing lessees as part of a plan to remedy the social and economic ills resulting from a land oligopoly on the islands. The court of appeals for the Ninth Circuit later found the legislation to be unconstitutional and enjoined enforcement. The HHA (D) appealed.

ISSUE: Is redistribution of fees simple to correct deficiencies in the market attributable to land oligopoly a rational exercise of the eminent domain power?

HOLDING AND DECISION: (O'Connor, J.) Yes. Redistribution of fees simple to correct deficiencies in the market is a rational exercise of the eminent domain power. The state legislature had determined that the deficiencies in the market attributable to land oligopoly were attributable to the land oligopoly. The Fifth Amendment does not prohibit Hawaii from taking property, with just compensation, from lessors and transferring it to lessees in order to reduce the concentration of ownership of fees simple in the state. The exercise of the eminent domain power was rationally related to a legitimate public purpose and was therefore constitutional. Reversed and remanded.

EDITOR'S ANALYSIS: The Court here found that the government itself did not have to use the land to legitimize its taking. Only the taking's purpose, not its mechanics, must pass constitutional scrutiny. Judicial deference was also due the findings of the state legislature.

QUICKNOTES
EMINENT DOMAIN - The governmental power to take private property for public use so long as just compensation is paid therefore.

FIFTH AMENDMENT - Provides that no person shall be compelled to serve as a witness against himself, or be subject to trial for the same offense twice, or be deprived of life, liberty, or property without due process of law.

MITCHELL v. UNITED STATES
Business owner (P) v. Government (D)
267 U.S. 341 (1925).

NATURE OF CASE: Review of denial of claim for compensation for government taking.

FACT SUMMARY: Mitchell (P) claimed that his business was destroyed when the U.S. government (D) took his land to use for military purposes.

CONCISE RULE OF LAW: It is the settled policy of Congress to limit the right to compensation for the taking of land to interest in the land taken.

FACTS: Mitchell (P) was growing a special grade of corn on land which was taken over by the federal government (D) for military use. The President fixed $76,000 as just compensation for the land, but made no allowance for the taking of the business. Mitchell (P) unsuccessfully sought additional compensation for the loss of his business. The U.S. Supreme Court granted certiorari.

ISSUE: Is it the settled policy of Congress to limit the right to compensation for the taking of land to interest in the land taken?

HOLDING AND DECISION: (Brandeis, J.) Yes. It is the settled policy of Congress to limit the right to compensation for the taking of land to interest in the land taken. In the absence of an agreement, losses due to the destruction of a business are considered unintended incidents of the taking of the land and are not compensable. Affirmed.

EDITOR'S ANALYSIS: The court here explained that many states require payment for such losses. In this case, there was no agreement and no statutory right. Consequential damages may be provided for by state law.

QUICKNOTES
CONSEQUENTIAL DAMAGES - Monetary compensation that may be recovered in order to compensate for injuries or losses sustained as a result of damages that are not the direct or foreseeable result of the act of a party, but that nevertheless are the consequence of such act and which must be specifically pled and demonstrated.

EMINENT DOMAIN - The governmental power to take private property for public use so long as just compensation is paid therefore.

TAKING - A governmental action that substantially deprives an owner of the use and enjoyment of his or her property, requiring compensation.

UNITED STATES v. FULLER
Government (P) v. Landowner (D)
409 U.S. 488 (1973).

NATURE OF CASE: Review of award of compensation for a government taking of land.

FACT SUMMARY: The trial court allowed Fuller (D) to introduce testimony as to the value of fee lands taken by the federal government (P), which considered value accruing to those lands by virtue of their proximity to federal grazing lands.

CONCISE RULE OF LAW: The government as condemnor may not be required to compensate a condemnee for elements of value that the government has created, or that it might have destroyed under the exercise of its authority other than the eminent domain power.

FACTS: The federal government (P) condemned 920 acres of Fuller's (D) ranch. In determining the just compensation for the lands taken, Fuller (D) claimed that the jury should be allowed to consider value accruing to the land as a result of its actual or potential use in combination with neighboring federal Taylor Grazing Act lands. The district court allowed the jury to consider those factors with respect to value, and the government (P) appealed.

ISSUE: May the government as condemnor be required to compensate a condemnee for elements of value that the government has created?

HOLDING AND DECISION: (Rehnquist, J.) No. The government as condemnor may not be required to compensate a condemnee for elements of value that the government has created, or that it might have destroyed under the exercise of its authority other than the eminent domain power. The Fifth Amendment does not require the government (P) to pay for that element of value based on the use of Fuller's (D) fee lands in combination with the United States' (P) permit lands. Reversed.

EDITOR'S ANALYSIS: The Court here analogized to cases involving the government's (P) navigational servitude. A long line of cases had established the precedent that compensation for fast lands taken does not include any benefits conferred by proximity to a potential portsite or hydroelectric gate site. Here, the permit lands were owned by the government (P) and could not be aggregated by the fee owners in order to determine the correct valuation of the fee lands.

QUICKNOTES

EMINENT DOMAIN - The governmental power to take private property for public use so long as just compensation is paid therefore.

JUST COMPENSATION - The right guaranteed by the Fifth Amendment to the United States Constitution of a person, when his property is taken for public use by the state, to receive adequate compensation in order to restore him to the position he enjoyed prior to the appropriation.

TAKINGS - A governmental action that substantially deprives an owner of the use and enjoyment of his or her property, requiring compensation.

TAYLOR GRAZING ACT - 48 Stat. 1270 as amended, 43 U.S.C. 315b - authorizes the Secretary of the Interior to issue permits to livestock owners for grazing their cattle on federal government lands.

NOTES:

GRIGGS v. ALLEGHENY COUNTY
Home owner (P) v. County (D)
369 U.S. 84 (1962).

NATURE OF CASE: Review of state supreme court ruling on taking of an air easement.

FACT SUMMARY: The supreme court of Pennsylvania held that Allegheny County (D) may have taken an air easement over Griggs' (P) property but that the County (D) was not liable.

CONCISE RULE OF LAW: Invasion of superadjacent airspace affects the use of the surface of the land itself.

FACTS: Allegheny County (D) owned and maintained an airport near the Griggs' (P) home. The noise from the planes taking off and landing made it impossible for the Griggs (P) to continue living in their house. When Griggs (P) sued the County (D), a hearing was ordered and the court then found that the County (D) had taken an air easement over Griggs' (P) property. The court set damages at $12,690. Both parties appealed, and the Pennsylvania Supreme Court found that the County (D) was not liable for damages. The United States Supreme Court granted certiorari.

ISSUE: Does invasion of superadjacent airspace affect the use of the surface of the land itself?

HOLDING AND DECISION: (Douglas, J.) Yes. Invasion of superadjacent airspace affects the use of the surface of the land itself. The use of land presupposes the use of some of the air space above it. When the County (D) designed the airport, it had to acquire some private property. By constitutional standards, it did not acquire enough. Reversed.

EDITOR'S ANALYSIS: This case involved inverse condemnation. Inverse condemnation is an action brought by a private citizen against the government, forcing the government to purchase the citizen's property. A court must first make a factual finding that a taking has occurred, despite the government's denials.

PHELPS v. BOARD OF SUPERVISORS OF MUSCATINE
Property owners (P) v. Government (D)
Iowa Sup. Ct., 211 N.W.2d 274 (1973).

NATURE OF CASE: Review of judgment for defendant in *mandamus* action.

FACT SUMMARY: Phelps (P) claimed that Muscatine County's (D) construction of a causeway and bridge caused his land to be intermittently flooded, and demanded compensation.

CONCISE RULE OF LAW: A permanent liability to intermittent but inevitably recurrent flooding is a taking of property.

FACTS: Phelps (P) alleged that the intermittent flooding over his land, resulting from the County's (D) construction of a bridge and causeway as part of a highway improvement constituted a taking of his property. When Phelps' (P) demand for compensation from the County (D) was denied, he petitioned the court for a writ of *mandamus.* The court denied his request and the Iowa Supreme Court granted review.

ISSUE: Is a permanent liability to intermittent but inevitably recurrent flooding a taking of property?

HOLDING AND DECISION: [Judge not stated in casebook excerpt.] Yes. A permanent liability to intermittent but inevitably recurrent flooding is a taking of property. It is the character of the invasion, not the amount of damage resulting therefrom, that determines whether there was a taking. If any substantial enjoyment of the land still remains to the owner, it may be treated as a partial, rather than a total, divesting of his interest in the land. Reversed and remanded.

EDITOR'S ANALYSIS: The trial court found that the flooding had substantially increased as a result of the highway improvements, and that future flooding was conjectural and speculative. The Iowa Supreme Court, however, took judicial notice that, despite the uncertainty as to time and security, there would inevitably be future flooding.

QUICKNOTES
FIFTH AMENDMENT - States that the right of citizens of the United States to vote shall not be denied on account of race, color, or previous condition of servitude.

TAKING - A governmental action that substantially deprives an owner of the use and enjoyment of his or her property, requiring compensation.

QUICKNOTES
FIFTH AMENDMENT - Provides that no person shall be compelled to serve as a witness against himself, or be subject to trial for the same offense twice, or be deprived of life, liberty, or property without due process of law.

TAKING - A governmental action that substantially deprives an owner of the use and enjoyment of his or her property, requiring compensation

UNITED STATES v. 531.13 ACRES OF LAND, ETC.
Government (D) v. Polluter (P)
366 F.2d 915 (4th Cir. 1966).

NATURE OF CASE: Appeal from lower court judgment for government (D).

FACT SUMMARY: 531.13 Acres (P) sued for damages incurred in constructing a disposal facility to comply with higher pollution standards imposed by the government (D).

CONCISE RULE OF LAW: A polluter has no absolute right to discharge industrial waste into a river.

FACTS: The government (P) converted a reservoir to recreational use and upgraded its classification. 531.13 Acres (P) dumped untreated waste into rivers feeding into the reservoir and alleged that it had to construct a disposal facility to comply with the new pollution standards set by the government (D). The government (D) won a lower court judgment which was reversed on appeal.

ISSUE: Does a polluter have an absolute right to discharge industrial waste into a river?

HOLDING AND DECISION: [Judge not stated in casebook excerpt.] No. A polluter has no absolute right to discharge industrial waste into a river. Even if the government prevented 531.1 Acres (P) from using the river to dispose of its waste, in doing so it took nothing belonging to 531.1 Acres (P). Utilization of the streams is subject to the rights of other riparian owners in South Carolina. If a lower riparian owner had adapted his riparian ownership to recreational use, 531.1 Acres (P) would not have been able to continue polluting. Reversed.

EDITOR'S ANALYSIS: The court did not find a taking here. Any riparian owner has the right to convert his use to recreational and thereby change the pollution standards for the river. The effluence could be stopped either under the common law or under the statute.

_____

QUICKNOTES

TAKING - A governmental action that substantially deprives an owner of the use and enjoyment of his or her property, requiring compensation.

ARKANSAS STATE HIGHWAY COMMISSION v. MCNEILL
Government (D) v. Land owners (P)
Ark. Sup. Ct., 238 Ark. 244, 381 S.W.2d 425 (1964).

NATURE OF CASE: Appeal from damages award for violation of restrictive covenant.

FACT SUMMARY: The McNeills (P) alleged that the Arkansas State Highway Commission's (D) construction of a highway cloverleaf interchange reduced the value of their property.

CONCISE RULE OF LAW: Where the reduction in value of property is due to the construction of a highway, and not to the breach of a covenant, no damages can be awarded.

FACTS: The construction of a highway interchange near the McNeills' (P) home violated a restrictive covenant. The McNeills (P) sued the Arkansas State Highway Commission (D) for damages on two grounds. The first ground, that the highway would reduce the value of their property, was rejected by the trial court. The trial court upheld the second ground, that the highway violated a restrictive covenant in the bill of assurances. The commission (D) appealed.

ISSUE: Where the reduction in value of property is due to the construction of a highway, and not to the breach of a covenant, can damages be awarded?

HOLDING AND DECISION: [Judge not stated in casebook excerpt.] No. Where the reduction in value of property is due to the construction of a highway and not to the breach of a covenant, no damages can be awarded. Compensation would be denied in the absence of the covenant. But there is no logical basis for awarding damages here since the McNeills' (P) damage cannot be attributed to the violation of the restrictive covenant. Reversed and dismissed.

EDITOR'S ANALYSIS: Jurisdictions are split as to whether to award compensation under such circumstances. Some jurisdictions deny damages on the basis that the restrictive covenant does not confer a property right. Other jurisdictions would allow damages for the decrease in the market value of the property.

QUICKNOTES

DAMAGES - Monetary compensation that may be awarded by the court to a party who has sustained injury or loss to his or her person, property or rights due to another party's unlawful act, omission or negligence.

RESTRICTIVE COVENANT - A promise contained in a deed to limit the uses to which the property will be made.

TAKING - A governmental action that substantially deprives an owner of the use and enjoyment of his or her property, requiring compensation.

NOTES:

PALM BEACH COUNTY v. COVE CLUB INVESTORS LTD.
County (D) v. Private owner (P)
Fla. Sup. Ct., 734 So. 2d 379 (1999).

NATURE OF CASE: Appeal from affirmance of judgment for plaintiff in inverse condemnation action.

FACT SUMMARY: Cove Club Investors Ltd. (Cove Club) (P), owner of Sandalfoot Cove Country Club, claimed that Palm Beach County (County) (D) took from it a property right compensable upon inverse condemnation when the County (D) acquired a lot through eminent domain in Sandalfoot Cove, a mobile home community adjacent to Sandalfoot Country Club, whose members were required to pay a monthly recreational fee to Cove Club (P) pursuant to a covenant benefitting Cove Club (P).

CONCISE RULE OF LAW: The right of a private owner to receive an income stream from a monthly fee assessed against an owner of adjacent property pursuant to a covenant running with the land constitutes a property right compensable upon inverse condemnation by a public authority for use of that adjacent property in a public road improvement project.

FACTS: Sandalfoot Cove was a mobile home community. Pursuant to a Declaration of Conditions, Covenants, Restrictions and Reservations Affecting Property Located in Sandalfoot Cove (Declaration), each lot owner was required to pay a monthly recreational fee in exchange for the right to use the recreational facilities of Sandalfoot Country Club, owned by Cove Club Investors Ltd. (Cove Club) (P). The Declaration specified that all restrictions were to "run with the land." Twenty years after the Declaration was recorded, Palm Beach County (County) (D) acquired a lot in Sandalfoot Cove through its eminent domain power for use in a public road widening project. Cove Club (P) filed an inverse condemnation action against the County (D) claiming that the County (D) took from it a property right in the form of the income generated from the monthly recreational fees. The trial court held for Cove Club (P), and reserved jurisdiction to determine valuation. The intermediate court of appeals (district court of appeal) affirmed, and the state's supreme court granted review.

ISSUE: Does the right of a private owner to receive an income stream from a monthly fee assessed against an owner of adjacent property pursuant to a covenant running with the land constitute a property right compensable upon inverse condemnation by a public authority for use of that adjacent property in a public road improvement project?

HOLDING AND DECISION: (Anstead, J.) Yes. The right of a private owner to receive an income stream from a monthly fee assessed against an owner of adjacent property pursuant to a covenant running with the land constitutes a property right compensable upon inverse condemnation by a public authority for use of that adjacent property in a public road improvement project. The County (D) argues that the covenant at issue here is a restrictive covenant, which is an interest akin to that arising from contract and which does not create a compensable property right in condemnation cases. Under the state's constitution, every person holding an interest in private property is entitled to reasonable compensation in the event the property is taken by the government. The compensability of restrictive covenants is not settled. The majority of courts now hold that the right to collect assessment fees constitutes a compensable property interest held by the owner of the property that the covenant benefits, whereas a minority has not found that such covenants constitute compensable property rights in the constitutional sense when such rights are condemned by a public authority. The minority view is that such restrictions were not intended to apply as against public improvements, as the eminent domain rights of the governmental condemner are impliedly excepted from the operation of the restrictive covenant, and because such restrictions cannot possibly inhibit the action of the sovereign, which has the right to condemn the fee prior to the imposition of the restriction; the placing of the additional burden on the land does not create a new compensable interest. Another argument for denial of compensation is that such restrictions are merely contract rights, enforceable against individuals, but not the state. The better view is that restrictive covenants, such as building restrictions, do not constitute compensable property rights because they are not true easements and do not convey an interest in land. Those restrictions curtail the type of use an owner may make of his property. In contrast, the covenant here imposes a continuing affirmative obligation on the owners of the burdened land, which in turn granted to those owners a right of way (to use the country club facilities). Under established law, and under the Declaration itself, Cove Club (P) has a right to assert a lien against any nonpaying lot owner who fails to pay the monthly fee. Also, in cases involving building restrictions, the public policy concern is that if the government must succumb to restrictions placed on the use of land, its ability to exercise eminent domain will likewise be curtailed. Here, those concerns are not present, as the government's taking of the lot is not being challenged and the covenant does not in any way interfere with the government's eminent domain power; the government must merely pay for exercising that power. Here, too, that compensation is clearly determinable and must be paid to only one owner, thus, not

Continued on next page.

imposing any unreasonable burden on the County (D). As one commentator has noted: "The constitutional guarantee of compensation does not extend only to cases where the taking is cheap or easy." To deprive Cove Club (P) of its right to collect recreational fees would be to deny it of its constitutional right. Where, as here, the assessment fees are mandatory and run with the land, the right to collect such fees is clearly a property right, which must be compensated upon a governmental taking. Affirmed.

DISSENT: (Overton, Sr.J.) The covenant at issue here was a mere contract right, not a property right, and this view is consistent with prior precedent. To hold otherwise would give Cove Club (P) an income windfall for a monthly fee from taxpayers, none of whom will be able to use the recreational facilities for which they are paying. Also, the majority's distinguishing of prior precedent is illogical.

EDITOR'S ANALYSIS: Commentators critical of the court's decision in this case fear that the decision will restrict some governmental functioning to the extent that the sovereign's condemnation power will be subject to an undefined number of private contractual affirmative promises evidenced by covenants running with the title.

QUICKNOTES

EMINENT DOMAIN - The governmental power to take private property for public use so long as just compensation is paid therefore.

14

CHAPTER 14
LAND USE REGULATION AND
ITS CONSTITUTIONAL LIMITS

QUICK REFERENCE RULES OF LAW

1. **The Early Cases.** Making the mining of certain coal commercially impracticable has very nearly the same effect for constitutional purposes as appropriating or destroying it. (Pennsylvania Coal Co. v. Mahon)

2. **The Early Cases.** The state does not exceed its constitutional power by deciding upon the destruction of one class of property in order to save another which is of greater value to the public. (Miller v. Schoene)

3. **Zoning as the Paradigm Land Use Regulation.** A zoning ordinance, as a valid exercise of the police power, will only be declared unconstitutional where its provisions are clearly arbitrary and unreasonable, having no substantial relation to the public health, safety, morals or general welfare. (Village of Euclid v. Ambler Realty Co.)

4. **Ten Years in Takings Law from 1978–1987.** Although governmental regulation is invalid if it denies a property owner all reasonable return on his property, there is no constitutional imperative that the return embrace all attributes or contributing external factors derived from the social complex in which the property rests. (Penn Central Transportation v. City of New York)

5. **Ten Years in Takings Law from 1978–1987.** Where an owner possesses a full bundle of possessory rights, the destruction of one strand of the bundle is not a taking. (Andrus, Secretary of the Interior v. Allard)

6. **The 1987 Cases.** Land use regulation can effect a taking if it does not substantially advance legitimate state interests or denies an owner economically viable use of his land. (Keystone Bituminous Coal Ass'n v. DeBenedictis)

7. **The 1987 Cases.** Complete abolition of both the descent and devise of a particular class of property may be a taking. (Hodel, Secretary of the Interior, v. Irving)

8. **Damages as the Requested Remedy for a Taking.** Temporary takings which deny a landowner all use of his property are not different in kind from permanent takings. (First English Evangelical Lutheran Church of Glendale v. County of Los Angeles, California)

9. **The Court Pits Purpose Against Effect.** The state must compensate a landowner when a regulatory action denies the owner economically viable use of the land, unless the prohibited use constitutes a nuisance. (Lucas v. South Carolina Coastal Council)

10. **The Court Pits Purpose Against Effect.** A purchaser or successive title holder is not barred from bringing a takings claim by the mere fact that the title was acquired after the effective date of the state regulation. (Palazzolo v. Rhode Island)

11. **The Court Pits Purpose Against Effect.** A moratorium on development imposed during the process of devising a comprehensive land-use plan does not constitute a *per se* taking of property requiring compensation under the Takings Clause. (Tahoe-Sierra Preservation Council, Inc. v. Tahoe Regional Planning Agency)

12. **Exactions and Traded Liberties in the Zoning Process.** Where individuals are given a permanent and continuous right to pass to and fro over real property, a permanent physical occupation has occurred. (Nollan v. California Coastal Commission)

13. **Exactions and Traded Liberties in the Zoning Process.** The government may not require a person to give up a constitutional right, such as the right to receive just compensation when property is taken for public use, in exchange for a discretionary government benefit where the property sought has little or no relationship to the benefit. (Dolan v. City of Tigard)

PENNSYLVANIA COAL CO. v. MAHON
Grantor v. Grantee (P)
260 U.S. 393 (1922).

NATURE OF CASE: Appeal from judgment for plaintiffs.

FACT SUMMARY: The trial court enjoined Pennsylvania Coal (D) from mining under a house to avoid subsidence.

CONCISE RULE OF LAW: Making the mining of certain coal commercially impracticable has very nearly the same effect for constitutional purposes as appropriating or destroying it.

FACTS: The Pennsylvania Coal Co. (D) deeded a house to the Mahons (D) but reserved the right to remove all the coal under the house. The Mahons (D) waived all claim for damages arising out of the mining. But the Mahons (P) later sued Pennsylvania Coal (D) to prevent them from mining under the house in such a way as to cause subsidence of the surface and of their house. The Mahons (P) claimed that a Pennsylvania statute forbidding mining that causes a subsidence of houses had taken away any rights the Coal Company (D) may have had. On appeal, the Pennsylvania Supreme Court found that the statute was a legitimate exercise of the police power and ruled in favor of the Mahons (P). The Coal Company (D) claimed that, as applied to this case, the statute destroyed existing rights of property and contract. The U.S. Supreme Court granted certiorari.

ISSUE: Does making the mining of certain coal commercially impracticable have very nearly the same effect for constitutional purposes as appropriating or destroying it?

HOLDING AND DECISION: (Holmes, J.) Yes. Making the mining of certain coal commercially impracticable has very nearly the same effect for constitutional purposes as appropriating or destroying it. The statute cannot be upheld as an exercise of the police power so far as it affects the mining of coal in places where the right to mine such coal has been reserved. While property may be regulated to a certain extent, if regulation goes too far it will be a taking. Reversed and remanded.

DISSENT: (Brandeis, J.) The restriction here in question is merely the prohibition of a noxious use. The property so restricted remains in the possession of its owner, the state does not appropriate it or make use of it.

EDITOR'S ANALYSIS: This landmark case is often cited for the proposition that government may execute laws or programs that adversely affect recognized economic values without compensating those affected. Taking challenges have since been held to be without merit in a wide variety of situations, including zoning, when the government action prohibited a beneficial use, causing substantial individualized harm. Justices Holmes and Brandeis represent the two perspectives of the continuing conflict between

the obligation of government to provide for the general welfare and the right of citizens to privately own property.

QUICKNOTES
CONDEMNATION - The taking of private property for public use so long as just compensation is paid therefor.

POLICE POWER - The power of a government to impose restrictions on the rights of private persons, as long as those restrictions are reasonably related to the promotion and protection of public health, safety, morals and the general welfare.

NOTES:

MILLER v. SCHOENE
Remainderman (P) v. Life tenant (D)
276 U.S. 272 (1928).

NATURE OF CASE: Appeal from order under the Cedar Rust Act of Virginia.

FACT SUMMARY: The trial court affirmed the state entomologist's order that the Millers (P) cut down a large number of ornamental red cedar trees on their property to prevent communication of a rust or plant disease which endangered the apple crop.

CONCISE RULE OF LAW: The state does not exceed its constitutional power by deciding upon the destruction of one class of property in order to save another which is of greater value to the public.

FACTS: The state entomologist ordered the Millers (P) to cut down their red cedar trees located within two miles of any apple trees to prevent the communication of a rust disease to the apple crop. The Millers (P) sued for damages. The trial court allowed them $100 to cover the cost of removing the cedars. The Millers (P) appealed, alleging that they should be compensated for the value of the standing cedars or the decrease in the value of their realty caused by their destruction. The Supreme Court of Appeals of Virginia affirmed.

ISSUE: Does the state exceed its constitutional power by deciding upon the destruction of one class of property in order to save another which is of greater value to the public?

HOLDING AND DECISION: (Stone, J.) No. The state does not exceed its constitutional power by deciding upon the destruction of one class of property in order to save another which is of greater value to the public. Where the public interest is involved, the police power has the authority to prefer that interest over the property interest of an individual. Affirmed.

EDITOR'S ANALYSIS: The court here said it did not matter whether or not the infected cedars constituted a common law nuisance. There was no denial of due process. Considerations of social policy were not unreasonable.

QUICKNOTES

DUE PROCESS - The constitutional mandate requiring the courts to protect and enforce individuals' rights and liberties consistent with prevailing principals of fairness and justice and prohibiting the federal and state governments from such activities that deprive its citizens of a life, liberty or property interest.

NUISANCE - An unlawful use of property that interferes with the lawful use of another's property.

POLICE POWER - The power of a government to impose restrictions on the rights of private persons, as long as those restrictions are reasonably related to the promotion and protection of public health, safety, morals and the general welfare.

NOTES:

VILLAGE OF EUCLID v. AMBLER REALTY CO.
Municipality (D) v. Realtor (P)
272 U.S. 365 (1926).

NATURE OF CASE: Action to enjoin enforcement of a zoning ordinance.

FACT SUMMARY: Euclid (D) zoned property of Amber Realty (P) in a manner which materially reduced its potential value.

CONCISE RULE OF LAW: A zoning ordinance, as a valid exercise of the police power, will only be declared unconstitutional where its provisions are clearly arbitrary and unreasonable, having no substantial relation to the public health, safety, morals or general welfare.

FACTS: Ambler Realty (P) was the owner of 68 acres in the village of Euclid (D). Though surrounded primarily by residential neighborhoods, the 68 acres also is bounded by a major thoroughfare to the south and a railroad to the north. Euclid (D) instituted zoning ordinances placing use, height and area restrictions. Restrictions were placed on Ambler Realty's (P) prohibiting (1) apartment houses, hotels, churches, schools, or any other public or semi-public buildings for the first 620 feet from Euclid Avenue, the above-described major thoroughfare, and (2) industry, theaters, banks, shops, *etc.*, for the next 130 feet after that. As a result of this zoning, the value of Ambler Realty's (P) property has declined from $10,000 per acre to $2,500 per acre. Ambler Realty (P) brought an action to enjoin Euclid (D) from enforcing the ordinance on the ground that it constitutes a violation of Fourteenth Amendment due process. From a decree in favor of Ambler Realty (P), Euclid (D) appeals, contending that the ordinance was a valid exercise of the police power of the state.

ISSUE: Is a zoning ordinance unconstitutional as a deprivation of property without due process because it results in a diminution of value in the property zoned?

HOLDING AND DECISION: (Sutherland, J.) No. A zoning ordinance, as a valid exercise of the police power, will only be declared unconstitutional where its provisions are clearly arbitrary and unreasonable, having no substantial relation to the public health, safety, morals, or general welfare. Zoning ordinances, and all similar laws and regulations, must find their justification in some aspect of the police power, asserted for the public welfare. Until recent years, urban life was comparatively simple; but with the great increase and concentration of population, problems have developed which require new restrictions on the use and occupation of private lands in urban communities. There is no serious difference of opinion on the state power to avoid the nuisances which industry may cause in a residential area. As for residential regulation, many considerations point toward their validity. Segregation of residential, business and industrial buildings makes it easier to provide appropriate fire apparatus, for

example. Further, it is often observed that the construction of one type of building destroys an area for other types. In light of these considerations, the court is not prepared to say that the end of public welfare here is not sufficient to justify the imposition of this ordinance. It clearly cannot be said that it passes the bounds of reason and assumes the character of a merely arbitrary "fiat." The decree must be reversed. No injunction may be had.

EDITOR'S ANALYSIS: *Village of Euclid v. Ambler Realty* is the landmark U.S. Supreme Court decision on zoning ordinances as valid exercises of the police power. Essentially, any zoning ordinance which is tied to public health, safety, morals or welfare will be upheld unless clearly arbitrary and unreasonable. So-called Euclidian Zoning, which resulted from this decision, usually consists in the division of areas into zones, in which building use, height and area are regulated in a manner designed to guarantee homogeneity of building patterns. All too often, however, zoning operates not so much lo protect the public interest as to protect the vested interest; in a community. Building restrictions may all too easily be used as an economic sanction by which social segregation is perpetuated. (Barring low-cost housing keeps out economically deprived segment of the population.) Note, however, that *Euclid* did not foreclose the possibility that government land-use regulations may constitute a "taking" which requires compensation. In *Pennsylvania Coal Co. v. Mahon*, the U.S. Supreme Court held that an anti-mining restriction which totally destroyed the interest which the party who owned only the mineral rights, constituted a taking as to that person which had to be compensated for. There, the diminution in value of the party's property was to zero, and this is clearly a "taking."

QUICKNOTES

TAKING - A governmental action that substantially deprives an owner of the use and enjoyment of his or her property, requiring compensation.

NOTES:

175

PENN CENTRAL TRANSPORTATION CO.
v. CITY OF NEW YORK
Railroad (P) v. City (D)
438 U.S. 104 (1978).

NATURE OF CASE: Appeal from an action seeking an injunction and a declaratory judgment.

FACT SUMMARY: Penn Central Transportation Co. (P), owner and proposed developer of the air rights above Grand Central Terminal, brought this action seeking a declaration that a landmark regulation as applied to the terminal property was unconstitutional.

CONCISE RULE OF LAW: Although governmental regulation is invalid if it denies a property owner all reasonable return on his property, there is no constitutional imperative that the return embrace all attributes or contributing external factors derived from the social complex in which the property rests.

FACTS: Penn Central Transportation Co. (Penn Central) (P), owner and proposed developer of the air rights above Grand Central Terminal, brought this action against the City of New York (D) seeking a declaratory judgment that the landmark preservation provisions as applied to the terminal property were unconstitutional. Penn Central (P) also sought to enjoin the City of New York (D) from enforcing the landmark regulation against the subject property. Penn Central (P) desired to construct an office building atop the terminal and contended that the landmark regulation deprived it from realizing a reasonable return on the property in violation of the due process clause of the Constitution. Trial term granted the requested relief, but the appellate division reversed. Penn Central (P) appealed.

ISSUE: Is a government regulation invalid if it denies a property owner of all reasonable return on his property?

HOLDING AND DECISION: (Brennan, J.) Yes. Although government regulation is invalid if it denies a property owner all reasonable return, there is no constitutional imperative that the return embrace all attributes or contributing external factors derived from the social complex in which the property rests. So many of these attributes are not the result of private effort or investment, but of opportunities for the utilization or exploitation which an organized society offers to any private enterprise, especially to a public utility, favored by government and the public. It is enough, for the limited purposes of a landmarking statute, that the privately created ingredient of property receive a reasonable return. All else is society's contribution. Moreover, in this case, the challenged regulation provides Penn Central (P) with transferable above-the-surface development rights which, because they may be attached to specific parcels of property, some already owned by Penn Central (P), may be considered as part of the owner's return on the terminal property. Thus, the regulation does not deprive Penn Central (P) of property without due process of law, and should be upheld as a valid exercise of the police power. Absent past heavy public governmental investment in the terminal, the railroads, and connecting transportation, it is indisputable that the terminal property would be worth but a fraction of its current economic value. Penn Central (P) may not now frustrate legitimate and important social objectives by complaining, in essence, that government regulation deprives them of a return on so much of the investment made not by private interests but by the people of the city and state through their government. The judgment of the appellate division is affirmed.

DISSENT: (Rehnquist, J.) Not every destruction or injury to property by the government is a taking. Examining the two exceptions where the destruction of property does not constitute a taking shows that a compensable taking has occurred here. The first is that there is no taking where the government is prohibiting a nuisance, which it is not here. The second, which applies to broad land use controls such as zoning, is where a prohibition applies over a broad cross section of land and thereby secures an average reciprocity of advantage. That, however, is not the case at hand. Here, a multimillion dollar loss has been imposed, but it is not offset by any benefits flowing from the preservation of less than one-tenth of one percent of other "landmarks" in New York City. Although the public may benefit, it is exactly this imposition of general costs on a few individuals at which the "taking" protection is directed.

EDITOR'S ANALYSIS: Landmark regulation is not a zoning problem. Restrictions on alteration of individual landmarks are not designed to further a general community plan, but to prevent the alteration or demolition of a single piece of property. To this extent, such restrictions resemble discriminatory zoning restrictions. There is, however, a significant difference. Discriminatory zoning is condemned because there is no acceptable reason for singling out one particular parcel for different and less favorable treatment. When landmark regulation is involved, there is such a reason: the cultural, architectural, historical, or social significance attached to the property.

QUICKNOTES
POLICE POWERS - The power of a state or local government to regulate private conduct for the health, safety and welfare of the general public.

TAKING - A governmental action that substantially deprives an owner of the use and enjoyment of his or her property, requiring compensation.

ANDRUS, SECRETARY OF THE INTERIOR v. ALLARD
Government (D) v. Merchants (P)
444 U.S. 51 (1979).

NATURE OF CASE: Appeal from judgment for plaintiff in takings case.

FACT SUMMARY: The trial court held that statutes protecting certain birds violated Allard's (P) property rights when they were construed to prohibit commercial transactions in pre-existing avian artifacts.

CONCISE RULE OF LAW: Where an owner possesses a full bundle of possessory rights, the destruction of one strand of the bundle is not a taking.

FACTS: The Eagle Protection Act and the Migratory Bird Treaty Act were conservation statutes designed to prevent the destruction of certain species of birds. Regulations were promulgated prohibiting the sale of bird parts lawfully acquired prior to the effective date of the legislation. Allard (P) alleged that the prohibition of the sale of pre-existing artifacts containing birds' parts obtained prior to the effective dates of the statutes violated the Fifth Amendment, and sought injunctive relief. The district court held that, as construed, the statute violated Allard's (P) Fifth Amendment property rights. Andrus (D) appealed.

ISSUE: Where an owner possesses a full bundle of possessory rights, is the destruction of one strand of the bundle a taking?

HOLDING AND DECISION: (Brennan, J.) No. Where an owner possesses a full bundle of possessory rights, the destruction of one strand of the bundle is not a taking. The regulations challenged here do not compel a surrender of the artifacts and there is no physical invasion or restraint on them. The simple prohibition of the sale of lawfully acquired property in this case does not effect a taking in violation of the Fifth Amendment. Reversed and remanded.

EDITOR'S ANALYSIS: The court here said that loss of future profits was a "slender reed upon which to rest a takings claim." The takings clause is used to spread the harm caused by economic injuries. If a few persons would be disproportionately penalized, the government must pay for the harm caused.

QUICKNOTES
FIFTH AMENDMENT - Provides that no person shall be compelled to serve as a witness against himself, or be subject to trial for the same offense twice, or be deprived of life, liberty, or property without due process of law.

TAKINGS - A governmental action that substantially deprives an owner of the use and enjoyment of his or her property, requiring compensation.

KEYSTONE BITUMINOUS COAL ASS'N v. DEBENEDICTIS
Coal mining companies (P) v. State agency (D)
470 U.S. 480 (1987).

NATURE OF CASE: Appeal from judgment for defendant in takings case.

FACT SUMMARY: The trial court held that a state statute did not violate the takings clause of the Fifth Amendment.

CONCISE RULE OF LAW: Land use regulation can effect a taking if it does not substantially advance legitimate state interests or denies an owner economically viable use of his land.

FACTS: Keystone (P), an association of coal mine operators, alleged that Pennsylvania's Subsidence Act, authorizing the state Department of Environmental Resources (DER) (D) to implement and enforce a program to prevent or minimize coal mine subsidence, constituted a taking. The DER (D) claimed that the Subsidence Act did not merely involve a balancing test of the private economic interests of coal companies against the private interests of the surface owners, but rather served important public interests. When the district court held that there was no regulatory taking, Keystone (P) appealed. The court of appeals affirmed and the U.S. Supreme Court granted certiorari.

ISSUE: May land use regulation effect a taking if it does not substantially advance legitimate state interests or denies an owner economically viable use of his land?

HOLDING AND DECISION: (Stevens, J.) Yes. Land use regulation can effect a taking if it does not substantially advance legitimate state interests or denies an owner economically viable use of his land. Here the government action leans heavily against finding a taking. Pennsylvania (D) has acted to halt what it believes is a significant threat to the common welfare. Secondly, there was no evidence that the Subsidence Act made it impossible for Keystone (P) to profitably engage in their business. Affirmed.

DISSENT: (Rehnquist, C.J.) Keystone's (P) interests in particular coal deposits have been completely destroyed. The coal in the ground constitutes a separate segment of property for taking purposes.

EDITOR'S ANALYSIS: The Court here found that the holding of *Pennsylvania Coal Co. v. Mahon*, 260 U.S. 393 (1922) did not apply. It based its decision on differences in the facts of the two cases. The right to sell property was also considered as only one strand or element of the owner's property interest.

HODEL, SECRETARY OF THE INTERIOR v. IRVING
Native-Americans (P) v. Government (D)
481 U.S. 704 (1987).

NATURE OF CASE: Appeal from judgment for plaintiffs in takings case.

FACT SUMMARY: The escheat provision of the Indian Land Consolidation Act of 1983 was challenged as an unconstitutional taking.

CONCISE RULE OF LAW: Complete abolition of both the descent and devise of a particular class of property may be a taking.

FACTS: The Irvings (P) were members of the Oglala Sioux Indian tribe who were heirs or devisees of members of the tribe who died in 1983. Under the terms of the Indian Land Consolidation Act, which was enacted to ameliorate the problem of fractionated ownership of Indian lands, the undivided fractional property interests that the Irvings (P) would have inherited escheated to the state. The Irvings (P) claimed that the escheat provision of the Act resulted in a taking of property without just compensation in violation of the Fifth Amendment because it abolished both descent and devise of property to the rightful heir even in cases where the passing of the property to the heir might have resulted in the consolidation of the property, which was the government objective sought to be advanced by the legislation. The court of appeals found that this regulation effected a taking. The U.S. Supreme Court granted certiorari.

ISSUE: May complete abolition of both the descent and devise of a particular class of property be a taking?

HOLDING AND DECISION: (O'Connor, J.) Yes. Complete abolition of both the descent and devise of a particular class of property may be a taking. Since the government objective was to end the fractionalization and to encourage consolidation of ownership of Indian lands, the escheat provision did not advance that legitimate governmental objective. Affirmed.

EDITOR'S ANALYSIS: The Court here suggested other ways of dealing with the problem of fractionalization of Indian lands. It may be possible to abolish the descent of such interests by rules of intestacy and thereby force the owner to formally appoint an heir to prevent escheat to the tribe. The total abolishment of both devise and descent, however, went too far.

QUICKNOTES

DESCENT - The transfer of property that occurs when a person dies without a will; usually accmoplished in accordance with statute.

DEVISE - The conferring of a gift of real or personal property by means of a testamentary instrument.

ESCHEAT - The transfer of property to the state because its owner died with no one legally entitled to claim it.

FIFTH AMENDMENT - Provides that no person shall be compelled to serve as a witness against himself, or be subject to trial for the same offense twice, or be deprived of life, liberty, or property without due process of law.

HEIRS - Those who succeed to one's interest in property pursuant to statute after he dies intestate.

INTESTATE SUCCESSION - The scheme pursuant to which property is distributed in the absence of a valid will or of a disposition of particular property.

TAKING - A governmental action that substantially deprives an owner of the use and enjoyment of his or her property, requiring compensation.

NOTES:

FIRST ENGLISH EVANGELICAL LUTHERAN CHURCH OF GLENDALE v. COUNTY OF LOS ANGELES, CALIFORNIA

Property owner (P) v. Government (D)

482 U.S. 304 (1987).

NATURE OF CASE: Review of judgment for defendant in government takings case.

FACT SUMMARY: First Evangelical Lutheran Church of Glendale (P) sought damages for inverse condemnation of its property prior to the time that it was finally determined that an L.A. County (D) regulation constituted a taking.

CONCISE RULE OF LAW: Temporary takings which deny a landowner all use of his property are not different in kind from permanent takings.

FACTS: The County of Los Angeles (D) adopted an ordinance creating a flood control area which prevented First English (P) from using its campground and recreational center in that area. First English (P) alleged that the Just Compensation Clause required the government to pay for its temporary regulatory taking. The California Court of Appeal held that First English (P) could not recover for the time before it was finally determined that there was a regulatory taking subject to the Fifth Amendment requirement for Just Compensation. The California Supreme Court denied review. The U.S. Supreme Court granted certiorari.

ISSUE: Are temporary takings which deny a landowner all use of his property different in kind from permanent takings?

HOLDING AND DECISION: (Rehnquist, C.J.) No. Temporary takings which deny a landowner all use of his property are not different in kind from permanent takings. Where a government's activities have already worked a taking of all use of the property, the government has a duty to provide compensation for the time during which the taking was effective. No subsequent action by the government can relieve it of this duty. Invalidation of the ordinance without payment of fair value for the prior use of the property would not be a constitutionally sufficient remedy. Reversed and remanded.

DISSENT: (Stevens, J.) The Court has reached out to address an issue which was not presented by the facts in this case. The Court distorts case precedents in the area of regulatory takings when it holds that all ordinances which would effect takings if allowed to remain permanently necessarily constitute takings even if imposed temporarily.

EDITOR'S ANALYSIS: This case went back to the California Court of Appeals. On remand, the California court held that there was no regulatory taking after all. Landowners may bring actions for inverse condemnation when the government has taken land by eminent domain without saying so.

QUICKNOTES

EMINENT DOMAIN - The governmental power to take private property for public use so long as just compensation is paid therefore.

FIFTH AMENDMENT - Provides that no person shall be compelled to serve as a witness against himself, or be subject to trial for the same offense twice, or be deprived of life, liberty, or property without due process of law.

JUST COMPENSATION - The right guaranteed by the Fifth Amendment to the United States Constitution of a person, when his property is taken for public use by the state, to receive adequate compensation in order to restore him to the position he enjoyed prior to the appropriation.

TAKINGS - A governmental action that substantially deprives an owner of the use and enjoyment of his or her property, requiring compensation.

NOTES:

LUCAS v. SOUTH CAROLINA COASTAL COUNCIL
Lot purchaser (P) v. Regulatory agency (D)
505 U.S. 1003 (1992).

NATURE OF CASE: Appeal of the denial of a taking claim in action for compensation of property value.

FACT SUMMARY: South Carolina's (D) Beachfront Management Act barred Lucas (P) from erecting homes on two parcels of land near the ocean.

CONCISE RULE OF LAW: The state must compensate a landowner when a regulatory action denies the owner economically viable use of the land, unless the prohibited use constitutes a nuisance.

FACTS: In 1986, Lucas (P) bought two residential lots near the ocean for $975,000. In 1988, South Carolina (D) enacted the Beachfront Management Act, which sought to counteract coastal erosion. The law restricted new development of beachfront areas and barred Lucas (P) from building homes on his lots as he intended. Lucas (P) brought suit contending that the Act was an unconstitutional taking of his property. The trial court ruled that the Act deprived Lucas (P) of any reasonable economic use of the land and was an uncompensated taking. The South Carolina Supreme Court reversed, holding that the regulation was designed to prevent serious public harm and did not constitute a taking. Lucas (P) appealed, and the U.S. Supreme Court granted review.

ISSUE: Must the state compensate a landowner when a regulatory action denies an owner economically viable use of the land?

HOLDING AND DECISION: (Scalia, J.) Yes. The state must compensate a landowner when a regulatory action denies an owner economically viable use of his land, unless the prohibited use constitutes a nuisance. Physical intrusions on property must always be compensated. A regulation that denies all economically beneficial and productive uses of land is the equivalent of physical appropriation and must also be compensated under the Takings Clause. The Court has previously acknowledged that regulations that restrict nuisance-like uses of land may provide an exception to the general rule on takings. The court of appeals attempted to distinguish laws that prevented harmful use from those regulations that confer benefits on the public. This distinction should not provide the basis for our determinations because it is impossible to objectively distinguish the two rationales. The better rule is that the government may only restrict uses that are already unlawful under existing nuisance and property laws. South Carolina's (D) Beachfront Management Act deprived Lucas' (P) land of all economically beneficial use and restricted uses which were previously permissible. Therefore, it was an unconstitutional taking. Reversed and remanded.

CONCURRENCE: (Kennedy, J.) The trial court's finding that Lucas' (P) land had been deprived of all beneficial use is highly questionable. Furthermore, the nuisance exception should not be the sole justification for severe restrictions when the state's unique concerns for fragile land systems are involved.

DISSENT: (Blackmun, J.) Lucas (P) may continue to use his land for recreation and camping and retains the right to alienate the land. Therefore, the trial court's ruling is certainly erroneous.

DISSENT: (Stevens, J.) The categorical rule established here is an unsound and unwise addition to the law and the Court's formulation of the exception to that rule is too rigid and narrow.

EDITOR'S ANALYSIS: Justice Souter wrote separately to indicate that he felt the writ of certiorari was improvidently granted because he also thought that the trial court's conclusion as to the value of Lucas' (P) land after the regulation was highly questionable. Souter also indicated that, contrary to Scalia's conclusion, nuisance law should not be the basis of regulatory takings because it focuses on conduct and not on the character of the property.

QUICKNOTES

NUISANCE - An unlawful use of property that interferes with the lawful use of another's property.

TAKING - A governmental action that substantially deprives an owner of the use and enjoyment of his or her property, requiring compensation.

NOTES:

PALAZZOLO v. RHODE ISLAND
Developer (P) v. State (D)
533 U.S. 606 (2001).

NATURE OF CASE: Inverse condemnation action.

FACT SUMMARY: Palazzolo (P) brought an inverse condemnation suit against the state (D) after his development proposals for a parcel of waterfront property were rejected.

CONCISE RULE OF LAW: A purchaser or successive title holder is not barred from bringing a takings claim by the mere fact that the title was acquired after the effective date of the state regulation.

FACTS: Palazzolo (P) owned a waterfront parcel of land, almost all of which was designated as coastal wetlands. After his development proposals were rejected, he filed suit in state court claiming the state's (D) application of its wetlands regulations constituted a taking in violation of the Fifth Amendment. The state supreme court rejected the claim that Palazzolo (P) was denied all economically beneficial use of the property since the regulation predated his ownership of the property. Palazzolo (P) appealed.

ISSUE: Is a purchaser or successive title holder barred from bringing a takings claim by the mere fact that the title was acquired after the effective date of the state regulation?

HOLDING AND DECISION: (Kennedy, J.) No. A purchaser or successive title holder is not barred from bringing a takings claim by the mere fact that the title was acquired after the effective date of the state regulation. We agree with the court's decision that all economically viable use of the property was not deprived since the uplands portion of the property could still be developed. Remanded.

CONCURRENCE: (O'Connor, J.) *Penn Central* still controls. Under that analysis interference with investment-backed expectations is one of a number of factors that a court must examine. The regulatory scheme at the time the property is acquired also shapes the reasonableness of the claimant's expectations.

CONCURRENCE: (Scalia, J.) The investment-backed expectations the law will take into account on remand do not include the assumed validity of a restriction that in fact deprives property of so much of its value that it is an unconstitutional taking.

CONCURRENCE IN PART, DISSENT IN PART: (Stevens, J.) Palazzolo is the wrong person to be bringing this action; if anyone is to be compensated it is the owner of the property at the time the regulations were adopted.

DISSENT: (Ginsburg, J.) The Rhode Island Supreme Court was correct in finding that the claim was not ripe for several reasons including that Palazzolo had not sought permission for development of the upland portion of the property only.

DISSENT: (Breyer, J.) As Justice O'Connor says in her concurrence, the simple fact that property has changed hands (*e.g.*, by inheritance) does not always and automatically bar a takings claim. Under partial regulatory takings precedent (*Penn Central*), much depends on whether, or how, the timing and circumstances of a change of ownership affect whatever reasonable investment-backed expectations might otherwise exist. Ordinarily, such expectation will diminish with the passing of time. The *Penn Central* framework can adequately take into account such factors. Moreover, allowing complete regulatory takings claims to survive changes in ownership will not permit owners to fabricate such claims by strategically transferring property until only a nonusable portion remains.

EDITOR'S ANALYSIS: The court here did away with the prior rule under *Lucas* and *Penn Central* that a purchaser or successive title holder was deemed to have notice of an earlier-enacted restriction and was barred from bringing a takings claim. The court also held that a state does not avoid the duty to compensate based on a "token interest." So long as a landowner is permitted to build a substantial residence on the parcel, then it is not deemed to constitute a deprivation of all economic value.

QUICKNOTES

FIFTH AMENDMENT - Provides that no person shall be compelled to serve as a witness against himself, or be subject to trial for the same offense twice, or be deprived of life, liberty, or property without due process of law.

NOTICE - Communication of information to a person by an authorized person or an otherwise proper source.

TAKING - A governmental action that substantially deprives an owner of the use and enjoyment of his or her property, requiring compensation.

TAHOE-SIERRA PRESERVATION COUNCIL, INC. v. TAHOE REGIONAL PLANNING AGENCY

Landowners (P) v. Regional planning agency (D)

535 U.S. 302 (2002).

NATURE OF CASE: Appeal from reversal of judgment finding a per se taking of property.

FACT SUMMARY: Tahoe Regional Planning Agency (TRPA)(D) imposed two moratoria, totaling 32 months, on development in the Lake Tahoe Basin while formulating a comprehensive land-use plan for the area. Landowners (P) affected by the moratoria filed suit, claiming that TRPA's (D) actions constituted a taking of their property without just compensation in violation of the Takings Clause.

CONCISE RULE OF LAW: A moratorium on development imposed during the process of devising a comprehensive land-use plan does not constitute a *per se* taking of property requiring compensation under the Takings Clause.

FACTS: Tahoe Regional Planning Agency (TRPA)(D) imposed two moratoria, one, from 1981 to 1983, and a more restrictive one, from 1983 to 1984, totaling 32 months, on development in the Lake Tahoe region while formulating a comprehensive land-use plan of environmentally sound growth for the area. During the moratoria, virtually all development was prohibited. Landowners (P) affected by the moratoria filed suit, claiming that TRPA's (D) actions constituted a taking of their property without just compensation in violation of the Takings Clause. The district court found a taking, but the court of appeals reversed. The U.S. Supreme Court granted review.

ISSUE: Does a moratorium on development imposed during the process of devising a comprehensive land-use plan constitute a per se taking of property requiring compensation under the Takings Clause?

HOLDING AND DECISION: (Stevens, J.) No. A moratorium on development imposed during the process of devising a comprehensive land-use plan does not constitute a per se taking of property requiring compensation under the Takings Clause. The attack on the moratoria is only facial. The landowners contend that the mere enactment of a temporary regulation that, while in effect, denies a property owner of all viable economic use of the property gives rise to an unqualified constitutional obligation to compensate for the value of the property's use during that period. The landowners want a categorical rule, but the Court's cases do not support such a rule. The answer to any given case depends on the particular circumstances of the case, and the circumstances in this case are best analyzed within the framework of *Penn Central Transp. Co. v. New York* (1978). The longstanding distinction between physical and regulatory takings makes it inappropriate to treat precedent from one as controlling

on the other. The landowners (P) in this case rely on *First English Evangelical Lutheran Church of Glendale v. County of Los Angeles,* 482 U.S. 304 (1987) and *Lucas v. South Carolina Coastal Council,* 505 U.S. 1003 (1992)—both regulatory takings cases—to argue for a categorical rule that whenever the government imposes a deprivation of all economically viable use of property, no matter how brief, it effects a taking. In *First English,* the Court addressed the separate remedial question of how compensation is measured once a regulatory taking is established, but not the different and prior question whether the temporary regulation was in fact a taking. Nor is *Lucas* dispositive of the question presented. Its categorical rule—requiring compensation when a regulation permanently deprives an owner of "*all* economically beneficial uses" of his land—does not answer the question whether a regulation prohibiting any economic use of land for 32 months must be compensated. The landowners (P) attempt to bring this case under the rule in *Lucas* by focusing exclusively on the property during the moratoria is unavailing. This Court has consistently rejected such an approach to the "denominator" question. To sever a 32-month segment from the remainder of each fee simple estate and then ask whether that segment has been taken in its entirety would ignore *Penn Central's* admonition to focus on "the parcel as a whole." Both dimensions of a real property interest—the metes and bounds describing its geographic dimensions and the term of years describing its temporal aspect—must be considered when viewing the interest in its entirety. A permanent deprivation of all use is a taking of the parcel as a whole, but a temporary restriction causing a diminution in value is not, for the property will recover value when the prohibition is lifted. *Lucas* was carved out for the "extraordinary case" in which a regulation permanently deprives property of all use; the default rule remains that a fact specific inquiry is required in the regulatory taking context. Nevertheless, the Court will consider the landowners' (P) argument that the interest in protecting property owners from bearing public burdens "which, in all fairness and justice, should be borne by the public as a whole," justifies creating a new categorical rule. "Fairness and justice" will not be better served by a categorical rule that any deprivation of all economic use, no matter how brief, constitutes a compensable taking. That rule would apply to numerous normal delays—in obtaining building permits, variances, zoning changes, etc.—and would require changes in practices that have long been considered permissible exercises of the police power. Such an important change in the law should be the product of legislative rulemaking, not adjudication. More importantly, the better approach to a temporary regulatory taking claim requires careful examination and weighing of all the relevant circumstances—only one of which is the length of the

Continued on next page.

delay. A narrower rule excluding normal delays in processing permits, or covering only delays of more than a year, would have a less severe impact on prevailing practices, but would still impose serious constraints on the planning process. Moratoria are an essential tool of successful development. The interest in informed decision-making counsels against adopting a *per se* rule that would treat such interim measures as takings—regardless of the planners' good faith, the landowners' reasonable expectations, or the moratorium's actual impact on property values. The financial constraints of compensating property owners during a moratorium may force officials to rush through the planning process or abandon the practice altogether. And the interest in protecting the decisional process is even stronger when an agency is developing a regional plan than when it is considering a permit for a single parcel. Here, TRPA obtained the benefit of comments and criticisms from interested parties during its deliberations, but a categorical rule tied to the deliberations' length would likely create added pressure on decision makers to quickly resolve land-use questions, disadvantaging landowners and interest groups less organized or familiar with the planning process. Moreover, with a temporary development ban, there is less risk that individual landowners will be singled out to bear a special burden that should be shared by the public as a whole. It may be true that a moratorium lasting more than one year should be viewed with special skepticism, but the district court found that the instant delay was not unreasonable. The restriction's duration is one factor for a court to consider in appraising regulatory takings claims, but with respect to that factor, the temptation to adopt *per se* rules in either direction must be resisted. Affirmed.

DISSENT: (Rehnquist, C.J.) The relevant time frame here is not, as the majority indicates, 32 months, but rather it is six years because the 1984 Regional Plan that was implemented after the moratoria were lifted also denied landowners (P) all use of their property until 1987, thus extending the period from 1981 to 1987. Neither the takings clause nor the Court's precedent support a distinction between "temporary" and "permanent" prohibitions. Such a distinction is tenuous—here, the "temporary" prohibition lasted six years, whereas the "permanent" prohibition in *Lucas* lasted only two years. Using this distinction, the government only has to label its prohibition "temporary" in order avoid compensation. Such a designation would not preclude the government from repeatedly extending the "temporary" prohibition into a long-term ban on all development. Even if a practical distinction between temporary and permanent deprivations were plausible, to treat the two differently in terms of takings law would be at odds with the justification for the *Lucas* rule. The *Lucas* rule is derived from the fact that a total deprivation of use is, from the landowner's point of view, the equivalent of a physical appropriation. Because the rationale for the *Lucas* rule applies just as strongly in this case, the "temporary" denial of all viable use of land for six years is a taking. The majority is concerned that applying *Lucas* here would compel a finding that many traditional, short-term, land-use planning devices are

takings. However, the Court has recognized that property rights are enjoyed under an implied limitation. When a regulation merely delays a final land use decision, there are other background principles of state property law that prevent the delay from being deemed a taking, as in the case of normal delays in obtaining building permits, changes in zoning ordinances, variances, and the like. Thus, the short-term delays attendant to zoning and permit regimes are a longstanding feature of state property law and part of a landowner's reasonable investment-backed expectations. But a moratorium prohibiting all economic use for a period of six years is not one of the longstanding, implied limitations of state property law. As is the case with most governmental action that furthers the public interest, here the preservation of Lake Tahoe should be borne by the public at large and not just by a few landowners.

DISSENT: (Thomas, J.) The majority's conclusion that the temporary moratorium at issue here was not a taking because it was not a "taking of 'the parcel as a whole.'" This position was rejected in the context of *temporal* deprivations of property by *First English,* which held that temporary and permanent takings "are not different in kind" when a landowner is deprived of all beneficial use of his land. Thus, a total deprivation of the use of a so-called "temporal slice" of property is compensable under the Takings Clause unless background principles of state property law prevent it from being deemed a taking. Regulations prohibiting all productive uses of property are subject to *Lucas' per se* rule regardless of whether the property retains theoretical useful life and value, if and when, the "temporary" moratorium is lifted. Such potential future value, which the majority assures will be recovered upon lifting the moratorium, bears on the amount of compensation due and not on whether there was a taking in the first place.

EDITOR'S ANALYSIS: With this case, the majority of the Court seems to have adopted the approach recommended by Justice O'Connor's concurring opinion in *Palazzolo v. Rhode Island,* 533 U.S. 606 (2001)—namely, an *ad hoc* approach that evaluates the circumstances of each case using the *Penn Central* framework—and rejected a categorical rule for all regulatory takings cases. The majority also seemed to resolve the "denominator" issue that had hitherto been unsettled in takings jurisprudence.

NOLLAN v. CALIFORNIA COASTAL COMMISSION
Landowner (P) v. Government (D)
483 U.S. 825 (1987).

NATURE OF CASE: Review of takings case.

FACT SUMMARY: The Nollans (P) alleged that imposition of a condition that a permanent easement be created constituted a taking and sought damages.

CONCISE RULE OF LAW: Where individuals are given a permanent and continuous right to pass to and fro over real property, a permanent physical occupation has occurred.

FACTS: The Nollans (P) sought a coastal development permit from the California Coastal Commission (D) to replace a small bungalow on their beachfront property with a three-bedroom house in keeping with the rest of the neighborhood. The Commission (D) conditioned the granting of the permit on the Nollans' (P) granting of a public easement over their land. The Nollans' (P) objections and request for just compensation were overruled. The U.S. Supreme Court granted certiorari.

ISSUE: Where individuals are given a permanent and continuous right to pass to and fro over real property, has a permanent physical occupation occurred?

HOLDING AND DECISION: (Scalia, J.) Yes. Where individuals are given a permanent and continuous right to pass to and fro over real property, a permanent physical occupation has occurred California (D) is free to advance a comprehensive coastal program by using its power of eminent domain for this public purpose. If it wants an easement over the Nollans' (P) land, it must pay them for it. Reversed and remanded.

EDITOR'S ANALYSIS: In common law a temporary invasion is considered a trespass. A permanent invasion is considered to be an ouster. Substantive due process requires a close nexus between the purported purpose of the governmental action and the means used to advance it.

QUICKNOTES

EMINENT DOMAIN - The governmental power to take private property for public use so long as just compensation is paid therefore.

FIFTH AMENDMENT - Provides that no person shall be compelled to serve as a witness against himself, or be subject to trial for the same offense twice, or be deprived of life, liberty, or property without due process of law.

TAKINGS - governmental action that substantially deprives an owner of the use and enjoyment of his or her property, requiring compensation.

NOTES:

DOLAN v. CITY OF TIGARD
Property owner (P) v. Government (D)
512 U.S. 374 (1994).

NATURE OF CASE: Review of judgment for defendant in takings case.

FACT SUMMARY: The Oregon Supreme Court held that the City of Tigard (D) could condition the granting of a building permit on the dedication of a portion of Dolan's (P) property for flood control and traffic improvements.

CONCISE RULE OF LAW: The government may not require a person to give up a constitutional right, such as the right to receive just compensation when property is taken for public use, in exchange for a discretionary government benefit conferred where the property sought has little or no relationship to the benefit.

FACTS: Dolan (P) applied to the City of Tigard (D) for a permit to redevelop and improve her plumbing and electric supply store which was located on a site on a floodplain. When the City (D) granted the permit application on the condition that Dolan (P) dedicate the portion of her property lying in the floodplain for improvement of a storm drainage system and another strip of land as a pedestrian bicycle pathway, Dolan (P) appealed, alleging that the City's (D) dedication requirements were not related to the proposed redevelopment. The Land Use Board of Appeals found that there was a reasonable relationship between the conditions and the impact of the expansion of Dolan's (P) business. The U.S. Supreme Court granted certiorari.

ISSUE: May the government require a person to give up a constitutional right, such as the right to receive just compensation when property is taken for public use, in exchange for a discretionary government benefit conferred where the property sought has little or no relationship to the benefit?

HOLDING AND DECISION: (Rehnquist, C.J.) No. The government may not require a person to give up a constitutional right, such as the right to receive just compensation when property is taken for public use, in exchange for a discretionary government benefit conferred where the property sought has little or no relationship to the benefit. The City (D) must make some type of individualized determination that the required dedication is related both in nature and in extent to the impact of the proposed development. Here, the imposition of the conditions deprives Dolan (P) of her right to exclude others from her property. The findings upon which the City (D) relied did not show the required reasonable relationship between the floodplain easement and Dolan's proposed new building. Reversed and remanded.

DISSENT: (Stevens, J.) The Court's narrow focus on one strand of the property owner's bundle of rights is misguided since this case involves the development of commercial property. The correct inquiry is whether the required nexus is present and should only venture beyond considerations of the condition's germaneness if the developer establishes that a concededly germane condition is so grossly disproportionate to the proposed development's adverse effects that it manifests motives other than land-use regulation.

DISSENT: (Souter, J.) The Court here erred by placing the burden of producing evidence of relationship on the City (D), despite the ordinary presumption that the government has acted constitutionally in exercising its police powers.

EDITOR'S ANALYSIS: The Court here invented a new rule of proportionality to apply in such cases. It was later decided that this rule would not apply to regulatory takings cases. Judge Stevens' dissent focused on the commercial nature of Dolan's improvements.

QUICKNOTES

FIFTH AMENDMENT - Provides that no person shall be compelled to serve as a witness against himself, or be subject to trial for the same offense twice, or be deprived of life, liberty, or property without due process of law.

FIFTH AMENDMENT JUST COMPENSATION TAKING CLAUSE - Provision of the Fifth Amendment to the United States Constitution prohibiting the government from taking private property for public use without providing just compensation therefor.

NEXUS - Presence; contact.

TAKINGS - A governmental action that substantially deprives an owner of the use and enjoyment of his or her property, requiring compensation.

NOTES:

15

CHAPTER 15
THE STRUCTURE OF ZONING

QUICK REFERENCE RULES OF LAW

1. **Separating Single-Family Homes from Apartments.** A partial deprivation of the best economic use land does not overcome the presumption that an ordinance is valid. (Krause v. City of Royal Oak)

2. **Regulating the Family Unit.** Reasonable social and economic legislation limiting the number of non-family members that may cohabit together to two, and that bears a rational relationship to a permissible state objective, does not violate the Equal Protection Clause. (Village of Belle Terre v. Boraas)

3. **Regulating the Family Unit.** Freedom of personal choice in matters of marriage and family life is one of the liberties protected by the due process clause of the Fourteenth Amendment and any zoning ordinance infringing on these freedoms is subject to strict scrutiny. (Moore v. City of East Cleveland, Ohio)

4. **Regulating the Family Unit.** Municipalities may not condition residence upon the number of unrelated people present within the household. (State v. Baker)

5. **Zoning with Discriminatory Intent.** To withstand equal protection review, legislation that distinguishes between the mentally retarded and others must be rationally related to a legitimate government purpose. (City of Cleburne, Texas v. Cleburne Living Center)

6. **The New Jersey Experience.** Municipal land use regulations must provide a realistic opportunity for low- and moderate-income housing unless the municipality can demonstrate circumstances which dictate that it should not be required to do so. (Southern Burlington County N.A.A.C.P. v. Township of Mountain Laurel)

7. **The New Jersey Experience.** The Fair Housing Act appears to be designed to remedy the low and moderate income housing shortage within a reasonable period. (Hills Development Co. v. Township of Bernards)

8. **Other Solutions to the Problem of Low-Income Housing: Mobile Homes.** The *per se* exclusion of mobile homes from all areas not designated as mobile home parks has no reasonable basis under the police power and is therefore unconstitutional. (Robinson Township v. Knoll)

9. **Variances.** To obtain a zoning variance it must be shown that the land cannot yield a reasonable return, that the plight of the owner is due to unique circumstances, and that the use to be authorized by the variance will not alter the essential character of the location. (Otto v. Steinhilber)

10. **Rezoning and Zoning Amendments.** To prove that a grant of a zoning change is in conformance with the comprehensive plan, it must be shown that there is a public need for the change and that the public need will be best served by changing the classification of that particular property. (Fasano v. Board of County Commissioners)

11. **Floating Zones and Contract Zoning.** Where a local municipality conditions an amendment of its zoning ordinance on the execution of a declaration of covenants providing, in part, that no construction may occur on the property so re-zoned without the municipality's consent, absent a provision that such consent may not be unreasonably withheld, the municipality may not be compelled to issue such consent or give an acceptable reason for failing to do so. (Collard v. Incorporated Village of Flower Hill)

12. **Initiatives and Referendums: "All in Favor..."** A zoning referendum is not an unlawful delegation of legislative power, but rather a power, that the people have reserved to themselves. (City of Eastlake v. Forest City Enterprises, Inc.)

KRAUSE v. CITY OF ROYAL OAK

Property owner (P) v. Government (D)
Mich. App. Ct., 11 Mich.App. 183, 160 N.W.2d 769 (1968).

NATURE OF CASE: Appeal from judgment for plaintiff in zoning ordinance case.

FACT SUMMARY: The trial court enjoined the City of Royal Oak (D) from enforcing a zoning ordinance.

CONCISE RULE OF LAW: A partial deprivation of the best economic use land does not overcome the presumption that an ordinance is valid.

FACTS: Krause (P) owned property in an area zoned for single-family residences and applied to the City (D) for a change in zoning. The trial judge held that the one-family zoning classification was void because it constituted an unreasonable and arbitrary exercise of the police power of the city of Royal Oak (D) and was confiscatory when it deprived Krause (P) of his property without due process of law. The City (D) appealed.

ISSUE: May a partial deprivation of the best economic use land overcome the presumption that an ordinance is valid?

HOLDING AND DECISION: (Burns, J.) No. A partial deprivation of the best economic use land does not overcome the presumption that an ordinance is valid. When a zoning classification is merely debatable, the decision of the legislative body in enacting the ordinance is presumptively valid. Judgment vacated.

EDITOR'S ANALYSIS: The court here applied the traditional rule in such cases. The zoning ordinance here had been enacted to avoid the overcrowding that would result from multiple-family units. Krause (P) was only concerned with his profits.

QUICKNOTES

DUE PROCESS - The constitutional mandate requiring the courts to protect and enforce individuals' rights and liberties consistent with prevailing principals of fairness and justice and prohibiting the federal and state governments from such activities that deprive its citizens of a life, liberty or property interest.

PRESUMPTION - A rule of law requiring the court to presume certain facts to be true based on the existence of other facts, thereby shifting the burden of proof to the party against whom the presumption is asserted to rebut.

ZONING ORDINANCE - A statute that divides land into defined areas and which regulates the form and use of buildings and structures within those areas.

VILLAGE OF BELLE TERRE v. BORAAS

Government (D)) v. Property owner (P)
416 U.S. 1 (1974).

NATURE OF CASE: Review of holding that local ordinance was unconstitutional.

FACT SUMMARY: Boraas (P) sought a declaratory judgment that an ordinance adopted by the Village of Belle Terre (D) was unconstitutional because it violated the Equal Protection Clause.

CONCISE RULE OF LAW: Reasonable social and economic legislation limiting the number of nonfamily members that may cohabit together to two, and that bears a rational relationship to a permissible state objective, does not violate the Equal Protection Clause.

FACTS: Boraas (P) leased a house to six unrelated college students and was cited for violation of an ordinance in the Village of Belle Terre (D) limiting all land-use in the village to one-family dwellings. This action was brought to declare the ordinance unconstitutional as violative of equal protection and the rights of association, travel, and privacy. The Village (D) claimed that the ordinance involved no fundamental right and was enacted to protect family values, quiet seclusion and clean air.

ISSUE: Does reasonable social and economic legislation limiting the number of nonfamily members that may cohabit together to two, and that bears a rational relationship to a permissible state objective, violate the Equal Protection Clause?

HOLDING AND DECISION: (Douglas, J.) No. Reasonable social and economic legislation limiting the number of nonfamily members that may cohabit together to two, and that bears a rational relationship to a permissible state objective, does not violate the Equal Protection Clause. The exercise of discretion in defining family units is a legislative, not a judicial function. If the validity of a classification for zoning purposes is fairly debatable, the legislative judgment must control. Reversed.

DISSENT: (Marshall, J.) The ordinance at issue here unconstitutionally burdens the students' fundamental right of association and privacy guaranteed by the first and fourteenth amendments by discriminating with respect to the personal lifestyle choice as to household companions.

EDITOR'S ANALYSIS: The court here applied the general rule that legislation that is fairly debatable is valid. The ordinance permitted any number of family members to live together, but limited the number of nonfamily members cohabiting to two. An ordinance need not seek to avoid a nuisance to be valid. The dissent points out that the ordinance was both overinclusive and underinclusive with respect to the means chosen to accomplish its stated goals.

MOORE v. CITY OF EAST CLEVELAND
Extended family (D) v. City (P)
431 U.S. 494 (1977).

NATURE OF CASE: Appeal from an action challenging the constitutionality of a housing ordinance.

FACT SUMMARY: Inez Moore (D), who lived with her own son and two grandsons, first cousins to each other, was directed to remove her grandson John from her home in compliance with a housing ordinance of Cleveland (P).

CONCISE RULE OF LAW: Freedom of personal choice in matters of marriage and family life is one of the liberties protected by the due process clause of the Fourteenth Amendment and any zoning ordinance infringing on these freedoms is subject to strict scrutiny.

FACTS: Inez Moore (D) lived in her Cleveland home together with her son and her two grandsons. The two boys were first cousins. Mrs. Moore (D) received a notice of violation of a housing ordinance from the City of Cleveland (P) stating that John, her grandson, was an illegal occupant and directing her to comply with the ordinance. Cleveland's (P) housing ordinance limited occupancy of a dwelling unit to members of a single family, but contained an unusual and complicated definitional section that recognized as a family only a few categories of related individuals. Mrs. Moore's (D) family did not fit into any of these categories. When Mrs. Moore (D) failed to remove her grandson from her home, Cleveland (P) filed a criminal charge. Mrs. Moore (D) moved to dismiss, claiming that the ordinance was constitutionally invalid on its face. The motion was overruled, and, upon conviction, Moore (D) was sentenced to five days in jail and a fine. The Ohio Court of Appeals affirmed and the Ohio Supreme Court refused review. Moore (D) appealed to the United States Supreme Court.

ISSUE: Is any zoning ordinance which infringes on a person's freedom of choice in matters of marriage and family life subject to the strict scrutiny of the due process clause?

HOLDING AND DECISION: (Powell, J.) Yes. This Court has long recognized that freedom of personal choice in matters of marriage and family life is one of the liberties protected by the due process clause of the Fourteenth Amendment. When government intrudes on choices concerning family living arrangements, this Court must scrutinize carefully the importance of the governmental interests advanced and the extent to which they are served by the challenged regulation. When thus examined, the Cleveland ordinance cannot survive. The City (P) sought to justify it as a means of preventing overcrowding, minimizing traffic and parking congestion, and avoiding an undue financial burden on the school system. Although these are legitimate goals, the ordinance serves them

marginally, at best. For example, the ordinance permits any family consisting only of husband, wife, and unmarried children to live together, even if the family contains a half-dozen licensed drivers, each with his own car. At the same time, it forbids an adult brother and sister to share a household, even if both faithfully use public transportation. The ordinance would permit a grandmother to live with a single dependent son and children, even if his school-age children number a dozen, yet it forces Mrs. Moore (D) to find another dwelling for her grandson, simply because of the presence of his uncle and cousin in the same household. The decision of the Ohio Court of Appeals is, therefore, reversed.

CONCURRENCE: (Brennan, J.) The ordinance's definition of "family" displays "a depressing insensitivity toward the economic and emotional needs of a very large part of our society." The nuclear family reflected by the ordinance is found primarily in white suburbia, but the Constitution cannot be interpreted to tolerate the imposition by government upon the rest of us white suburbia's preference in family living patterns. The "extended family" remains a prominent pattern for large numbers of the poor and deprived minorities of our society; compelled pooling of scant resources requires compelled sharing of a household. If these unfortunates were required to abandon extended, for nuclear, living patterns, they would be even worse off than they are now.

DISSENT: (Stewart, J.) To suggest that the biological fact of common ancestry necessarily gives related persons constitutional rights of association superior to those of unrelated persons is to misunderstand the nature of the associational freedoms that the Constitution protects. Freedom of association has been constitutionally recognized because it is often indispensable to effectuation of explicit First Amendment guarantees. The association in this case is not for any purpose relating to the promotion of speech, assembly, the press, or religion.

DISSENT: (White, J.) The emphasis of the Due Process Clause is in "process." Justice Harlan observed, it has been "...argued in response to what were felt to be abuses by this Court of its reviewing power," that the Clause should be limited "to a guarantee of fairness."

EDITOR'S ANALYSIS: The U.S. Supreme Court relied on the *Pierce* case, 268 U.S. 535, to support its decision here. *Pierce* struck down an Oregon law requiring all children to attend the

Continued on next page.

state's public schools, holding that the Constitution excludes any general power of the state to standardize its children by forcing them to accept instruction from public teachers only. The Court, in *Moore*, reasoned that by the same token the Constitution prevents East Cleveland from standardizing its children and its adults by forcing all to live in certain narrowly defined family patterns.

QUICKNOTES

FREEDOM OF ASSOCIATION - The right to peaceably assemble.

TAKING - A governmental action that substantially deprives an owner of the use and enjoyment of his or her property, requiring compensation.

STATE v. BAKER
Government (P) v. Home owner (D)
N.J. Sup. Ct., 81 N.J. 99, 405 A.2d 368 (1979).

NATURE OF CASE: Appeal from judgment for plaintiff in zoning violation case.

FACT SUMMARY: The State (P) sought to enforce a local zoning ordinance prohibiting the cohabitation of over four unrelated persons in a single-family dwelling.

CONCISE RULE OF LAW: Municipalities may not condition residence upon the number of unrelated people present within the household.

FACTS: Baker (D) shared a single-family dwelling with another family. When convicted for violating a local zoning ordinance, Baker (D) alleged that the regulation violated the New Jersey Constitution.

ISSUE: May municipalities condition residence upon the number of unrelated people present within the household?

HOLDING AND DECISION: (Pashman, J.) No. Municipalities may not condition residence upon the number of unrelated people present within the household. As long as a group bears the generic character of a family unit as a relatively permanent household, it should be equally entitled to occupy a single family dwelling as its biologically related neighbors. Local governments may act to preserve a family style of living in certain residential neighborhoods. This ordinance's classification system, however, prohibits many uses which pose no threat to the accomplishment of the end sought to be achieved. Affirmed.

DISSENT: (Mountain, J.) This decision will deprive homeowners of the protection they hitherto enjoyed against the possibility that other dwellings in the same zone would be used for multi-family purposes or for occupancy by groups of unrelated individuals unrestricted as to size.

EDITOR'S ANALYSIS: The court here found that there were less restrictive means available to accomplish the goal of the zoning ordinance. The ordinance prohibited more than four unrelated people from living together as a family. The ordinance was also found to prohibit social diversity.

QUICKNOTES

EQUAL PROTECTION - A constitutional guarantee that no person shall be denied the same protection of the laws enjoyed by other persons in like circumstances.

ZONING ORDINANCE - A statute that divides land into defined areas and which regulates the form and use of buildings and structures within those areas.

CITY OF CLEBURNE, TEXAS v. CLEBURNE LIVING CENTER
City (D) v. Private institution (P)
473 U.S. 432 (1985).

NATURE OF CASE: Appeal from order invalidating zoning ordinance as applied.

FACT SUMMARY: The Court of Appeals for the Fifth Circuit held that mental retardation was a quasi-suspect classification and that a housing ordinance requiring a special permit for the operation of a group home for the mentally retarded was unconstitutional.

CONCISE RULE OF LAW: To withstand equal protection review, legislation that distinguishes between the mentally retarded and others must be rationally related to a legitimate government purpose.

FACTS: Cleburne Living Center (CLC) (P) wanted to operate a group home for the mentally retarded in a residential area. The City (D) informed CLC (P) that a special use permit was required. After a hearing, the City (D) turned down CLC's (P) application for the permit. CLC (P) then filed suit in federal court, alleging that the zoning ordinance was invalid on its face because it discriminated against the mentally retarded in violation of equal protection. The Court of Appeals held that mental retardation was a quasi-suspect classification and held the ordinance to be unconstitutional. The City (D) appealed.

ISSUE: To withstand equal protection review, must legislation that distinguishes between the mentally retarded and others be rationally related to a legitimate government purpose?

HOLDING AND DECISION: (White, J.) Yes. To withstand equal protection review, legislation that distinguishes between the mentally retarded and others must be rationally related to a legitimate government purpose. Requiring a permit for a facility for the mentally retarded when other care and multiple-dwelling facilities are freely permitted results from an irrational prejudice against the mentally retarded. Although mental retardation is not a quasi-suspect class, the record does not reveal any rational basis for believing that the group home would pose any special threat to the City's (D) interests. Affirmed.

EDITOR'S ANALYSIS: The court here applied the rational basis test. There are three levels of scrutiny the U.S. Supreme Court applies in considering Equal Protection cases. They are rational basis, somewhat heightened review; and strict scrutiny.

QUICKNOTES

EQUAL PROTECTION - A constitutional guarantee that no person shall be denied the same protection of the laws enjoyed by other persons in life circumstances.

QUASI-SUSPECT CLASS - A class of persons that have historically been subject to discriminatory treatment; statutes drawing a distinction between persons based on a quasi-suspect classification, i.e., gender or legitimacy, are subject to an intermediate scrutiny standard of review.

RATIONAL BASIS TEST - A test employed by the court to determine the validity of a statute in equal protection actions, whereby the court determines whether the challenged statute is rationally related to the achievement of a legitimate state interest

STRICT SCRUTINY - Method by which courts determine the constitutionality of a law, when a law affects a fundamental right. Under the test, the legislature must have a compelling interest to enact law and measures prescribed by the law must be the least restrictive means possible to accomplish goal.

NOTES:

SOUTHERN BURLINGTON COUNTY N.A.A.C.P. v. TOWNSHIP OF MOUNT LAUREL

Civil rights organization (P) v. Township (D)
N.J. Sup. Ct., 67 N.J. 151, 336 A.2d 713 (1975).

NATURE OF CASE: Appeal from invalidation of zoning ordinance.

FACT SUMMARY: The N.A.A.C.P. (P) sued a municipality because it failed to provide for low-income housing.

CONCISE RULE OF LAW: Municipal land use regulations must provide a realistic opportunity for low- and moderate-income housing unless the municipality can demonstrate circumstances which dictate that it should not be required to do so.

FACTS: The N.A.A.C.P. (P) sued the Township of Mount Laurel (Mount Laurel) (D), contending the municipality's zoning scheme violated the New Jersey constitution by failing to provide for low-income housing outside of depressed areas. The residential zoning ordinance permits only single-family, detached dwellings, one house per lot. Attached townhouses, apartments and mobile homes are not allowed. The reason for this conduct was to keep down taxes on property, as the fewer the school children, the lower the tax rate. The trial court found that the zoning ordinances exhibited economic discrimination and declared the ordinance invalid.

ISSUE: Must municipal land use regulations provide a realistic opportunity for low- and moderate- income housing?

HOLDING AND DECISION: (Hall, J.) Yes. Municipal land use regulations must provide a realistic opportunity for low- and moderate-income housing unless the municipality can demonstrate circumstances which dictate that it should not be required to do so. A zoning enactment which is contrary to the general welfare is invalid. When regulation has a substantial external impact, the welfare of the state's citizens beyond the borders of the particular municipality cannot be disregarded and must be recognized and served. Each municipality must, therefore, plan and provide a reasonable opportunity for an appropriate variety of housing to meet the needs of all categories of people. Since the township's general ordinance permits only one type of housing that it believes will have sufficient taxable value to come close to paying its own governmental way, low- and moderate-income housing has been excluded. Its ordinance is therefore contrary to the general welfare and outside the intended scope of the zoning power and is thus invalid. A favorable tax structure cannot be accomplished by restricting the types of housing through the zoning process. The judgment of the law division is modified.

CONCURRENCE: (Mountain, J.) The result of the majority opinion is correct, but the majority was incorrect in reaching that result by relying on the state constitution. Instead, the court should have rested its opinion on a state statute providing for "general welfare." Accordingly, the court should not have reached the constitutional argument.

CONCURRENCE: (Pashman, J.) The Court should go farther and faster in its implementation of the principles it announces, which have been long overdue. Also, exclusionary zoning can assume a multiplicity of forms, and, ultimately, the existence of such practices must be measured by exclusionary intent and actual or potential exclusionary effect.

EDITOR'S ANALYSIS: The rationale behind the Mount Laurel case is that the use of all land is controlled by the State. The State has constitutional obligations to all of its residents whether rich or poor. Municipalities, as state subjects, must set aside a fair share of its land for lower income housing. They cannot allocate only dilapidated land for the poor and retain valuable land for the rich exclusively. While this rationale appears clear in theory, in execution it had proven very difficult. The main difficulty is in developing an equitable formula for determining "fair share." Until a definitive formula is developed, this will prevent widespread application of this rule.

QUICKNOTES

EQUAL PROTECTION - A constitutional guarantee that no person shall be denied the same protection of the laws enjoyed by other persons in life circumstances.

ZONING ORDINANCE - A statute that divides land into defined areas and which regulates the form and use of buildings and structures within those areas.

NOTES:

HILLS DEVELOPMENT CO. v. TOWNSHIP OF BERNARDS

Construction company (P) v. Government (D)
N.J. Sup. Ct., 103 N.J. 1 (1986).

NATURE OF CASE: Review of constitutional validity of statute.

FACT SUMMARY: Hills (P) alleged that the Fair Housing Act would not rectify the shortage of low and moderate income housing in the area.

CONCISE RULE OF LAW: The Fair Housing Act appears to be designed to remedy the low and moderate income housing shortage within a reasonable period.

FACTS: Hills Development (P) claimed that the new Fair Housing Act, enacted as a result of litigation claiming constitutional violations of equal protection, would not work. The Act created an overall plan for the state to increase the availability of lower income housing. Hills (P) claimed the Act was unconstitutional because it would result in delay in implementing the constitutional obligations.

ISSUE: Does the Fair Housing Act appear to be designed to remedy the low and moderate income housing shortage within a reasonable period?

HOLDING AND DECISION: (Wilentz, C.J.) Yes. The Fair Housing Act appears to be designed to remedy the low and moderate income housing shortage within a reasonable period. Legislative action was the proper vindication of the constitutional obligation imposed by the earlier litigation. The Act promises results beyond those achieved by the judicial doctrine administered by the courts. Affirmed.

EDITOR'S ANALYSIS: The court here found that the statewide plan should be given a chance. If it proved to be ineffective, further relief could be requested from the courts. A council was created to oversee the implementation of the state plan. This decision was the culmination of ten years of litigation pitting the Township of Mt. Laurel against an activist state supreme court determined to end economic discrimination in housing. In the first *Mt. Laurel* case, *Southern Burlington County NAACP v. Township of Mt. Laurel (Mt. Laurel I)*, 336 A.2d 713 (1975), the court found that Mt. Laurel's zoning ordinance was designed to permit construction of only middle- and upper-income housing, effectively excluding those people who would not add favorably to its tax base. The court ordered Mt. Laurel to amend its zoning law, resulting in *Southern Burlington County NAACP v. Mt. Laurel (Mt. Laurel II)*, 456 A.2d 390 (1983), wherein the court expanded its ruling to require each developing municipality in New Jersey to provide for its fair share of the regional needs for low- and moderate-income housing—the so-called *Mt. Laurel* obligation.

QUICKNOTES

EQUAL PROTECTION - A constitutional guarantee that no person shall be denied the same protection of the laws enjoyed by other persons in like circumstances.

NOTES:

ROBINSON TOWNSHIP v. KNOLL
Government (P) v. Mobile home owners (D)
Mich. Sup. Ct., 410 Mich. 293, 302 N.W.2d 146 (1981).

NATURE OF CASE: Review of constitutional challenge of zoning ordinance.

FACT SUMMARY: The trial court found that an ordinance prohibiting mobile homes was unconstitutional.

CONCISE RULE OF LAW: The *per se* exclusion of mobile homes from all areas not designated as mobile home parks has no reasonable basis under the police power and is therefore unconstitutional.

FACTS: The Knolls (D) placed a mobile home on their 80-acre parcel of land. The land had not been approved for use as a mobile home park but later the Knolls (D) developed plans for such development. Robinson Township (P) sued the Knolls (D) to remove the mobile home because it violated the township's zoning ordinance. The Knolls (D) claimed that the ordinance was unconstitutional because it was arbitrary and capricious. The Court of Appeals held that it was unconstitutional. The Township (P) appealed.

ISSUE: Does the per se exclusion of mobile homes from all areas not designated as mobile home parks have a reasonable basis under the police power?

HOLDING AND DECISION: (Levin, J.) No. The per se exclusion of mobile homes from all areas not designated as mobile home parks has no reasonable basis under the police power and is therefore unconstitutional. The Township's (P) building code allows for prefabricated housing which is assembled at the site. There can be no reasonable basis for distinguishing between mobile homes and other prefabricated dwellings. Affirmed and remanded.

DISSENT: (Coleman, C.J.) The Knolls (D) have not sustained their burden of showing that no governmental interest is being advanced by the present classification system.

EDITOR'S ANALYSIS: The dissent discussed the appropriate standard for determining the constitutional validity of a zoning ordinance. It must be shown that no reasonable governmental interest is being advanced by the legislation itself, or the plaintiff must show that the ordinance is unreasonable because of the purely arbitrary and capricious exclusion of other types of legitimate land use.

QUICKNOTES
ARBITRARY AND CAPRICIOUS - Standard imposed in reviewing the decision of an agency or court that the decision was made in disregard of the facts or law.

OTTO v. STEINHILBER
Land owner (P) v. Government (D)
N.Y. Ct. of App., 282 N.Y. 71, 24 N.E.2d 851 (1939).

NATURE OF CASE: Appeal from grant of a variance.

FACT SUMMARY: The Board of Appeals granted Otto (P) a variance in the application of zoning laws on the ground of unnecessary hardship.

CONCISE RULE OF LAW: To obtain a zoning variance it must be shown that the land cannot yield a reasonable return, that the plight of the owner is due to unique circumstances, and that the use to be authorized by the variance will not alter the essential character of the location.

FACTS: Otto (P) wanted to build a skating rink which would include both the commercial and residential portions of his land. He applied to the Board of Appeals for a variance from the zoning ordinance to do so. The Board of Appeals granted the variance on the grounds of unnecessary hardship. The appellate division confirmed and Steinhilber (D) appealed.

ISSUE: To obtain a zoning variance must it be shown that the land cannot yield a reasonable return, that the plight of the owner is due to unique circumstances, and that the use to be authorized by the variance will not alter the essential character of the location?

HOLDING AND DECISION: [Judge not stated in casebook excerpt.] Yes. To obtain a zoning variance it must be shown that the land cannot yield a reasonable return, that the plight of the owner is due to unique circumstances, and that the use to be authorized by the variance will not alter the essential character of the location. Here, no evidence was presented that the portion of his land which is in the residential zone could not be reasonably employed in conformity with the existing zoning regulation. Nor has Otto (P) shown that his situation is any different the from that of his neighbors. Reversed.

EDITOR'S ANALYSIS: The court here set forth the general rule which has been applied to such cases ever since. The three factors from the hearing of this case are applied. A fourth element has been added: that the hardship was not of the petitioner's making.

QUICKNOTES
VARIANCE - Exemption from the application of zoning laws.

ZONING ORDINANCE - A statute that divides land into defined areas and which regulates the form and use of buildings and structures within those areas.

FASANO v. BOARD OF COUNTY COMMISSIONERS

Homeowners (P) v. Government (D)

Or. Sup. Ct., 264 Or. 574, 507 P.2d 23 (1973).

NATURE OF CASE: Review of reversal of zone change.

FACT SUMMARY: The trial court reversed the Board of County Commissioners' (D) grant of a zone change to Fasano and other homeowners (P) so that they could construct a mobile home park.

CONCISE RULE OF LAW: To prove that a grant of a zoning change is in conformance with a comprehensive plan, it must be shown that there is a public need for the change and that the public need will be best served by changing the classification of the particular property.

FACTS: Fasano and other homeowners (P) wanted to build a mobile home park and the Board of County Commissioners (D) granted their request for a zone change in a residential area. The trial court reversed the order because the commissioners (D) had not shown any change in the character of the neighborhood which would justify the rezoning. Fasano (P) appealed.

ISSUE: To prove that a grant of a zoning change is in conformance with a comprehensive plan must it be shown that there is a public need for the change and that the public need will be best served by changing the classification of the particular property?

HOLDING AND DECISION: [Judge not stated in casebook excerpt.] Yes. To prove that a grant of a zoning change is in conformance with a comprehensive plan it must be shown that there is a public need for the change and that the public need will be best served by changing the classification of the particular property. The burden of proof is on the party seeking the change. The more drastic the change, the greater the burden. Judicial review of a county commissioners' (D) determination to change the zoning of part of the property is not limited to a determination that it was not arbitrary or capricious. In this case, there has been no adequate showing that the zoning change was in accord with the comprehensive plan. Affirmed.

EDITOR'S ANALYSIS: The court here admitted that zoning ordinances are legislative acts. But such activities are administrative, *quasi*-judicial or judicial in character. For that reason they are not always presumptively valid.

QUICKNOTES

PRESUMPTION - A rule of law requiring the court to presume certain facts to be true based on the existence of other facts, thereby shifting the burden of proof to the party against whom the presumption is asserted to rebut.

ZONING ORDINANCE - A statute that divides land into defined areas and which regulates the form and use of buildings and structures within those areas.

NOTES:

COLLARD v. INCORPORATED VILLAGE OF FLOWER HILL
Homeowner (P) v. Municipality (D)
N.Y. Ct. of App., 52 N.Y.2d 594, 421 N.E.2d 818, 439 N.Y.S.2d 326 (1981).

NATURE OF CASE: Appeal from dismissal of claim for reasonableness review of a conditional zoning decision.

FACT SUMMARY: The trial court granted Flower Hills' (the Village) (D) motion to dismiss Collard's (P) action seeking review of the decision of the Board of Trustees of the Village (the Board) (D) to deny the Collards' (P) plan to enlarge a structure on their property.

CONCISE RULE OF LAW: Where a local municipality conditions an amendment of its zoning ordinance on the execution of a declaration of covenants providing, in part, that no construction may occur on the property so re-zoned without the municipality's consent, absent a provision that such consent may not be unreasonably withheld, the municipality may not be compelled to issue such consent or give an acceptable reason for failing to do so.

FACTS: When the Village of Flower Hill (the Village) (D) granted a re-zoning application, Collard's (P) predecessor-in-interest had agreed that no building situated on the premises would be enlarged without the prior consent of the Board of Trustees of the Village (D). When Collard's (P) request for proposed enlargement was denied, he alleged that the Board's (D) determination was arbitrary and capricious and that a phrase should be read into the agreement requiring that any denial by the Board (D) be reasonable. The court granted the village's (D) motion to dismiss for failure to state a cause of action. Collard (P) appealed.

ISSUE: Where a local municipality conditions an amendment of its zoning ordinance on the execution of a declaration of covenants providing, in part, that no construction may occur onthe property so re-zoned without the municipality's consent, absent a provision that such consent may not be unreasonably wthheld, may the municipality be compelled to issue such consent or give an acceptable reason for failing to do so?

HOLDING AND DECISION: [Judge not stated in casebook excerpt.] No. Where a local municipality conditions an amendment of its zoning ordinance on the execution of a declaration of covenants providing, in part, that no construction may occur on the property so re-zoned without the municipality's consent, absent a provision that such consent may not be unreasonably withheld, the municipality may not be compelled to issue such consent or give an acceptable reason for failing to do so. Where the language in such a covenant is not uncertain or ambiguous, courts may not imply additional requirements in the agreement. The standards for judging the validity of conditional re-zoning are no different than those used to judge unconditional re-zoning. The terminology employed in the declaration here is explicit. If it had been the intent of the parties to include an additional requirement of reasonableness, they could easily have done so. There is no authority in the court to reform the zoning enactment of 1976 retroactively. Affirmed.

EDITOR'S ANALYSIS: The court here found that the Board (D) was not required to explain why it had denied the Collards' (P) petition. The court could not compel the Board (D) to issue its consent to the change. Only when there is ambiguous language in the contract is the court permitted to construe an agreement.

QUICKNOTES

ZONING ORDINANCE - A statute that divides land into defined areas and which regulates the form and use of buildings and structures within those areas.

NOTES:

CITY OF EASTLAKE v. FOREST CITY ENTERPRISES, INC.

Municipality (D) v. Real estate developer (P)

426 U.S. 668 (1976).

NATURE OF CASE: Review of reversal of referendum.

FACT SUMMARY: The Ohio Supreme Court held that a zoning referendum had violated due process.

CONCISE RULE OF LAW: A zoning referendum is not an unlawful delegation of legislative power, but rather a power that the people have reserved to themselves.

FACTS: Forest City (P), a real estate devveloper, applied for a zoning change to permit construction of a high-rise apartment in Eastlake, Ohio (D). While the application was pending, the City Council added a requirement to its charter that a public referendum be held on such changes in land use. The proposed zoning change was defeated in a referendum and the charter amendment requiring the referendum was upheld as constitutional by the Ohio Court of Appeals. The Ohio Supreme Court reversed, holding that the amendment constituted a delegation of power that violated federal due process standards because voters were given no standards to guide their decisions. Forest City (P) appealed and the United States Supreme Court granted certiorari.

ISSUE: Is a zoning referendum an unlawful delegation of legislative power rather than a power that the people have reserved to themselves?

HOLDING AND DECISION: (Burger, C.J.) No. A zoning referendum is not an unlawful delegation of legislative power, but rather a power that the people have reserved to themselves. The referendum provision was not an unlawful delegation of power, as the Ohio Supreme Court had held. Under our Constitution, all power derives from the people, who can delegate it to representative instruments which they create. In establishing legislative bodies, the people can reserve to themselves the power to deal directly with matters which might otherwise be assigned to the legislature. The referendum is a means for direct political participation and does not violate the Due Process Clause of the Fourteenth Amendment. Reversed.

DISSENT: (Powell, J.) Here the only issue concerned one small parcel owned by a single person and the procedure used, affording no realistic opportunity for the affected person to be heard, was fundamentally unfair.

DISSENT: (Stevens, J.) The two critical issues here are whether the procedure employed by the city in deciding to grant or deny a property owner's request for a change in zoning complies with the Due Process Clause, and if so, whether the procedure employed here is fundamentally fair. An individual owner has a right to fair procedure. The opportunity to apply for an amendment or an individual exception is an aspect of property ownership protected by due process.

EDITOR'S ANALYSIS: This case involved what some have entitled the "spot" referendum technique. If only one party or one parcel is at stake, normal due process constraints are bypassed. The Court assumed that the Due Process Clause of the Fourteenth Amendment applied to this case.

QUICKNOTES

DUE PROCESS - The constitutional mandate requiring the courts to protect and enforce individuals' rights and liberties consistent with prevailing principals of fairness and justice and prohibiting the federal and state governments from such activities that deprive its citizens of a life, liberty or property interest.

FOURTEENTH AMENDMENT - Declares that no state shall make or enforce any law which shall abridge the privileges and immunities of citizens of the United States.

REFERENDUM - Right constitutionally reserved to people of state, or local subdivision thereof, to have submitted for their approval or rejection, under prescribed conditions, any law or part of law passed by a lawmaking body.

NOTES:

GLOSSARY
COMMON LATIN WORDS AND PHRASES ENCOUNTERED IN THE LAW

A FORTIORI: Because one fact exists or has been proven, therefore a second fact that is related to the first fact must also exist.

A PRIORI: From the cause to the effect. A term of logic used to denote that when one generally accepted truth is shown to be a cause, another particular effect must necessarily follow.

AB INITIO: From the beginning; a condition which has existed throughout, as in a marriage which was void ab initio.

ACTUS REUS: The wrongful act; in criminal law, such action sufficient to trigger criminal liability.

AD VALOREM: According to value; an ad valorem tax is imposed upon an item located within the taxing jurisdiction calculated by the value of such item.

AMICUS CURIAE: Friend of the court. Its most common usage takes the form of an amicus curiae brief, filed by a person who is not a party to an action but is nonetheless allowed to offer an argument supporting his legal interests.

ARGUENDO: In arguing. A statement, possibly hypothetical, made for the purpose of argument, is one made arguendo.

BILL QUIA TIMET: A bill to quiet title (establish ownership) to real property.

BONA FIDE: True, honest, or genuine. May refer to a person's legal position based on good faith or lacking notice of fraud (such as a bona fide purchaser for value) or to the authenticity of a particular document (such as a bona fide last will and testament).

CAUSA MORTIS: With approaching death in mind. A gift causa mortis is a gift given by a party who feels certain that death is imminent.

CAVEAT EMPTOR: Let the buyer beware. This maxim is reflected in the rule of law that a buyer purchases at his own risk because it is his responsibility to examine, judge, test, and otherwise inspect what he is buying.

CERTIORARI: A writ of review. Petitions for review of a case by the United States Supreme Court are most often done by means of a writ of certiorari.

CONTRA: On the other hand. Opposite. Contrary to.

CORAM NOBIS: Before us; writs of error directed to the court that originally rendered the judgment.

CORAM VOBIS: Before you; writs of error directed by an appellate court to a lower court to correct a factual error.

CORPUS DELICTI: The body of the crime; the requisite elements of a crime amounting to objective proof that a crime has been committed.

CUM TESTAMENTO ANNEXO, ADMINISTRATOR (ADMINISTRATOR C.T.A.): With will annexed; an administrator c.t.a. settles an estate pursuant to a will in which he is not appointed.

DE BONIS NON, ADMINISTRATOR (ADMINISTRATOR D.B.N.): Of goods not administered; an administrator d.b.n. settles a partially settled estate.

DE FACTO: In fact; in reality; actually. Existing in fact but not officially approved or engendered.

DE JURE: By right; lawful. Describes a condition that is legitimate "as a matter of law," in contrast to the term "de facto," which connotes something existing in fact but not legally sanctioned or authorized. For example, de facto segregation refers to segregation brought about by housing patterns, etc., whereas de jure segregation refers to segregation created by law.

DE MINIMUS: Of minimal importance; insignificant; a trifle; not worth bothering about.

DE NOVO: Anew; a second time; afresh. A trial de novo is a new trial held at the appellate level as if the case originated there and the trial at a lower level had not taken place.

DICTA: Generally used as an abbreviated form of obiter dicta, a term describing those portions of a judicial opinion incidental or not necessary to resolution of the specific question before the court. Such nonessential statements and remarks are not considered to be binding precedent.

DUCES TECUM: Refers to a particular type of writ or subpoena requesting a party or organization to produce certain documents in their possession.

EN BANC: Full bench. Where a court sits with all justices present rather than the usual quorum.

EX PARTE: For one side or one party only. An ex parte proceeding is one undertaken for the benefit of only one party, without notice to, or an appearance by, an adverse party.

EX POST FACTO: After the fact. An ex post facto law is a law that retroactively changes the consequences of a prior act.

EX REL.: Abbreviated form of the term ex relatione, meaning, upon relation or information. When the state brings an action in which it has no interest against an individual at the instigation of one who has a private interest in the matter.

FORUM NON CONVENIENS: Inconvenient forum. Although a court may have jurisdiction over the case, the action should be tried in a more conveniently located court, one to which parties and witnesses may more easily travel, for example.

GUARDIAN AD LITEM: A guardian of an infant as to litigation, appointed to represent the infant and pursue his/her rights.

HABEAS CORPUS: You have the body. The modern writ of habeas corpus is a writ directing that a person (body) being detained (such as a prisoner) be brought before the court so that the legality of his detention can be judicially ascertained.

IN CAMERA: In private, in chambers. When a hearing is held before a judge in his chambers or when all spectators are excluded from the courtroom.

IN FORMA PAUPERIS: In the manner of a pauper. A party who proceeds in forma pauperis because of his poverty is one who is allowed to bring suit without liability for costs.

INFRA: Below, under. A word referring the reader to a later part of a book. (The opposite of supra.)

IN LOCO PARENTIS: In the place of a parent.

IN PARI DELICTO: Equally wrong; a court of equity will not grant requested relief to an applicant who is in pari delicto, or as much at fault in the transactions giving rise to the controversy as is the opponent of the applicant.

IN PARI MATERIA: On like subject matter or upon the same matter. Statutes relating to the same person or things are said to be in pari materia. It is a general rule of statutory construction that such statutes should be construed together, i.e., looked at as if they together constituted one law.

IN PERSONAM: Against the person. Jurisdiction over the person of an individual.

IN RE: In the matter of. Used to designate a proceeding involving an estate or other property.

IN REM: A term that signifies an action against the res, or thing. An action in rem is basically one that is taken directly against property, as distinguished from an action in personam, i.e., against the person.

INTER ALIA: Among other things. Used to show that the whole of a statement, pleading, list, statute, etc., has not been set forth in its entirety.

INTER PARTES: Between the parties. May refer to contracts, conveyances or other transactions having legal significance.

INTER VIVOS: Between the living. An inter vivos gift is a gift made by a living grantor, as distinguished from bequests contained in a will, which pass upon the death of the testator.

IPSO FACTO: By the mere fact itself.

JUS: Law or the entire body of law.

LEX LOCI: The law of the place; the notion that the rights of parties to a legal proceeding are governed by the law of the place where those rights arose.

MALUM IN SE: Evil or wrong in and of itself; inherently wrong. This term describes an act that is wrong by its very nature, as opposed to one which would not be wrong but for the fact that there is a specific legal prohibition against it (malum prohibitum).

MALUM PROHIBITUM: Wrong because prohibited, but not inherently evil. Used to describe something that is wrong because it is expressly forbidden by law but that is not in and of itself evil, e.g., speeding.

MANDAMUS: We command. A writ directing an official to take a certain action.

MENS REA: A guilty mind; a criminal intent. A term used to signify the mental state that accompanies a crime or other prohibited act. Some crimes require only a general mens rea (general intent to do the prohibited act), but others, like assault with intent to murder, require the existence of a specific mens rea.

MODUS OPERANDI: Method of operating; generally refers to the manner or style of a criminal in committing crimes, admissible in appropriate cases as evidence of the identity of a defendant.

NEXUS: A connection to.

NISI PRIUS: A court of first impression. A nisi prius court is one where issues of fact are tried before a judge or jury.

N.O.V. (NON OBSTANTE VEREDICTO): Notwithstanding the verdict. A judgment n.o.v. is a judgment given in favor of one party despite the fact that a verdict was returned in favor of the other party, the justification being that the verdict either had no reasonable support in fact or was contrary to law.

NUNC PRO TUNC: Now for then. This phrase refers to actions that may be taken and will then have full retroactive effect.

PENDENTE LITE: Pending the suit; pending litigation underway.

PER CAPITA: By head; beneficiaries of an estate, if they take in equal shares, take per capita.

PER CURIAM: By the court; signifies an opinion ostensibly written "by the whole court" and with no identified author.

PER SE: By itself, in itself; inherently.

PER STIRPES: By representation. Used primarily in the law of wills to describe the method of distribution where a person, generally because of death, is unable to take that which is left to him by the will of another, and therefore his heirs divide such property between them rather than take under the will individually.

PRIMA FACIE: On its face, at first sight. A prima facie case is one that is sufficient on its face, meaning that the evidence supporting it is adequate to establish the case until contradicted or overcome by other evidence.

PRO TANTO: For so much; as far as it goes. Often used in eminent domain cases when a property owner receives partial payment for his land without prejudice to his right to bring suit for the full amount he claims his land to be worth.

QUANTUM MERUIT: As much as he deserves. Refers to recovery based on the doctrine of unjust enrichment in those cases in which a party has rendered valuable services or furnished materials that were accepted and enjoyed by another under circumstances that would reasonably notify the recipient that the rendering party expected to be paid. In essence, the law implies a contract to pay the reasonable value of the services or materials furnished.

QUASI: Almost like; as if; nearly. This term is essentially used to signify that one subject or thing is almost analogous to another but that material differences between them do exist. For example, a quasi-criminal proceeding is one that is not strictly criminal but shares enough of the same characteristics to require some of the same safeguards (e.g., procedural due process must be followed in a parol hearing).

QUID PRO QUO: Something for something. In contract law, the consideration, something of value, passed between the parties to render the contract binding.

RES GESTAE: Things done; in evidence law, this principle justifies the admission of a statement that would otherwise be hearsay when it is made so closely to the event in question as to be said to be a part of it, or with such spontaneity as not to have the possibility of falsehood.

RES IPSA LOQUITUR: The thing speaks for itself. This doctrine gives rise to a rebuttable presumption of negligence when the instrumentality causing the injury was within the exclusive control of the defendant, and the injury was one that does not normally occur unless a person has been negligent.

RES JUDICATA: A matter adjudged. Doctrine which provides that once a court of competent jurisdiction has rendered a final judgment or decree on the merits, that judgment or decree is conclusive upon the parties to the case and prevents them from engaging in any other litigation on the points and issues determined therein.

RESPONDEAT SUPERIOR: Let the master reply. This doctrine holds the master liable for the wrongful acts of his servant (or the principal for his agent) in those cases in which the servant (or agent) was acting within the scope of his authority at the time of the injury.

STARE DECISIS: To stand by or adhere to that which has been decided. The common law doctrine of stare decisis attempts to give security and certainty to the law by following the policy that once a principle of law as applicable to a certain set of facts has been set forth in a decision, it forms a precedent which will subsequently be followed, even though a different decision might be made were it the first time the question had arisen. Of course, stare decisis is not an inviolable principle and is departed from in instances where there is good cause (e.g., considerations of public policy led the Supreme Court to disregard prior decisions sanctioning segregation).

SUPRA: Above. A word referring a reader to an earlier part of a book.

ULTRA VIRES: Beyond the power. This phrase is most commonly used to refer to actions taken by a corporation that are beyond the power or legal authority of the corporation.

ADDENDUM OF FRENCH DERIVATIVES

IN PAIS: Not pursuant to legal proceedings.

CHATTEL: Tangible personal property.

CY PRES: Doctrine permitting courts to apply trust funds to purposes not expressed in the trust but necessary to carry out the settlor's intent.

PER AUTRE VIE: For another's life; in property law, an estate may be granted that will terminate upon the death of someone other than the grantee.

PROFIT A PRENDRE: A license to remove minerals or other produce from land.

VOIR DIRE: Process of questioning jurors as to their predispositions about the case or parties to a proceeding in order to identify those jurors displaying bias or prejudice.

REV 1-95

CASENOTE LEGAL BRIEFS